Rising States, Rising Institutions

Rising States, Rising Institutions

CHALLENGES FOR GLOBAL GOVERNANCE

ALAN S. ALEXANDROFF
ANDREW F. COOPER
editors

THE CENTRE FOR INTERNATIONAL
GOVERNANCE INNOVATION
Waterloo, Ontario

BROOKINGS INSTITUTION PRESS
Washington, D.C.

ABOUT CIGI

The Centre for International Governance Innovation (CIGI) is an independent, non-partisan think tank led by distinguished practitioners and scholars that addresses international governance challenges. Based in Waterloo, Ontario, Canada, CIGI conducts in-depth research and engages experts and partners worldwide from its extensive networks to craft policy proposals and recommendations for multilateral and other governance improvements relating to economic, diplomatic, and global security challenges. For more information about CIGI please visit www.cigionline.org.

ABOUT BROOKINGS

The Brookings Institution is a private nonprofit organization devoted to research, education, and publication on important issues of domestic and foreign policy. Its principal purpose is to bring the highest quality independent research and analysis to bear on current and emerging policy problems. Interpretations or conclusions in Brookings publications should be understood to be solely those of the authors.

Copyright © 2010
THE CENTRE FOR INTERNATIONAL GOVERNANCE INNOVATION

Brookings Institution Press, c/o HFS, P.O. Box 50370, Baltimore, MD 21211-4370
Tel.: 800/537-5487; 410/516-6976; Fax: 410/516-6998
Internet: www.brookings.edu

Library of Congress Cataloging-in-Publication data

Rising states, rising institutions : challenges for global governance / Alan S. Alexandroff and Andrew F. Cooper, editors.
   p.   cm.
   Includes bibliographical references and index.
   ISBN 978-0-8157-0422-5 (pbk. : alk. paper)
   1. International organization. 2. International cooperation. 3. Middle powers. 4. World politics—21st century. I. Alexandroff, Alan S. II. Cooper, Andrew Fenton, 1950– III. Title.

   JZ1318.R574 2010
   341.2—dc22   2010007109

9 8 7 6 5 4 3 2 1

Printed on acid-free paper

Typeset in Minion

Composition by Cynthia Stock
Silver Spring, Maryland

Printed by R. R. Donnelley
Harrisonburg, Virginia

Contents

Rising Institutions

Acknowledgments

This edited volume continues the collaborative work between two distinctive partners, the Centre for International Governance Innovation (CIGI) with respect to its Global Institutional Reform Project (GIR) and the Project on the Future of Multilateralism at the Woodrow Wilson School of Public and International Affairs, Princeton University, led by its director, John Ikenberry. In a similar manner to an earlier collection, *Can the World Be Governed? Possibilities for Effective Multilateralism,* this edited volume analyzes the ongoing evolution of contemporary global governance. At its core, this volume aims to examine and evaluate the leadership and the institutional settings of global governance.

John Ikenberry was an admirable host of the preliminary conference held at Princeton University, August 25–27, 2008. He also contributed a chapter on U.S. leadership. Many of our authors were able to prepare and deliver first drafts of their chapters and to obtain valuable feedback from invited discussants at the Princeton conference: Steven Bernstein, University of Toronto; Patricia Goff, Wilfrid Laurier University; Jonathan Hausman, Ontario Teachers' Pension Plan; Miles Kahler, University of California, San Diego; Parag Khanna, New America Foundation; Jeffrey Legro, University of Virginia; and Arthur Stein, University of California, Los Angeles. We would also like to thank John Kirton, Director, G-8 Research Group, for coming in after the Princeton conference to prepare and/or partner on chapters on the G-20 Leaders' Summit and the G-20 finance ministers' meetings.

The production of the book benefited from the hard work of many individuals. At CIGI Agata Antkiewicz and Andrew Schrumm were effective managers of this and other research projects. Logistical support was invaluable to the successful August 2008 workshop. In that regard we wish to thank CIGI's Colleen Fitzpatrick and Princeton's Tim Waldron. Joe Turcotte assisted in the preparation of the introduction. Max Brem provided sophisticated guidance throughout the publication process, and the assistance of CIGI Publications' Jessica Hanson at communications is much appreciated. As on the previous volume, Barry Norris worked his magic as copy editor.

The support of Thomas A. Bernes, CIGI's vice president of programs and acting executive director, and John English, former CIGI executive director, was vital, as was the enthusiasm of Daniel Schwanen, CIGI's deputy executive director. As on many other components of our research agenda, CIGI's International Advisory Board of Governors provided great encouragement and intellectual guidance. CIGI was founded in 2002 by Jim Balsillie, co-CEO of Research In Motion (RIM), and collaborates with and gratefully acknowledges support from a number of strategic partners, in particular the governments of Canada and Ontario. Interpretations and opinions expressed in this book are those of the authors alone.

Our final thanks go to our colleagues at Brookings Institution Press, Robert Faherty, Mary Kwak, and Janet Walker, whose support and encouragement are much appreciated.

ANDREW F. COOPER *and* ALAN S. ALEXANDROFF

Introduction

The global order is shifting in an appreciable but awkward fashion. The global governance fabric set up in the post-1945 era, the crux of the U.S.-dominated liberal international order, is now seriously frayed. The Bretton Woods and UN institutions face fundamental crises of efficiency. The G-x process modifications added in recent decades, most notably the G-7/8, are seen as illegitimate because of their limited membership.

Questions of leadership have also arisen. The center of gravity of the global power structure is arguably no longer in the United States, a transition that reflects the erosion of U.S. leadership capabilities. The George W. Bush administration abdicated both the normative and practical responsibilities of liberal internationalism, and its unilateral overstretch in Iraq and poor economic policies seem to have drained U.S. resources. Added to these rash policies, the issues of renditions and Guantanamo Bay detainees have undermined the United States' normative credentials.

Still, an analysis of the shifting global order that focuses only on fading U.S. hegemony and leadership is insufficient. The world is also changing at the beginning of the twenty-first century as a result of the emergence of new powers—especially China, India, and Brazil. The challenges these states pose to global governance differ from previous challenges to U.S. leadership. These countries neither accede to a Western-centric order nor view themselves as beneficiaries of the liberal international system. Distance from the liberal world order does not necessarily mean, however, a fundamental rejection of the tenets of the established system. Thus the rise of these states from among the global South does not preclude the emergence of new institutions that can serve the interests of both the traditional powers and the rising powers.

These different components related to "the crunching and grinding of geo-political plates"[1] stand at the center of this volume. What jumps out in an evaluation of the global system is the distinctive context of the shift in global power. Unlike many previous transformations the contemporary shift in the global order has not emerged in the aftermath of armed struggle. The classic model for reconstruction is the creation of the system of global governance that followed World War II.[2] The current reconfiguration, though, is not the result of a dramatic rupture, nor even analogous to the end of the cold war; rather, in the post–cold war era a new order has emerged but without a comprehensive form of settlement.[3]

The financial tsunami of 2008–09 does suggest the image of a sharp break with the status quo, but even this "made in the U.S." economic crisis should not lead one to exaggerate the extent of the transition of power. Although it faces severe fiscal and military constraints, the United States retains a privileged standing in global politics, maintained through a combination of material and normative attributes.[4]

The Contemporary G-x Process

What, then, has altered in the global system? The primary change appears to be that no longer can the United States simply impose its will on others. Many of the initiatives put in train by President Barack Obama require the United States to exert a new style of diplomatic skill that places the onus on negotiation and compromise. Rather than imposing discipline in an arbitrary fashion, the United States needs to demonstrate that it too can be a rules keeper as well as a rules maker. To compensate for the relative decline of both its capabilities and its legitimacy, and to displace some of the responsibilities of leadership, the United Stares must act in a more inclusive fashion. Indeed it was the United States that convened the most dramatic illustration of a "rising institution," the transition of the G-20 from a forum for finance ministers and central bank governors to an expanded Leaders' Summit.

Although the G-20 points to the capacity of the international system to adjust and to accommodate both rising states and rising institutions, it also raises a number of open-ended questions about contemporary global governance.

---

1. The phrase is from Philip Stevens, "Four Things You Must Know about the Global Puzzle," *Financial Times*, September 24, 2009.

2. Ikenberry (2001).

3. Clark (1991).

4. See Joffe (2009).

The first of these questions relates to the specific format of rising institutions. A hallmark of the liberal international order has been its universalist appeal; even amid its most severe crisis, in the move toward the U.S.-led invasion of Iraq, assumptions of legitimacy rested squarely on UN authorization. The G-x bodies, however, are quite distinct—the G-20 and before it the G-7/8 and the many associated bodies make no such claim of universalism but instead are quite self-consciously created as clubs of the few. At the same time the G-x process also uses transgovernmental networks: G-7/8 finance ministers, G-20 finance ministers, and a variety of other groupings, such as trade ministers and foreign ministers. The legitimacy attached to these groups is functional in nature, with weight (or influence) and efficiency as the core rationales; for example, the Major Economies Forum on Energy and Climate consists of seventeen countries responsible for the large majority of greenhouse gas emissions. Whether traditional powers or a combination of traditional powers and global South countries, however, only "major" countries with a big stake in the system are accorded representation in any of these G-x bodies. And even in this mix there is frequently an implicit hierarchy of powers.

A second question about contemporary global governance deals with the ingredients that bind the mix of rising states and rising institutions. One thing that is different about the G-20 is that, unlike earlier plurilateral forums such as the G-7, it lacks like-mindedness. While the G-7 could and would often disagree on policies and decisions, the steering group ethos reflected a sense that this exclusive club could guide international public policy not just on the basis of rich countries' preferences but by making a collective appeal through shared democratic values and similar ways of looking at the global system. If not a club of the likeminded, then, what is the G-20? Could it be an updated "central committee" reminiscent of a nineteenth-century concert of European powers?[5] The G-20 differs from historical concerts, however, in that its priority is global governance, not the division of territorial spoils. Global public goods were to be derived from the effective performance of the G-20 as a crisis committee in the face of the near-death experience of the global financial system. And indeed the effects of the rescue efforts put in place by the new G-20 architecture extended well beyond the club to the wider international arena. If the G-20 eschewed fairness it generated systematic benefits.

A third question concerns the issue of scope in contemporary global governance. Any targeting of rising states must focus on the big three of China, India, and Brazil. Does this concentration of attention minimize the roles of other states? The same question arises concerning the nature of rising institutions.

5. Rosecrance (1992, p. 65).

The G-20 receives a good deal of scrutiny in this volume, and the G-x process certainly represents the dynamic evolution of institutions and rising states in global governance. The G-x process is far more dynamic and purposive than the more traditional—and in most cases far more formal and treaty-based—UN and Bretton Woods institutions, although changes are occurring in these more traditional institutions as well. Informal institutions increasingly are the means of addressing complex global problems in a more diverse way. Compared to other bilateral or institutionalized groupings, "multilateral institutions are weaker and fragmented but they also matter in shaping and directing the flow of politics and economics."[6] While these rising institutions lack the binding mechanisms of formalized, traditional forums, they are increasingly setting the agenda for further discussion.

One source of awkwardness in the contemporary international order arises from the disconnect between the forums of rising states and the rising states themselves. Novel forms of networks represent key ingredients for the rising institutions. What is evident is that the G-x process is not just about leaders' clubs but is also built on trangovernmental networks. Thus the G-7 Leaders' Summit is built on its precursor, the G-7 finance ministers' forum. These networks may reinforce the older traditional powers as opposed to rising states from the global South. Conversely, rising states may seek alternative forms of institutions in competition with established structures—such as the BRICs and the G-5. From this perspective the G-20 might be a significant exception to the rule, with its signaling of a "coming in" of these rising powers and their integration in a revamped and rather exclusive club.

It is not always obvious where rising states are acting in tandem with rising institutions. Much of the process of change is occurring on an incremental basis in highly technical forums and thus proceeds "below the radar." The accumulated effect nonetheless is a dramatic one that holds promise for a fundamental transformation of the main arena of international politics. Albeit replete with built-in constraints about durability, the array of opportunities for rising states to drive the formation of rising institutions and for rising institutions to necessitate new recipes for relations with rising states merits a comprehensive assessment.

Beyond a Single Rising State

Of the cluster of rising states, the only one whose rise is seen by some as analogous to past systemic challengers is China. Although this interpretation is

---

6. Ikenberry and Inoguchi (2007, p. 2).

strongly contested, some have labeled China a new "Prussian" threat: disruptive, potentially revisionist, and a challenge to the status quo.[7] Nonetheless it is the differences with the past, not the similarities that stand out as China rises. One key difference is the economic interdependence of the contemporary global system, seen in the image of "Chimerica"—the intertwined dependence of China and the United States on each other. Another difference with the past is the nature of accepted forms of diplomacy. Historically a disruptive emerging power like Germany combined coercion and bilateral arrangements, but China increasingly embraces an extended form of multilateral diplomacy. If the Chinese are still suspicious about surveillance and the accompanying intrusion into its sovereignty, they are at least beginning to appreciate that the promotion of a stable international order requires some degree of coordination of domestic policies.

Importantly, however, the current shift in the global order differs from past changes in that China is rising in tandem with other countries of the global South.[8] This plurality of actors among the rising states has led to a vigorous debate about whether the twenty-first century will belong to China or India as economic (and nuclear) superpowers; in other bodies of literature China and India are linked as the "Asian drivers" of the global economy.[9]

One aspect of the shift in the global order is the novel manner in which states—especially rising states—are interacting with market forces and the wider dynamics of globalization, reinforced by the opening of different forms of networks across the global system. Rising states and rising institutions are often seen as independent variables, but in fact rising states and institutions are much intertwined: rising states are often at the forefront of the emerging institutions—the domestic and international concerns must be juxtaposed to highlight the differing nature of these rising actors.

The volume is broadly separated into three distinct sections. The first, "Great Powers and International Structure," explores leadership and emerging forms of governance. These chapters address the evolving nature of international structures and state engagement. With the move of rising powers to the forefront of international affairs, new mechanisms are needed for collaboration in global governance. How the traditional powers, such as the United States, respond

---

7. See the recent debate between Niall Ferguson and James Fallows on the China-Prussia analogy in "Niall Ferguson and James Fallows on 'Chimerica.'" FORA.tv (fora.tv/2009/07/01/Niall_Ferguson_and_James_Fallows_on_Chimerica); James Fallows, "More Chimerica, Ferguson, Fallows, Kaiser Wilhelm, etc.," *The Atlantic*, July 5, 2009; and Niall Ferguson, "'Chimerica' Is Headed for a Divorce," *Newsweek*, August 15, 2009.

8. See Bergsten and others (2008); and Julian Borger, "David Miliband: China Ready to Join U.S. as World Power," *The Guardian*, May 17, 2009.

9. See Messner and Humphrey (2008); and Scott (2008).

will have a large impact on the outcome of contemporary engagement. In that regard transgovernmental networks represent a benign environment where traditional and rising power officials can interact collaboratively in meeting the challenges of global governance.

The second section, "Rising States," shifts attention to the emerging powers. The domestic concerns of these increasingly important international actors ultimately will influence how they engage with rising institutions and traditional powers alike. The chapters in this section provide an appreciation of how the global system is evolving by explaining the ways in which rising states are becoming increasingly implicated with and integrated into the contemporary international system and their reasons for doing so.

The final section, "Rising Institutions," examines the emergence on the international scene of various institutions and the changes they are bringing about in global governance. In stark contrast to the traditional UN and Bretton Woods institutions, these new forums typically are informal clubs and networks, but even the traditional institutions are adapting to tackle new global governance issues, most particularly counterterrorism. Whether traditional or emerging from the G-x process, however, these new governance organizations raise concerns about their effectiveness.

Rising Institutions and Rising States: In Competition or in Tandem?

With rising states come big questions about modifications to global governance. In the past rising states muscled their way into elevated status, or tried to. In some cases, the challenge was defeated in war; in other cases, most notably that of the USSR, some degree of accommodation was achieved diplomatically via the United Nations through the granting of veto power, if not via institutions covering military or economic spheres.

A key test of the twenty-first-century order will be how the rising states relate to the organizational machinery of global governance. The problem is highlighted by efforts to preserve the privileges of the old elite. This status quo orientation stands out on UN reform, where the five permanent members of the Security Council cling together to ward off demands for expanded membership. The same resistance shapes the response to efforts to reform Bretton Woods financial institutions such as the International Monetary Fund, where China has less voting power than the Benelux states.

The challenge of meshing rising states and rising institutions is made more difficult by the existence of other factors. The first of these concerns the legacy of North-South relations. Each of the big rising states has its own national interests that it seeks to defend and promote, but each also sees itself in some form or another as a defender and promoter of the collective concerns of the global South and as a bridge between the top tier, to which it has now moved, and the bottom rungs.[10] Such "developmentalism" represents a serious limitation to collaborative global governance.[11] One explicit form of this ideology is the creation of the India-Brazil-South Africa (IBSA) dialogue forum, which stresses "the need to make the structures of global governance more democratic, representative and legitimate by increasing the participation of developing countries in the decision-making bodies of multilateral institutions."[12] The post-1945 order revolved around specific pivotal points—above all, formal international institutions such as the UN, the Bretton Woods system, the General Agreement on Tariffs and Trade, and later the World Trade Organization (WTO). Although these structures allowed the global South a degree of access, these clubs—the economic ones in particular—remained hierarchical. As the traditional rules of the game have become increasingly contested over time, however, participation has expanded but the capacity to generate collective decisions has badly eroded.

Institutionally the established formal structures—such as the Organisation for Economic Cooperation and Development (OECD) and the G-8—have been joined by a number of exclusive clubs and informal forums in which countries from either the North or the South are dominant. "Coalitions of the willing" exemplify the former,[13] while the latter notably includes the G-77, the Non-Aligned Movement, and the United Nations Conference on Trade and Development, as well as groupings such as IBSA, the G-5, and the BRICs (Brazil, Russia, India, China). This dynamic could make the relationship between rising states and aspects of the institutional structure far messier, with their amplified voices making it extremely difficult to come to consensus on economic issues—the immobilized Doha Development Round of trade negotiations is a clear case in point. Yet rising institutions provide some positive signs of new conduits between the established powers and the rising states. The G-20 finance ministers' meetings are an example of this trend. The Asian financial crisis gave birth in 1999 to this institution with a mix of North and South and creditor and debtor countries. In turn the 2008 global financial crisis saw this forum upgraded to the leaders level.

---

10. See Cooper and Antkiewicz (2008).

11. Hurrell (2007).

12. IBSA (2008); see also "Brazil, India, South Africa to Broaden 'Voice of the South'," *Medilinks,* September 2, 2009 (medilinkz.org/news/news2.asp?NewsID=28652).

13. See Cooper (2008).

There is a temptation to see China simply as authoritarian—as a more sophisticated version of a resurgent and seemingly belligerent Russia.[14] Equally, however, China can be viewed as the archetypal globalization success story. From the perspective of the global economy China is not so much a "spoiler" of the global order as a stabilizer, and the solution to managing the "products of success" is seen as enhanced cooperation.[15] Indeed it has been pointed out that China "has made a huge bet on integration into the world economy."[16] Misreading this situation through calls for a unilateral, or wholly Atlanticist, version of the global order will alienate, and possibly provoke, the rising states.[17]

There are, furthermore, arenas of cooperation beyond the economic where the traditional powers might be beneficiaries. In the case of the war on terrorism, coordinated action, information sharing, and common international forums of current and rising powers will be mutually helpful.[18] What began as a partnership of convenience ultimately could become a strategic commitment as all powers develop shared goals of security and prosperity.

Yet the obstacles to meshing current institutions and rising powers should not be underestimated. There is distrust on both sides. Rising states remain wary about approaches that attempt to lock (or "socialize") them into obligations where their interests and values are subordinated to those of the traditional powers. In the North there is anxiety about losing control of a system that has proved beneficial to their economic and diplomatic interests. If the rising powers gain more prominent seats at the international table, do others lose privileges?

Any new condominium of old and new powers will meet diplomatic resistance from those excluded. Amply illustrating this inevitability is the June 2009 Summit of the "192" UN countries amply, where North and South "battled to a standoff."[19] The populist left in Latin America is another source of discontent. But similar sentiment extends to the "uninvited" among more traditional but smaller powers such as the Nordic countries, left out of the G-20 notwithstanding a stellar record of good international citizenship, and Switzerland and Lichtenstein, which face mounting assaults on their status as secretive "offshore" finance centers.

14. See Freedom House (2009).

15. Fareed Zakaria, "The Capitalist Manifesto: Greed Is Good (to a Point)," *Newsweek,* June 13, 2009.

16. Martin Wolf, "What the Presidential Choice Could Mean," *Financial Times,* September 3, 2008.

17. Kagan (2008).

18. Shen (2004).

19. See Bretton Woods Project (2009); and Edith M. Lederer, "Summit Gives UN Role in Solving Economic Crisis," *The Guardian,* June 27, 2009.

Expanding Global Governance Interaction among the Platforms

The challenges associated with integrating the rising states into the established international architecture are both conceptual and practical. The varied nature of the rising states and the wide array of institutional formats in place or in train determine that there will not be one all-encompassing way for this process to take place; nonetheless, the chapters in this volume examine various approaches to a reconfigured global governance architecture, one that is both open and responsive.

The volume begins with an introductory section analyzing the choices and changes that face the established world powers and the current architecture of global governance. John Ikenberry focuses on the current state and role of the traditional powers—most notably the United States—and on whether the liberal internationalist order can be remade. In doing so, he helps to frame how the United States and the current architecture need to adapt to challenges to their leadership on the part of the rising powers. Ikenberry charts the history of the liberal internationalist order before discussing how the current configuration of established and rising powers must adapt to meet changing times. As he notes, "The U.S. hegemonic organization of liberal order no longer appears to offer a solid foundation for the maintenance of an open, rules-based system—an impasse to which the very success of the old order is partly responsible for bringing us." Ikenberry argues that, for a new liberal internationalist order to emerge, the United States must play an active role in ensuring the participation of the rising powers in international institutions—at the expense, of course, of a reduction of its own level of influence. It remains to be seen how the United States will respond to this challenge. Ikenberry concludes that the new liberal international order will need to become less hegemonic and "flatter," with a hierarchy that includes a greater number of voices in the top tier.

Anne-Marie Slaughter and Thomas Hale present a compelling case for the importance of less rigid and formal mechanisms for global governance and crisis resolution. They argue that informal transgovernmental networks would afford rising powers a greater voice and more influence on the world stage, and provide the flexibility necessary to organize groups of different countries around common problems. Slaughter and Hale also suggest the possibility of sidestepping potentially divisive issues or organizational arrangements. They caution, however, that these networks are not suited to all instances or conditions and, in fact, might discourage participation by emerging powers that feel alienated from such processes. Still, transgovernmental networks create mutually beneficial relationships, as the actors involved are able to learn from the experience and perspectives of others, thus building their own capacity and knowledge. And while such networks might not solve all problems, they allow for long-term convergence and the sharing of conventions on a variety of issues.

Andrew F. Cooper, in examining changes in global architecture and the challenge of rising states and actors, argues that it is important to address how these actors interact with one another and with international institutions. Rising states are establishing both formal and informal clubs, the development logic and influence of which need to be understood. In analyzing some of these groups Cooper looks through various lenses. In this sense "labels matter," as different rising state groupings allow for distinct ways of approaching global governance. IBSA, for example, is a dialogue forum based on three countries— India, Brazil, and South Africa—that share a common identity in that they are all "champions" of the global South, with normative power derived from their respective histories and common situations. In contrast the much-touted BRIC grouping, coined by the investment bank Goldman Sachs, focuses mainly on economic weight and potential. As Cooper argues, however, this focus fails to take into account other attributes— including military, diplomatic, and soft power—necessary to become Great Powers on the world scene. An extension of the BRICs that does take these factors into account and fills in some of the gaps is BRIC-SAM—the BRICs group plus South Africa, the ASEAN countries and Mexico.

The Core States in Question

Moving away from the overarching concerns and implications of the rising states as a group, the volume turns to the character and role of individual rising states. Despite their involvement in various clubs, the rising states remain focused on national sovereignty and the promotion of their domestic interests. Understanding these priorities offers insight into how these states are becoming key players in international affairs.

Gregory Chin provides a fresh perspective on China, whose rising status has been widely acknowledged. By focusing on a tangible set of actions and international policies Chin explores what kind of global leader China might become and how it will affect the established world order, both strategically and financially. Chin also looks at whether China will accept or challenge the established norms and powers, and argues that China has found a middle path between a status quo and revisionist power. China is operating as part of—and appears to be creating change within—the global governance system, while developing hedging options and reaching out to other countries and regions to develop its own international clout.

Amrita Narlikar takes up the task of examining India, the other rising Asian power often compared with China, and assesses whether it is cooperative or antagonistic in the face of the current and evolving global governance system. By focusing on India's involvement in WTO discussions and the bilateral nuclear nonproliferation deal with the United States, Narlikar demonstrates the multiple personalities of India's foreign policy. In the former example, India's domestic concerns and historic positioning toward such international institutions have led to a combative position, with the country showing little interest in compromises that would both benefit India's rise and preserve the strength and integrity of the WTO. On the nuclear file, though, India's pragmatic negotiation with the United States demonstrates a willingness to make concessions on issues where doing so enhances its interests.

Andrew Hurrell focuses on Brazil, which has now established itself as an influential global power, and on the problems Brazil must navigate to maintain its elevated position. For Hurrell, Brazil's two largest challenges come in the forms of ideas and institutions. Brazil now has an important stake in how international institutions are transformed, but it must look beyond the immediate challenges of the recent global financial crisis and attendant calls for institutional reforms, and it must make an active contribution to the dialogue necessary to make viable, long-term reforms possible.

The rising states of China, India, and Brazil capture much of the attention, but Andrew Moravcsik reminds us of the continuing importance of the relatively quiet "other superpower," the European Union. The EU accounts for a significant portion of the world's economy, is the world's "second" military power (when combined), and its members have a great deal of influence in the world's international institutions. The EU's success in bridging national governments has been extraordinary. It is, as Moravcsik writes, "the most ambitious and successful international organization of all time, pioneering institutional practices far in advance of anything viewed elsewhere." While idiosyncratic on a comparative basis and fraught with internal constraints, the model of European integration proves a constructive example of how to move ahead with innovations to the global governance system.

Expanding the Range of Global Governance Institutions

Rising States, Rising Institutions concludes by examining various international groupings that are emerging and threatening to alter or even to displace established institutions. Central in this examination is the evolving G-x process.

Alan S. Alexandroff and John Kirton begin this section by focusing on the role that the newly emergent G-20 Leaders' Summit played in dealing with the global financial crisis. Coming dramatically into prominence, the G-20 has reoriented club summitry away from the G-8 and the "likeminded" membership of developed Western countries to an integration of traditional, rising, and developing countries. Revealing that a crisis can trigger opportunities for substantive institutional change, Alexandroff and Kirton herald this new expanded forum. By comparing and contrasting the Washington (November 2008), London (April 2009) and Pittsburgh (September 2009) Summits, the authors focus on how the G-20 process is serving as an important bridging exercise and as a way to enmesh the rising powers within the current global governance system. Alexandroff and Kirton cautioned, though, that these Summits were held with the global financial crisis as a guiding context; it will be interesting to see if the G-20 remains focused on financial issues, where many of its members have common interests, or expands into an ongoing dialogue on a more comprehensive agenda.

John Kirton then amplifies the discussion of the G-x process by focusing on the transgovernmental network of finance ministers that originated in the late 1990s. Kirton argues that the G-20 finance ministers' meeting is at the forefront of global governance networks of ministerial forums and summits that allow for horizontal relationships and influence. It has worked well, although questions remain about the effectiveness of this forum and of the whole G-x process. Still, talk of expanding the sphere of influence of rising states should be accompanied by discussion of the importance of normative considerations for entry into the group. The diversity of the G-20 refers not just to considerations of geography or economic size but also to governance styles, with traditional Western democracies intermingled with newer democracies in the global South, as well as Russia (a "managed democracy") and China (a single-party state).

In his chapter Daniel Drezner focuses on the emergence of sovereign wealth funds (SWFs) as an influential force in international relations. The growth of SWFs from rising states can be viewed as a test of how these countries are interacting with existing institutions. Drezner also touches on the geopolitical and economic concerns associated with SWFs. Financially, Drezner argues, SWFs do not pose a serious threat to global financial governance, as the established powers remain integral actors in this arena. But if these funds continue to grow and begin to outpace the wealth of the OECD countries, they would become a significant challenge for the global financial system, particularly if rising states gradually shift their resources away from the established powers and institutions. That the BRICs have expressed a willingness to begin diversifying their investments highlights that such a scenario is not exaggerated.

Flynt Leverett uses energy security as a meeting point for rising institutions and to express how sovereign states work in international institutions. After a brief look at the history of international energy regulation, Leverett ties this into how energy affects global governance itself, noting that supply and demand (and price) issues can have a dramatic impact on the lives of people around the world, and that national governments as well as international institutions must be attuned to the geopolitical ramifications of energy. Finally, he looks at the effectiveness and the possibilities of the International Energy Agency (IEA) and, in keeping with the theme of this volume, discusses the challenges and opportunities that rising states present for international energy cooperation.

Steven E. Miller finishes this section with a look at global security in the post-9/11 era. He focuses not only on how the United States responded to the terrorist attacks and other threats to its security, but also on how the international community and institutions of global governance reacted. These simultaneous responses proved to be very different. Washington moved toward a unilateral approach that sought to use whatever means were necessary to assert its national interests and security. In the global governance institutions, however, there was an increased emphasis on multilateralism and cooperative approaches to dealing with transnational threats. By reviewing these two responses in tandem, Miller highlights the complex nature of international reality. In an increasingly interconnected world, the ripple effects of attacks such as those on 9/11 can spread far and wide. The responses of institutions such as the UN, NATO, and the EU have been promising: law, cooperation, and diplomacy are privileged as much of the world looks to global governance for security. With a new administration in Washington—apparently one more committed to multilateralism—there is hope that the collaborative precedent set following 9/11 will have a positive, lasting, and consequential legacy for global governance institutions.

Teasing Out the Implications

The international governance architecture is in the midst of substantial change. Rising states are engaging with the established powers. Countries that have remained on the margins of the global governance system for so long are now asking for a place at the table. These demands are accompanied by significant implications for global governance. Will rising states—notably China, India, and Brazil—play a productive role in the processes of greater integration or strike a more combative pose? Equally, how will countries that have previously enjoyed a privileged position—in the case of the United States, hegemonic power— respond to influential new actors?

One view points to the desire among traditional powers and rising states to be embedded in institutions across the board, covering strategic as well as economic and social arenas. Another perspective, however, posits that, as the tightened patterns of global economic integration—that is to say, globalization—become more fully recognized, so will the dynamics of leadership diversity and a kind of "unlikemindedness." Although each of the contributions to this volume has a different emphasis, they uniformly focus the discussion on how the global governance system might adapt to these changing pressure points. Together they offer needed conceptual and practical insights into how the dynamic of an emergent cluster of rising states can be meshed with an adaptive set of rising institutions. Only by bringing both elements to the fore can there be a keener understanding of whether and how the world of the twenty-first century can be governed more legitimately and effectively.

References

Bergsten, C. Fred, and others. 2008. *China's Rise: Challenges and Opportunities*. Washington: Peterson Institute for International Economics.

Bretton Woods Project. 2009. "Economic Crisis: Rich Countries Block Reform at UN Summit." London, June 26 (www.brettonwoodsproject.org/art-564772).

Clark, Ian. 1991. *The Post–Cold War Order: The Spoils of Peace*. Oxford University Press.

Cooper, Andrew F. 2008. "Stretching the Model of 'Coalitions of the Willing.'" In *Global Governance and Diplomacy: Worlds Apart?* edited by Andrew F. Cooper, Brian Hocking, and William Maley. New York: Palgrave Macmillan.

Cooper, Andrew F., and Agata Antkiewicz, eds. 2008. *Emerging Powers in Global Governance: Lessons from the Heiligendamm Process*. Wilfrid Laurier University Press.

Freedom House. 2009. "Undermining Democracy: 21st Century Authoritarians." Washington: Freedom House/Radio Free Europe (June 4) (www.underminingdemocracy.org/).

Hurrell, Andrew. 2007. *On Global Order: Power, Values, and the Constitution of International Society*. Oxford University Press.

IBSA. 2008. "III Summit Joint Declaration." New Delhi, October 15 (www.ibsa-trilateral. org//index.php?option=com_content&task=view&id=36&Itemid=16).

Ikenberry, G. John. 2001. *After Victory*. Princeton University Press.

Ikenberry, G. John, and Takashi Inoguchi. 2007. *The Uses of Institutions: The US, Japan, and Governance in East Asia*. New York: Palgrave.

Joffe, Josef. 2009. "The Default Power: The False Prophecy of U.S. Decline." *Foreign Affairs* 88, no. 5: 21–35.

Kagan, Robert. 2008. *The Return of History and the End of Dreams*. New York: Vintage Books.

Messner, Dirk, and John Humphrey. 2008. "China and India in the Global Governance Arena." In *Governance and Legitimacy in a Globalized World*, edited by Ruediger Schmitt-Beck, Tobias Debiel, and Karl-Rudolf Korte. Berlin: Nomos.

Rosecrance, Richard. 1992. "A New Concert of Powers." *Foreign Affairs* 71, no. 2: 64–82.

Scott, David. 2008. "The Great Power 'Great Game' between India and China: 'The Logic of Geography.'" *Geopolitics* 13, no. 1: 1–26.

Shen, Dingli, 2004. "Can Alliances Combat Contemporary Threats?" *Washington Quarterly* 27, no. 2: 166–69.

Sotero, Paulo, and Leslie Elliott Armijo. 2007. "Brazil: To Be or Not to Be a BRIC?" *Asian Perspective* 31, no. 4: 43–70.

Great Powers and International Structure

G. JOHN IKENBERRY

1 *The Three Faces of Liberal Internationalism*

Over the past century the liberal international "project" has evolved and periodically reinvented itself. The liberal international ideas championed by Woodrow Wilson were extended and reworked by Franklin Roosevelt and Harry Truman. Today's liberal internationalist agenda is evolving yet again, with the new Obama administration adding its distinctive mark to this long tradition. The actual orders themselves, built after the two world wars and in the aftermath of the cold war, have also differed in their logic and character. Liberal international order—both its ideas and real-world political formations—is not embodied in a fixed set of principles or practices.[1] Open markets, international institutions, cooperative security, democratic community, progressive change, collective problem solving, shared sovereignty, the rule of law—these are aspects of the liberal vision that have appeared in various combinations and changing ways over the decades.[2]

In grand historical perspective, this makes sense. The most important macro-transformation in world politics unfolding over the past two centuries has been what might be called the "liberal ascendancy." This has involved the extraordinary rise of liberal democratic states from weakness and obscurity in the late eighteenth century to power and wealth in the twentieth century, propelling the West and the liberal capitalist system of economics and politics to world preeminence. All this occurred in fits and starts amid world war and economic upheaval. At historical junctures along the way, liberal states have pursued

---

1. International order refers to the settled arrangements among states that define the terms of their interaction. Liberal international order refers to international order that is open and rule-based. As noted, the more specific features of liberal international order—in particular the character and location of sovereignty and political authority—can vary widely within liberal orders.

2. An earlier version of this paper was published as Ikenberry (2009).

various efforts to establish rules and institutions of international governance. Adaptation and innovation, necessity and choice, success and failure—all of these are aspects of liberal internationalism's movement along its twentieth-century pathway.

It is possible to identify three major versions or models of liberal international order—call these versions 1.0, 2.0, and 3.0. The first is associated with the ideas that Wilson and Anglo-American liberals brought to the post–World War I international settlement; the second is the cold war liberal internationalism of the post-1945 decades; and the third version is a sort of posthegemonic liberal internationalism that has appeared only partially and whose full shape and logic is still uncertain. In its early twentieth century form, liberal order was defined in terms of state independence and the building of an international legal order that reinforced norms of state sovereignty and nonintervention. In the early twenty-first century, liberal order is being defined in terms of the reverse, as an evolving order marked by increasingly far-reaching and complex forms of international cooperation that erode state sovereignty and reallocate on a global scale the sites and sources of political authority.

The United States was the major champion and sponsor of the liberal international "project" in the twentieth century. But at each turn, the role and function of the United States in the liberal international order have differed. Indeed, the ways in which the preeminent geopolitical position of the United States has simultaneously facilitated and impeded the operation of an open, rules-based liberal order is a critical aspect of the shaping of the character and logic of liberal order itself. In the post-1945 period, the United States gradually became the hegemonic organizer and manager of Western liberal order. The U.S. political system—and its alliances, technology, currency, and markets—became fused to the wider liberal order. The United States supported the rules and institutions of liberal internationalism but it was also given special privileges. In the shadow of the cold war, the United States became the "owner and operator" of the liberal capitalist political system. The questions today are, How will the system evolve—and how will the United States respond—to a successor liberal order in which the United States plays a less dominating role? How necessary is the United States as a liberal hegemonic leader to the stability and functioning of liberal internationalism? And will the United States remain a supporter of liberal order in an era when it has fewer special privileges? For half a century, the United States essentially had liberal order built to its specifications. What will happen when this special status ends?

This chapter has two goals. One is to map the various models of liberal international order—both in ideal-typical terms and in their historical setting. This entails specifying the dimensions along which liberal international order can vary and identifying the logic and functions of these ideal-typical orders. The second goal is to probe the alternative and changing ways in which the United States has interacted with international liberal order. In particular I delineate the alternative liberal pathways that might lead away from the post-1945 U.S.-centered order—that is, the movement from liberal internationalism 2.0 to version 3.0.

I begin by looking at the major dimensions around which liberal order can vary. I then survey the major historical eras of liberal international order, including the transitional contemporary era. I argue that the "third era" of liberal international order hinges in important ways on whether and how the United States can accommodate itself to diminished authority and sovereignty. The question for U.S. policymakers is whether they can make bargains and other arrangements—particularly in security cooperation—that allow the United States to remain at the center of liberal international order. New forms of governance—networks and informal steering groups—will become more important in a post–U.S.-centered liberal international order.

Dimensions of Liberal Internationalism

The liberal imagination is vast, and the ideas and designs for liberal international order are also extraordinarily wide ranging. At its most basic, liberal internationalism offers a vision of an open, rules-based system in which states trade and cooperate to achieve mutual gains.[3] Liberals assume that peoples and governments have deep common interests in the establishment of a cooperative world order organized around principles of restraint, reciprocity, and sovereign equality. An optimistic assumption lurks in liberal internationalism that states can overcome constraints and cooperate to solve security dilemmas, pursue collective action, and create an open, stable system. There is also an optimistic assumption that powerful states will act with restraint in the exercise of their power and find ways credibly to convey commitments to other states. Across the decades, liberal internationalists have shared the view that trade and exchange have a modernizing and civilizing effect on states, undercutting illiberal tendencies and strengthening the fabric of international community. Liberal internationalists also share the view that democracies—in contrast to autocratic and authoritarian states—are particularly able and willing to operate within a open, rules-based international system and to cooperate for mutual gain. Likewise, liberal internationalists share the view that institutions and rules

---

3. For surveys of liberal international theory, see Keohane (1990); Doyle (1997); Deudney and Ikenberry (1999); and Russett and Oneal (2001).

Table 1-1. *Dimensions of Liberal International Order*

Dimension	Characteristic	
Scope	Universal	Regional
Sovereign-independence	Autonomous	Shared
Sovereign-equality	Equal	Hierarchical
Rule of law	Rules based	Ad hoc
Policy domain	Narrow	Expansive

established between states facilitate and reinforce cooperation and collective problem solving.[4]

Beyond these general shared liberal convictions, there is a great deal of variation in the ordering ideas of liberal internationalism. In particular, liberal internationalist ideas and real-world orders differ in regard to how sovereignty, rules, institutions, and authority are to be arrayed within the international system. How liberal order is to be governed—that is, the location of rules and authority—is the great unresolved, contested, and evolving issue of liberal internationalism.

Looking back at the various visions of liberal order in the twentieth century, it is possible to identify five key dimensions of variation: participatory scope, sovereign independence, sovereign equality, rule of law, and policy breadth and depth. These dimensions are summarized in Table 1-1.

Scope refers to the size of liberal order—whether it is a selective grouping or global in scope. This is a distinction between order that is built around an exclusive grouping of states (defined by regional or other shared characteristics) or open in access and membership to all states (defined by universal principles). Liberal order can be constructed among Western democracies or within the wider global system. In one case it is situated within an exclusive grouping of like-minded states—the West, the "free world," the Atlantic community—and in the other it is open to the entire world.

Sovereign independence refers to the degree to which liberal order entails legal-political restrictions on state sovereignty. Sovereignty in this sense refers

---

4. No single modern theorist captures the whole of liberal international theory, but a variety of theorists provide aspects. On the democratic peace, see Doyle (1983). On security communities, see Deutsch, Burrell, and Kann (1957); and Adler and Barnett (1998). On the interrelationship of domestic and international politics, see Rosenau (1969). On functional integration theory, see Haas (1964). On international institutions, see Krasner (1981); and Keohane (1984). On the fragmented and complex nature of power and interdependence, see Keohane and Nye (1977). On domestic preferences and foreign policy, see Moravsik (1997). On transgovernmentalism and networks, see Slaughter (2004). On the modernization theory underpinnings of the liberal tradition, see Morse (1976); and Rosenau (1991).

to the state's exclusive claims to authority within its territory, manifest in the internationally recognized domestic formal-legal right to issue commands and enforce obligations. States can possess full Westphalian legal sovereignty and interact with other states on this basis, or agreements and institutions can be constructed that involve the sharing and abridgement of state sovereignty: states can cede sovereign authority to supranational institutions or reduce the autonomy of their decisionmaking by making commitments to other states, or they can retain their legal and political rights within wider frameworks of inter-state cooperation.[5]

Sovereign equality refers to the degree of hierarchy within liberal order. Hierarchy, in turn, refers to the degree of differentiation of rights and author-ity within the international system. Liberal order can be organized around the sovereign equality of states—a horizontal ordering based on principles of equal access, rights, and participation—or it can be more hierarchical in the sense that one or several states possess special rights and authority. In an order marked by sovereign equality, there is little differentiation of roles and responsibilities. States enter into agreements and cooperate as more-or-less equal parties. In a hierarchical order the roles and responsibilities are more differentiated, and states are organized, formally or informally, around superordinate and subordi-nate authority relationships.[6]

Rule of law refers to the degree to which agreed-on rules infuse the opera-tion of liberal order. The "ruliness" of liberal order can vary. The interaction of states might be informed by highly articulated sets of rules and institutions that prescribe and proscribe actions, or the interaction of states can be informed by more ad hoc and bargained relations.[7] Even ad hoc and bargained relations are informed by some minimal sense of rules—if only by the notion of reciprocity. Nonetheless variations exist in the degree to which generalized rules and prin-ciples of order prevail or whether specific powers and bargaining advantages of states shape interaction. Hierarchical order, which confers unequal privileges and authority on the most powerful state or states, also can be more-or-less rules based.

Finally, liberal order can vary in terms of the breadth and depth of its pol-icy domains. International order can be organized to deal with only a nar-row policy domain—essentially focused on, say, traditional inter-state secu-rity challenges—or it can be organized to deal with a more expansive set of

5. On the dimensions of sovereignty, see Krasner (1999).

6. For discussions of hierarchy in international relations as defined in terms of rights and authority relationships, see Lake (2003); and Hobson and Sharman (2005).

7. See Goldstein and others (2001).

Table 1-2. *Three Versions of Liberal Internationalism*

Liberal Internationalism 1.0	Liberal Internationalism 2.0	Liberal Internationalism 3.0
• universal membership, not tied to regime location or character • Westphalian sovereignty, defined in terms of an international legal order affirming state independence and nonintervention • flat political hierarchy • rules and norms operate as international law, enforced through moral suasion and global public opinion • narrow policy domain, restricted to open trade and collective security system	• Western-oriented security and economic system • modified Westphalian sovereignty, where states compromise legal independence to gain greater state capacity • hierarchical order, with U.S. hegemonic provision of public goods, rules-based and patron-client relations, and voice opportunities • dense intergovernmental relations, enforcement of rules and institutions through reciprocity and bargaining • expanded policy domains, including economic regulation and human rights	• universal scope, expanding membership in core governing institutions to rising non-Western states • post-Westphalian sovereignty, with increasingly intrusive and interdependent economic and security regimes • posthegemonic hierarchy in which various groupings of leading states occupy governing institutions • expanded rules-based system, coupled with new realms of network-based cooperation • further expansion of policy domains

social, economic, and human rights challenges. The more expansive the policy domains of liberal order, the more the international community is expected to be organized to intervene, control, regulate, and protect aspects of politics and society within and across states.

These dimensions of liberal order help identify and contrast the various historical manifestations of liberal international order. See Table 1-2 for a summary of these differences.

The logic of liberal international order has evolved and, at specific historical moments, it has been transformed. I do not offer a theory of why liberal order has evolved over the past century—such explanatory efforts have been attempted elsewhere;[8] rather, the effort here is typological—that is, to identify the changing ways in which liberal international order has been envisaged and constructed.

8. For arguments about why and how powerful states build international order, liberal or otherwise, see Organski (1958); Gilpin (1981); Ikenberry (2001); and Legro (2007).

Liberal International Order 1.0

The first efforts to construct a liberal international order came in the aftermath of World War I with ideas famously advanced by Woodrow Wilson. The Wilsonian vision was of an international order organized around a global collective security body in which sovereign states would act together to uphold a system of territorial peace. Open trade, national self-determination, and a belief in progressive global change also undergirded the Wilsonian world view. It was a "one world" vision of nation-states trading and interacting in a multilateral system of laws that would create an orderly international community. "What we seek," Wilson declared at Mount Vernon on July 4, 1918, "is the reign of law, based on the consent of the governed and sustained by the organized opinion of mankind." Despite its great ambition, the Wilsonian plan for liberal international order entailed little in the way of institutional machinery or formal Great Power management of the system. It was to be an institutionally "thin" liberal order in which states would act cooperatively through the shared embrace of liberal ideas and principles.

At the center of the Wilsonian vision was the League of Nations, which was to provide the forum for collective security. This was to be a universal membership organization, and nation-states that joined it would make diffuse commitments to act in concert to protect territorial borders and enforce the peace, with mechanisms for dispute resolution provided by the League itself. There is some tension in the Wilsonian notion of a universal liberal order. Wilson held the view that a stable and peaceful international order needed to be built around liberal democratic states: accountable governments that respected the rule of law were essential building blocks of a peaceful and just world order. As he argued in his war address, "A steadfast concert of peace can never be maintained except by a partnership of democratic nations."[9] Wilson also understood, however, that the architecture of liberal order needed to be universal and open in scope and membership; therefore all states, regardless of their regime type, should be able to join the League.

The Wilsonian vision reconciled this apparent contradiction with the understanding that all aggressive states could be brought to heel within a collective security system and that, in the long run, nondemocratic states would make democratic transitions and eventually come to embrace liberal international rules and norms. Wilson believed, indeed, that a worldwide democratic revolution was under way; beyond this, he tended to emphasize the democratic bases of peace in his war speeches, but less so later on in his efforts to secure the

9. Woodrow Wilson, War Message to Congress, Washington, April 2, 1917.

Covenant of the League of Nations. Wilson never thought that all members of the League had to be democracies in order for the organization to succeed. In neither his original proposal for the Covenant presented in Paris on February 14, 1919, nor in the final version adopted on April 28 does the word "democracy" appear. The League's mission was mainly the avoidance of war, essentially by means of arbitration and a reduction of armaments and then the threat of collective sanctions. The spread of democracy was seen more as a consequence of an effective League than an essential source of that effectiveness; hence the universalist architecture.[10]

Wilsonian-era liberal internationalism was also predicated on Westphalian state sovereignty. The nation-state was championed, and ideas of a progressive liberal order were closely associated with anti-imperial movements and struggles for national self-determination. Wilson did not see the liberal "project" involving a deep transformation of states themselves as sovereign legal units. Nationalism was a dominant force in world politics, and Wilson's support for rights of national self-government gave voice to it. In May 1916, he proclaimed that "every people has a right to choose the sovereignty under which they shall live," and argued that "small states" as well as "great and powerful nations" should enjoy sovereignty and territorial integrity free from aggression."[11] To be sure, at the Paris peace conference, Wilson was hesitant to recognize new nations, particularly outside Europe. As historian Lloyd Ambrosius observes, "As in the Philippines earlier, he [Wilson] applied the principle of national self-determination with great caution. He did not undermine British rule in Ireland, Egypt, and India, or French rule in Indochina. Wilson recognized only new nations that emerged from the collapse of the Russian, German, Austro-Hungarian, and Ottoman empires."[12] Wilson's notion of national self-determination was decidedly developmental—and patronizing. Sovereign self-rule required the emergence of an "organic" nation whose people were politically mature enough to govern themselves independently. Hence the mandate system, a League of Nations innovation to replace formal colonial rule, which would operate to maintain order in backward areas until national self-rule was possible.

The Wilsonian concept of liberal internationalism similarly embraced the notion of sovereign equality of states. Among the established nation-states—most of whom were Western—there was little formal institutional hierarchy in the postwar order. The League of Nations was to be an organization of states that came together as equals. It would not have the institutional framework for special Great Power authority and rights of the later United Nations. It would

10. I thank Thomas Knock for discussions that clarified these points.
11. Woodrow Wilson, Speech to the League to Enforce Peace, Washington, May 27, 1916.
12. Ambrosius (2002, p. 130).

have an Executive Council, but, adhering closely to the principle of the equality of states, its powers would be simply to initiate investigations and make recommendations to the body of the whole. The hierarchies of Wilsonian liberal internationalism were more implicit and informal, manifest in notions of racial and civilizational superiority. Wilson himself was notoriously unenlightened in these respects. Hierarchical arrangements of Wilsonian-style international order were also manifest in the ways in which the major powers of the League would remain responsible for supervision of postcolonial territories. Again, Wilson's progressive developmental vision provided the intellectual coherence.

Regarding the rule of law, Wilson of course championed a world ordered by international law. As he put it, "the same law that applies to individuals applies to nations."[13] Yet he had a very nineteenth-century view of international law. That is, Wilson did not see international law primarily as formal, legally binding commitments that transferred sovereignty upward to international or supranational authorities. In his view international law had more of a socializing dynamic, creating norms and expectations that states slowly would come to embrace as their own. As Thomas Knock notes, "Wilson emphasized that international law actually was 'not made,' as such. Rather it was the result of organic development—'a body of abstract principles founded upon long established custom.'"[14] International law and the system of collective security anchored in the League of Nations would provide a socializing role, gradually bringing states into a "community of power."

Finally, liberal internationalism 1.0 had a relatively narrow view about the domain of international cooperation. It was essentially a system of collective security and free trade bound together by rules and norms of multilateralism. Wilsonian internationalism did not call on the international community to organize to promote expansive notions of human rights, social protections, or economic development. To be sure there was an underlying assumption that the international system was modernizing in a liberal direction. But liberal internationalism during this period did not contain an explicit agenda of building international capacity to defend or advance ambitious social ends. Indeed the Versailles Treaty has been widely depicted as a flawed blueprint for postwar order with little understanding of the economic and social underpinnings of stable order and progressive change.[15]

The Wilsonian vision of liberal internationalism was both breathtakingly ambitious and surprisingly limited. It sought to transform the old global system based on the balance of power, spheres of influence, military rivalry, and

---

13. Woodrow Wilson, Address to the Senate, Washington, January 22, 1917.
14. Knock (1992, p. 8).
15. See Keynes (1920).

alliances into a unified liberal international order based on nation-states and the rule of law. Power and security competition would be decomposed and replaced by a community of nations. But Wilsonian liberal internationalism did not involve the construction of deeply transformative, legally binding political institutions. Instead liberal international order was to be constructed around the "soft law" of public opinion and moral suasion. The League of Nations was, according to Wilson, to "operate as the organizing moral force of men throughout the world" that would turn the "searching light of conscious" on wrong doing around the world. "Just a little exposure will settle most questions," Wilson optimistically asserted.[16]

The liberal internationalism Wilson envisaged was a historical failure, not simply because the U.S. Senate failed to ratify the Versailles Treaty, but also because the underlying conditions needed for a collective security system to function failed to emerge. The Wilsonian version of liberal internationalism was built not just around a "thin" set of institutional commitments, but also on the assumption that a "thick" set of norms and pressures—public opinion and the moral rectitude of statesmen—would activate sanctions and enforce the territorial peace. Wilson got around the problem of sovereign autonomy—which the United States Senate would not give up—by emphasizing the informal norms that would take hold and bring countries together to maintain a stable peace. The sovereignty of states—sovereignty as it related to both legal independence and equality—would not be compromised or transformed. States would be expected just to act better, which for Wilson meant they would become socialized into a "community of power."

Looking back it is clear that the security commitments were too thin and the norms of compliance and collective action were not thick enough. As a result, the interwar era did not see the full implementation of liberal international order 1.0. Instead the United States pulled back from active involvement in peace and security. The internationalism of the 1920s and 1930s was a sort of internationalism 0.5. That is, it was essentially a private internationalism of banks and commercial firms that struggled during these decades to cooperate to manage the effects of a contracting world economy. There was also a revival of legal internationalism manifest in the Kellogg-Briand Pact, which sought to return to the early nineteenth-century uses of arbitration treaties to settle international disputes.[17] This multilateral treaty, which gave governments an opportunity to renounce war against other treaty members except in self-defense or other circumstances, was even less a formal security pact than was the League

---

16. Quoted in Ambrosius (2002, p. 52).
17. See Ninkovich (1999, chap. 3).

of Nations. And it shared with Wilson's liberal internationalism 1.0 the conviction that public opinion and moral suasion were the mechanisms that would activate cooperation and collective security.

Liberal International Order 2.0

When the United States found itself in a position to relaunch the liberal international project in the 1940s, it initially did not seek to transform its basic logic. Franklin Roosevelt wanted to inject a bit more realism into its operation by building a more formal role for the Great Powers. Like Wilson's version, it would be a "one world" system in which the major powers would cooperate to enforce the peace. The United States would take the lead in creating the order, but the order would be collectively run. In this sense, FDR's wartime vision of postwar order was liberal internationalism 1.5. But the unexpected and evolving challenges of forging a viable postwar order—rebuilding Europe, integrating Germany and Japan, making commitments, opening markets, providing security, containing Soviet communism—forced the United States along a pathway that led to a transformation of the foundations of liberal international order. In the shadow of the cold war a new logic of liberal internationalism emerged. It was a logic of U.S.-led liberal hegemonic order—that is, liberal internationalism 2.0.

From the moment it began to plan for peace, the Roosevelt administration wanted to build a postwar system of open trade and Great Power cooperation. "The United States did not enter the war to reshape the world," the historian Warren Kimball argues, "but once in the war, that conception of world reform was the assumption that guided Roosevelt's actions."[18] It would be a reformed "one world" global order. In the background, the Great Powers would operate together to provide collective security within a new global organization. The Atlantic Charter provided the vision. Wartime conferences at Bretton Woods, Dumbarton Oaks, and elsewhere provided the architectural plans. The Roosevelt vision anticipated more compromises in sovereign equality than Wilson did—that is, the system would be more hierarchical. There was also a substantially more developed notion of how international institutions might be deployed to manage economic and political interdependence. Roosevelt's wartime proclamation of the Four Freedoms and the Atlantic Charter's advocacy of a postwar order that would support full employment and economic growth gave liberal internationalism a more expansive agenda. The Great Powers and governance institutions would have more authority than Wilson proposed, but

18. Kimball (1994, p. 17); see also Divine (1971); and Dalleck (1979).

the system would remain a unified one in which Roosevelt's "family circle" of states would manage openness and stability.

The order that actually took shape in the decades after the war, however, came to have a more far-reaching and complex logic. It was more Western-centered, multilayered, and deeply institutionalized than originally anticipated, and it brought the United States into direct political and economic management of the system. The weakness of Europe, the looming Soviet threat, and the practical requirements of establishing institutions and making them work drove the process forward—and in new directions. In the decades that followed, the United States found itself not just the sponsor of and leading participant in the new liberal international order, it was also its owner and operator. The vision of liberal order turned into liberal hegemonic order.

In both security and economic realms, the United States found itself steadily taking on new commitments and functional roles. Its own economic and political system became, in effect, a central component of the larger liberal hegemonic order. The U.S. domestic market, the dollar, and cold war alliances emerged as crucial mechanisms and institutions through which postwar order was founded and managed. The United States and Western liberal order became fused into one system. The United States had more direct power in running the postwar order but it also found itself more tightly bound to the other states within that order. It became a provider of public (or at least of club) goods, upholding a set of rules and institutions that circumscribed how U.S. power was exercised and developing mechanisms for reciprocal political influence. In the late 1940s security cooperation moved from the UN Security Council to NATO and other U.S.-led alliances. The global system of Great Power–managed collective security became a Western-oriented security community organized around cooperative security. Likewise the management of the world economy moved from the Bretton Woods vision to a U.S.-dollar-and market system. In effect the world "contracted out" to the United States the provision of global governance.

A critical characteristic of liberal internationalism 2.0 is its Western foundation. The United States found it possible to make binding security commitments as it shifted from Wilsonian collective security to alliance security built around democratic solidarity within the Atlantic region. The nature of this shift was twofold. One was the movement toward more specific and explicit security commitments. Alliance partnerships entailed obligations but they were also limited-liability agreements. Commitments were not universal and open ended but were tied to specific security challenges, with treaty-based understandings about roles and responsibilities.[19] The second aspect of the shift was

19. The shift was from a logic of collective security to one of cooperative security. For the classic discussion of collective security, see Claude (1962, esp. chap. 2).

that commitments were backed by a political vision of a Western security community. The sense that the United States and Europe were imperiled by a common threat strengthened the feeling of Western solidarity, but the notion of a Western core to liberal international order also suggested that unusual opportunities existed—because of common culture and democratic institutions—to cooperate and build postwar institutions.

Liberal internationalism 2.0 also moved beyond the Wilsonian vision with its more complex notions of sovereignty and interdependence. Westphalian sovereignty remained at the core of Truman-era liberal internationalism, but there was a new understanding of the dangers and opportunities of economic and security interdependence—views that were informed by the economic calamities of the 1930s and the successes of New Deal regulation and governance. Advanced societies were seen to be deeply and mutually vulnerable to international economic downturns and to bad policies pursued by other states. As a result, nations would need to become involved in more intense and more institutionalized forms of joint management of the global system. Jacob Viner, a leading international economist and postwar planner, captured this view: "There is wide agreement today that major depressions, mass unemployment, are social evils, and that it is the obligation of governments . . . to prevent them." Moreover, there is "wide agreement also that it is extraordinarily difficult, if not outright impossible, for any country to cope alone with the problems of cyclical booms and depressions . . . while there is good prospect that with international cooperation . . . the problem of the business cycle and of mass unemployment can be largely solved."[20] New institutions would be needed in which states worked side by side on a continuous basis to regulate and reduce the dangers inherent in increasingly interdependent societies.

This emerging view that it was necessary to reduce the sovereign independence of states had several aspects. One was that the vision was essentially intergovernmental rather than supranational. At least in the advanced world, governments would remain the primary sources of authority and decision, but they would bargain, consult, and coordinate their policies with other governments, facilitated through international institutions. Another aspect was that the new international institutional machinery would bolster, rather than diminish, the ability of governments to deliver on their economic and political obligations to their societies; states within liberal internationalism 2.0 would give up some sovereign independence but gain new governmental capacities.[21]

20. Viner (1942, p. 168).

21. This is the argument I make about the Bretton Woods agreements; see Ikenberry (1993). A similar logic holds for the human rights regimes in postwar Europe, in which countries employed international commitments to consolidate democracy—"locking in" the domestic political status quo against their nondemocratic opponents; see Moravcsik (2000).

Similarly the norms of sovereign equality embodied in Wilsonian internationalism gave way to a much more hierarchical form of liberal order. The United States took on special functional-operational roles. It positioned itself at the center of the liberal international order. It provided public goods of security protection, market openness, and sponsorship of rules and institutions. The U.S. dollar became an international currency and the U.S. domestic market became an engine of global economic growth. The U.S. alliance system and the forward deployed military forces in Europe and East Asia gave the United States a direct and ongoing superordinate role in the capitalist-democratic world. Other states established clientalistic and "special relationships" with Washington. In NATO the United States was first among equals. It led and directed security cooperation across the regions of the world. In short the United States exported security and imported goods. The resulting order was hierarchical, with the United States the most powerful state in the order, a position manifest in its roles, responsibilities, authority, and privileges.

At the same time the hierarchical character of the order was to be more liberal than imperial. The United States engaged in public goods provision, but it operated within agreed-on rules and institutions while opening itself up to "voice opportunities" from subordinate states. To be sure these liberal features of hierarchy differed across regions and over time. The United States was more willing to make multilateral commitments to Western European partners than to others. In East Asia the United States built a "hub-and-spoke" set of security pacts that made the regional order more client based than rules based.[22] Generally speaking the dominant global position of the United States made de facto hierarchy an inevitable feature of the postwar order. But that dominant global position—together with cold war bipolar competition—also gave Washington strategic incentives to build cooperative relations with allies, integrate Japan and Germany, share the "spoils" of capitalism and modernization, and, generally, operate the system in mutually acceptable ways.[23]

The rules-based character of liberal order also evolved in the 1940s beyond the Wilsonian vision. In the aftermath of depression and war, U.S. liberal internationalists had a new appreciation of the ways in which capitalist modernization and interdependence had created growing functional needs for cooperation; they also had new views about the role and importance of rules and institutions.[24] Wilsonian internationalists had strong convictions about the moral and political virtues of international law and its socializing effects

22. See Press-Barnathan (2003).
23. See Ikenberry (2001).
24. For an important study of these evolving views, see Murphy (1994).

on states. Truman-era internationalists had convictions about the utility and functions of institutions and rules-based order. More so than in earlier decades, U.S. officials saw that their country's interests—national economic, political, and security—could be advanced only with the building of a stable, articulated, and institutionalized international environment. That is, the U.S. commitment to rules-based order was not simply a concession to other states, driven by cold war alliance imperatives; it was an incentive that the United States would have had even without the Soviet threat. As the 1950 National Security Council strategic planning document that launched containment argued, the United States had a need "to build a healthy international community," which "we would probably do even if there were no international threat." The felt need was to build a "world environment in which the American system can survive and flourish."[25]

The 1940s-era rules-based order had several distinctive features. One involved an innovation in the uses of institutions. Not only would intergovernmental institutions provide functional tools to manage interdependence, they would also be created to bind states together. This was most important in the reintegration of Germany into the West, in which European and Atlantic-wide institutions provided frameworks to bind, commit, and reassure.[26] Beyond this the U.S. approach to a multilateral, rules-based order was to insist on flexibility and privileges: in return for its support, there would need to be accommodations, exceptions, weighted voting, and opt-out clauses.[27] These were the compromises that allowed liberal internationalism 2.0 both to reflect commitment to the rule of law and to accommodate the realities of hierarchy. Finally rules-based order was also supplemented by bilateral ties and agreements. States were not mainly or simply asked to abide by treaty-based rules and norms; rather, and crucially, they agreed to operate in a rules-based system that primarily created ongoing political processes. That is, rules-based order did not, strictly speaking, create "laws" that states were to obey; instead it created mechanisms and processes in which states would bargain, communicate, and adjust—all within agreed-on normative and institutional parameters.

As the foregoing suggests, 1940s-era liberal internationalism expanded the policy domain of liberal order. A denser and more complex international environment was necessary to allow governments to fulfill their roles and obligations

25. Quoted in May (1993, p. 40).

26. See Ikenberry (2001, chap. 6).

27. For a survey of these "exemptionalist" tendencies in U.S. foreign policy, see Ruggie (2004). For a sympathetic portrayal, see Robert Kagan, "Multilateralism American Style," *Washington Post*, September 13, 2002.

domestically. The domestic liberal agenda had expanded as well, and it required liberal states to be more internationally active and committed. Indeed the shift from liberal internationalism 1.0 to 2.0 involved a new definition of "national security." The Depression and the New Deal brought into existence the notion of "social security," but the violence and destruction of world war brought into existence the notion of "national security." It was more than just a new term of art; it was a new and more expansive internationalist notion of security.[28] In earlier decades the notion of "national security" did not really exist. The term most frequently used was national "defense," and its meaning was restricted to protection of the homeland against traditional military attack. The new term emerged sometime during World War II, capturing a vision of an activist and permanently mobilized state seeking security across economic, political, and military realms. National security required the United States to be attempting actively to shape its external environment by coordinating agencies, generating resources, building alliances, and laying the groundwork.

What the New Deal and national security liberalism brought to postwar U.S. internationalism was a wider constituency for liberal order building than in earlier eras. The desirable international order had more features and moving parts; it was more elaborate and complexly organized. In several senses, the stakes had grown since the end of World War I: more had to be accomplished, more was at risk if the right sort of postwar order was not constructed, and more of U.S. society had a stake in a successful U.S. liberal internationalist project.

Throughout the cold war era, this U.S.-led liberal international order was the dominant reality in world politics. Along the way the United States itself—its economy, military, and political institutions—became tightly tied to the wider order. Some aspects of that liberal order, however, did change and evolve. In the 1970s the dollar-gold standard collapsed and monetary and financial relations became less tightly tied to Washington. The expansion of the world economy in the decades before and after the end of the cold war also reduced the centrality of Atlantic relations within the wider global liberal order. During the cold war, liberal international order existed "inside" the global bipolar system. With the end of the cold war, this inside order became an "outside" order, a global system now largely tied together through the markets, relations, and institutions of the postwar U.S.-led system. At the same time, amid these sweeping changes, the underling logic of liberal internationalism 2.0 seemed to be increasingly problematic. Why, then, is this order in trouble, and what would liberal internationalism 3.0 look like?

28. See Borgwardt (2005).

The Crisis of Liberal Internationalism 2.0

Liberal internationalism 1.0 ended in a crisis of failure. Liberal internationalism 2.0 is in crisis today, but it is a crisis of success. The Wilsonian vision of liberal order was coherent; it simply did not fit the realities of the time, having been built on assumptions that did not hold. In contrast the liberal internationalism of the post-1945 period was highly adapted to existing realities. Ironically its coherence was less obvious, at least at first. Indeed, unlike its Wilsonian predecessor, liberal internationalism 2.0 was never really articulated in a single statement but cobbled together in a protracted political process. Its logic and operation emerged gradually from the shifting imperatives, negotiations, and adaptations of the early postwar decades. Eventually, in the context of a weakened Europe and a threatening Soviet Union, the United States found itself taking responsibility for organizing and operating the system—and the liberal hegemonic order took shape.

But U.S. liberal hegemony no longer appears to be an adequate framework to support liberal international order. Shifts in the underlying circumstances of world politics again are forcing change in the organizing ideas and institutions of the liberal project. The authority of the United States, its hegemonic bargains with other states, and the rules and institutions of liberal internationalism 2.0 are increasingly contested.[29] What has changed?

First, most obviously, the end of the cold war altered the logic of hegemony. During the decades of bipolar competition, the United States provided "system-function" services as it balanced against Soviet power. Under conditions of bipolarity the United States was a global security provider. U.S. power was functional for system stability and security, and it disciplined and restrained the way Washington exercised power. It made the United States more willing to undertake global responsibilities, provide public goods, and support and operate within a system of rules and institutions. Other countries received services and benefits from the United States' bipolar global power position. The United States needed allies and allies needed the United States. This provided the basis for bargains—and it created incentives for cooperation in areas outside of national security. The end of the cold war did not eliminate these security-driven incentives for cooperation, but it altered and weakened these incentives.[30]

---

29. For discussions of the dilemmas and troubled character of liberal internationalism, see Hoffmann (1998); Bernstein and Pauly (2007); and Hurrell (2007).

30. See Ikenberry (forthcoming).

Second, the rise of unipolarity has made U.S. power more controversial and raised the level of uncertainty around the world about the bargains and institutions of liberal order. With the end of the cold war, the primacy of the United States in the global distribution of capabilities has become one of the most salient features of the international system. No other major state has enjoyed such advantages in material capabilities—military, economic, technological, geographical—and this historically unique unipolar distribution of power has ushered in a new set of dynamics that is still working its way through the organization of world politics.[31] But the rise of unipolarity has brought with it a shift in the underlying logic of order and rule in world politics. In a bipolar or multipolar system, powerful states "rule" in the process of leading a coalition of states in balancing against other states. When the system shifts to unipolarity, this logic of rule disappears: power is no longer based on balancing or equilibrium, but on the predominance of one state. This is new and different, and potentially threatening to weaker and secondary states.[32]

Third, a more gradual shift in the global system has been the unfolding revolution of human rights and the "responsibility to protect," the result of which has been an erosion over the postwar decades of norms of Westphalian sovereignty. The international community is now seen as having a legitimate interest in what goes on inside countries—that is, in the domestic governance practices of states. This growing interest is driven by considerations of both human rights and security.[33] The result is that norms of sovereignty are seen as more contingent, and powerful states now have a "license" to intervene in the domestic affairs of weak and troubled states. Over the past several centuries Westphalian sovereignty in many ways has been the universal and agreed-on norm of international politics.[34] It underlies international law, the United Nations, and the great historical movements of anticolonialism and national self-determination. So when the norm weakens it is not surprising that there are consequences.

31. On the character and consequences of unipolarity, see Ikenberry, Mastanduno, and Wohlforth (2009).

32. See Ikenberry (2006).

33. For a survey of the shifting norms of state sovereignty, see Richard Haass, "The Changing Nature of Sovereignty" (remarks given at Georgetown University, Washington, January 14, 2003). The emerging doctrine of the "responsibility to protect" is the most systematic notion that captures the changing terms of sovereignty and interventionism; see International Commission on Intervention and State Sovereignty (2001); and Evans (2008).

34. Krasner (1999) argues that Westphalian norms have been consistently and continually violated by Great Powers over the centuries, and honored primarily in the breach. The argument here is not that violations of state sovereignty have increased—a proposition that would be difficult to measure—but that the norms of state sovereignty have eroded as a defining feature of liberal international order.

But the erosion of state sovereignty norms have not been matched by the rise of new norms and agreements about how the international community should make good on human rights and the responsibility to protect. Unresolved disagreements mount about the standards of legality and legitimacy that attach to powerful states that profess to act on behalf of the international community. As a result the erosion of norms of sovereignty has ushered in a new global struggle over the sources of authority in the international community. This problem is made worse by U.S. unipolarity: only the United States really has the military power to engage systematically in the large-scale use of force around the world. If the United Nations has no troops or military capacity of its own, what precisely is the "community of states" and who speaks for it? The problem of establishing legitimate international authority grows.

Fourth, the sources of insecurity in world politics have also evolved since the early decades of liberal internationalism 2.0. The threat to peace is no longer primarily from Great Powers engaged in security competition. Nuclear deterrence, democratic peace, and the decline in gains from conquest are key to explaining the persistence of stable peace among the major states over the past half-century, the longest period of Great Power peace in the modern era.[35] The result has been a shift in the ways in which violence is manifest. In the past only powerful states were able to threaten other societies. Today technology and globalization create opportunities for non-state actors—or even transnational gangs of individuals—to acquire weapons of mass destruction.[36] Now the weakness of states and their inability to enforce internal law and order provide the most worrisome dangers to the international system.

Fifth, the growth of the world economy and its incorporation of many new countries, or "stakeholders," has raised questions about participation and decisionmaking in global governance. For the first time in the modern era, economic growth is bringing fast-growing non-Western countries such as China and India into the top ranks of the world economic system. Developing countries now produce half of global GNP, hold most of the world's financial reserves, and are placing huge new demands on energy and raw materials. As Fareed Zakaria notes, "For the first time ever, we are witnessing genuinely global growth. This is creating an international system in which countries in all parts of the world are no longer objects or observers but players in their own right."[37] These are remarkable developments with potentially far-reaching implications for power and governance in world politics.[38]

35. See Jervis (2002).
36. See Keohane (2002).
37. Zakaria (2008, p. 3).
38. See Ikenberry and Wright (2007).

The foundation on which liberal internationalism 2.0 was built has shifted. It is no longer a system based on equilibrium or balance among the Great Powers. The unipolar distribution of power and the rise of new powers and participants in the global system have made the old bargains and institutions less tenable. The building of liberal international order was more successful than anyone in the 1940s really imagined was possible. But the erosion of old norms of sovereignty, the spread of international norms of human rights, and the rise of new threats of collective violence have created in a fundamental sense a crisis of authority in today's liberal order. During the cold war U.S. leadership was acceptable to other liberal states because it provided protection from Soviet communism. That authority is now less securely established, and the U.S.-centered, hierarchical character of the postwar international order is more problematic. Now the great challenge to liberal international order is how to establish legitimate authority for concerted international action on behalf of the global community—and to do so when old norms of order are eroding.

Liberal International Order 3.0

Liberal internationalism 2.0 is in crisis, and pressures and incentives are growing for reform and reorganization. The U.S.-led order is giving way, but to what? It is not easy to specify the organizational logic of the posthegemonic liberal international order, but three sets of issues are particularly important in shaping what comes next.

One set of issues concerns scope and hierarchy. A reformed liberal international order will need to become more universal and less hierarchical—that is, the United States will need to cede authority and control to a wider set of states and give up some of its hegemonic rights and privileges. But a "flatter" international order will also be one in which the United States plays a less central role in providing functional services—generating public goods, stabilizing markets, and promoting cooperation. So the questions are several. What is the logic of a posthegemonic liberal order, and is it viable? Can these functional services be provided collectively? Will the United States agree to relinquish the special rights and privileges built into liberal internationalism 2.0? It is possible, of course, for more incremental shifts away from liberal hegemony. The United States could continue to provide functional services for liberal order but do so in wider concert with other major states. Liberal order might be endangered if there is too much hierarchy—indeed hierarchy in its extreme form is empire—but it also might also endangered if there is too little hierarchy, as the Wilsonian-era experiment in liberal order revealed.

A second issue concerns legitimate authority and post-Westphalian sovereignty. A reformed liberal international order will need to find ways to reconcile more intrusive rules and institutions with legitimate international authority. The human rights revolution makes the international community increasingly concerned with the internal workings of states. So too does the new international threat environment, where growing "security interdependence" makes each country's security increasingly dependent on what goes on elsewhere, including inside states. The international community will need the capacity and legitimate authority to intervene in weak and troubled states.[39] It will also need monitoring, surveillance, and inspection capacities to ensure that increasingly lethal technologies of violence do not get into the hands of dangerous groups. Finding consensus on the norms of intervention in a post-Westphalian world is deeply problematic—yet short of establishing such legitimate authority, the international order will continue to be troubled and contested.

A third issue relates to democracy and the international rule of law. Here the question is how to build authority and capacity in international bodies and agreements without jeopardizing popular rule and accountability inherent in liberal democratic states. Can the authority and capacity of the international community to act be strengthened without sacrificing constitutional democracy at home? This is a deep unresolved problem in the liberal international project.[40] Liberals anticipate a growing role for the international community in the functioning of the global system even though the postwar era already saw a radical increase in the norms and cooperative efforts launched on its behalf. The human rights revolution and the rise of international norms of "deviance" carry with them expectations that the outside world will act when governments fail to behave properly.[41] The growing interdependence of states is also creating rising demands for governance norms and institutions. But how can one square the domestic and international liberal visions?

Out of these tensions and dilemmas will be shaped the next phase of the liberal international project. There are at least three paths away from liberal internationalism 2.0, each involving a different array of sovereignty, rules, institutions, and authority.

---

39. For discussions of post-Westphalian forms of international supervision and the management of weak or collapsed states, see Keohane (2003); Fearon amd Laitlin (2004); and Krasner (2005). See also Ferguson (2004).

40. On the accountability of international institutions, see Keohane and Nye (2003); and Grant and Keohane (2005).

41. On the evolving norms of "deviance" in international relations, see Nincic (2007).

The first possibility is liberal internationalism 3.0, a far-reaching reworking of the U.S.-led liberal hegemonic order in which the United States exercises less command and control of the rules and institutions. The special rights and privileges of the United States would contract as other states gained more weight and authority at the high table of global governance. The "private" governance the United States provided through NATO and its dominance of multilateral institutions would give way to more "public" rules and institutions of governance. At the same time the intrusiveness and reach of liberal order would also continue to expand, placing demands on governance institutions to forge consensual and legitimate forms of collective action.

In this liberal order 3.0, authority would move toward universal institutions—or at least to international bodies with wider global membership. These would include a reformed United Nations, with a Security Council whose permanent membership would expand to include rising and non-Western countries such as Japan, India, Brazil, and South Africa. Other bodies such as the G-20—which, unlike the G-8, includes representatives from both developed and emerging states—would grow in importance. The Bretton Woods institutions—the International Monetary Fund and the World Bank—would expand and reapportion voting shares to give countries such as China and India significant voices in the governance of these institutions while those of the United States and European countries would contract.

Liberal international order 3.0 would also see a further erosion of norms of Westphalian sovereignty and increasing importance of the notion of a "responsibility to protect." The idea that the international community has a right—indeed, a responsibility—to intervene inside states for reasons of human rights and security would be increasingly embraced worldwide. This movement toward post-Westphalian norms of sovereignty, however, leaves unanswered the question of which states—and international bodies—should acquire the right and the authority to decide where and how to act. The logical move would be to turn to the authority of a reformed UN Security Council, but if the recent past is a guide the ability of the Security Council actually to reach agreement and to sanction the use of force is highly problematic.[42] Other, less universal bodies—such as NATO or a proposed League or Concert of Democracies—might provide alternative sources of authority for intervention, but the legitimacy of these bodies is only partial and contested.[43] Liberal internationalism 3.0 might

---

42. A large literature explores the problems of legitimacy and the use of force; for the classic exploration of these issues, see Claude (1966).

43. Several proposals for a new grouping of democracies have been advanced; see, for example, Ikenberry and Slaughter (2006); and Daalder and Lindsay (2007).

solve this problem by fostering greater agreement among Security Council permanent members on the rights and obligations of the international community to act. More likely, questions about intervention and the use of force will remain contested, and regional bodies and nonuniversal groupings of like-minded states will continue to offer alternative sources of authority.

Beyond questions of humanitarian intervention and the "responsibility to protect," security threats coming from the potential diffusion of technologies of violence into the hands of terrorist groups will continue to generate incentives for more intrusive international arms control and counterproliferation capacities. Over the past two decades, the International Atomic Energy Agency (IAEA)—the leading organizational edge of these efforts—has developed scientific and technical competence and legal frameworks for monitoring and inspecting nuclear programs around the world. As nuclear, biological, and chemical weapons technologies grow more sophisticated and diffuse into troubled parts of the world, governments no doubt will seek to expand IAEA-type capacities for monitoring, inspection, verification, and safeguarding. Pressures will grow for norms of Westphalian sovereignty to continue to give way incrementally to intrusive international security regimes.[44]

The hierarchical character of liberal internationalism 3.0 would be "flatter," but hierarchy would remain—it simply would not be dominated by the United States. Instead it would be found in an expanded grouping of leading states occupying positions in the UN Security Council, the Bretton Woods institutions, and other less formal international bodies that collectively would provide security, uphold open markets, and perform other functional services that were once the responsibility of the United States. In some ways the character of hierarchy would look similar to Roosevelt's vision of liberal internationalism 1.5, in which a grouping of leading states claims authority and institutional positions to oversee the stability and peace of the global system. In liberal internationalism 3.0, however, their leadership responsibilities would multiply to include a wider array of security, economic, and political governance duties.

The character of the rule of law would also evolve under liberal internationalism 3.0. In some areas, such as trade and investment, rules-based norms would continue to apply—indeed the World Trade Organization is already a liberal internationalism 3.0–type global system of rules. Under international trade law the United States does not have special rights or privileges. Leading trade states do exercise power in various ways owing to their market size and overall standing in the international order, but the norms of trade law are based

---

44. For discussions of the evolving technical and legal frameworks for arms-control monitoring and enforcement, see Kessler (1995); and Cirincione, Wolfsahl, and Rajkmar (2005).

fundamentally on notions of equality and reciprocity. All contracting parties have access to opt-out and escape clauses, and mechanisms exist for dispute resolution.[45] In areas where economic interdependence generates incentives for states to coordinate and harmonize their policies, rules-based order should increase. But in other areas where states resist legal-institutional forms of cooperation, less formal networks of cooperation likely will grow.[46] Such network-style cooperation allows states to circumvent politically difficult or costly formal, treaty-based commitments. Network cooperation would appear particularly attractive to the United States as it loses the power advantages and rights and privileges it had under liberal internationalism 2.0. In a posthegemonic order, the United States would find informal and network-oriented agreements tolerable substitutes that allow it to gain the benefits of cooperation without offering up formal-legal restrictions on its sovereign independence.

Liberal internationalism 3.0 would draw on the logics of both its predecessors. Like the post-1945 liberal order, it would be a governance system that did a great deal of work. The policy domains in which states would cooperate would be expansive—indeed even more so than was liberal internationalism 2.0. The breadth and depth of the rules and institutions of liberal order would continue to grow. As a nonhegemonic order, however, the actual functioning of the system would look a lot like Wilsonian-style liberal internationalism—a universal order tied less to the United States or to the West. But also like the Wilsonian version, it would be an order in which cooperation depended on shared norms that fostered collective action. It remains a question whether the norms—or ideology of liberal order—are sufficiently coherent and widely embraced to make this posthegemonic order function effectively over the long haul.

A second path is also possible in which liberal internationalism 2.0 is less fully transformed—this would be liberal internationalism 2.5. In this adaptation the United States would renegotiate the bargains and institutions of the past decades but retain its position as hegemonic leader. In some sense this is what is already happening today.[47] In this reformed liberal hegemonic order the United States would continue to provide functional services for the wider system; in return, other countries would acquiesce in the hierarchical rules and institutions presided over by Washington. The order would remain hierarchical but the terms of hierarchy—the bargains and rules—would be altered in ways mutually acceptable to states within the order.

45. On the rules-based character of the World Trade Organization, see Lloyd (2001).

46. The leading study of network-based international cooperation is Slaughter (2004); see also Slaughter (2000).

47. See Drezner (2007).

In this 2.5 order the United States would give up some of its hegemonic rights and privileges but retain others. In economic and political realms it would yield authority and accommodate rising states. Within the reformed Bretton Woods institutions the United States would share authority, but in security realms it would retain its hegemonic position and offer security to other states in a worldwide system of alliances. The U.S. economy would remain a leading source of markets and growth, even if its relative size declined. In short the United States would remain positioned to support and uphold the renegotiated rules and institutions of the liberal order.

In some respects the George W. Bush administration sought to save the U.S.-led hegemonic order by renegotiating its bargains, envisioning the United States as the unipolar provider of global security and upholder of an international order of free and democratic states.[48] In this version the United States would provide functional services to the world, but in return it would ask for new rights and privileges. It would remain aloof from various realms of rules-based order—including the International Criminal Court and other sovereignty-restraining treaties and international agreements. Under this new hegemonic bargain the United States would provide security and stable order, but it would receive special dispensation to remain unattached to the multilateral, rules-based system. In the end this was a bargain the rest of the world did not accept.[49] The question is whether a different set of bargains might be acceptable whereby the United States provides functional services—particularly security protection—but also agrees to operate within a renegotiated system of rules and institutions. The Bush administration tried to use the unrivaled military capabilities of the United States to reduce its exposure to rules-based order. Is it possible for the United States to increase its exposure to such order while retaining aspects of authority and privilege within a renegotiated hegemonic order—that is, liberal internationalism 2.5?

A final possibility is the breakdown of liberal international order, which would occur if the order were to become significantly less open and rules based. The collapse of the system of open, multilateral trade could usher in a 1930s-style world of mercantilism, regional blocs, and bilateral pacts. The political and security rules and institutions of liberal internationalism 2.0 could also fragment into competing geopolitical blocs. Such a breakdown would not necessarily entail a complete collapse of order, but it would mean an end to its open, rules-based, multilateral character. The U.S. hegemonic order might

---

48. The best statement of this vision is President George W. Bush's speech at the 2002 West Point commencement.

49. For critiques of the Bush doctrine, see Daalder and Lindsay (2003); and Shapiro (2007).

simply yield to an international system in which several leading states or centers of power—for example, China, the United States, and the European Union—establish their own economic and security spheres. The global order would become a less unified and coherent system of rules and institutions, while regional orders would emerge as relatively distinct, divided, and competitive geopolitical spheres.[50]

Several factors, or variables, will shape the path away from liberal internationalism 2.0. One is the actual willingness of the United States to cede authority to the international community and accommodate itself to a system of more binding rules and institutions. Short of a radical shift in the international distribution of power, the United States will remain the world's most powerful state for decades to come, so there is reason to think that other countries would be willing to see the United States play a leading role—and provide functional services—if the terms are right. Under almost any circumstances these terms would entail a reduction in its hegemonic rights and privileges while operating within agreed-on rules and institutions. The United States might also come to believe that this renegotiated hegemonic arrangement was better than any of the alternatives. But would the United States be willing to make the political commitments implicit in a renegotiated liberal international order 2.5, let alone reconcile itself to version 3.0? In the end the United States might opt for a more fragmented system in which it built more selective partnerships with key allies that remain tied to the provision of U.S. security.

A second variable is the degree to which the security capacities of the United States could be leveraged into wider economic and political agreements. The United States has extraordinary advantages in military power: its expenditures on military capacity equal the rest of the world's combined, it operates a worldwide system of alliances and security partnerships, and it "commands the commons" in alone having the power to project force in all regions of the world. This situation will not change anytime soon, even with the rapid economic growth of China and India. To what extent, however, do these advantages and disparities in military capabilities translate into bargaining power over the wider array of global rules and institutions? If the answer is very little, then the United States will find it necessary to reconcile itself to liberal internationalism 3.0. But if other countries value U.S. security protection, this would allow the United States to negotiate a modified hegemonic system.

A third variable is the degree of divergence among the leading states' visions of global governance. The EU is clearly more interested in moving to a world

---

50. This fragmented order might have characteristics similar to the those of the U.S. airlines industry, in which the major power centers (airlines) have their own distinct and competing hub-and-spoke systems; see Aaltola (2005).

of liberal internationalism 3.0 than is China—at least to the extent that this would entail further reductions in Westphalian sovereignty. But would China and India seek to use their rising power to usher in a substantially different sort of international order? Do these countries see their interests as well served within liberal international order,[51] or are they not inclined to embrace the open, rules-based logic of liberal internationalism at all, whether it is 1.0, 2.0, or 3.0?[52] If the former is the case, the character of the negotiations on the movement away from liberal internationalism 2.0 will focused more on participation and the sharing of authority and less on shifts in the substantive character of liberal order.

Conclusion

The liberal international "project" has continued to evolve over the past century. Previous shifts in the logic and character of liberal international order came in the aftermath of war and economic upheaval. In contrast the current troubles that are besetting U.S.-led liberal internationalism 2.0 are not manifesting in the breakdown of the old order; rather, the crisis is one of authority. At issue is the way liberal international order is governed, which is generating pressures and incentives for a reorganization of the way sovereignty, rules, institutions, hierarchy, and authority are arrayed in the international system. The U.S. hegemonic organization of liberal order no longer appears to offer a solid foundation for the maintenance of an open, rules-based system—an impasse to which the very success of the old order is partly responsible for bringing us.

What comes after liberal internationalism 2.0? In the absence of war or economic calamity, the old order is not likely to breakdown completely or to disappear. As in the past, liberal international order will evolve, with the character of governance shifting with changes in the way states share and exercise power and authority. Precisely because the current crisis of liberal order is one of success, leading and rising states are not likely to seek to overturn the basic logic of liberal internationalism as a system of open, rules-based order. Instead the pressures and incentives for change are motivated by a desire to rearrange the way roles and responsibilities are allocated in the system.

The way in which liberal order evolves will hinge in important respects on the willingness and ability of the United States to make new commitments to rules and institutions while agreeing to a reduction of its rights and privileges within the order. The United States historically has been deeply ambivalent about

---

51. I make this argument in Ikenberrry (2008).
52. See Leonard (2008).

making such institutional commitments, however—a feeling that the end of the cold war and the rise of U.S. unipolarity and new security threats have served to exacerbate. Nevertheless the United States still possesses profound incentives to build and operate within a liberal, rules-based order. Just as important, that order is now not simply an extension of U.S. power and interests but has taken on a life of its own. U.S. power might rise or fall and its foreign policy ideology might wax and wane between multilateral and imperial impulses, but a wider and deeper liberal global order is now a reality to which the United States must accommodate itself.

References

Aaltola, Mika. 2005. "The International Airport: The Hub-and-Spoke Pedagogy of the American Empire." *Global Network* 5, no. 3: 261–78.

Adler, Emanuel, and Michael Barnett, eds. 1998. *Security Communities*. Cambridge University Press.

Ambrosius, Lloyd E. 2002. *Wilsonianism: Woodrow Wilson and His Legacy in American Foreign Relations*. New York: Palgrave.

Bernstein, Steven, and Louis W. Pauly, eds. 2007. *Global Liberalism and Political Order: Toward a New Grand Compromise*. State University of New York Press.

Borgwardt, Elizabeth. 2005. *A New Deal for the World: America's Vision for Human Rights*. Harvard University Press.

Cirincione, Joseph, Jon B. Wolfshal, and Miriam Rajkmar. 2005. *Deadly Arsenals: Nuclear, Biological and Chemical Threats*, 2nd ed. Washington: Carnegie Endowment for International Peace.

Claude, Inis L. 1962. *Power and International Relations*. New York: Random House.

———. 1966. "Collective Legitimation as a Political Function of the United Nations." *International Organization* 20, no. 3: 367–79.

Daalder, Ivo, and James Lindsay. 2003. *America Unbound: The Bush Revolution in Foreign Policy*. Brookings.

———. 2007. "Democracies of the World, Unite." *The American Interest* 2, no. 3: 5–19.

Dallek, Robert. 1979. *Franklin Roosevelt and American Foreign Policy, 1932–1945*. Oxford University Press.

Deudney, Daniel, and G. John Ikenberry. 1999. "The Nature and Sources of Liberal International Order." *Review of International Studies* 25 (Spring): 179–96.

Deutsch, Karl, Sidney Burrell, and Robert Kann. 1957. *Political Community and the North Atlantic Area: International Organization in the Light of Historical Experience*. Princeton University Press.

Divine, Robert A. 1971. *Second Chance: The Triumph of Internationalism in America during World War II*. New York: Atheneum.

Doyle, Michael. 1983. "Kant, Liberal Legacies, and Foreign Affairs." *Philosophy and Public Affairs* 12 (Summer-Fall): 205–35, 323–53.

———. 1997. *Ways of War and Peace*. New York: Norton.

Drezner, Daniel. 2007. "The New New World Order." *Foreign Affairs* 86 (March-April): 34–46.

Evans, Gareth. 2008. *The Responsibility to Protect: Ending Mass Atrocity Crimes Once and for All*. Brookings.

Fearon, James, and David D. Laitin. 2004. "Neotrusteeship and the Problem of Weak States." *International Security* 28, no. 4: 5–43.

Ferguson, Niall. 2004. *Colossus: The Rise and Fall of the American Empire*. New York: Penguin Books.

Gilpin, Robert. 1981. *War and Change in World Politics*. Cambridge University Press.

Goldstein, Judith, and others, eds. 2001. *Legalization and World Politics*. MIT Press.

Grant, Ruth, and Robert O. Keohane. 2005. "Accountability and Abuses of Power in World Politics." *American Political Science Review* 99, no. 1: 1–15

Haas, Ernst. 1964. *Beyond the Nation-State: Functionalism and International Organization*. Stanford University Press.

Hobson, John M., and J.C. Sharman. 2005. "The Enduring Place of Hierarchy in World Politics: Tracing the Social Logic of Hierarchy and Political Change." *European Journal of International Relations* 11, no. 1: 63–98.

Hoffmann, Stanley. 1998. *World Disorders: Troubled Peace in the Post–Cold War Era*. Lanham, Md.: Rowman and Littlefield.

Hurrell, Andrew. 2007. *On Global Order: Power, Values, and the Constitution of International Society*. Oxford University Press.

Ikenberry, G. John. 1993. "Creating Yesterday's New World Order." In *Ideas and American Foreign Policy: Beliefs, Institutions, and Political Change*, edited by Judith Goldstein and Robert Keohane. Cornell University Press.

———. 2001. *After Victory: Institutions, Strategic Restraint, and the Rebuilding of Order after Major War*. Princeton University Press.

———. 2006. "The Security Trap." *Democracy: A Journal of Ideas*, no. 2.

———. 2008. "The Rise of China and the Future of the West." *Foreign Affairs* 87, no. 1: 23–37.

———. 2009. "Liberal Internationalism 3.0: America and the Dilemmas of Liberal World Order." *Perspectives on Politics* 71, no. 1: 71–87.

———. Forthcoming. "The Restructuring of the International System after the Cold War." In *Cambridge History of the Cold War*, vol. 3, edited by Melvyn Leffler and Odd Arne Westad. Cambridge University Press.

Ikenberry, G. John, Michael Mastanduno, and William Wohlforth. 2009. "Unipolarity and International Relations Theory." *World Politics* 61, no. 1: 1–27.

Ikenberry, G. John, and Anne-Marie Slaughter. 2006. *Forging a World of Liberty under Law*, Final Report of the Princeton Project on National Security. Princeton University.

Ikenberry, G. John, and Thomas Wright. 2007. "Rising Powers and Global Institutions." Working paper. New York: Century Foundation.

International Commission on Intervention and State Sovereignty. 2001. *The Responsibility to Protect*. Ottawa.

Jervis, Robert. 2002. "Theories of War in an Era of Leading-Power Peace." *American Political Science Review* 96, no. 1: 1–14.

Keohane, Robert O. 1984. *After Hegemony: Cooperation and Discord in the World Political Economy*. Princeton University Press.

———. 1990. "International Liberalism Reconsidered." In *Economic Limits to Modern Politics*, edited by John Dunn. Cambridge University Press.

———. 2002. "The Globalization of Informal Violence, Theories of World Politics, and 'The Liberalism of Fear.'" In *Understanding September 11*, edited by Craig Calhoun, Paul Price, and Ashley Timmer. New York: New Press.

———. 2003. "Political Authority after Intervention: Gradations in Sovereignty." In *Humanitarian Intervention: Ethical, Legal, and Political Dilemmas*, edited by J. L. Holzgrefe and Robert O. Keohane. Cambridge University Press.

Keohane, Robert O., and Joseph Nye, Jr. 1977. *Power and Interdependence*. Boston: Little, Brown.

———. 2003. "Redefining Accountability for Global Governance." In *Governance in a Global Economy: Political Authority in Transition*, edited by Miles Kahler and David Lake. Princeton University Press.

Kessler, J. Christian. 1995. *Verifying Nonproliferation Treaties: Obligations, Process, and Sovereignty*. National Defense University Press.

Keynes, John Maynard. 1920. *The Economic Consequences of the Peace*. New York: Harcourt Brace Jovanovich.

Kimball, Warren F. 1994. *The Juggler: Franklin Delano Roosevelt as Wartime Statesman*. Princeton University Press.

Knock, Thomas Knock. 1992. *To End All Wars: Woodrow Wilson and the Quest for a New World Order*. Oxford University Press.

Krasner, Stephen, ed. 1981. *International Regimes*. Cornell University Press.

———. 1999. *Sovereignty: Organized Hypocrisy*. Princeton University Press.

———. 2005. "Sharing Sovereignty: New Institutions for Collapsed and Failing States." *International Security* 29, no. 2: 85–120.

Lake, David A. 2003. "The New Sovereignty in International Relations." *International Studies Review* 5, no. 3: 303–23.

Legro, Jeff. 2007. *Rethinking the World: Great Power Strategies and International Order*. Cornell University Press.

Leonard, Mark. 2008. *What Does China Think?* New York: Public Affairs Press.

Lloyd, P. J. 2001. "The Architecture of the WTO." *European Journal of Political Economy* 17, no. 2: 327–53.

May, Ernest, ed. 1993. *American Cold War Strategy: Interpreting NSC-68*. New York: St. Martin's Press.

Moravcsik, Andrew. 1997. "Taking Preferences Seriously: A Liberal Theory of International Relations." *International Organization* 51, no. 4: 513–53.

———. 2000. "The Origins of Human Rights Regimes: Democratic Delegation in Postwar Europe." *International Organization* 54, no. 1: 217–52.

Morse, Edward. 1976. *Modernization and the Transformation of International Relations*. New York: Free Press.

Murphy, Craig. 1994. *International Organization and Industrial Change: Global Governance since 1850*. Oxford University Press.

Nincic, Miroslav. 2007. *Renegade Regimes: Confronting Deviant Behavior in World Politics.* Columbia University Press.

Ninkovich, Frank. 1999. *The Wilsonian Century: U.S. Foreign Policy since 1900.* University of Chicago Press.

Organski, A. F. K. 1958. *World Politics.* New York: Alfred A. Knopf.

Press-Barnathan, Galia. 2003. *Organizing the World: The United States and Regional Cooperation in Asia and Europe.* New York: Routledge.

Rosenau, James, ed. 1969. *Linkage Politics: Essays on the Convergence of National and International Systems.* New York: Free Press.

———. 1991. *Turbulence in World Politics: A Theory of Change and Continuity.* Princeton University Press.

Ruggie, John. 2004. "American Exceptionalism, Exemptionalism, and Global Governance." In *American Exceptionalism and Human Rights*, edited by Michael Ignatieff. Princeton University Press.

Russett, Bruce, and John Oneal. 2001. *Triangulating Peace: Democracy, Interdependence and International Organization.* New York: Norton.

Shapiro, Ian. 2008. *Containment: Rebuilding a Strategy against Global Terror.* Princeton University Press.

Slaughter, Anne-Marie. 2000. "Governing the Global Economy through Government Networks." In *The Role of Law in International Politics*, edited by Michael Byers. Oxford University Press.

———. 2004. *A New World Order.* Princeton University Press.

Viner, Jacob. 1942. "Objectives of Post-War International Economic Reconstruction." In *American Economic Objectives*, edited by William McKee and Louis J. Wiesen. New Wilmington, Pa.: Economic and Business Foundation.

Zakaria, Fareed. 2008. *The Post-American World.* New York: Norton.

ANNE-MARIE SLAUGHTER *and* THOMAS HALE

2

Transgovernmental Networks and Emerging Powers

Transgovernmental networks are informal institutions linking regulators, legislators, some ministers, judges, and other actors across national boundaries to carry out various aspects of global governance. They exhibit "pattern[s]
of regular and purposive relations among like government units working across
the borders that divide countries from one another and that demarcate the
'domestic' from the 'international' sphere."[1] They allow domestic officials to
interact with their foreign counterparts directly, without much supervision by
foreign offices or senior executive branch officials, and feature "loosely structured, peer-to-peer ties developed through frequent interaction rather than formal negotiation."[2]

Transgovernmental networks occupy a middle place between traditional
international organizations and ad hoc communication. They have emerged
organically in response to the increasing complexity and transnational nature
of contemporary problems, to which they are uniquely suited, challenging the
distinction between domestic and foreign policy. They appear most commonly
in the realm of regulatory policy—for example, commercial and financial regulation, environmental protection—but also extend to judicial and even legislative areas of government.

Transgovernmental networks provide opportunities to include rising powers
in global governance beyond those available from traditional intergovernmental organizations. The flexible and quasi-formal nature of networks can make
it easier both to bring new countries into transnational decisionmaking and
to give their voices greater weight. The very flexibility of networks, however,
does not make them suited to every cooperation problem that states face, so

---

1. Slaughter (2004b, p. 14).
2. Raustiala (2002, p. 1); see also Risse-Kappen (1995).

transgovernmental networks are no silver bullet. Still transgovernmental networks represent a useful and underexploited tool for interstate cooperation that can help resolve some, if not all, the dilemmas rising powers pose.

Overview of Transgovernmental Networks

Transgovernmental networks have arisen in response to the complex governance challenges posed by increasing transnational interdependence.[3] The phenomenon dates back at least to the 1970s, when Keohane and Nye noted the growing importance of "transgovernmental" activities.[4] In 1972 Harvard University's Francis Bator testified before the U.S. Congress that "it is a central fact of foreign relations that business is carried on by the separate departments with their counterpart bureaucracies abroad, through a variety of informal as well as formal connections."[5]

By the late 1990s, however, transgovernmental networks had increased so dramatically in degree as to amount to a difference in kind. As the latest intense wave of globalization has made international cooperation increasingly necessary on a range of issues—from the economy to the environment to policing—"traditional" forms of diplomacy have sometimes proven cumbersome. By strictly bifurcating the international and domestic spheres, traditional diplomacy—conducted through foreign ministries, ambassadors, and international organizations—has been outstripped by the transnationality of many contemporary policy issues, which operate simultaneously in the domestic and international realms.

By associating "domestic" officials in networks that stretch between nations, transgovernmental networks perform three important functions. First, they expand the state's capacity to confront transnational issues. So many areas of policymaking now require international coordination that foreign ministries alone are simply unable to handle the full portfolio of extra-national assignments. Similarly, domestic officials find they are unable to fulfill their responsibilities adequately without consulting and coordinating with their foreign counterparts.

Second, and related to the first point, international cooperation now extends to many highly technical issues—for example, financial regulation or environmental monitoring—about which foreign ministries simply lack expertise. The expanded scope and depth of contemporary interdependence

---

3. Parts of this section are drawn from Slaughter (2004b); and Slaughter and Zaring (2006).
4. Keohane and Nye (1974, p. 43).
5. Quoted in Keohane and Nye (1974, p. 42).

sometimes necessitates technocratic responses that only specialized domestic officials can provide.

Third, networks allow for flexibility and responsiveness in a way that traditional diplomatic channels and international institutions often do not, which increases efficiency. Because networks are not formal institutions, they often reach outcomes with lower transaction costs than do international institutions. Networks focus attention on information exchange, discussion, and coordination, avoiding many of the obstacles that inevitably draw out efforts to negotiate formal treaties or pass resolutions. Moreover, by bringing together the actual officials responsible for a certain policy area—as opposed to diplomats responsible for liaising with other countries—networks can also increase the efficiency of international coordination.

Transgovernmental networks can be categorized by both the relationships they establish and the functions they perform. As noted above, transgovernmental relationships can be either horizontal or vertical. Most transgovernmental networks are horizontal—that is, between actors at the same level, such as judge to judge or regulator to regulator. Some networks, however, are vertical—for example, between supranational officials and national-level officials; in the European Union, supranational officials work closely with their domestic counterparts to ensure that EU policy is implemented in the national context.

Networks come in many different varieties, but can be grouped in three basic types: information networks, enforcement networks, and harmonization networks. Horizontal information networks, as the name suggests, bring together regulators, judges, or legislators to exchange information and to collect and distill best practices. This information exchange can also take place through technical assistance and training programs provided by one country's officials to another's. The direction of such training is not always from a developed country to a developing country; it can also be from one developed country to another, as when U.S. antitrust officials spent time training their counterparts in New Zealand.

Enforcement networks typically spring up due to the inability of government officials to enforce the laws of their own country, either by means of a regulatory agency or through a court. But enforcement cooperation inevitably also involves a great deal of information exchange, and might involve assistance programs of various types. Legislators can also collaborate on how to draft complementary legislation to avoid enforcement loopholes.

Finally, harmonization networks—typically authorized by treaty or executive agreement—bring regulators together to ensure that their rules in a particular substantive area conform to a common regulatory standard. Judges can also engage in equivalent activity, but in a much more ad hoc manner.

Harmonization is often politically controversial, with critics charging that the technical process of achieving convergence ignores the many winners and losers in domestic publics, most of whom have no input into the process.

The Proliferation and Evolution of Transgovernmental Networks

Transgovernmental networks have proliferated in almost every area of government regulation. They are used to address issues ranging from high politics, questions of national security, and official corruption to more mundane concerns such as common policies on airplane regulation. Legal scholars have identified and considered the implications of cooperation in such areas as tax, antitrust, food and drug, and telecommunications regulation.[6] Indeed, in the European Union alone, forms of coordinative governance have been documented in privatized network infrastructure, public health and safety, employment and social protection, other forms of regulation, and even rights-sensitive areas such as the protection of race, gender, and disabled status.[7]

A few examples may prove instructive. Consider the International Network for Environmental Compliance and Enforcement (INECE), a "partnership among government and non-government compliance and enforcement practitioners from over 150 countries."[8] Founded in 1989, this network of some 4,000 domestic environmental regulators allows participants to share experiences and best practices, to develop common standards, and to coordinate on transboundary issues. Originally a joint project of the U.S. and Dutch environmental agencies, INECE has evolved into a global and increasingly institutionalized organization.

The International Competition Network (ICN) has followed a similar trajectory in the antitrust sphere. In the mid-1990s antitrust regulators felt that the growing size and number of transnational corporations required coordinated responses from regulators across jurisdictions. In 2001, after much consultation, fourteen countries launched the ICN to provide "competition authorities with a specialized yet informal venue for maintaining regular contacts and addressing practical competition concerns" with the hope of allowing "a dynamic dialogue that serves to build consensus and convergence towards sound competition policy principles across the global antitrust community."[9]

---

6. A full list of references is given in Slaughter and Zaring (2006, p. 216).

7. See Sabel and Zeitlin (2006), who refer to such network-like forms as examples of "directly-deliberative polyarchy."

8. International Network for Environmental Compliance and Enforcement, "Overview: International Network for Environmental Compliance and Enforcement" (www.inece.org/ [2008]).

9. International Competition Network, "About the ICN" (www.internationalcompetition network.org/index.php/en/about-icn [2008]).

The ICN does not make antitrust laws; rather, it relies on working groups to develop recommendations and guidelines to solve specific problems that are then implemented by national regulators.

The Basel Committee on Banking Supervision, one of the most prominent transgovernmental networks, was founded in 1974 by the central bank governors of the G10 industrialized economies "to enhance understanding of key supervisory issues and improve the quality of banking supervision worldwide ... by exchanging information on national supervisory issues, approaches and techniques, with a view to promoting common understanding." By the 1970s the need for greater coordination and centralized information exchange among central bankers had become apparent. Once created the Basel Committee also took on a policymaking function by promulgating a global accord on capital adequacy standards (Basel I). In 1997 the committee issued a "Set of Core Principles for Effective Banking Supervision," which its members have worked actively to promote in many other countries.[10] By the 2000s the Basel Committee had developed four subcommittees, one of which is a regular liaison to sixteen supervisory authorities around the world and to regional and international financial institutions. The committee also undertook an elaborate consultative process to revise Basel I and issued new "Basel II" standards for capital adequacy and other banking issues. The committee meets regularly with central bankers from important emerging markets, holds biannual international conferences of banking supervisors, circulates published and unpublished papers to banking supervisors around the world, and offers technical assistance on banking supervision in many countries.

Expanding even more, the Basel Committee Secretariat now acts as secretariat to the Joint Forum and the Coordination Group, entities created to foster cooperation among central bankers, insurance supervisors, and securities commissioners. The Bank for International Settlements, the traditional international institution that hosts the Basel Committee and other regulatory networks, now describes itself in part as a "hub for central bankers," linking to central bank websites and related sources of information and expertise all over the world. It also provides secretariat functions for related organizations of financial regulators, such as the Financial Stability Forum, now the Financial Stability Board, and the International Organization of Insurance Supervisors. The result is nothing less than a new global financial architecture, but one created by informal networks rather than by formal institutions.

---

10. Bank for International Settlements, "About the Basel Committee" (www.bis.org/bcbs/index.htm [2008]).

Governmental networks are also increasingly important at the regional level, especially in Asia, where formal institutions remain weak. The Association of Southeast Asian Nations (ASEAN), arguably the most institutionalized inter-governmental organization in Asia, was founded not by a formal treaty but through a "multilateral declaration." In the beginning, formal governance of the organization was placed in an annual meeting of foreign ministers and most of the bargaining and negotiation occurred in the Senior Officials Meeting, a net-work of senior officials in foreign ministries that did not even have formal sta-tus within ASEAN. The informality and decentralization of ASEAN's structure is complemented by its institutional principles. Instead of emphasizing legal commitments and mutual obligations, ASEAN takes as its guiding precepts *musyawarah* (consultation) and *mufakat* (consensus), concepts originating in the practice of southeast Asian village life.

Apart from ASEAN, the most important transgovernmental networks in Asia today are horizontal information networks focused on economic policy, a response to the region's deepening economic integration. The ASEAN+3 net-work (consisting of the ten ASEAN member states plus China, South Korea, and Japan) has become the region's premier forum for financial coordination. It is complemented by the ASEAN Surveillance Process, the Manila Framework Group, the Executives Meeting of East Asia-Pacific Central Banks, and trans-regional forums such as Asia-Pacific Economic Cooperation and Asia-Europe Meeting. The premier security institution for China, the Shanghai Cooperation Organization, also exhibits much more of a network structure than more for-malized defense institutions such as NATO.

The informal nature of transgovernmental networks thus far has foiled efforts to generate a comprehensive list of them, so scholars cannot say precisely how broad their impact has been. Calls at the highest levels for the expansion of these networks indicate, however, that they will become even more impor-tant to multilateral cooperation in the future. To take just one example, the experience of Julie Geberding, director of the U.S. Centers for Disease Control (CDC), in managing the SARS pandemic is affirmed the extreme difficulty of coordinating the response to a global crisis affecting hundreds of agencies and authorities at different levels of national and international governance through a national hierarchy, the CDC itself.[11] Faced with responsibility for the problem but lacking the authority to command all the necessary actors, Gerberding dis-covered that a networked approach was the only way to confront the pandemic.

Beyond specific issues, a major study by the Brookings Institution recom-mends expanding the G-8 to a G-16 and creating a network that would include

---

11. Geberding (2003).

leaders of both developed and developing countries.[12] The 2004 UN High-level Panel on Threats, Challenges and Change endorsed a similar proposal for a leaders' network of some twenty countries. Another proposal, aimed at addressing climate change, is to form an E8, a group of the largest polluters. From high politics to the more mundane realms of everyday technical cooperation, networks are necessary.

How Transgovernmental Networks Work

The Basel Committee describes its own authority and role as follows:

> The Committee does not possess any formal supranational supervisory authority, and its conclusions do not, and were never intended to, have legal force. Rather, it formulates broad supervisory standards and guidelines and recommends statements of best practice in the expectation that individual authorities will take steps to implement them through detailed arrangements—statutory or otherwise—which are best suited to their own national systems. In this way, the Committee encourages convergence towards common approaches and common standards without attempting detailed harmonisation of member countries' supervisory techniques.[13]

That, in a nutshell, is how most transgovernmental networks—at least information networks—function. They have no formal legal authority, but instead operate through exchanging and distilling information and expertise. They are able to exploit the institutional benefits unique to the network form, which are produced in a variety of ways.

First, on the informational level, networks serve as forums for experimentation and sharing, which leads to learning. As one observer puts it, networks are "based on complex communication channels," and so are able not only to communicate information but also to generate new meanings and interpretations of the information transmitted, thereby providing "a context for learning by doing."[14] These types of learning networks are an increasingly common feature of domestic governance in many countries.[15] They are also important in many *private* transnational networks, such as the UN Global Compact, which

---

12. Jones, Pascual, and Stedman (2009).

13. Bank for International Settlements, "About the Basel Committee" (www.bis.org/bcbs/index.htm [February 2008]).

14. Powell (1990, p. 325). The mechanics of this kind of learning- and experiment-based governance have been explored in depth, principally in the domestic context, by Sabel and Zeitlin (2006).

15. See, for example, Sorensen and Torfing (2007).

serves, in part, as a platform for multinational corporations to share methods for making their business practices more environmentally and socially sustainable.[16] This "wiki-government" remains underused, however, in the realm of state-to-state relations.[17]

Second, regarding coordination, networks might provide a platform for mutual influence. In very few networks do participants have direct influence over one another; instead, they must try to convince their counterparts to follow a certain course of action through argumentation and persuasion. Influence thus comes not solely from a nation's power or wealth, but from an actor's ability to earn the trust of his peers, a process that can lead to significant policy coordination. Looking at regulatory networks in the securities, competition, and environmental fields, one analyst shows that transgovernmental networks serve as channels for "regulatory export" from advanced nations to developing countries. Through technical advice and example setting, networks in each of these areas have served to strengthen regulatory capacity within and across states.[18]

Third, simply by offering a regularized environment in which relevant actors can interact with one another, networks provide a way to coordinate actions such as enforcement or rulemaking across states without many of the transactions costs associated with international institutions or traditional diplomacy. The role of traditional international institutions in providing information and lowering the transaction costs of coordination is well established in international relations theory.[19] Networks bring many of the benefits of traditional organizations—such as information sharing, monitoring, or the creation of focal points—without many of the costs, such as decreased autonomy, principal-agent dilemmas, or administrative burdens. Consequently, however, this lighter, more flexible form of institutionalism cannot achieve some of the deeper benefits of traditional institutions, such as allowing states to make credible, enforceable commitments to one another. Nor does it allow states to delegate tasks to an international organization, because state officials themselves comprise the network. Networks thus represent a form of international cooperation that is distinct from traditional institutions.

Fourth, transgovernmental networks can be a normatively attractive form of global governance. Traditional international institutions and other forms of global governance are sometimes said to suffer from a "democratic deficit." Far removed from public pressure and electoral politics, international institutions such as the World Bank and the International Monetary Fund (IMF)—to

16. Ruggie (2002).
17. Noveck (2008).
18. Raustiala (2002).
19. The seminal work is Keohane (1984).

cite two of the most prominent examples—have been accused of trampling the interests of marginalized peoples or poor countries to promote their preferred policies. Because transgovernmental networks are composed of *national* officials, they are more closely linked to states and thus, in theory, are bound by the same accountability mechanisms that control national governments. By giving states a way to solve transnational problems directly, governmental networks elide a potential legitimacy problem that bedevils many other areas of global governance.

No Network Is Perfect: Problems and Open Questions

Transgovernmental networks also suffer from some deficiencies, of course, and are by no means the ideal institutional arrangement for every setting. The very flexibility that makes networks useful also might render them toothless when strong enforcement powers are necessary to sustain international cooperation. For example, it is difficult to imagine the World Trade Organization (WTO) functioning as a network. Formal rules and the possibility of enforcing those rules through the regulated withdrawal of trade concessions are necessary to make the parties agree to liberalization. Moreover, although transgovernmental networks avoid the accountability concerns of delegating to international institutions, they can face legitimacy problems of their own.[20] To the extent that they empower domestic officials to act without the approval of their domestic superiors, networks might take power out of the hands of elected officials and place it in the hands of enterprising bureaucrats. This problem is reinforced by the technical nature of many transgovernmental networks. By bringing together experts and specialists from different countries, transgovernmental networks gain efficiency and capacity but might lose sight of potential trade-offs with other policy areas. For example, the U.S. public interest organization Public Citizen has criticized harmonization networks—which seek to facilitate economic coordination—for being secretive and biased toward industry. Moreover, because they are not official government agencies but simply ad hoc transnational committees, they are shielded from the accountability guarantees enshrined in domestic administrative law.[21]

Projects aimed at developing global administrative law could address some of these defects.[22] In other cases the participants in government networks themselves have realized the need for much greater transparency and participation.[23]

20. Slaughter (2004a).
21. Slaughter (2004b, pp. 221–22).
22. See, for example, Kingsbury, Krisch, and Stewart (2005).
23. See, for example, Barr and Miller (2006).

One of the authors of this paper has also called repeatedly for the creation of legislative networks that correspond to regulatory networks in order to enhance national legislative oversight.[24] In EU member states, national parliamentarians serving on committees focused on EU affairs realize that they need to network with one another quite independently of the EU Parliament so as not to be left out of the action. As transgovernmental networks grow not only in number but also in the number and types of tasks they are asked to undertake, mechanisms for increased accountability will grow with them.

In addition to these problems and possible reforms, transgovernmental networks are a relatively young form of international cooperation.[25] Their potential uses, and their potential pitfalls, are not fully understood or explored. Several questions remain.

First is the question of how the *social* nature of networks affects their political functions. Networking is a form of creating and storing relational capital, but do the government officials who participate in networks also develop a common sense of values and norms? Most observers of transgovernmental networks—and most scholars of networks of all kinds—believe this kind of socialization is at least possible. In the transgovernmental context, such socialization can enhance trust and coordination between countries, thus making networks more effective. Some observers worry, however, that socialization also might lead bureaucrats to place the values of the network over national interests, although no specific instances are cited in the literature.

In general, socialization—the transfusion of norms, values, and identities among actors—is not well understood in the political literature. More research is needed to understand the mechanisms through which socialization might occur within transgovernmental networks, the relationship between socialization and the operation of networks, and the conditions under which socialization does and does not occur.[26]

Second, a better understanding of the effect of networks on their participants can contribute to our understanding of how best to manage networks for maximum efficiency and impact. In the business literature much is made of "orchestrating networks"; for example, Hong Kong–based Li and Fung Ltd., the largest sourcing company in the world, essentially links different partners at

24. Slaughter (2004b, pp. 104–30).

25. It is difficult to measure the age of this phenomenon or to track its growth precisely because, as we have noted, no definitive list of these networks exists. Few of the networks mentioned in the literature predate the 1970s, however, and most date only from the 1990s. They can thus be associated with the most recent epoch of globalization.

26. Wang (2000), for example, finds little evidence that multilateral institutions have socialized Chinese foreign policy. See, generally, Checkels (2005).

different times to produce different products around the world. Orchestration differs from management in a vertical organization by purportedly requiring "a more fluid approach that empowers partners and employees, yet demands that control be maintained at the same time."[27] The aim is to unleash the kind of creativity and collaboration that produces, say, Wikipedia, while maintaining quality control and enough discipline to ensure that holes get filled and new projects undertaken. Fung, Fung, and Wind write about moving from a firm to a network, from control to empowerment, and from specialization to integration.[28] Other business authors write about "team leadership" and working within decentralized organizations where no one individual is really in charge.[29] Indeed the mantra of team leadership is "strength through shared responsibility," which is a way of describing collective responsibility for a common problem, a requirement for solving global problems such as terrorism and climate change that cannot be contained within national borders.

It is, of course, not clear how management practices in the business community can translate into the government arena. But as national governments and international organizations adapt to operating in a networked world, it will become important to understand the optimal functions of a small secretariat or "central node" of a horizontal network and which functions are best allocated to traditional organizations and which are better handled by networks. Government officials can also learn from some of the large nongovernmental organizations; CARE, for instance, operates supply networks that in some ways resemble those of a company such as Li and Fung, using information technology to identify individuals all over the world who can take part in disaster relief teams ready to be deployed at once.

Third, scholars need to understand better the way in which influence and power operate in transgovernmental networks. In formal international institutions, a state's influence is often a function of its power vis-à-vis other states. Power relations are often even institutionalized in the laws governing an institution—consider the proportional voting system in the WTO or the IMF or the veto power of the permanent members of the UN Security Council. Influence within a transgovernmental network is certainly also a function of state power, but it also might include other factors. The goal of many networks is to share experience, deliberate over experiences, learn from colleagues, and coordinate action around "best practices." To become influential, actors must win colleagues over to their point of view by means of their technical expertise, practical experience, or the power of reasoned argument.

27. Fung, Fung, and Wind (2007, p. 11).
28. Fung, Fung, and Wind (2007, p. 15).
29. See, for example, Barna (2001); Kelly, Ferguson, and Alwon (2001).

Conventional economic or diplomatic levers might play a role where national interests are directly at stake, but much of the work of transgovernmental networks falls outside the realm of competitive diplomatic wrangling. In this way networks favor a different set of skills and competencies than do traditional institutions. Convincing one's peers of the rightness of a common course of action is qualitatively different from lobbying an interlocutor to do what you want him to do. While networks certainly include both kinds of interactions, their ability to highlight the former might broaden the range of successful cooperation beyond that available in traditional institutions.

A last but fundamental question is the effectiveness of transgovernmental networks. Measuring the effectiveness of any institution or policy typically is difficult given the usual lack, in the policy world, of an appropriate counterfactual for comparison. To our knowledge, no systematic studies of transgovernmental network effectiveness exist. For many networks, however, the appropriate counterfactual is not a formal institution—which would be politically infeasible—but ad hoc cooperation, or even none at all. To evaluate networks' effectiveness, observers must first ask themselves what other structures are possible. If none is, then the question is not, are networks better than formal institutions, but, are networks better than nothing?

Transgovernmental Networks and Emerging Powers

In some cases transgovernmental networks might provide an ideal way to increase the participation of emerging powers in global governance. Because they are not suited to all conditions, however, networks cannot "solve" the challenge of including new powers. Moreover some characteristics of networks in fact might discourage the participation of certain emerging powers. Consider the opportunities that transgovernmental networks offer the so-called BRIC countries (Brazil, Russia, India, and China) and the challenges that their participation in networks likely will entail.

On the plus side the flexibility and informality of networks is useful for including new countries. Joining a formal international organization requires a number of potentially costly steps: the institution might have explicit or implicit criteria for membership, existing members might be able to veto new members or impose conditions on their ascension, or the institution's treaties or charters must be signed and ratified, potentially involving other domestic political actors such as legislatures or interest groups that might oppose the institution. These transaction costs do not disappear with networks, but they are often greatly diminished—for example, while legislative consent is often needed for a country to join a formal organization, a senior administrator typically authorizes bureaucratic participation in a network.

Informality also lessens existing members' concerns about including new countries, particularly rising powers. In a formal organization, voting shares, obligations, and other legal commitments must be worked out explicitly, decisions that have significant implications for power and the distribution of resources and thus can forestall agreement. Such difficulties are likely to be particularly salient for rising powers. Networks, however, because they are informal, can elude many of these problems. To the extent that network forms of cooperation contribute to effective global governance, they will be an attractive way to engage new powers.

Consider a concrete example. One of the most vexing institutional issues raised by the BRIC countries is representation on the UN Security Council. With the exception of China and Russia, emerging powers in the international system have expended enormous effort to gain greater influence on what is arguably the most important intergovernmental decisionmaking body in the world. These labors have been in vain: the veto power of the current five permanent members and the politics of the General Assembly time and again have rendered Security Council reform impossible. Contrast this stalemate with the (relative) speed and ease with which the G7 Finance Ministers became the G20 Finance Ministers in 1999 (see the chapter by Kirton in this volume). Despite the concerns of some European countries, especially France and Italy, that an expanded group of finance ministers would dilute the authority of the IMF and of themselves, support from Canada, Japan, and the United States proved sufficient to open the doors of one of the world's most important financial forums to a number of emerging markets in a single stroke. The G20 has since proved an invaluable component of global financial governance.

It is not only the flexibility and informality of networks that make them an attractive way to include the BRIC countries; the very logic of their functioning also might help. Information networks benefit, as we have noted, from increasing returns to scale: the more countries are involved in sharing and learning from information, the more effective is the network. Including more emerging powers in such networks thus would represent not just a way to accommodate rising powers, but also a mutually beneficial arrangement for existing and potential members.

Despite these advantages the limitations of networks will prevent them from solving all the challenges posed by the rise of the BRICs. It is often those areas of international relations where strains between existing and rising powers are most tense that networks are least effective. Consider, for example, the decade-plus of negotiations that preceded Chinese membership in the WTO and difficulty of the ongoing Russian negotiations. A network style of governance would not be able to provide the credible commitment and enforcement mechanisms that underpin the WTO, and so would offer no answer in this case, although it might be the best of a set of bad alternatives. It also might help produce gradual convergence over the longer term. In general, however, when hard rules and institutions are necessary, the network form offers no magical solution through which emerging powers might be included in global governance.

Third, the domestic politics of some BRICs might make it harder for them to participate in transgovernmental networks effectively. Networks of government officials now stretch across all regions of the world, but are most concentrated in North America and especially Europe. There are likely many reasons for this distribution: interdependence in these areas is particularly intense; states in these regions possess vast, sophisticated bureaucracies and liberal political systems that diffuse power throughout government; and a high level of trust exists among these states. The same is not necessarily true of emerging powers, whose governments might favor greater central control over their bureaucracies (as in China or Russia). The BRICs' relative lack of bureaucratic capacity to engage with their developed counterparts, especially on many of the highly technical issues around which networks form, also might their participation in transgovernmental networks.

In sum, although transgovernmental networks cannot solve all the challenges of governing the globe in a world of rising powers, they are already playing a crucial role and likely will become increasingly common. It is thus important for scholars and policymakers to learn more about how such networks operate and to apply that knowledge and experience to create increasingly sophisticated policy mechanisms. For example, networks might be able to incorporate some formalized legal commitments—like those typical of traditional international organizations—while maintaining a desirable degree of flexibility. Most existing networks have emerged organically from the needs of an increasingly interconnected world. But as states seek to include rising powers in the shared task of global governance, more purposeful development of network structures likely will be an important part of the solution.

References

Barna, George. 2001. *The Power of Team Leadership: Finding Strength in Shared Responsibility*. Colorado Springs, Colo.: Waterbrook Press.

Barr, Michael, and Geoffrey Miller. 2006. "Global Administrative Law: The View from Basel." *European Journal of International Law* 17 (1): 15–46.

Checkels, Jeffery. 2005. "International Institutions and Socialization in Europe." *International Organization* 59 (4, special issue).

Fung, Victor K., William K. Fung, and Yoram (Jerry) Wind. 2007. *Competing in a Flat World: Building Enterprises for a Borderless World*. Upper Saddle River, N.J.: Wharton Publishing.

Geberding, Julie. 2003. "Faster . . . but Fast Enough? Responding to the Epidemic of Severe Acute Respiratory Syndrome." *New England Journal of Medicine* 348 (20): 2030–31.

Jones, Bruce, Carlos Pascual, and Stephen John Stedman. 2009. *Power and Responsibility: Building International Order in an Era of Transnational Threats*. Washington: Brookings Institution Press.

Kelly, Mark, Robert Ferguson, and George Alwon. 2001. *Mastering Team Leadership: 7 Essential Coaching Skills*. Raleigh, N.C.: Mark Kelly Books.

Keohane, Robert O. 1984. *After Hegemony: Cooperation and Discord in the World Political Economy*. Princeton University Press.

Keohane, Robert O., and Joseph S. Nye. 1974. "Transgovernmental Relations and International Organizations." *World Politics* 27 (1): 39–62.

Kingsbury, Benedict, Nico Krisch, and Richard Stewart. 2005. "The Emergence of Global Administrative Law." *Law and Contemporary Problems* 38 (3–4): 15–61.

Noveck, Beth Simone. 2008. "'Wiki-Government': How Open-Source Technology Can Make Government Decision-making More Expert and More Democratic." *Democracy* 7 (Winter): 31–43.

Powell, Walter W. 1990. "Neither Market nor Hierarchy: Network Forms of Organization." *Research in Organizational Behavior* 12: 295–336.

Raustiala, Kal. 2002. "The Architecture of International Cooperation: Transgovernmental Networks and the Future of International Law." *Virginia Journal of International Law* 43 (1): 1–92.

Risse-Kappen, Thomas. 1995. *Bringing Transnational Relations Back In: Non-State Actors, Domestic Structures and International Institutions*. Cambridge University Press.

Ruggie, John Gerard. 2002. "The Theory and Practice of Learning Networks: Corporate Social Responsibility and the Global Compact." *Journal of Corporate Citizenship* 5 (Spring): 27–36.

Sabel, Charles F., and Jonathan Zeitlin. 2006. "Learning from Difference: The New Architecture of Experimentalist Governance in the European Union." Paper presented to the Theory of the Norm workshop, FP6 project "Reflexive Governance in the Public Interest," Brussels, October 27.

Slaughter, Anne-Marie. 2004a. "Disaggregated Sovereignty: Toward the Public Accountability of Global Government Networks." *Government and Opposition* 39 (2): 159–90.

———. 2004b. *A New World Order*. Princeton University Press.

Slaughter, Anne-Marie, and David Zaring. 2006. "Networking Goes International: An Update." *Annual Review of Law and Social Science* 2: 211–29.

Sorensen, Eva, and Jacob Torfing. 2007. *Theories of Democratic Network Governance*. New York: Palgrave Macmillan.

Wang, Hongying. 2000. "Multilateralism in Chinese Foreign Policy: The Limits of Socialization." *Asian Survey* 40 (3): 475–91.

ANDREW F. COOPER

3

Labels Matter:
Interpreting Rising States
through Acronyms

Acronyms are playing an increasing importance in evaluating the rise of emerging powers in international relations and their effects both on traditional powers and on the architecture of global governance. These labels, indeed, are accorded privileged status, shaping the manner in which rising states operate together both normatively and practically, and in establishing distinctive platforms that allow a collective interpretation of these countries' diplomatic profiles.

This emphasis on labeling is not to downplay the distinctive individual roles rising states play. The emerging powers, whether the big three of China, India, and Brazil or others such as South Africa and Mexico, have unique political cultures and capabilities. All, however, possess multiple identities that need to be taken into account. Although each country operates as a distinct actor in international affairs, a strong component of their identity relates to how they work together and are seen to do so. Key additions and subtractions considerably alter the image and the purpose of these processes of institutionalized interactions.

This chapter focuses on three contemporary groupings of rising states: IBSA (India, Brazil, and South Africa), the BRICs (Brazil, Russia, India, and China), and BRICSAM (the BRICs countries plus South Africa and Mexico). The definitional spaces occupied by these groupings provide insight into how each functions in the global system of governance. To varying degrees, each captures key elements of the phenomenon of rising states. As particular sets of lenses, IBSA, the BRICs, and BRICSAM contain a combination of aspiration and normative force, economic heft and growth potential, and institutional engagement. In combination, when set off against one another, these three acronyms highlight the scope of interpretations through which the contrasting sum of alternative parts vis-à-vis rising states can be analyzed.

63

Acronyms as Interpretative Lenses for Rising States

The tendency to group rising states through interpretive lenses is not new. A decade ago Jeffrey Garten set the standard terminology for representing rising countries by using the label "the Big Ten," or Big Emerging Markets.[1] In attempting to pick the substantive "winners" on the ascendant in the post–cold war era, Garten established a standard by which the current cycle can be judged and guided.

Jumping forward a decade it is now possible to pick from a much wider array of labels to portray rising powers. At one end of the spectrum the cluster of acronyms can be sharply compressed—for example, the term CHINDIA has gained popularity as a means to differentiate the supersized character of China and India.[2] At the other end of the spectrum "diffuseness" is added in constellations such as the Next Eleven or N-11. To be sure this latter group contains some of Garten's original choices—including Indonesia, Mexico, South Korea, and Turkey—but it also has some of the flavor of the newly industrializing countries, reflecting a concern with potential, though widely varying, "up and comers" such as Bangladesh, Egypt, Iran, Nigeria, Pakistan, the Philippines, and Vietnam.[3]

What these conceptualizations lack is the degree of balance between economic clout and geopolitical agency that Garten built into his original model. The criteria for assessing the status of these countries are material and commercial strength, while their capabilities concerning diplomatic will and skill are completely neglected. Economic GDP is showcased; "diplomatic GDP," or leverage, is not.[4]

Although all these approaches are interesting, these labels do not provide the comprehensive lens that is needed in the twenty-first century to appraise rising powers. Only hinted at by Garten, all the rising powers have multiple personalities in the international arena, and increasingly operate out of multiple clubs—some universal, but others restricted to the emerging powers themselves.[5]

In contemporary global governance IBSA, the BRICs, and BRICSAM capture the general perspectives of the collective rise of key ascendant actors and identify the shades of individual differences and distinctive points of diplomatic convergence. These acronyms narrow the scope of analysis by reducing the various rising states to three, four, and finally five large emerging powers.

1. Garten (1997).
2. See, for example, John Lloyd and Alex Turkeltaub, "India and China Are the Only Real Brics in the Wall," *Financial Times*, December 4, 2006.
3. Goldman Sachs (2007).
4. See Gregory and de Almeida (2008).
5. Rosecrance and Stein (2001).

The overlap in membership is striking; significantly, however, it is not the most ascendant of the emerging powers, China, that dominates the acronyms but rather India and Brazil, while South Africa, noticeably absent from the Next Eleven, is present in two of the three identified clubs.[6]

As the number of actors goes down, however, the conceptual space expands. Although only a sketch of these implications is attempted in this chapter, even a basic overview of the purpose and trajectory of IBSA, the BRICs, and BRIC-SAM reflects very different modes of analysis and expectations about how these acronyms—and clubs—play out in international relations scholarship.

IBSA: A Shared Identity with Normative Power

Of the three club labels under examination, IBSA is the only one with some form of official endorsement. This formal standing conditions its contradictory attributes. At its outset IBSA was a state-led project, with the establishment of the IBSA Dialogue Forum in Brasilia in June 2003.[7] IBSA is also the most expansive of the three labels in privileging a shared or collective identity in the construction of perception in relation to global affairs.[8]

There is, however, a material underpinning for the IBSA club. From the outset the three countries have placed a good deal of emphasis on the prospects of building cooperative components in their relationship via collaborative activity in the areas of trade, energy, transport, and security. The IBSA partners created a Trilateral Business Council, and umbrella business organizations signed agreements aiming to promote contacts and contracts. Brazilian president Luiz Inácio Lula da Silva has stated that the "the Group of Three are getting together . . . to change or at least improve the economic geography of the Planet."[9] Indeed trade among the IBSA countries has grown: India's trade with South Africa expanded from $2.4 billion in fiscal year 2003/04 to $4 billion in 2005/06 and to $6.2 billion in 2007/08,[10] while Brazil's trade with South Africa was estimated

6. Lampton (2008).

7. The pioneer meeting of the group was held in Brasilia on June 6, 2003, and was attended by the foreign ministers of the three countries. That initial meeting set the stage for the official IBSA Dialogue Forum, which was formalized through the Brasilia Declaration. There have now been four such meetings: New Delhi, 2004; Cape Town, 2005; Rio de Janeiro, 2006; and New Delhi, 2008. It was at the New Delhi summit of October 15, 2008, that the scope increased with the participation of the leaders of the three countries. For more information, see www.ibsa-trilateral.org.

8. Hopf (1998).

9. Quoted in Nafey (2005, p. 53).

10. "Ansari Leaves for South Africa to Attend Inauguration of President Zuma," *Sakaal Times,* May 8, 2009.

to have doubled from $750 million in 2004/05 to $1.5 billion in 2005/06.[11] Trilaterally the IBSA countries have set a trade target of $15 billion by 2010.[12] Still, it has been the limitations of IBSA rather than the positive outcomes that have attracted the most scrutiny.

IBSA cannot be viewed, however, simply as an enterprise that combines three regional anchors, hubs, or powerhouses in a common project.[13] One of the commonalities among the IBSA countries is how they dominate their immediate neighborhood, but this reality has a negative aspect: in fact, all three, but especially India and South Africa, are too big for their neighborhood.[14]

The sense of core primacy in IBSA was accorded not to a rationalist design or to material goals but to the shared identity with normative power among the IBSA countries. In terms of causation, the existence of some significant similarities among the three countries in terms of their historical sense of victimization cannot be ignored. The still relatively recent experiences of colonialism, apartheid, and military dictatorship provided India, South Africa, and Brazil, respectively, some considerable weight as champions against injustice and inequity on a global basis. Uncommonly, moreover, all three have the ability to transcend this shared legacy through the expression of a robust form of democracy, albeit with many faults in the form of corruption and tolerance for criminality, and in marked contrast to the authoritarian regimes that rule China and Russia as well as neighbors such as Pakistan (in the case of India) and Zimbabwe (South Africa). A similar dichotomy between (moderate left) Brazil and (populist/authoritarian) Venezuela has become a standard feature of the recent literature on Latin America.[15]

Reinforcing this shared democratic image is the impressive profile of leaders of the IBSA countries. The stature of Brazil's president Lula da Silva can be attributed not only to his resilience as a long-time opposition leader but also to his position as a repeat winner of democratic presidential elections. After his appointment in 2004, Indian prime minister Manmohan Singh recalibrated his

---

11. Antoine Roger Lokongo, "Brazil, Russia and India Join Africa Resources Grab," *Dow Jones*, December 14, 2006. For more information on the rise of IBSA trade, see Puri (2007, table 4.5), who also notes that the United Nations Conference on Trade and Development refers to IBSA as "An emerging trinity in the new geography of international trade," a result of the dramatic increase in their trade, which doubled its global share from 0.8 percent to 1.6 percent between 2000 and 2005.

12. Manmohan Singh, "PM's Remarks after the Presentation of IBSA Reports" (New Delhi: Prime Minister of India's Office, October 15, 2008) (pmindia.nic.in/speech/content.asp?id=730 Singh).

13. See Council on Hemispheric Affairs (2006).

14. Alden and Soko (2005).

15. See Cooper amd Heine (2009).

international reputation as a leading economist (notably his role as secretary-general of the South Commission from 1987 to 1990) into that of a technically oriented crisis manager. His 2009 reelection, the first for an Indian prime minister since Jawaharlal Nehru in 1962, demonstrated the confidence his country has in him. And in South Africa, for all of the controversy surrounding the perceived handover of power from Thabo Mbeki to Jacob Zuma, the country remains free of any taint of constitutional crisis, a position that Zuma's election 2009 win should consolidate further.[16]

What is most striking about the IBSA partners' diplomatic performance is how disjointed it is. All the IBSA countries had high expectations of their club membership. India and Brazil campaigned as part of the so-called Group of 4 (with Germany and Japan) for permanent UN Security Council membership, while South Africa, if content to pursue this goal in a more low-key fashion, remains a prime African contender for this status. Through other means, however, this form of club diplomacy has given way to a multifaceted, society-oriented, networked diplomacy. This hybrid posture is reinforced by the contrast between the hard-headed commercial approaches developed by Indian, Brazilian, and South African firms and the magnified expression of soft-power capabilities on the part of their governments. All three countries have closely identified national champions: Tata, Reliance, Jet Airways, and Infosys in the case of India; Petrobras, CVRD, and Embraer in Brazil; and Anglo-American, SABMiller, MTN, and Nando's in South Africa.[17] At the same time all three countries exhibit a high degree of soft power as a means of selling cultural products, developing global brands—Carnival, Bollywood, the Rainbow Nation—and attracting tourism and economic investment. They also promote their own national interest, an approach complemented by increases in foreign aid. Moreover all three countries showcase their presence in global communities based not only on their ethnic diasporas, but also on culture and language: India and South Africa are key members of the English-speaking Commonwealth, while Brazil plays a lead role in the Commonwealth of Portuguese-Speaking Countries.

To a great extent, then, the construction of a sense of collective identity among the IBSA countries in relation to global affairs is built on a shared diplomatic style. Although only a portion of a wider multitiered personality, a good deal of weight of the shared attributes of the IBSA diplomatic makeup has been fixed on normative power. At its core the IBSA enterprise revolves around the global projection of democratic principles.[18]

16. See Jorge Heine, "Zuma's Presidency & the Rainbow Nation," *The Hindu*, May 5, 2009; and Hamilton Wende, "Why the World Will Be Watching Zuma," *CNN.com*, May 13, 2009.

17. See Goldstein (2007); Shaw, Cooper, and Antkiewicz (2007); and Van Agtmael (2007).

18. See Cooper, Higgott, and Nossal (1993); and Cooper (1997).

The three also exhibit common efforts in substantive policy areas. It would be misleading to write off the national and political calculations of Indian, Brazilian, and South African approaches to high-profile activities—such as in World Trade Organization (WTO) negotiations.[19] Shining through is a principled advocacy of a reformist mode on behalf of the South as a wider constituency, the main purpose of which is to ensure the delivery of results that are compatible with the instrumental interests of the South. The ability to say no on a repeated basis to a North-imposed agenda remains a marked feature of their approach.

In addition to the capacity to "generate new forms of resistance" comes the "search for new alternatives."[20] There are noticeable signs that the IBSA countries are increasingly committed to shaping some sort of joint vision of global governance, and they remain a strong collective advocate for the UN Millennium Development Goals and debt eradication for the least-developed countries. Although these aspirational impulses—and even a sense of entitlement—come out in all three countries, perhaps most strongly in South Africa, this attitude is found in equipoise with an appreciation that more needs to be done at home to address inequitable development.[21] The IBSA countries retain as a fundamental part of their diplomatic personality the duality that goes with seeing themselves as both powerful and developing.

The main criticism of IBSA is what the grouping leaves out. By focusing on identity rather than on material attributes (if not interests), it distorts the relationship between economic clout and diplomatic will and skill, which is at the core of earlier analysis. In comparison to the BRICs or BRICSAM, IBSA lacks substance in its ability to act as a guide for future collective action: to break or bend the established global governance order.

The BRICs: "Economism" of Size with an Overlay of Realism

The second of the labels, the BRICs, refocuses attention to the perspective that size matters. As conceived by Goldman Sachs (2003), the concentration on Brazil, Russia, India, and China was justified strictly on an economistic rather than an ideational or value-driven basis. The preferred imagery was not that of norm entrepreneurs but of vehicles progressively gaining traction because of their material attributes and catching up to the current world leaders.

19. Signs of IBSA working in tandem were also seen in the trade context during the G-20 Cancun Ministerial in 2005; see Garth Le Pere and Lyal White, "South-South Cooperation: IBSA Is about More than Just Trade," *The Star* (Johannesburg), October 25, 2005.

20. Ozkan (2007).

21. See Hurrell (2006).

In this race size is everything. the 2003 Goldman Sachs publication, *Dreaming with BRICs: The Path to 2050*, provided a comprehensive overview of the sheer bigness of the BRICs, with reference to land coverage (25 percent), demographics (40 percent of the world's population), and GDP in terms of purchasing power parity (GDP/PPP) (with China as the fourth largest, India sixth, Russia ninth, and Brazil eleventh). Each of the four BRIC countries holds massive foreign exchange reserves, and the combined weight of their economies accounts for 15 percent of the global economy. According to the 2005 *World Investment Report,* the BRICs constitute four out of the five most attractive foreign direct investment destinations for multinational corporations.[22]

With such a size-focused approach the gaps are obvious. The BRICs framework is largely silent on most political, strategic, and social matters. No differentiation is made between those that are democracies with functioning civil societies and media and those that are not. Nor is any attention devoted to the significant rich-poor, urban-rural inequalities that their booming economies are opening up. Further, internal instabilities—concerning ethnic minorities in China, for example—are ignored. Moreover the portrayal of the BRICs as similar distorts the complexity of their economic structures: no distinctions are made among the relationship between the state and the private sector in the four countries. Nor is there any reference to their systemic problems with corruption—at odds with the optimism of the Goldman Sachs appraisal is the BRICs' rankings on Transparency International's corruption perceptions index, with Brazil, China, and India sharing the lowly position of seventy-second and Russia even further behind at one hundred and forty-third.[23]

Goldman Sachs does recognize aspects of development in the individual BRICs countries. A later study of India, for instance, raises the need for reforms in key sectors such as power and telecommunications, improvement in education, and concerns about the lack of an independent judiciary and property rights, and the presence of infrastructural bottlenecks and red tape.[24] Even while recognizing these limitations, however, Goldman Sachs continues to be bullish about the BRICs. As the world financial crisis deepened in 2008, it predicted that the BRICs would be able to use the crisis to catch up with the traditional pacesetters among the G-8 industrialized countries: "on a relative basis [the crisis] definitely allows the BRICs to develop faster as they are going to take an even bigger share of GDP sooner."[25]

22. UNCTAD (2005); see also Goldstein (2007).
23. Transparency International (2007, p. 27).
24. Goldman Sachs (2007).
25. Guy Faulconbridge, "BRICs Helped by Western Finance Crisis, Goldman," *Reuters,* June 8, 2008.

Amid these gaps and difficulties, though, the fundamental strength of the focus on the BRICs as opposed to the IBSA club becomes apparent. For example, although South Africa retains a pivotal status as a diplomatic actor and regional economic powerhouse, it does not have the economic clout of the other IBSA members. The BRICs also might include authoritarian regimes but their economic strength is evident: Russia is a resource giant and, *inter alia*, China is the world's manufacturing shop and the largest holder of U.S. Treasury bills.[26] Additionally these two countries retain strategic clout in their possession of nuclear weapons and permanent membership in the UN Security Council.

To extend the analysis of the BRICs label beyond Goldman Sachs's "economism," an overlay of Realism might help. The most explicit type of this instrumental activity comes out in the BRICs' connections with Africa. In terms of summit diplomacy, China initiated the Forum on China-Africa Cooperation (FOCAC) in 2000; the third FOCAC Summit in Beijing in October 2006 was attended by forty-eight African heads of state or government leaders.[27] The summit was preceded by close to a year of intense consultations between Chinese diplomats and their African counterparts in the participating countries to work out a consensus on the China-African Strategic Partnership, which was announced at the summit. Beijing followed the summit by hosting the annual general meeting of the African Development Bank in Shanghai in May 2007, only the second time the meeting had not been held in Africa. In early 2008 India followed suit by hosting a more selective India-Africa Forum with fourteen African leaders.

The BRICs' summit diplomacy complements their outreach efforts toward Africa at the bilateral level. Chinese president Hu Jintao has made four tours of Africa since 2003, the latest one in February 2009 when he visited Mali, Senegal, Tanzania, and Mauritius. Former Russian president Vladimir Putin visited South Africa in September 2006, the first trip by a Russian leader to sub-Saharan Africa since the fall of the Soviet Union. Current Russian president Dimitry Medvedev has continued this trend, leading a trade delegation to Egypt, Nigeria, Namibia, and Angola in June 2009.[28] Brazilian president Lula da Silva's diplomatic outreach

26. The importance of this came to the fore when Chinese premier Wen Jiabao expressed "worry" about the safety of Chinese investment in the face of the United States' economic troubles; see Rana Foroohar, Mac Margolis, and Jason Overdorf, "The world Has Long Expected China to Emerge as an Economic Superpower, but the Downturn May Cause It to Happen Sooner," *Newsweek*, April 20, 2009.

27. Analysts described the meeting as a "charm offensive," a term to which Chinese officials objected, as they believed it suggested China was exploiting the continent to satisfy its growing economic needs; see Nicholas Kralev, "African Leaders, China to Meet on Investment; Beijing Says It Is No Threat," *Washington Times*, 2 November 2, 2006.

28. See Steven Eke, "Medvedev seeks closer Africa Links," *BBC News*, June 23, 2009.

to Africa has gone even further, involving six official visits since November 2003. In November 2006, Lula cohosted the first ever African-South American Summit in Abuja with Nigerian president Olusegun Obasanjo. Adding to the involvement with Africa, Brazil recently hosted a major climate change conference, promoting alternative fuels, especially ethanol as automobile fuel.

The question is whether this parallel activity will coalesce into some form of new grouping or club, and if so, what might be the purpose of such a group and what would be the implications for other actors in the interstate system.[29] There are signs that the BRICs concept is being reconfigured in such a fashion. In October 2007 the foreign ministers of Russia, India, and China (RIC) met in Harbin, China, and in May 2008 after another meeting of these three, the foreign ministers of all the BRICs met for a day in Yekaterinburg, Russia. This was followed by the first official BRICs Summit, also in Yekaterinburg, in June 2009. The meeting, which came on the heels of the Shanghai Cooperation Organization, was hailed as a "historic event" by Medvedev. The BRICs demonstrated unity on many issues and called for a larger role for developing countries in the global system.[30]

Yet from one perspective the BRICs as a grouping might be akin to an IBSA-like club. According to this interpretation the key message from the BRICs Summit was the sense of an ideational commitment similar to that of the IBSA countries toward universalistic values—favoring equity and justice for the less powerful and seeking curtailment of unilateral or plurilateral or coalitional activity by the most powerful. An alternative view argues instead that the summit should be seen as part of a more comprehensive process of realignment of power, with a new concert of oppositional or adversarial states taking shape. Any interpretation along these lines, however, requires one to distinguish the 2008 meeting of the RIC foreign ministers from meetings of all four BRIC countries. The reason is that, although Brazil seems prepared to share the common sense of resistance to the North on economic issues, it has not joined the others in discussing a common response to security questions relating to Afghanistan, North Korea, and Iran. As the director of the first Asian department in Russia's foreign ministry commented, "BRIC will be based on economic ties and financial ties. While RIC will not exclude economic issues from its discussions, it will chiefly concentrate on international problems."[31] At the 2009 summit these security matters were noticeably absent. This differentiation has been underlined by Brazil's absence from other complementary forums in which the RICs

29. See Armijo (2007).

30. See Ira Iosebashvili, "BRIC Leaders Search for Greater Influence," *St. Petersburg Times,* June 19, 2009.

31. Quoted in Deb Swati, "BRIC Nations Heroes of 2050," *Rediff news,* April 8, 2008.

have participated, most notably the Shanghai Cooperation Organization. As India was drawn in beyond its original status as associate to full member, the contrast between Brazil and the other BRICs has become evident. As *The Economist* put it, "Unlike China and Russia it is a full-blooded democracy; unlike India it has no serious disputes with its neighbours. It is the only BRIC without a nuclear bomb."[32]

The emphasis on the projection of economic growth (and leverage) into considerations of hard security and new hard balancing coalitions—the crux of Realists in international relations—leaves open the possibility that the Harbin and Yekaterinburg meetings constitute harbingers of a more divisive future global architecture. Yet there are strong countervailing forces to the promotion of divisiveness in global governance. Each of the BRICs retains deep and specific ties with pivotal countries of the North in the context of the complex interdependent nature of the global economy. And of course rivalries exist between BRIC members themselves over borders, resources, and even status.

BRICSAM (or the Heiligendamm 5): The Promise of Institutional Engagement

The third of the labels under review, BRICSAM, provides for greater flexibility, albeit with a far more limited form of institutional engagement and reform. This acronym overlaps with the BRICs, given that its members include Brazil, Russia, India, and China. The addition of South Africa and Mexico, however, changes the context of the relationships among these countries. The BRICs label implies that these four big countries are separate from the other two, while BRICSAM, because of its association with a specific initiative through the Heiligendamm process, which refers to the 2007 G-8 Summit in Heiligendamm, Germany where the process was formalized,[33] assumes that this separateness can be mitigated. As such BRICSAM is most appropriately viewed through an institutionalist lens, with a tilt toward cooperative behavior.[34] Ideas are not neglected completely, neither is state power ignored, but for BRICSAM the institutionalist process—with space for either socialization or voice opportunities or both—matters most.

The focus of the Heiligendamm process, the interplay between the established powers and the BRICSAM countries, was often overshadowed by more dramatic calls for enlargement of the G-7/8. Then-Canadian prime minister

---

32. "Land of Promise," *The Economist*, April 12, 2007.
33. See Cooper and Antkiewicz (2008).
34. See Keohane (1984); Ikenberry (2001).

Paul Martin was the first to raise the idea of a summit of twenty key countries,[35] but other G-8 leaders—especially French president Nicolas Sarkozy—have been tempted as well. In the wake of the November 2008 G-20 meeting in Washington, it was recognized at the G-7/8 meetings themselves that more countries needed to be included. At L'Aquila, Italy, in July 2009, the G-8 were joined by a constellation of other countries revolving around what can be termed the Heiligendamm 5 but extended outward through a variable geometry.[36] And at the G-20 Summit in Pittsburgh in September 2009, it was announced that that forum would become the hub of global economic governance.

What has become salient about the Heiligendamm process is that it builds a specific format of institutional engagement, a "structured dialogue," between the G-8 and the G-5 (Brazil, China, India, South Africa, and Mexico). In terms of intensity it shifts the onus from a grand or big-bang approach to a more incremental process. In terms of membership it takes the focus away from specific countries—whether because of their economic size or democratic credentials—and gives a wider group of countries equivalent status in the engagement process.

In keeping with the dominant assumptions of institutionalists, the most optimistic scenario relating to the Heiligendamm process is that the provision of a seat at the (elevated) table of the G-8 will enhance cooperative practices. The sense of precedent or social trust is given due attention as the BRICSAM countries now have attended four summits in a row, going back to the 2005 Gleneagles Summit, when then-U.K. prime minister Tony Blair invited them (as the Outreach 5) to participate in discussions on climate change and energy security. Once in on such a long-term basis it is hard to let them go. The "structured dialogue" within the Heiligendamm process also features a unique blend of animation from specific G-8 leaders. The technical orientation of the process, however, encourages cooperation between sherpas and other state officials as well.

Although the future of the relationship between the world's industrialized and key emerging countries was the major result of the 2007 G-8 Heiligendamm Summit, enlargement of the G-8 was not on the agenda. China, India, and Brazil—along with South Africa and Mexico—were invited to participate as a group of five in an on-going dialogue with the G-8 over the next two years, which was extended for another two-year term at the 2009 L'Aquila Summit. This Heiligendamm process engagement has focused on four specific issues: the promotion of innovation; the enhancement of free investment and corporate

---

35. See English, Thakur, and Cooper (2005); Martin (2005).

36. See Peter Baker and Rachel Donadio, "Group of 8 Is Not Enough, Say Those Waiting In," *New York Times*, July 10, 2009. For more on the various manifestations of the G-8, see Andrew Schrumm and Ruth Davis, "Is the G8's Variable Geometry Sustainable?" *CIGIOnline.org*, July 7, 2009.

social responsibility; common responsibilities with respect to African development; and knowledge exchange on technologies to fight climate change.[37]

Initially, the seat at the table offered to the BRICSAM countries—or the Heiligendamm 5—fell far short of equal status. Apart from France and the United Kingdom, the other G-8 members remain ambivalent or staunchly opposed to the Heiligendamm process. The United States, for its part, is in the midst of a serious debate about the future of the G-8, which played out during the 2008 presidential election campaign. The approach by Republican candidate John McCain focused on an "us against them," values-oriented perspective with his proposal for a "league of democracies." President Obama views institutional reform in functional terms, with an emphasis on both rationalization of the G-X process (accented by a tilt away from the G-8 toward the G-20) and the ability of such forums to feed into coalitions intended to tackle energy and environmental issues. Obama embraced the 2009 G-20 meetings in London as a "turning point" for worldwide economic recovery. At the G-8 Summit in L'Aquila, the president's sherpa, Mike Froman, indicated that the meetings were "a midpoint between the London G20 and the Pittsburgh G20 summit."[38] The consecutive G-X summits in Canada in 2010 will reflect the contemporary condition of international relations. As a White House press release indicates, "This decision brings to the table the countries needed to build a stronger, more balanced global economy, reform the financial system, and lift the lives of the poorest."[39]

Reinforcing the negative attitudes toward BRICSAM has been the performance of Russia. Brought into the G-8 in 1998 after a lengthy transition period as a reward for its democratic momentum, Russia has not acted as expected. It enjoys its elevated status over the other members of BRICSAM through its membership in the G-8 (although it remains excluded from the G-7 finance ministers' meetings), but it has also strengthened its relationships with the core BRICs group.

The real distinguishing, and innovative, features of BRICSAM—or, more accurately, B(R)ICSAM, given Russia's distinctive position—are twofold. First, BRICSAM privileges "diplomacy" as the engine for institutional engagement, a dynamic that highlights not the core BRICs countries but the SAM dimension. Although their economies are below the top tier of BRICs, the expansion of the process of engagement to take in South Africa (ranked twenty-seventh in terms of GDP/PPP) and Mexico (ranked fourteenth) was predicated on their special

37. Heiligendamm Summit Declaration, "Growth and Responsibility in the World Economy" (June 7, 2007, p. 36).

38. Quoted in Baker and Donadio (2009).

39. White House, Office of the Press Secretary, "Fact Sheet: Creating a 21st Century International Economic Architecture" (Washington, September 24, 2009) (www.whitehouse.gov/the_press_office/Fact-Sheet-Creating-a-21st-Century-International-Economic-Architecture/).

diplomatic attributes as bridging countries. Second, such an approach assumes that the gap between the G-8 and the Heiligendamm 5 could be bridged by institutional means.[40]

South Africa at least plays up to the ranks of the other BRICs in the diplomatic domain—as president, Thabo Mbeki attended all of the G-7/8 Summits from 2000 through 2008, the same number as President George W. Bush, the senior G-8 leader. Moreover, while its credentials as Africa's leader have always faced challenge, South Africa has taken on the role of continental champion on a host of issues, above all the New Partnership for Africa's Development.[41] Furthermore, as the Heiligendamm process demonstrates, these capabilities are not framed through IBSA. Grouped together with China, India, Brazil, and Mexico, South Africa showed that it was able to participate on an equal status in a structured forum for ongoing dialogue with the G-8 in the run-up to the 2008 Summit in Toyako, Japan. Under Mbeki's successor, Jacob Zuma, this trend does not appear to have altered.

Mexico, because of its unique stature within BRICSAM as the only member of the Organization for Economic Cooperation and Development (OECD), plays a bridging role in a specific fashion. Such a role has proved highly valuable since the OECD was tasked with facilitating the Heiligendamm process over its initial two-year period through the establishment of a Support Unit.[42] Mexico, in fact, has become the central organizational hub of the BRICSAM/ Heiligendamm 5. It hosted the first autonomous meeting of the group in Berlin shortly before the 2007 G-8 Summit, as well as the first meeting of sherpas taking part in the Heiligendamm process. Lourdes Aranda, Mexico's deputy foreign minister, has served as the coordinator for the Heiligendamm 5 group.

Still, the translation of the Heiligendamm process into novel and constructive forms of institutionalized engagement are far from ensured. In the months following Heiligendamm, stories began to emerge about the BRICSAM countries' unhappiness with both their treatment at the summit and the OECD's involvement in the Heiligendamm process. The *Financial Times* reported that the Outreach 5 leaders felt snubbed by the announcement of the communiqué, which proclaimed the Heiligendamm process's establishment prior to the group's joining the G-8 meetings.[43] Indian prime minister Manmohan Singh voiced his displeasure to the media about the limited role that the Outreach 5

40. For more detail concerning the economics and diplomacy of the BRICSAM states, see Cooper, Shaw and Antkiewicz (2006); Cooper (2007); Cooper, Antkiewicz, and Shaw (2007); and Shaw, Cooper, and Antkiewicz (2007).

41. See Miller (2005, pp. 54–55).

42. See Benterbusch and Seifert (2008).

43. Hugh Williamson, "Rich Nations Stall Dialogue with 'G5' Partners," *Financial Times,* July 2, 2008.

were given, arguing that these countries had much to offer in terms of addressing a wider array of global governance challenges than those on the summit agenda. This disquiet of the BRICSAM leaders appears to be confirmed by the decision of the big rising states to support the transformation of the G-20 as the hub of global economic governance, notwithstanding the decision made at L'Aquila to extend the Heiligendamm process for another two-year period until 2011, renamed the Heiligendamm-L'Aquila process, and reconfigured as "a dialogue among equals." Although still in train, the evolution of the relationship between the G-8 and the G-5 through this process has lost momentum as a privileged label with the primacy accorded to the G-20.

Conclusion

The analysis of different clubs shows how expansive, fluid, and contested the depiction of rising powers has become. No one acronym has the field to itself. Although the BRICs label has achieved the clearest sense of popular exposure, it has not become the dominant label. Instead of marginalizing other acronyms, the trend remains tilted toward discovering other brands—whether the ones detailed in this paper or alternatives. Indeed the various labels highlight the degree to which these countries possess multiple identities, national interests, and institutional connections. In the past unidimensional labels, such as the South, might have been enough, but such depictions are no longer satisfactory in contemporary global governance.

Size has its advantages, and it is understandable why Goldman Sachs would try to locate the new big countries to watch for (and invest in). But even the logic of the BRICs can be contested. If "bigness" were the critical criteria, CHINDIA might be the key club. On climate change, in the context of the Copenhagen Accord, the BASIC (Brazil, South Africa, India and China) has come to the fore.[44] And if rising powers are to be identified by geopolitical clout, then the RIC might be the key acronym.

Looking at the labels more closely, it becomes evident that assessing economic clout might be valuable but insufficient. The labels unnecessarily exclude some rising powers, so it is useful to stretch the constellation of such powers to understand fully the contemporary dynamics of international relations. Indeed a fixation with bigness arguably is likely to return the debate to more familiar discussions about which country is thought to be the new challenger of the apex of power, an impression borne out by the growing literature on "Rising"

44. Charles Babington and Jennifer Loven. "Obama Raced Clock, Chaos, Comedy for Climate Deal," Associated Press, December 19, 2009.

China, whether as "peaceful" and "responsible" or as a new neo-Bismarckian challenger.[45]

Taking into account the diplomatic dimension opens up the debate along lines that are valuable for various reasons. For one, it gives pride of place not just to economic and geopolitical power but also to identity and institutional factors. IBSA is not all that important a club when viewed through an economic and geopolitical lens, but through a lens that highlights identity reframing and norm promotion it takes on added significance. The BRICSAM grouping has had the disadvantage of being brought into operational existence as part of the G-8 "outreach." But even as this acronym has been preempted by the ascendancy of the G-20, there continue to be signs of logic for its existence, both as a separate site for dialogue with the G-8 and as a distinctive label of identity for a core cluster of G-20 members beyond the established power club.

In conformity with the concept of identity reframing and norm promotion,[46] however, there is acknowledgment that these countries can take on and maintain different group memberships at the same time. It is compelling that the three central club acronyms examined in this paper have an overlap of members, with India and Brazil being in all three. But when examined through these club acronyms, these countries come out in very contrasting shapes, demonstrating their multiple identities in international affairs. The lens used by the particular label makes a significant difference, and so does the addition or subtraction of a single actor.

The examination of the various acronyms, then, has a serious analytic edge to it. Calling these rising powers by a group shorthand, whether IBSA, BRICs, or BRICSAM, helps to determine not just the shape of our mental map about emerging powers but also how their diplomatic behavior is taken as playing out in practice. If the saying "where you sit is where you stand" is borne out in practice, it is equally accurate that the choice of one label over another matters. Which acronym is favored reflects whether identity, power, or institutionalization is privileged.

References

Alden, Chris, and Mills Soko. 2005. "South Africa's Economic Relations with Africa: Hegemony and Its Discontents." *Journal of Modern African Studies* 43, no. 3: 367–92.

Armijo, Leslie Elliott. 2007. "The BRICs Countries (Brazil, Russia, India, and China) as Analytical Category: Mirage or Insight?" *Asian Perspective* 31, no. 4: 7–42.

45. See, for example, Goldstein (2003); Ross and Feng (2008).
46. See Rosecrance and Stein (2001).

Benterbusch, Ulrich, and Juliane Seifert. 2008. "The Heiligendamm Dialogue Process: Joining Forces to Meet the Challenges of the World Economy." Dialogue on Globalization 3. Berlin: Friedrich Ebert Foundation (March).

Cooper, Andrew F. 1997. *Niche Diplomacy: Middle Powers After the Cold War*. London: Macmillan.

———. 2007. "The Logic of the B(R)ICSAM Model for G8 Reform." CIGI Policy Brief in International Governance 1. Waterloo, Ont.: Centre for International Governance Innovation (May).

Cooper, Andrew F., and Agata Antkiewicz, eds. 2008. *Emerging Powers in Global Governance: Lessons from the Heiligendamm Process*. Wilfrid Laurier University Press.

Cooper, Andrew F., Agata Antkiewicz, and Timothy M. Shaw. 2007. "Lessons from/for BRICSAM about South-North Relations at the Start of the 21st Century: Economic Size Trumps All Else?" *International Studies Review* 9, no. 4: 673–89.

Cooper, Andrew F., and Jorge Heine, eds. 2009. *Which Way Latin America? Hemispheric Politics Meets Globalization*. United Nations University Press.

Cooper, Andrew F., Richard Higgott, and Kim Richard Nossal. 1993. *Relocating Middle Powers: Australia and Canada in a Changing World Order*. University of British Columbia Press/University of Melbourne Press.

Cooper, Andrew F., Timothy M. Shaw, and Agata Antkiewicz. 2006. "Economic Size Trumps All Else? Lessons from BRICSAM." Working Paper 12. Waterloo, Ont.: Centre for International Governance Innovation (December).

Council on Hemispheric Affairs. 2006. "India-Brazil-South Africa: The Southern Trade Powerhouse Makes its Debut." Washington (March 15).

English, John, Ramesh Thakur, and Andrew F. Cooper, eds. 2005, *Reforming from the Top: A Leaders' 20 Summit*. United Nations University Press.

Garten, Jeffrey E. 1997. *The Big Ten: The Big Emerging Markets and How They Will Change Our Lives*. New York: Basic Books.

Goldman Sachs. 2003. "Dreaming with BRICs: The Path to 2050." Global Economics Paper 99. New York: Goldman Sachs Global Research Center.

———. 2007. "BRICs & Beyond." New York (www2.goldmansachs.com/ideas/brics/BRICs-and-Beyond.html).

Goldstein, Andrea. 2007. *Multinational Companies from Emerging Economies*. London: Palgrave Macmillan.

Goldstein, Avery. 2003. "An Emerging China's Emerging Grand Strategy." In *International Relations Theory and the Asia-Pacific*, edited by G. John Ikenberry and Michael Mastanduno. Columbia University Press.

Gregory, Denise, and Paulo Roberto de Almeida. 2008. "Brazil and the G8 Heiligendamm Process." In *Emerging Powers in Global Governance: Lessons from the Heiligendamm Process*, edited by Andrew F. Cooper and Agata Antkiewicz. Wilfrid Laurier University Press.

Hopf, Ted. 1998. "The Promise of Constructivism in International Relations Theory." *International Security* 23, no. 1: 171–200.

Hurrell, Andrew. 2006. "Hegemony, Liberalism and Global Order: What Space for Would-be Great Powers?" *International Affairs* 82, no. 1: 1–19.

Ikenberry, G. John. 2001. *After Victory: Institutions, Strategic Restraint, and the Rebuilding of Order after Major Wars*. Princeton University Press.

Keohane, Robert O. 1984. *After Hegemony: Cooperation and Discord in the World Political Economy*. Princeton University Press.

Lampton, David M. 2008. *The Three Faces of Chinese Power: Might, Money and Minds*. University of California Press.

Martin, Paul. 2005. "A Global Answer to Global Problems." *Foreign Affairs* 84, no. 3: 2–6.

Miller, Darlene. 2005. "South Africa and the IBSA Initiative: Constraints and Challenges." *Africa Insight* 35, no. 1: 52–55.

Nafey, Abdul. 2005. "IBSA Forum: The Rise of 'New' Non-Alignment." *India Quarterly* 61, no. 1: 1–79.

Ozkan, Mehmet. 2007. "Economic Development and the Global South: What Role for IBSA Dialogue Forum." Paper presented at the AEGIS second biennial conference, Leiden: July 11–14.

Puri, Lakshmi. 2007. "IBSA: An Emerging Trinity in the New Geography of International Trade." Policy Issues in International Trade and Commodities, Study Series 35. New York: United Nations Conference on Trade and Development.

Rosecrance, Richard, and Arthur A. Stein. 2001. "The Theory of Overlapping Clubs." In *The New Great Power Coalition: Toward a World Concert of Nations*, edited by Richard Rosecrance. Lanham, Md.: Rowman & Littlefield.

Ross, Robert S., and Zhu Feng, eds. 2008, *China's Ascent: Power, Security and the Future of International Politics*. Cornell University Press.

Shaw, Timothy M., Andrew F. Cooper, and Agata Antkiewicz. 2007. "Global and/or Regional Development at the Start of the 21st Century? China, India & (South) Africa." *Third World Quarterly* 28, no. 7: 1255–70.

Transparency International. 2007. *Corruptions Perceptions Index*. Berlin.

UNCTAD. 2005. *World Investment Report 2005: Transnational Corporations and the Internationalization of R&D*. New York: United Nations Conference on Trade and Development.

Van Agtmael, Antoine. 2007. *The Emerging Markets Century: How a New Breed of World-class Companies Is Overtaking the World*. New York: Free Press.

Rising States

GREGORY CHIN

4

China's Rising Institutional Influence

China's rise is ultimately about power and purpose.[1] There is wide-spread international debate—though little consensus—on the exact relationship between China's growing global importance and its long-term strategic intentions. Debate in the West has focused on how the traditional powers should respond. In the United States the debate is often vague and contradictory, hardening around "engagement" versus "containment" approaches.[2] More recent debate has coalesced around whether China's growing power will lead Beijing to challenge international norms, rules, and institutions, and generate conflict among the major powers.[3] Will the combination of a growing middle class, increased integration into the global economy, and growing participation in international institutions lead to deeper Chinese commitment to the existing order? With the recent global financial crisis the debate has evolved once again, focusing on whether China is using the current global crisis, and its status as an international creditor, to strengthen its international influence.[4]

I thank the Chinese officials and researchers, officials from G-7 countries, and representatives of the World Bank, United Nations, and OECD who were interviewed for this study. I also thank the workshop participants, particularly Daniel Drezner, John Ikenberry, Flynt Leverett, Miles Kahler, Jeffrey Legro, and Amrita Narlikar, for their comments. My thanks to Andrew F. Cooper and Alan S. Alexandroff for their editorial suggestions. I acknowledge the support of the Social Science and Humanities Research Council of Canada.

1. See Legro (2007, 2008).

2. See Johnston and Ross (1999, p. xii).

3. Medeiros and Fravel (2003); Thomas (2009).

4. Simon Romero and Alexei Barrioneuvo, "Deals Help China Expand Sway in Latin America," *New York Times,* April 15, 2009; Ariana Eunjung Cha, "China Uses Global Crisis to Assert Its Influence," *Washington Post,* April 23, 2009. For a discussion of China's rising creditor power see: Chin and Helleiner (2008).

This chapter examines the intersection of power and purpose in China's foreign policy behavior, and the prospects for engaging China in rebuilding the existing multilateral institutional order. It leaves to one side the prediction of China's longer-term behavior and focuses instead on deciphering Beijing's medium-range intentions by examining the concrete evidence of its international behavior.[5] The chapter focuses on two areas of Chinese norm diffusion and organizational innovation—international security and foreign aid—as seen through China's involvement in the Shanghai Cooperation Organization (SCO) and its evolving relations with the World Bank. The two critical case studies are useful for analyzing normative and organizational intentions in China's evolving multilateral outlook and foreign policy. Underpinning China's approach to the SCO is the "New Security Concept" (NSC), which has been portrayed as reflecting a new set of principles and norms that Beijing has advanced as an alternative framework for Asian-exclusive regional politics and security.[6] The NSC is also said to illustrate growing Chinese resistance to the influence of other major powers in the region, particularly the United States.

Foreign aid is described as another area of Chinese normative opposition to Western influence. International commentators have focused on Beijing's adherence to "nonintervention" and its "absence of conditionality" in its foreign aid strategies for Asia, Africa, and Latin America and the Caribbean. China's approach is said to offer normative opposition to Western donors' requirements for aid monitoring and universalist norms of civil political rights and individual freedoms.[7] How accurate are these depictions of China's stance on international norms and institutions? The argument here is that the conventional wisdom offers only partial understanding on the range of Chinese institutional behavior. More important, such partial comprehension of Chinese international behavior can lead to strategic miscalculation if it becomes the starting point for developing grand strategy in response to China's rise.

The central question guiding this chapter is whether, or to what extent, China is pursuing status quo or revisionist policies in engaging the existing global institutional order. The purpose is to determine whether there is a shared basis of political will and institutional interest to engage China effectively on institutional reform. The main conclusion is that, on balance, Beijing is exhibiting moderately reformist forms of institutional behavior. Although China

5. The analysis builds on the assumption that China's long-term foreign policy objectives ultimately will be the outcome of the convergence of path-dependent factors and unpredictable contingencies, and shaped by a combination of its relative national power *and* deepening ties of economic interdependence.

6. This perception is discussed in Thomas (2009, pp. 121–22).

7. See Naim (2007); and Hubbard (2008).

was a "status quo" power during the first two decades of the post-Mao reform period, it has not been so since the late 1990s, especially at the regional level inside East Asia.[8] Over the past three decades, China's national power capabilities have expanded exponentially, leading to changes in its international interests and behavior. Since the late 1990s China has shifted toward a more activist multilateral role,[9] and its behavior can be categorized as beyond the status quo, though not "radically revisionist." China has pressed for changes *within* the major global institutions, while also fostering secondary hedging options at the regional level. In many respects China is acting in ways similar to those of the United States in the twilight of British hegemony.[10]

Rethinking Revisionist Power

Iain Johnston[11] has highlighted five indicators of revisionist foreign policy: i) the actor has a low participation rate in institutions that regulate the behavior of members of the community; ii) the actor participates in international institutions, but breaks rules and norms; iii) the actor temporarily abides by the rules and norms of the institution, but will try to change them in ways that defeat the institution's original purposes; iv) the actor has internalized a preference for a radical redistribution of material power in the international system; v) by its behavior the actor aims at realizing such a redistribution of power, and is willing to dedicate military tools to this end. The indicators related to "the rules" and international preferences on the international distribution of power as observed in a country's approach to the major multilateral institutions are of relevance to this study.

China's growing capabilities are enabling it to take a more proactive approach to the major multilateral institutions. Its increased integration with the institutional order over the past few decades has also enabled China to increase its influence over the system itself. This has led to interventions at both the regional and global level that go beyond the status quo. In so doing, Beijing's objective has not been to *defeat* the original purposes of the global multilateral institutions or to destabilize the international system. It is, however, supporting a shift in the balance of global influence toward multipolarity. The balancing of this broader systemic reform objective with allowances for a degree of contingency

---

8. See Ravenhill (2008).

9. Mederos and Fravel (2003).

10. One example is the U.S. "Good Neighbor" policy toward Latin America in international financial assistance in the period before World War II; see Helleiner (2006).

11. Johnston (2003).

in institutional intentions and desired outcomes in current Chinese strategy suggests a need to rethink the conventional meaning of "revisionist power."

The Shanghai Cooperation Organization: "New Security" Principles and Norms

China's attitude toward the "norms" and "rules" of international security has been somewhat ambiguous. In terms of actual behavior it has participated in the construction of some of the most important international security institutions of the post–World War II era.[12] China has signed onto norms such as nuclear nonproliferation and arms control and is a member of the key institutions, the Comprehensive Nuclear Test Ban Treaty and the Nuclear Non-Proliferation Treaty (NPT).[13] It has established a military dialogue and armed forces exchange relationship with the United States and a security hotline between Beijing and Washington for key issues such as antiterrorism. It has integrated international export control measures related to nuclear and small arms into domestic law. There are few overt signs that China is dissatisfied with the existing rules, norms, or guiding principles of the main global security institutions. Its officials and scholars stress that China wants only to have serious nuclear deterrent capability and is looking to work with the United States and other NPT signatories to prevent nuclear proliferation. China's initial dissenting views appeared to have been largely worked out during the bargaining that led to the founding of the institutions.

China specialist Iain Johnston suggests that Beijing does not appear to be interested in building coalitions that aim to undermine or dramatically alter the main existing global security institutions.[14] He adds that the tensions that do exist appear less about whether China is a status quo actor and more about its bilateral conflicts of interest with the United States. And yet in the intervening period since Johnston's definitive study, Beijing has begun to put significant resources into establishing new *regional* security arrangements with its immediate neighbors—although it has not championed new *global* security institutions. Asian regional relations have been consistently listed as China's second-highest foreign policy priority, just behind Great Power relations.[15]

Beijing has developed a "New Security Concept" for building regional political and security relations in Asia that emphasizes cooperation and dialogue

---

12. See Johnston (2003, p. 23).
13. China has signed and ratified every single extension of the NPT.
14. Johnston (2003, p. 23).
15. See China (2005), pp. 33–36.

for resolving inter-state conflict. Guided by the NSC, China has taken a more proactive approach to multilateralism. For example, it established the Six Party Talks on North Korea's nuclear program; signed onto the security pact with the Association of Southeast Asian Nations (ASEAN), the Treaty of Amity and Cooperation, which is a nonaggression pact among ASEAN members that includes a "substantive political promise" that China will conduct its relations with ASEAN members according to the TAC principles.[16] In all these areas of Asian security Chinese foreign policy has been broadly oriented toward the status quo. Beijing has not given any indication that it is interested in forcing the United States out of East Asia in the immediate future— indeed it has avoided pushing *directly* for any radical alteration of the region's existing U.S.-centered security complex. A strong motivation in so doing has been Beijing's desire to avoid Japanese rearmament.

The question of China and revisionism in international security rests on whether, or to what degree, China's leadership ultimately has a preference and a plan for establishing Chinese hegemony in the region. On the scale from moderate reformism to radical revisionism, is China trying to shift the balance away from U.S. military power in the region or does it prefer merely to reduce U.S. influence in the immediate to medium-term future? Some observers have suggested that the SCO—the main force behind the establishment of which was China—is indeed a signal of Beijing's desire to establish regional hegemony.[17] Opinion varies, however, as to how the SCO compares to other international security institutions such as NATO or to arrangements between China and ASEAN. Despite its brief history, some experts see the SCO as potentially evolving into one of the more powerful international organizations to emerge out of post—cold war Asia. China scholar Bates Gill suggests that "China's ongoing efforts to strengthen the salience and impact of the [SCO] are clearly an attempt by Beijing to more effectively establish an *alternative* regional security approach in Asia."[18] Mark Lanteigne suggests that, although the SCO lacks the material and diplomatic capabilities to directly challenge Western interests in central Asia, "it has sought, largely successfully, to become an *alternative force* in regional cooperation."[19] Since the 2005 SCO Summit declaration that U.S. military bases should be removed from the region, some Western analysts have

---

16. See Chin and Stubbs (2008, pp. 15–16).

17. See, for example, Ong (2005); Chung (2006); and Khana (2009).

18. Bates Gill, "Contrasting Visions: United States, China and World Order" (remarks to the U.S.-China Economic and Security Review Commission, Session on U.S.-China Relationship and Strategic Perceptions, Washington, August 3, 2001); emphasis added.

19. Lanteigne (2006-2007, p. 606; emphasis added).

viewed the SCO as a "nascent alliance" in which autocratic states are making common cause against liberal Western states.[20] Concerns have also arisen that the group might become a new "energy club" that eventually could include Iran. One analyst has referred to the SCO as China's "premier defense institution,"[21] while another notes that the SCO marks a fundamental break from previous Chinese security policy and organizational arrangements.[22]

Chinese proponents of the SCO, not surprisingly, provide a more positive assessment. Some suggest the SCO demonstrates the continuing strategic relevance of China's long-standing foreign policy doctrine, the "Five Principles of Peaceful Coexistence," and is a clear demonstration of the utility of China's NSC, which emphasizes security cooperation based on 'mutual interest, confidence building, nonalignment, and consensus-based collaboration.[23] According to Chinese accounts the SCO supports "friendship," "cooperation," "dialogue," and "good neighborly relations," and troop reductions are seen as the chief means for building security and confidence in border areas. The Chinese approach is said to contrast with that of U.S. security policy in East Asia, which is underpinned by bilateral alliances and "forward deployment." The Chinese government's praise for the SCO is meant implicitly to emphasize normative differences between "Eastern" and "Western" approaches to international security.[24] Other Chinese scholars offer a more measured and status-quo-oriented view of what the SCO represents. Zhang Yunling and Tang Shiping, for example, suggest that "the SCO is becoming an anchor for stability in the Eurasian heartland" and is mainly a response to the growing Western presence in the region. They see China as simply adopting an approach toward Russia and central Asia similar to its approach to east Asia: a "comprehensive relationship" with regional states.[25]

The unique principles and norms that underlie the SCO are not evident, however, from its own rather generic self-description as a "permanent intergovernmental international organization." At first glance, the SCO looks like an Asian equivalent of NATO. SCO members have signed a charter[26] and a number of agreements; there is a permanent secretariat in Beijing, a Regional Counter-Terrorism Structure headquarters in Tashkent, Uzbekistan, and a business council office in Moscow; and its heads of state and government meet on

20. See, for example, Deudney and Ikenberry (2009).
21. Slaughter (2008, p. 64).
22. Blank (2005, p. 13).
23. Pan (2005, 2007).
24. Oreseman (2004).
25. Zhang and Tang (2006, p. 55).
26. The charter was signed at the second conference of the SCO in St. Petersburg in June 2002.

an annual basis. A closer inspection, however, reveals important differences between the SCO and NATO. The SCO charter explicitly states that the organization is "neither a bloc nor a closed alliance," but is based on respect for mutual interests and common approaches to dealing with shared problems rather than on uniting against an outside adversary (read: NATO).[27] SCO members are not bound by the clear set of legal obligations of a multilateral security *alliance*, but have pledged to work together gradually to forge a collective mission and identity through consensus building. In 2003 SCO members issued a declaration that formally expanded the organization's mandate beyond building trust and cooperation on traditional security matters to promoting increased cooperation in trade, science and technology, culture, energy, and the environment, a move that was described as fostering "comprehensive cooperation."

Chinese officials emphasize that the SCO adheres to the so-called Shanghai spirit—meaning that the *internal policies* of the organization must conform to the "principles of mutual trust, mutual benefit, equal rights, consultations, respect for the diversity of cultures and aspiration toward common development," and to *external policies* that accord with the "principles of nonalignment, nontargeting anyone, and openness." The SCO's charter also emphasizes organizational "openness," explicitly referencing the organization's support of other peace-building initiatives in the Asia-Pacific region, such as the ASEAN Regional Forum, the Six Party Talks on the Korean Peninsula, and multilateral security initiatives in South Asia.

While it is tempting to write off the SCO as a "talk shop" rather than a *bona fide* military alliance, the approach of making a long-term investment in building intersecting networks of human relationships means that its members will have close and trusted working relationships to draw on in times of crises. Given its ever-expanding scope, the SCO has developed broad networks among officials and technical experts, not just among the heads of state and government that meet regularly. Mechanisms have also been established for meetings of parliamentarians, security officials, foreign ministers, defense ministers, economic officials, heads of law enforcement agencies, courts, prosecutors general, officials for emergency relief, transportation, culture, education, and health. These investments bring immediate benefits in terms of exchange of information, on sharing best practices, and developing ideas for further cooperation.

SCO members share a normative preference for "regime stability," adherence to the principle of state sovereignty, and what could be called "supportive

---

27. See Russia, Ministry of Foreign Affairs, Press Department, "Declaration of the Heads of the Member States of the Shanghai Cooperation Organization" (Moscow, June 10, 2002) (www. ln.mid.ru/Bl.nsf/arh/CBC1E4D4C4C826A43256BD400330C09?OpenDocument).

intervention with noninterference." Regime stability is emphasized in the members' agreement collectively to combat the so-called three evils: "terrorism, separatism, and extremism." Although the sanctity of regime stability, state sovereignty, and supportive intervention are not officially listed in the SCO's mandate, these norms and principles have provided the glue for SCO members for what *they do*. It is this set of traditional Westphalian values, rather than an expanding conception of the "responsibility to protect," that underpins the grouping. The group's common purpose has been given further impetus by rising concern over the narcotics trade, a fallout from the conflict in Afghanistan, that is threatening to engulf the region.[28] The SCO also reflects other particular characteristics of its Asian membership and their state-societal relations in terms of the top-down leadership exercised by the executive offices of the member states over the SCO's (permanent) secretariat. No state executive authorities have been formally delegated to the international organization, even though significant state resources are being invested by SCO members to build and maintain the broad socio-political networks at every level and part of government (as well as between business groupings from the member countries).

The SCO is distinct from other Asian regional security arrangements, including China's security arrangements with ASEAN states, in that its mandate has expanded well beyond traditional security concerns. In its approach to central Asia Beijing appears more willing (or feels it necessary) to take a proactive role in dealing with security issues and to take "preventative measures" through the SCO to counter political destabilization and threats to regime stability.[29]

The SCO is also distinct from China's other regional security arrangements in that Beijing increasingly uses it to advance the concept of "preventative diplomacy." Leading SCO members emphasize, however, that they are not promoting the liberal international human rights regime—the "right to intervene" or "preemptive intervention," as advanced by the Western powers. SCO members insist that their collective security approach to supporting regime stability—to "supportive intervention"—is built on strong adherence to the norm of state sovereignty. In this respect it is traditional Westphalian sovereignty norms, rather than an expanding notion of "the responsibility to protect," that underpin the grouping. The SCO's preventative diplomacy initially was carried out in areas of nontraditional security and involved a range of state agencies. Recent SCO documents indicate that the grouping is considering expanding the realm

---

28. See "SCO Foreign Ministers Council Meets in Moscow," *SCO Website*, May 15, 2009 (www.sectsco.org/EN/show.asp?id=73).

29. See Li (2009, p. 159).

of preventative diplomacy into traditional security issues—most notably, providing support in dealing with "domestic crises."[30]

China and the World Bank: Remaking, not Breaking

In the area of the rules, norms, and principles for foreign aid and development financing, China also offers a number of challenges to the status quo. Starting around 2003 China suddenly came back onto the international aid and development radar.[31] Western newspaper and magazines offered sensational reports of China's huge new aid program.[32] By 2006 China's role as a donor had turned into a hot topic, with concerns being raised about a new cycle of debt, lack of concern for supporting human rights and good governance, environmental impacts, and a growing threat to the World Bank and the International Monetary Fund (IMF), and the OECD's Development Assistance Committee.

China scholars had noted earlier that, since joining the IMF, the World Bank, and the World Trade Organization (WTO), China basically had accepted and operated within the norms, principles, and rules of these multilateral economic institutions. Margaret Pearson suggested that China had acted like a status quo power in relation to the major multilateral economic institutions, preoccupying itself mainly with "learning" the norms and rules of the game.[33] Iain Johnston argued, "there is little evidence that, in joining these institutions, China was either compelled by U.S. power or motivated by a desire to undermine capitalist institutions upon being a member."[34]

Since the early 2000s, however, there has been a gradual but marked shift in China's behavior toward the Bretton Woods institutions. Since acceding to the WTO, for example, Beijing has actually been quite active in advancing a

30. The "Declaration on the Fifth Anniversary of the Shanghai Cooperation Organization" highlights the SCO's potential role in safeguarding stability and security in the region, by holding immediate consultations on how to aid member states in emergency situations. The 2007 "Joint Communiqué of the Meeting of the Council of Heads of SCO Members States" calls for implementation of preventative measures against phenomena that threaten peace, stability, and security in the region, including creating a mechanism for joint responses. The SCO's support for preventative diplomacy to safeguard peace in the region was again affirmed at the SCO Summit in Dushanbe, Tajikistan; see SCO Summit, "Dushanbe Declaration," *Xinhua*, August 8, 2008.

31. China's foreign aid programs have been operating since the late 1950s. Beijing sees its "foreign assistance" programs as dating back to the early 1950s, with its intervention in the Korean War.

32. See Naim (2007).

33. See Pearson (1999a, 1999b, 2006); see also Lardy (1999).

34. Johnston (2003, p. 11).

series of proposals to modify its rules and rules-making bodies, usually speaking on behalf of "developing country interests."[35] China has also been practicing new forms of economic statecraft, using its newly accumulated state resources and capital as economic tools for its foreign policy, and recently has elevated its use of foreign aid as a means to advance its influence and interests.[36] Chinese authorities explain that the country's foreign assistance operations are based on a set of principles, norms, and values that differ from those of "traditional donors."[37] Although China's foreign aid programming has changed since its inception in the late 1950s, Chinese officials maintain that the "Eight Principles for China's Aid to Third World Countries," first espoused by Premier Zhou Enlai during a trip to Mali in 1964, continue to guide today's foreign assistance. The eight principles are: emphasize equality and mutual benefit; respect sovereignty and never attach conditions; provide interest-free or low-interest loans; help recipient countries develop independence and self-reliance; build projects that require little investment and can be accomplished quickly; provide quality equipment and material at market price; ensure effective technical assistance; and pay experts according to local standards.

While the exact figures for Chinese aid lending are not in the public domain, lending has increased annually over the past five years and appears set to continue to increase for the near future.[38] Chinese sources list its donor assistance for 2004 at $731.02 million, while foreign analysts suggest that Chinese aid (including grant and loans) likely totaled as much as $10 billion that year.[39] The Export-Import Bank of China alone received $5 billion (in July 2005) from the central bank's State Administration of Foreign Exchange to finance its policy lending.[40] At a speech at the UN in September 2005, China pledged $10 billion for the 2005–08 period in concessional loans and preferential export buyers' credits to developing countries to improve infrastructure and promote economic cooperation. At the Forum on China-Africa Cooperation (FOCAC)

35. See Chin (2009).

36. See Chin and Helleiner (2008).

37. Author's interviews with officials from China's ministries of foreign affairs, commerce, and science and technology, Beijing, April 2007.

38. See Chin and Frolic (2007).

39. Author's interviews with officials of the OECD's Development Assistance Committee, February and April 2007. The major discrepancy between the official Chinese figures and international estimates is likely due to differences in the definition of foreign aid and assistance, and to the Chinese figure's being based only on the grant portion of its aid contributions. The Chinese aid figure does not include concessional lending; it is unclear whether the figure includes China's no-interest foreign assistance loans.

40. "China Pledges US$20 Billion for Africa," *Financial Times*, May 18, 2007.

meeting in October 2006, Chinese authorities pledged $3 billion in preferential loans and $2 billion in export credits to Africa over the 2006–09 period.

China's new development financing presents a major challenge to the authority and influence of both the World Bank and the IMF. The threat is compounded by the fact that both institutions have been facing intense popular scrutiny since the late 1990s.[41] In addition, Beijing has registered its displeasure over both its voting share in the IMF and its relative influence in World Bank decisionmaking.[42] The sense of siege that China's actions have caused is reflected in statements from senior World Bank officials such as "the Bank cannot turn around in Africa without bumping into China."[43] In summing up the new reality of China's involvement in Africa, the World Bank's then-country director for China, David Dollar, noted that "China's trade with Africa has quadrupled in just a few years [reaching $US40 billion in 2005]. China's foreign direct investment in Africa has [also] quadrupled in just a few years. China is almost certainly going to emerge fairly soon as a larger trading partner for Africa than the United States is." He added, "China's foreign aid to Africa is growing extremely rapidly. But to the best that we can estimate, China's commitments of concessional assistance to Africa were in the order of $2 billion [in 2006], and President Hu Jintao is committed to doubling that within a relatively short period of time." Dollar noted that the World Bank had just finished a "very successful year" of assistance to Africa in 2007, amounting to $2.4 billion in new commitments that year, and added, "Very soon, China is likely to be a more substantial provider of concessional assistance to Africa than the World Bank's flagship assistance program in Africa."[44]

China's bilateral aid lending in Africa has undercut the *direct* leverage that the IMF and the World Bank have exercised over loan recipients. For example, in 2006 Beijing made itself available as an alternative source of capital for Chad, which weakened the position of the World Bank in its negotiations over the use of funds from the Chad-Cameroon pipeline project.[45] Beijing's new lending in Africa also diminishes the *indirect* or systemic influence of the IMF and the World Bank in terms of how announcements of their loans affect the direction and scale of commercial bank lending. This "announcement effect" has enabled the IMF and the World Bank to influence credit allocation in the developing world and, in turn, exert policy influence over recipient countries to promote

41. See, for example Stiglitz (2002); Woods (2006); and Helleiner and Momani (2008).

42. I thank an anonymous reviewer for highlighting this factor as a consideration.

43. Author's notes from a discussion with a World Bank official, May 2007.

44. David Dollar, presentation to "China: Developing Giant and Emerging Development Actor," Center for Global Development, Washington, June 21, 2007.

45. This case is cited in Moss and Rose (2006, p. 3).

economic policy models and lessons, even with a relatively small amount of financing. In applying conditionality on the countries receiving IMF and World Bank loans, which is an exercise of international influence, the seal of approval from the IMF and World Bank "money doctors" also means a much greater likelihood of increased private capital flows to recipient countries.[46] The new waves of Chinese development financing reduce the direct and indirect influence of the two Bretton Woods institutions.

China has further challenged the World Bank's international authority by increasing its financial support of regional development banks, which compete indirectly with the World Bank. Chinese authorities caught the attention of World Bank officials, when, for example, Chinese central bank governor Zhou Xiaochuan called on the Asian Development Bank and other regional banks to play a greater role in helping to manage international financial crises because they have the "competitive edge" of "being more familiar, more trusted and having better information on regional specifics."[47] China has been a main participant, contributor, and benefactor in two regional development programs coordinated by the Asian Development Bank: the Greater Mekong Subregional and the Central Asian Regional Economic Cooperation projects. The Chinese government also recently increased its financial contributions to regional development banks outside of Asia. In summer 2007 China hosted the annual meeting of the African Development Bank, and the Chinese government is working through that bank to deliver $5 billion to support Chinese investment in Africa. As promised at the 2006 FOCAC meeting, China announced it would double its 2006 grant assistance to build hospitals, malaria prevention and treatment centers, and rural schools, as well as a conference center for the African Union.[48] Beijing has also increased its contributions to the Caribbean Development Bank (CDB),[49] and has formally joined the Inter-American Development Bank (IDB),[50] which was eager to receive China's financial support in its efforts to

46. See Kahler (1992, p. 89).

47. John Garnaut, "China's Money Mandarins Take the Hard Line," *Sydney Morning Herald,* April 20, 2009.

48. At the 2006 FOCAC meeting, the Chinese government also announced it was canceling all interest-free loans owed by eligible African countries that had matured by the end of 2005.

49. China joined the CDB in 1998 as a nonregional member, taking a 5.57 percent capital stake; by 2005 the value of its stake had increased to $56 million. In 2002 Beijing provided the CDB $1 million to establish a new Caribbean regional development fund; its contributions to the fund have since grown to more than $33 million. See Kathy M. Higgins, "China in the Caribbean Region: Some Observations," *The Trinidad Express,* February 28, 2007.

50. After attending annual meetings of the IDB for sixteen consecutive years as an "observer," Beijing finally overcome U.S. opposition and joined the IDB in January 2009. On joining China agreed to contribute $350 million to the IDB's various funds and programs.

triple its capital and increase lending to $18 billion for 2009.[51] Chinese analysts note that China benefits from its membership in regional development banks by gaining opportunities to bid on infrastructure projects and to deepen economic relations generally.

For aid lending—as distinct from "grant" aid—a key actor has been the Export-Import Bank of China, (China EXIM Bank), the "operating bank for the concessional loans of the Chinese government," which is "sharing China's successful experience in reform and development with recipient countries to help address their problems of economic development." According to China EXIM Bank president Li Ruogu, the bank's concessional loans should contribute to establishing "strategic partnerships," build "mutual trust, mutual benefit, and common development," and foster "win-win results between China and other developing countries."[52] The principles guiding China EXIM Bank's aid financing are specified as "carefully implement the state economic and diplomatic strategies through providing financial services to publicize China's path and experience of peaceful development and the concept of building a harmonious world." The norms and values underpinning the bank's "foreign assistance and cooperation lending" are "to play an active role in maintaining a peaceful and stable international environment, a good neighborly and friendly surrounding environment, a cooperative environment based on equality and mutual benefit, a security environment based on mutual trust and reciprocal cooperation, and an environment of objective and friendly public opinion."[53] The above suggests that the Chinese government has established a coherent set of principles and values, norms, rules, and operational standards for its foreign aid lending; it is rooted in the government's long-established "Eight Principles," and portrayed as being distinct from the norms and principles of the World Bank, IMF, and the OECD.

Toward Institutional Rivalry?

In responding to the frenzy of Chinese aid lending, the World Bank has considered two options. One is to try to contain Beijing's rising influence as a development financier by creating disincentives for states to borrow from China. A second, arguably more enlightened option is to reach out to Beijing, build new consensus, and strengthen its sense of "stakeholdership," if not stewardship,

51. Simon Romero and Alexei Barriounuevo, "Deals Help China Expand Its Sway in Latin America," *New York Times*, April 16, 2009, pp. A1, A8.

52. Export-Import Bank of China (2006, p. 21).

53. Export-Import Bank of China (2006, p. 38).

inside the Bank. One such move was the appointment of an eminent Chinese economist, Justin Yifu Lin, as the Bank's chief economist and executive vice president. As one senior UN official stated, "This decision [to appoint Justin Lin] amounts to the new Bank president's [Robert Zoellick] acknowledgement of China's new weight in the global economy, the growing importance of South-South economic flows, of China's new place in the world."[54]

The World Bank has also attempted to forge a new institutionalized arrangement with China for aid lending by initiating a formal partnership with the Export-Import Bank of China.[55] In 2007 the two banks signed a formal Memorandum of Understanding (MOU) on cooperation[56] pledging them to collaborate in "certain common development areas" and in cases where this partnership is welcomed by the recipient developing country (primary recipients are in Africa). Article 1.1 of the MOU stipulates that a main purpose of the partnership is to "enhance their ongoing cooperation within their respective authority (including staff secondments, knowledge sharing and exchange on various aspects of development assistance, such as fiduciary and financial management, procurement, and environmental and social impact analyses)."[57]

The "general principles" of the MOU also highlight the norms and rules of the partnership. China has accepted some of the existing rules and norms of the World Bank, while at the same time promoting some rethinking and adjustment on the part of the Bank. For instance, in agreeing to the third principle—appropriate measures should be taken to identify, minimize, and mitigate potentially adverse environmental and social consequences of development initiatives—Beijing clearly has taken on the Bank's environmental protection standards, which Bank officials view as a major accomplishment. The second principle—assistance should contribute to measurable results and impacts—makes results-based management, based on quantifiable and qualitative project planning and monitoring, the managerial norm for the partnership. This signals Beijing's acceptance not only of the operational norms of Western donors in terms of financial accountability and aid transparency, but also of some degree of convergence with the "aid effectiveness principles" of the OECD's Development Assistance Committee.

It is with the MOU's fourth guiding principle—to ensure sustainable development, there should be appropriate levels of concessionality on development

---

54. Interview with the author, November 2008.

55. Author's interview with World Bank official, Beijing, April 2007.

56. The agreement is officially entitled "Memorandum of Understanding on Cooperation between the Export-Import Bank of China and International Bank of Reconstruction and Development and International Development Association," dated May 21, 2007.

57. Memorandum of Understanding, p. 2.

financing—where Beijing has most clearly advanced its thinking on the rules and norms of development financing within the new partnership. Here the Chinese government can claim to be achieving gains for developing countries. The chair and president of the Export-Import Bank of China, Li Ruogu, emphasizes that, in setting the level of concessionality, the bank has valuable lessons to share: "We have actively explored new modes of promoting international economic cooperation, and have disseminated a basket of cooperative models with developing nations . . . . Our Bank has started a series of package cooperation projects with African nations, and won high praise and appreciation from them."[58]

In brief China's evolving engagement with the World Bank suggests that, rather than exhibiting behavior that aims to undermine the Bank's operations, Beijing sees its relations as being useful. For now China still has much to learn from the Bank and the international donor community on how to strengthen its aid effectiveness and efficiency. It continues to reap international public relations gains if it is seen as a cooperative stakeholder in the World Bank, so turning away from this institutional affiliation would be costly on a number of levels. Thus China likely will continue to put significant resources into the lower-risk strategy of engaging with the World Bank even as it shares some of its developmental lessons and experiences internationally. Beijing suggests that its new partnership with the World Bank could bring new credibility to the Bank in the eyes of Southern borrowers.

In the realm of international security, Beijing is also picking and choosing its way forward. The Chinese leadership is putting significant resources into fostering new institutional arrangements, such as the SCO, that lie outside the status quo, while at the same time contributing to maintaining existing global security institutions, including UN security agreements. China is seeking to engage the United States in building a new condominium of power, rather than trying to overturn the existing international order. Yet it is also gradually building "supplemental" institutions that could eventually serve as parallel alternate options if needed. The analysis above suggests that China does not appear to have an explicit motive to turn the SCO into an oppositional force to the Western alliance or against the existing global security regime. Rather its primary motivation in fostering the SCO seems to be to protect China's sovereign cohesion and territorial integrity. The Chinese leadership knows that it faces formidable challenges in ensuring the country's sustainable and equitable development. At a secondary level the SCO is about promoting growth and development in the broader regional zones, to help stabilize the states on China's borders. The SCO

58. See Export-Import Bank of China (2007, p. 11).

members themselves have emphasized at every turn that the organization is not "Asia's NATO" and that it is not formed "against anyone."

Even if Beijing were to choose realignment on a global scale, it would not be a straightforward matter for China to detach itself from the institutional systems that the United States has nurtured since World War II or to create an alternative institutional architecture.[59] It is in China's immediate and medium-term interests to keep the United States involved in the Asian security scene, even if it would prefer Washington to be an increasingly *distant* balancer. Beijing is aware that any substantial U.S. military disengagement from Asia would cause Japan to rethink its security situation. Beijing also appears to recognize that, despite the shift to a multipolar world order, the United States is still the predominant power. The Chinese leadership seems to share a foreign policy view that is similar to the "new thinking" arguments of Wang Jisi and Yan Xuetong. Wang suggests that China must remain responsive to the enduring centrality of the United States as the lone superpower, while also supporting the shift to a more multipolar order consisting of a group of major powers.[60] Yan suggests that, even while accepting the continuing predominance of the United States, China should promote greater acceptance of its "Five Principles of Peaceful Co-Existence" as guiding norms for the international system, in which "Eastern" values of collective and national interest are accepted as legitimate norms and China acts as a powerful defender of the interests of developing countries.[61] According to this "new thinking," a multipolar order in which the United States is the "first among equals" is not necessarily a problem for China as long as it allows for China's continued rise.

What could cause China to shift from its hedging strategy in the realm of global security and trigger a shift toward a more contentious approach of pursuing rival institutions? In the case of the SCO the most likely cause would be if the region were to experience more "color revolutions" in the future, and if the United States chose to intervene to support these revolutions. According to Alexander Cooley, the SCO provides regional public goods that member states see as vital to their long-term development, but without involving itself in the internal decisionmaking or domestic politics of member countries.[62] Unlike Western international organizations, such as the OSCE, the World Bank, or the EU, the SCO is willing to foster cooperative initiatives with the only condition

59. See Ikenberry (2008).
60. Wang (1997, 2008).
61. Yan (1999).
62. Alexander Cooley, "The Rise of the Shanghai Cooperation Organization: Western Perspectives" (lecture delivered to the American University in Central Asia Research Center, Bishkek, Kyrgyzstan, January 17, 2008). See also Bobokulov (2006).

placed on members being that they support the struggle against the "three evils." The question of how SCO members should respond collectively to any such internal revolutions is now a key research topic among them. What has been especially worrisome to SCO governments is when revolutions exhibit pro-Western sentiment and people-power aspects, such as in the Rose Revolution in Georgia (December 2003) and the Orange Revolution in Ukraine (November–December 2004). There is evidence that the SCO's maturation and its expanding definition security cooperation are rooted in a desire to promote a more activist role in supporting the internal stability of its weaker member states and reducing the influence of "outside" factors.[63]

The effort to build up the SCO, and the alternative set of norms and principles that it espouses, is clearly beyond the status quo. It is also undeniable that the formation and institutional and organizational growth of the SCO have altered the balance of influence in the Asian region, with broader geostrategic implications. The new reality of the SCO means that China, Russia, and the central Asian members of the SCO are not leaving the provision of international security in the region to the United States or NATO. It is not clear, however, that the ultimate aim of the SCO is to undermine the position of the United States as the leading military nation in the world, nor is it self-evident that Beijing's ultimate security objective is to "defeat" the role of the United States in the security of the Greater Asian region.

Conclusion

In this chapter I have made an initial effort to compile the sets of international norms, rules, and principles that are guiding China's international behavior, and to map the concrete steps China is taking to engage the major multilateral institutions in the areas of international security and foreign aid. China has been simultaneously pursuing foreign policies that are partially supportive of existing global institutions in the areas of international security and foreign aid. It is even helping, in some ways, to rejuvenate the global institutional order. At the same time it is supporting the growth of alternative options that lie outside the established global institutional mix. In the language of the conventional debate, some of Beijing's positioning is within the status quo, while in other instances it is supportive of alternative norms, principles, rules, and organization. The key challenge in this area of research is to determine how much of

---

63. These concerns have grown despite the fact that the unrest in Kyrgyzstan in 2005 (The Tulip Revolution) lacked a pro-West dimension and was more focused on a transfer of elite power rather than a people's revolution; see Lanteigne (2006-2007, pp. 616–18).

Beijing's effort is dedicated to supporting existing versus alternative—or parallel—institutional options. For the Western alliance this means deciphering how much the Chinese state is operating "inside" versus "outside" the established global institutional order.

At this stage China does not appear to be promoting a set of meta-norms that go against those of the current institutional order.[64] Some experts conclude from this that China's role in international governance is largely that of a status quo power, but a more accurate assessment is that, in the realms of international security and foreign aid, China's institutional strategy is to "integrate but hedge." In supporting a shift in the balance of power toward a multipolar order, Beijing is not looking to overturn the international system; rather, it is acting more like a moderate revisionist power—one that prefers gradual reform of the international order. It is in the interests of the West—especially the United States—to encourage the "integrate" side of the equation and to provide China with incentives to be a principal stakeholder in the existing system. Moreover the other policy implication is to recognize that, if current global growth trends continue, there is a finite window of time in which to build a more sophisticated and robust engagement strategy. To be effective such a new strategy would need to be recalibrated to the shifting balance of power and influence, in which China takes on more leadership authorities and responsibility.

China, which has yet to face a more sophisticated multilateral engagement strategy from the Western alliance, has been engaging with the global security environment in ways that could be characterized as moderately revisionist. It is supporting the global nuclear nonproliferation and arms-control regimes while also championing the SCO as a new regional security organization that promotes a set of values, norms, and principles quite distinct from that of the NATO alliance. China is also building a new partnership with the World Bank, even as it greatly increases its provision of bilateral foreign aid. In neither case is it self-evident that these alternative Chinese arrangements are aimed at undermining the established global multilateral arrangements, even if they do entail a shift in the balance of institutional influence.

This chapter has also examined the factors that might lead China either to integrate more closely into the existing order or to drive it to take on the mantle of alternative leadership. In the latter scenario it goes without saying that the rules, norms, and institutions that would guide the alternative projects of international governance would look very different from those of the Western liberal order. If the Sino-U.S. bilateral economic relationship is not properly managed, and if the rivalry intensifies without adequate institutional adjustment at

64. See Thomas (2009, p. 135).

the global level to offset bilateral tensions, China could seek greater autonomy from the existing global multilateral institutions pursue alternative options, and eventually help establish a parallel institutional order. So far Beijing has tried to dispel concerns about such possibilities at every turn. It is disconcerting, however, that while the normative gap might be narrowing in the area of foreign aid lending practices, it appears to be widening gradually in the realm of international security.

To the extent that China actually wants to pursue security cooperation with the Western alliance, a bold gesture from the United States and its NATO allies to increase cooperation with China—and, arguably, with Russia—on Afghan security, for example, could help to narrow the gap on the security front. Former U.S. State Department official Evan Feigenbaum suggests that, despite existing barriers to joint efforts, the "Special Conference on Afghanistan" held in Moscow in March 2009 "offered an opportunity for the U.S. and the SCO to try to turn what are ostensibly common interests into complimentary interests."[65] In such a scenario the SCO could be a new platform on which to forge a transatlantic-Eurasian security cooperation framework for dealing with this troubled zone.

To the extent that China continues along its current upward growth trajectory—even if there are temporary setbacks—it would be useful for Western strategists to give more serious attention to the type of international bargains that might be struck with China, to help persuade Beijing to give up a degree of its autonomy, to close the institutional gaps that are emerging, and to choose greater integration into the existing system. To forge such an institutional bargain, it would be useful to consider what gains China could be offered to offset losses in autonomy. If current trends continue, the Western alliance will need to rethink the degree of malleability in the liberal order, and whether it is willing to formally renegotiate the range of acceptable civilizational norms and values that would provide the foundation for reconstituting the existing institutional order. The offer of such institutional reordering could ultimately be key to eliciting the autonomy trade-offs that would facilitate a higher level of Chinese integration into the existing global institutional arrangements.

In the current global scenario, China's *potential* willingness to embrace the above rational calculation is complicated by two factors. First, we are not dealing with a definitive global context in which the old order has been destroyed, for example, through a large-scale violent interstate conflict and where the hierarchy of interstate power is clearly demarcated. Second, the extended period of U.S.

---

65. Quoted in Robert McMahon, "The SCO's Role in Afghanistan (Interview with Evan Feigebaum)," Council on Foreign Relations Podcast, March 26, 2009 (www.cfr.org/publication/18944/sco_role_in_afghanistan.html).

unilateralism during the Bush administration diminished the attractiveness of predictability gains from "going multilateral,"[66] and damaged the perception of utility in exchanging policy autonomy for rules-based predictability.[67] There is much work for the current Obama administration to do to restore the *anticipated* value that other states could derive from going multilateral—in other words, for the United States to demonstrate the tangible benefits it could provide states that make the trade-off. In short, to the extent that China's leaders want to work in concert with the United States and are willing to go beyond relying strongly on bilateral mechanisms for such cooperation, they will agree to throw more weight behind the established global multilateral arrangements *only* if the United States shows greater willingness, over a sustained period, also to work within multilateral constraints and to restrain the impulse toward unilateralism.

References

Blank, Stephen. 2005. "The Shanghai Cooperative Organization: Post-Mortem or Prophecy." *China and Eurasia Forum Quarterly* 3, no. 2: 13–18.

Bobokulov, Inomjon. 2006. "Central Asia: Is There an Alternative to Regional Integration?" *Central Asian Survey* 25, nos. 1-2: 75–91.

Chin, Gregory. 2009. "Reforming the WTO: China, the Doha Round, and Beyond." In *Leadership and Change in the Multilateral Trading System*, edited by Amrita Narlikar and Brendon Vickers. Leiden: Martinus Nijhoff/Brill Academic.

Chin, Gregory, and B.M. Frolic. 2007. "Emerging Donors in International Development Assistance: The China Case." Ottawa: International Development Research Centre.

Chin, Gregory, and Eric Helleiner. 2008. "China as a Creditor: Rising Financial Power?" *Journal of International Affairs* 61, no. 2: 87–102.

Chin, Gregory, and Richard Stubbs. 2008. "Economic Diplomacy and Feedback Effect in the China-ASEAN FTA: Explaining 'Giving Six and Taking Four.'" Paper prepared for the International Studies Association conference, San Francisco, March 26–29; revised version.

China. 2005. Ministry of Foreign Affairs. Department of Policy Planning. *China Foreign Affairs, 2005 Edition*. Beijing: World Affairs Press.

Chung Chien-peng. 2006. "China and the Institutionalization of the Shanghai Cooperation Organization." *Problems of Post-Communism* 53, no. 5: 3–14.

Deudney, Daniel, and G. John Ikenberry. 2009. "The Myth of the Autocratic Revival: Why Liberal Democracy Will Prevail." *Foreign Affairs* 88, no. 1: 77–99.

Export-Import Bank of China. 2006. *Annual Report*. Beijing.

———. 2007. *Annual Report*. Beijing.

66. See Stein (1990, 2008).
67. I thank Miles Kahler for highlighting this point.

Helleiner, Eric. 2006. "Reinterpreting Bretton Woods: International Development and the Neglected Origins of Embedded Liberalism." *Development and Change* 37, no. 5: 943–67.

Helleiner, Eric, and Bessma Momani. 2008. "Slipping into Obscurity: Crisis and the Institutional Reform of the IMF." In *Can the World Be Governed? Possibilities for Effective Multilateralism*, edited by Alan S. Alexandroff. Wilfred Laurier University Press.

Hubbard, Paul. 2008. "Chinese Concessional Loans." In *China into Africa: Trade, Aid, and Influence*, edited by Robert I. Rotberg. Brookings.

Ikenberry, G. John. 2008. "The Rise of China and the Future of the West: Can the Liberal System Survive?" *Foreign Affairs* 87, no. 1: 23–37.

Johnston, Alastair Iain. 2003. "Is China a Status Quo Power?" *International Security* 27, no. 4: 5–56.

Johnston, Alastair Iain, and Robert S. Ross. 1999. "Preface." In *Engaging China: The Management of an Emerging Power*, edited by Alastair Iain Johnston and Robert S. Ross. New York: Routledge.

Kahler, Miles. 1992. "External Influence, Conditionality, and the Politics of Adjustment." In *The Politics of Economic Adjustment: International Constraints, Distributive Conflicts, and the State*, edited by Stephan Haggard and Robert R. Kaufman. Princeton University Press.

Khana, Parag. 2009. "The Road to Kabul Runs through Beijing (and Tehran)." *Foreign Policy* (web exclusive, February) (www.foreignpolicy.com/story/cms.php?story_id=4664).

Lanteigne, Mark. 2006-2007. "*In Medias Res*: The Development of the Shanghai Cooperation Organization as a Security Community." *Pacific Affairs* 79, no. 4: 605–22.

Lardy, Nicholas. 1999. "China and the International Financial System." In *China Joins the World: Progress and Prospects*, edited by Elizabeth Economy and Michael Oksenberg. New York: Council on Foreign Relations Press.

Li Mingjiang. 2009. "China's Participation in Asian Multilateralism: Pragmatism Prevails." In *Rising China: Power and Reassurance*, edited by Ron Huisken. Australia National University E-Press.

Legro, Jeffrey W. 2007. "What China Will Want: The Future Intentions of a Rising Power." *Perspectives on Politics* 5, no. 3: 1–21.

———. 2008. "Purpose Transitions: China's Rise and the American Response." In *China's Ascent: Power, Security, and the Future of International Politics*, edited by Robert S. Ross and Zhu Feng. Cornell University Press.

Medeiros, Evan S., and M. Taylor Fravel. 2003. "China's New Diplomacy." *Foreign Affairs* 82, no. 6: 22–35.

Moss, Todd, and Sarah Rose. 2006. "China ExIm Bank and Africa: New Lending, New Challenges." Washington: Center for Global Development.

Naim, Moises. 2007. "Rogue Aid." *Foreign Policy* 96 (March/April): 95–96.

Ong, Russell. 2005. "China's Security Interests in Central Asia." *Central Asian Survey* 24, no. 4: 425–39.

Oresman, Matthew. 2004. "Catching the Shanghai Spirit." *Foreign Policy* 142 (May/June): 78–79.

Pan Guang. 2005. "Shanghai Cooperation Organization and the 'Shanghai Spirit': Successful Practice and Innovative." Beijing: China Institute of International Studies (February).

———. "Shanghai Cooperation Organization: Challenges, Opportunities, and Prospects." In *Islam, Oil, and Geopolitics: Central Asia after September 11*, edited by Elizabeth Van Wie Davis and Rouben Azizian. Lanham, Md.: Rowman & Littlefield.

Pearson, Margaret M. 1999a. "China's Integration into the International Trade and Investment Regime." In *China Joins the World: Progress and Prospects*, edited by Elizabeth Economy and Michael Oksenberg. New York: Council on Foreign Relations Press.

———. 1999b. "The Major Multilateral Economic Institutions Engage China." In *Engaging China: The Management of an Emerging Power*, edited by Alastair Iain Johnston and Robert S. Ross. New York: Routledge.

———. 2006. "China in Geneva: Lesson from China's Early Years in the World Trade Organization." In *New Directions in the Study of China's Foreign Policy*, edited by Alastair Iain Johnston and Robert S. Ross. Stanford University Press.

Ravenhill, John. 2008. "China's 'Peaceful Development' and Southeast Asia: A Positive Sum Game?" In *China's Rise and the Balance of Influence in Asia*, edited by William W. Keller and Thomas G. Rawski. University of Pittsburgh Press.

Slaughter, Anne-Marie. 2008. "Networking Government to Government: The Asian Way." *International Review* (Autumn).

Stein, Arthur A. 1990. *Why Nations Cooperate: Circumstance and Choice in International Relations*. Cornell University Press.

———. 2008. "Incentive Compatibility and Global Governance: Existential Multilateralism, a Weakly Confederal World, and Hegemony." In *Can the World Be Governed? Possibilities for Effective Multilateralism*, edited by Alan S. Alexandroff. Wilfred Laurier University Press.

Stiglitz, Joseph. 2002. *Globalization and Its Discontents*. New York: Norton.

Thomas, Nicholas. 2009. "China's Regional Governance: Developing Norms and Institutions." In *Governance and Regionalism in Asia*, edited by Nicholas Thomas. New York: Routledge.

Wang Jisi. 1997. "Multipolarity versus Hegemonism: Chinese Views on International Politics." Paper prepared for the conference on Conflict or Convergence: Global Perspectives on War, Peace, and International Order, Harvard Academy of International and Area Studies, November 13–15.

———. 2008. "China's Grand Strategy." *International Studies*.

Woods, Ngaire. 2006. *The Globalizers: The IMF, the World Bank, and Their Borrowers*. Cornell University Press.

Yan Xuetong. 1999. *Zhongguo jueqi: Guoji huanjing pingu* [An assessment of the international environment for China's rise]. Tianjin: People's Publishing House.

Zhang Yunling and Tang Shiping. 2006. "China's Regional Strategy." In *Power Shift: China and Asia's New Dynamics*, edited by David Shambaugh. University of California Press.

AMRITA NARLIKAR

5

Reforming Institutions, Unreformed India?

International institutions, in order to preserve and improve their perceived fairness and efficiency, must evolve to reflect the changing balances of power. But equally important is another gain that emerges from institutional evolution. Appropriate changes in the structures and processes of global governance can facilitate smooth power transitions by giving rising powers a greater stake in the preservation of the existing international order.[1] Rather than act as disruptive or passive members of the international system, new powers are more likely to assume greater responsibility and leadership as their sense of ownership of international regimes increases.

The economic and diplomatic rise of certain developing countries has prompted a growing recognition by the established powers, which either manage existing clubs of global governance or constitute inner circles within multilateral organizations, that institutional reform is necessary. This recognition is manifest in the creation of the "Outreach Group" or the G-5, comprising Brazil, China, India, Mexico, and South Africa, as part of the G-8's Summit diplomacy.[2] It is also to be found in debates on the reform of other international

---

1. Ikenberry (2008) makes this argument in terms of accommodating China's rise: "The United States cannot thwart China's rise, but it can help ensure that China's power is exercised within the rules and institutions that the United States and its partners have crafted over the last century, rules and institutions that can protect the interests of all states in the more crowded world of the future." See also Ikenberry, in this volume.

2. For instance, Cooper and Jackson (2007) make the following case with reference to the G-8: "The group's under-representation of the global South (via regional participation) erodes its ability to set priorities for the international community and detracts from its capacity to mobilize governments to broker solutions to pressing global problems . . . As a number of big emergent countries become increasingly engaged global actors, the rationale for widening the summit process has been strengthened." The same logic is applicable to other forums of global governance.

organizations ranging from the Bretton Woods institutions (and quota changes within them) to the UN Security Council (particularly an expansion of its inner circle of veto-wielding permanent members).

In this chapter, I focus specifically on two international regimes—multilateral trade and nuclear nonproliferation—and analyze the extent to which reform within them has accommodated India's rise. In response to the rise of Brazil, India, and China, the former regime, under the auspices of the World Trade Organization (WTO), has introduced several important changes in both the substance of the negotiations as well as process, in response to the rise of Brazil, India, and China.[3] The second regime, which comprises a mix of treaties such as the Nuclear Non-Proliferation Treaty and the Comprehensive Test Ban Treaty, organizations such as the International Atomic Energy Agency, and other mechanisms of governance such as the Nuclear Suppliers Group, is for all practical purposes being renegotiated via the Indo-U.S. nuclear deal.

The first case study offers an opportunity to arrive at more definite conclusions, as reform has already taken place and there already exists a repertoire of evidence of India's behavior under the reformed regime. The second case study inevitably is more speculative, as the signing of the agreement and the approval of the Nuclear Suppliers Group are only initial steps in the reform of the nonproliferation regime (which actually encompasses several other treaties and institutions), thereby making it harder to predict India's behavior post reform. Nonetheless it provides an example of a regime in high politics where reform has moved beyond the discussion stage (where it remains stalemated in the UN Security Council) and is already under way—reform that is directed specifically to win over India's allegiance to the nonproliferation regime. Together the two cases provide insights into the extent to which India has proven responsive to Western overtures, and how far it has begun to demonstrate signs of greater leadership that conform to its rising power.

Reform in the two regimes has yielded considerably different outcomes as far as changes in India's negotiation behavior go, even though the agenda in both regimes conforms perfectly to Indian interests. In trade, despite having been welcomed at the high table of multilateral negotiations, India has continued to play its traditional and unreformed role of naysayer. Its continued use of a strict distributive strategy has jeopardized the Doha Round of multilateral trade negotiations and dented the credibility of the WTO. Insofar as responsible leadership goes beyond the ability to assert one's own interests and includes an ability to broker compromises in one's own favor that ensure the preservation

---

3. Russia, the fourth of the so-called BRICs (see Goldman Sachs 2003), is still not a member of the WTO.

of the regime, there is little sign of it in India's behavior in the WTO. In the nonproliferation case, however, the results so far are more positive. Even as part of its bilateral negotiations with the United States, India has reformed its foreign policy behavior in key areas and bound itself to the significant commitments necessary for the United States to agree to the deal and then persuade the Nuclear Suppliers Group to agree to a waiver. What explains these different outcomes?

In considerable measure India's recalcitrant behavior in the reforming WTO versus its relatively more regime-conforming behavior on nuclear nonproliferation (under the reforming regime) can both be partly explained in terms of its domestic politics, particularly the scale and nature of its poverty and the long-standing peculiarities of its worldview. As I go on to argue in this chapter, these features of India's domestic politics mean that unless institutional reform takes a significantly radical shape, India is unlikely to embrace existing governance structures and take on the responsibilities of a "normal" Great Power. The concluding section draws out the implications of this finding for the shape institutional reform might take in the future.

India in the World Trade Organization

India's standing in the WTO has evolved considerably, but its behavior has not. In this section, I trace the ways in which the WTO has evolved to better accommodate the needs of developing countries, particularly the rising powers among them. I then demonstrate that India's negotiating behavior has not proven responsive to these changes, and explain why India shows such great reluctance to assume more responsibility in the running of the multilateral trading system.

Transformations in the "Rich Man's Club": From the GATT to the WTO

India was one of the founding members of the General Agreement on Tariffs and Trade (GATT) and, along with Brazil, also had played an active role in the failed negotiations to form an International Trade Organization. But having invested in the process did not automatically lead to India's actually buying into it. Throughout the life of the GATT, India (along with other developing countries) protested against the content and process of multilateral trade negotiations, and not without reason.

The GATT's principal supplier principle automatically meant that developing countries would not be able to act as agenda setters. The exclusion of issues of key importance to developing countries via exceptions, such as textiles and agriculture, reinforced the voluntary marginalization of the developing world. Further, given the commitment of many developing countries to import-substituting industrialization, incentives to play an active role in an agreement that was based on the principle of trade liberalization were limited.

It was not just the content of the negotiations that led India to use a distributive strategy; decisionmaking processes within the GATT also led to India's alienation. Theoretically all the contracting parties to the GATT were equal, enjoying one vote each. In practice, however, decisions were taken by consensus, rather than by voting, and consensus, in turn, was built in small-group, invitation-only meetings of the so-called Green Room. Interestingly, Brazil and India were among the few developing countries invited to these consultations, but even this did not translate into effective influence. Key decisionmaking power, driven partly by the principal supplier principle, lay with the so-called Quad group, comprising Canada, the European Union, Japan, and the United States. Unsurprisingly, a Quad-dominated GATT was labeled the "Rich Man's Club" by developing countries.

Rather than attempt to improve its influence in a forum that seemed procedurally and substantively biased against its interests, India chose a path of resistance. Against the liberalizing content of multilateral negotiations, India took the lead in challenging the GATT's most fundamental principles: most-favored nation (MFN) and reciprocity. In 1954 Sir N. Raghavan Pillai, India's delegate to the GATT, argued that "Equality of treatment is equitable only among equals. A weakling cannot carry the same load as a giant."[4] In 1960 Pillai's successor, S. T. Swaminathan, argued:

> We feel that the contracting parties have, in the past, not been able to sufficiently come to grips with the problems of expanding the trade of less developed countries . . . . It would, in our view, be a thousand pities if the concentration of pressures from imports on certain limited sectors of production in particular countries leads to a general reversal of the efforts to expand international trade and, in particular, exports from the less-developed countries.[5]

Besides making individual submissions India also joined the Informal Group of Developing Countries in putting forth proposals to grant preferential treatment for their exports.[6] Some of these efforts bore fruit in the special and

---

4. Quoted in Kock (1969, p. 289).

5. S.T. Swaminathan, "Disruption of Market Access: Statement at the Meeting of the Contracting Parties, May 31, 1960," GATT Document L/1229 (Geneva: General Agreement on Tariffs and Trade, June 20, 1960).

6. These proposals can be accessed in "Minutes of a Group of Less Developed Countries" and "Minutes of the Informal Group of Developing Countries" Library under the LDC Document Series in the GATT Digital Library, Stanford University (gatt.stanford.edu).

differential treatment (SDT) provisions incorporated in the GATT enabling clause in 1979. But the graduation principle that went hand in hand with SDT, and the expanding agenda of the GATT under the Uruguay Round, meant that India would continue to plead the special case of developing countries in the later years of the GATT and even after the creation of the WTO. In making this case India took the lead in forming traditional third world, bloc-type coalitions. Alone and as part of coalitions such as the G-10 in the Uruguay Round and the Like-Minded Group in the run-up to the Doha Ministerial, India's negotiating strategy was strictly distributive: refusal to make any concessions, and threats to hold up the negotiations until its demands were met.[7]

Besides advancing an agenda of development, India also took the lead in pursuing an agenda of institutional reform. In the 1960s this involved the creation of a parallel organization—the United Nations Conference on Trade and Development (UNCTAD)—that was more sympathetic to concerns of development. In the 1990s it involved taking a leading role in improving the transparency of the WTO's decisionmaking procedures. One illustration of this is the vitriolic indictment by Indian minister of commerce, Murasoli Maran, of the Doha draft Ministerial text and the process whereby it was arrived at:

> The draft Ministerial Declaration is neither fair nor just to the view points of many developing countries including my own on certain key issues. It is negation of all that was said by a significant number of developing countries and least-developing countries. We cannot escape the conclusion that it accommodates some view points while ignoring 'others' . . . The only conclusion that could be drawn is that the developing countries have little say in the agenda setting of the WTO. It appears that the whole process was a mere formality and we are being coerced against our will.[8]

Compare the process and content of trade negotiations in the WTO today, and the contrast with the GATT (and the early years of the WTO, for that matter) is striking. First, in response to the critique presented by the India-led Like-Minded Group and other developing countries and nongovernmental organizations, the WTO has reformed key decisionmaking processes. The most important of these changes is the transformation of the GATT's invitation-only

7. Even though India launched its program of economic liberalization in 1991, its commitment to the cause of development in the WTO has continued under different guises. In the GATT years, that commitment took the shape of a call for SDT; in the WTO, particularly in the run-up to the launch of the Doha Development Agenda, India shifted its focus to the "implementation" concerns that had carried over from the Uruguay Round.

8. Murasoli Maran, Statement to the World Trade Organization, November 10, 2001 (WT/MIN(01)/ST/10).

and secretive Green Room meetings into small-group meetings whose agendas are publicized and whose deliberations are reported back to the membership. These meetings are explicitly consultative, rather than decisionmaking, in nature. Further, and again in contrast to the GATT and the early years of the WTO, the WTO Secretariat has maintained considerably greater transparency, and details of the process can be easily accessed on the WTO's website.[9]

Second, although these developments show the WTO's receptivity to evolving international norms of transparency, accountability, and democracy, another set of important changes reveals the organization's responsiveness to evolving balances of power. The old Quad has undergone various permutations in the Doha Development negotiations: the "New Quad," Five Interested Parties or the "Quint," the G-6, and the G-7. In all these groups that represent the core of the consensus-building process, four parties appear as constants: the European Union, the United States, Brazil, and India. The G-7, which was brought together by WTO director-general Pascal Lamy in the latest Geneva talks consisted of Australia, the European Union, Japan, the United States, Brazil, China, and India. India thus acquired a position of considerable importance at the high table of trade negotiations. And it is a position of some power: both Brazil and India have demonstrated their ability to veto a deal, and all members (including the European Union and the United States) recognize that the conclusion of the Doha Round will be impossible unless the new powers are on board.

Third, the responsiveness of the WTO to the diplomatic activism and economic rise of developing countries (including India) is borne out in the content of its negotiations. The Doha Development Agenda attaches unprecedented attention to the concerns highlighted by developing countries. Paragraph 2 of the Main Doha Declaration states: "The majority of WTO Members are developing countries. We seek to place their needs and interests at the heart of the Work Programme adopted in this Declaration."[10] The Doha negotiations not only cater to the needs of the least developed countries through a consideration of SDT provisions and specific issues such as cotton, but also incorporate the demands of larger developing countries, including Brazil, China, and India, on agriculture and nonagricultural market access (NAMA). Issues that India had labored hard in the GATT years to get included in the mainstream of the negotiations now finally form the very core of the WTO's agenda.

Finally, these institutional changes have been complemented by some significant changes in India's trade policy that should facilitate greater conformity

9. For instance, for details of the negotiating process in the latest round of trade talks, see www.wto.org/english/tratop_e/dda_e/meet08_circles_popup_e.htm; see also www.wto.org/english/tratop_e/dda_e/meet08_org_e.htm#green_room.

10. World Trade Organization (2001).

with multilateral trade liberalization. The launch of its liberalization program—partially in the late 1980s, and then in full swing in the early 1990s—showed how India's interests (and the epistemic consensus underpinning them) had evolved. In contrast to their famous defensiveness in the GATT, India's negotiators now had an incentive to play an aggressive role in trade liberalization. Yet despite developments in India's trade policy, and even though the WTO itself has undergone procedural and substantive reform to accommodate the aspirations of this rising power, India's negotiating behavior in the WTO remains largely unreformed to this day.

India's Negotiating Behavior Post Reform

Given the evolution of its own trade policy, its participation in the core of the negotiation process, and its impact on the modification of the WTO's trade liberalization agenda into a trade and development one, one might legitimately expect to see a greater willingness on India's part now to conform to a system that reflects its interests. Accompanying the expectation of regime conformity is also an expectation of greater leadership.

Such expectations are reflected in the statements of India's negotiating counterparts. In the (failed) attempt to reach a July Package in 2006, U.S. agriculture secretary Mike Johanns stated: "Now advanced developing countries are world class competitors. This would be China, this would be India, this would be Brazil, this would be other countries around the world that quite honestly can compete with anybody very effectively."[11] In the latest round of talks in Geneva, as part of the attempt to negotiate the July Package 2008, U.S. ambassador Susan Schwab made the following opening statement: "Today's dynamic economy brings to the table a broad and unprecedented spectrum of active and fast-growing economic players as never seen before. Our negotiations can succeed only if that same broad array of key trading partners come forward together to contribute and work toward solutions."[12] EU trade commissioner Peter Mandelson was even more direct:

> Rising powers are reshaping the post war world and existing institutions like the WTO, like multilateral negotiations have to adapt to these new realities . . . . Now Doha happens to be the first test of that new order . . . an attempt to reach a global pact involving not just the leadership of Europe and the United States but the exercise of responsibility by the

---

11. Mike Johanns, Statement, July 24, 2006 (geneva.usmission.gov/Press2006/0724Doha.html).

12. Susan Schwaab, Statement, July 21, 2008 (www.wto.org/english/tratop_e/dda_e/meet08_stat_usa_21jul_e.doc).

rising powers: China, India, Brazil and others. Now, if collectively, we fail this test in Geneva it will reduce our ability to pass future tests.[13]

But at least from the Indian side there is little evidence of a newfound responsibility to accompany India's rising power.

India's trademark "just say no" diplomacy that characterized its participation in the GATT has persisted into the WTO despite its greater stake in the multilateral trading system, which derives partly from its commitment to economic liberalization but even more from its improved influence within the system. The July Package 2008 talks in Geneva, where the India's chief negotiator got branded as "Dr. No," presented no departure from the norm of India's trade diplomacy. Two features of India's negotiating behavior stood out in the recent negotiations, raising important implications for its leadership potential.[14]

First, and patently obvious, was India's continued use of a strict distributive strategy on the content of the negotiations. The opening statement of Minister Kamal Nath at the 2008 Geneva talks was not one of compromise: "The position of developed counties is utterly self-righteous . . . . This self-righteousness will not do. If it means no deal, so be it . . . . I am obviously not here to hand around freebies without getting something in return."[15]

India persisted with this stance through the rest of the meeting. While several issues had the potential to cause a breakdown in the talks, the proximate cause for the collapse of this round of talks was again agriculture, where India dug its heels in on the issue of the special safeguard mechanism (SSM). Pascal Lamy had proposed a compromise between developing countries with a defensive interest in agriculture (including India and China) and developed countries seeking access to their markets, which would have allowed developing countries to resort to the SSM and even surpass pre-Doha tariff bindings by 15 percent

13. Peter Mandelson, Excerpts from Press Conference ahead of the Doha Ministerial, Brussels, July 17, 2008 (ec.europa.eu/commission_barroso/mandelson/speeches_articles/sppm211_en.htm).

14. The logic of focusing on the latest set of trade talks, as opposed to earlier iterations that also form a part of the Doha Agenda, is that the former is the harder test case. The earlier the case, the easier it would be to argue that India's continued nay saying and refusal to assume responsible leadership are simply a product of a lag in its learning and socialization; the later the case, the harder it becomes to explain away India's lack of synch between institutional changes in the WTO (along with changes in India's domestic trade policy) and its negotiating behavior in these terms. It is worth noting that the features of Indian behavior that I highlight in the context of the July 2008 talks are also common to its negotiating behavior in all the previous Doha years, the pre-launch phase of the Doha Development Agenda, and the aborted attempts to launch the Millennium Round.

15. Kamal Nath, Statement at the WTO Trade Negotiations Committee, July 23, 2008.

when their imports surged by 40 percent over a three-year average. India and China, however, led a large number of developing countries in demanding a lower trigger for the SSM to kick in and a higher cap on the percentage points they would be allowed above current bound levels. India's strict adherence to the principle of SSM with a high trigger was ironic, not only because of the current crisis in food prices (as pointed out by Susan Schwab), but also because of the "water in the tariffs" of India's bound versus applied tariff rates that allows it considerably more flexibilities and reduces the urgency of its need for the SSM.[16] By rejecting the deal primarily because of its disagreements with the United States in particular, on the SSM, India lost an important part of the "insurance policy" that was entailed in the U.S. offer to bind its trade-distorting subsidies to $14.5 billion. Admittedly this ceiling was higher than the United States was then spending on subsidies, but in eight out of the past ten years the United States has spent higher amounts than that. Having the binding in place would have ensured that the United States would no longer be able to hike spending over the $14.5 billion mark, even if prices declined. India's refusal to make or broker concessions on the SSM meant that the world has lost this significant guarantee.[17]

Second, India's commitment to coalitions involving developing countries remains steadfast. This is an interesting phenomenon: given India's increased stake and improved position in the system, it would have been more reasonable to expect it to abandon its third-worldist, developmentalist, bloc-type coalitions. Adherence to such coalitions is usually a weapon of the weak—hence India's enthusiastic leadership of the G-77 in the UNCTAD and the Informal Group of Developing Countries in the GATT.[18] But as countries acquire greater influence their ability to free themselves of ideological alliances and strike a more confident and independent foreign policy also increases; some prominent Indian analysts have indeed made such predictions regarding Indian foreign policy.[19] And yet India's negotiating behavior in the WTO presents a very different picture.

16. In contrast, for China, whose bound tariff rates are very close to its applied ones, its dependence on the SSM (or other measures) will be higher; see International Centre for Trade and Sustainable Development (2008).

17. I have focused on agriculture in this section as it provided the proximate cause of the Geneva 2008 deadlock. But it is worth bearing in mind that India (along with some other developing countries) had not been conciliatory on NAMA negotiations either. It also expressed reservations on some other issues—even those in which it did not have a particular interest at stake. See Ujal Singh Bhatia, Statement at the WTO Trade Negotiations Committee, July 28, 2008.

18. See Narlikar (2003).

19. See, for example, Mohan (2003).

Since the days of the GATT India has been instrumental in creating several coalitions, and even today most of its allies are developing countries.[20] India has been a leading member of the G-20, a coalition that was created on the initiative of Brazil and India just before the Cancun Ministerial conference and that is reminiscent of older coalitions India had led in that it unites some developing countries with fairly diverse interests on agriculture around a third-worldist, bloc-type agenda. Akin to coalitions such as the G-10 in the Uruguay Round and the Like-Minded Group in the run-up to the Doha Ministerial, which India also led, this one too had an explicitly developmentalist agenda. While the G-20 brings together developing countries with both offensive and defensive interests in agriculture that share the agenda of reducing agricultural protectionism in the developed world (particularly in the European Union and the United States), India has also been an active player in the G-33. As another coalition constituted entirely by developing countries, the G-33 seeks to protect the agricultural markets of developing countries against import surges through the designation of certain products as "special products" that are exempt from commitments and the use of an SSM. India also participates proactively in the NAMA-11 grouping, again a developing country coalition that seeks to secure greater market excess in the industrial world while protecting the developing world from excessive tariff cuts and ensuring greater flexibility for "policy space." All these coalitions thus have a strong development-oriented agenda.[21]

It is also noteworthy that, despite being a part of the all key decision-making groups in the WTO, India still draws on the backing of these coalitions, as well as other broader affinities with the larger group of developing countries, to legitimize its demands. For example, in support of India's position on the SSM, Minister Kamal Nath is reported to have stated that developing countries supporting a beefed-up SSM numbered close to a hundred.[22]

India continues to draw strength from the power of large numbers, exactly as it had done in the days of the GATT when it was still an outsider in key decisionmaking meetings—it has, if anything, further developed its ability to

20. Except for the one instance—on services at the Hong Kong Ministerial—when it was seen to be colluding with the developed world (see Ray and Saha 2008), India has been reluctant to make overtures to the North but has continued to work in coalitions of the South.

21. It is worth bearing in mind that the development-oriented agenda of these coalitions differs from that of coalitions like the G-10 in the GATT or the G-77 in the UNCTAD in that the new coalitions do not challenge the benefits of trade liberalization or present an alternative view of development. They do still focus on addressing development concerns, however, and are similar to the old third world-ist blocs in that their members often are all developing countries even though they focus on particular issue areas. On the processes of learning and adaptation that have led such coalitions to take the shape they have today, see Hurrell and Narlikar (2006).

22. Reported in International Centre for Trade and Sustainable Development (2008).

maintain the unity of its coalitions and to build synergies and "Alliances of Sympathy" among coalitions of developing countries. Unlike older coalitions that India led militantly—such as the G-10 and the Like-Minded Group—and that ended up isolated in the endgame as all the other members were bought off through side payments, today's developing country coalitions (including those led by India) show much greater longevity. This is partly a result of the willingness of countries such as Brazil and India to lend research and capacity-building assistance to their coalition allies and to offer side deals (such as preferential access to less developed countries) to reduce the temptation of weaker members to defect.[23] As a result of these developments, India's influence in the negotiations—whether as part of the Trade Negotiations Committee or as part of the elite G-7 in the WTO—has improved further. Having the weight of the G-20 or the G-33 behind it in agricultural negotiations—coalitions that have so far stood firm against side payments—gives India greater bargaining power due to both the very large market that such coalitions collectively represent and the legitimacy they impart to India's demands.

Interestingly, both the continued use of its distributive strategy and improvements in the coherence of its coalitions mean that India has increased the proclivity of the WTO to deadlock. The persistent use of a strict distributive strategy might lead to getting an agreement on one's own terms, but it also entails the serious risk that the other party will prefer the cost of no agreement rather than the price of reaching a deal.[24] Additionally, negotiating in coalitions can also detract from the ability to compromise and make concessions. The collective agenda of the coalitions that India leads today—such as the G-20—is arrived at through considerable logrolling that incorporates the diverse interests of all its members. Were the agenda not far reaching and ambitious, the benefits of defection would outweigh those of cooperation, leading to the unraveling of the coalition. But an ambitious agenda that brings together diverse interests also makes it difficult for the coalition to negotiate with flexibility. Compromise, under such circumstances, becomes especially difficult because a concession on any one issue risks antagonizing some members of the coalition and triggering defection. Bernard Hoekman has also noted this point: "The move towards the creation of negotiating coalitions of groups of countries may reduce the number of 'principals' but possibly at the cost of greater inflexibility and a higher risk of breakdown, especially in [a] setting where there is little time to consult."[25] Evidence of the recurrence of deadlock in the Doha negotiations

23. Narlikar (2009).
24. Narlikar and Odell (2006).
25. Hoekman (2003, p. 5).

reinforces the point that India's entry onto the center stage in the WTO has not improved the organization's efficiency. India has no incentive to undermine an institution in whose core it has only recently become a key player—and yet this is precisely the effect its newfound status in the organization has had. So what explains India's behavior in the WTO?

Explaining India's "Just Say No" Strategy

There are three reasons institutional reform to accommodate India (and other rising powers) has not produced greater regime conformity or socialization but has heightened the crisis of multilateralism in trade, rather than helped resolve it.

The first explanation is straightforward and lies in India's domestic politics. It has found frequent reference in the speeches of Minister Kamal Nath. For example, "For us, agriculture involves the livelihoods of the poorest farmers who number in the hundreds of millions. We cannot have a development Round without an outcome which provides full comfort to livelihood and food security concerns in developing countries . . . . The poor of the world will not forgive us if we compromise on these concerns. These concerns are too vital to be the subject of trade-offs."[26] In fact, the share of agriculture in India's GDP is small and declining (from 23 percent in fiscal year 2000/01 to 18 percent in 2005/06);[27] a Doha deal, even after having made concessions on agriculture, in fact would work to India's overall advantage through other issue areas (especially services). But any indication of making concessions on agriculture, which employs between 60 and 70 percent of India's population, would be electoral suicide for any government. Eighty-one percent of Indian farmers are small or marginal farmers of two hectares or less, and constitute the major proportion of India's rural poor.[28] Corruption and indebtedness are especially high here. India's ability to make concessions in this area is reduced not only because of the poor safety nets and welfare mechanisms available to farmers that would help tide them over any difficult transition, but also because of India's industrial sector, which is relatively small (accounting only for 16 percent of GDP in fiscal year 2005/06), especially compared with the services sector, and ridden with infrastructural weaknesses. Thus farmers forced out of agriculture due to any reform instituted under the provisions of the WTO would have few alternative avenues of employment to which to turn. Minister Nath was not exaggerating when he argued that, were there to be a sudden surge of agricultural imports into the country, millions of farmers would die.

26. Kamal Nath, Statement at the WTO Trade Negotiations Committee, July 23, 2008
27. World Trade Organization (2007a).
28. World Trade Organization (2007b).

This sorry state of affairs means that, until and unless the government is better able to institute welfare policies to combat rural poverty and indebtedness, which would involve radical reform of its domestic institutions, India will find it extremely difficult to show any flexibility on agriculture. These constraints also raise serious questions about India's future as a responsible Great Power. Extreme income inequalities, lack of infrastructure, high levels of corruption, and highly skewed patterns of development make it a qualitatively different aspiring power to deal with in comparison to, say, the rise of Japan and Germany in the 1980s or even China today.

While the domestic problems India faces with respect to agriculture help explain why it dug in its heels on the issue of the SSM, they do not tell the full story. It is worth recalling that India's use of a distributive strategy is not unique to agriculture. Would India have shown a greater willingness to make concessions were it not required to make *any* concessions on agriculture? The answer probably would still be no. Even more than the domestic politics of poverty, the second and third explanations—its ideational proclivity and unique worldview, and the source of its power within the WTO thus far—show why India's behavior remains unreformed in a reforming WTO.

In India, even today, suspicion of liberalization at home remains strong. Its negotiation positions of resistance abroad have been accompanied by a cautious and gradual policy of liberalization at home.[29] The Congress Party in power today under Dr. Manmohan Singh represents perhaps the most liberal face of India's economic power, but even under this government India is not giving in easily to pressures from the North. At first glance this might seem partly a function of party politics: after all, irrespective of its liberal proclivities, the previous Singh government was reined in by the leftist parties that formed part of the governing coalition.[30] Interestingly, however, even after its resounding 2009 election victory, the new Singh government displayed evidence of India's ability to stand firm at the G-8 Summit at L'Aquila, Italy, where Prime Minister Singh firmly placed the onus on the developed world to address the problem of climate change, rather than offer any significant concessions by India. India's position was also evident in the G-5 Declaration, which reiterated that "The needs and interests of developing countries must be placed at the centre of the Doha negotiations."[31]

The Indian government's caution in trade negotiations, rather than a function of party politics, is more a reflection of the suspicions of its populace.

29. On Indian liberalization, see Jenkins (1999); Athreye (2004); and Kohli (2004).

30. See Jenkins (2004) for an analysis of the lack of legitimacy of the neoliberal global market.

31. See G-5 Declaration, July 8, 2009 (www.g7.utoronto.ca/summit/2009laquila/2009-g5 declaration.pdf).

Deriving partly from its post-colonial development that was based on models of import-substituted industrialization, there remains "'a very strong colonial mindset" in India, where the WTO is seen as an "instrument of neocolonialism."[32] In a country where "'the spirit of liberalization has simply not seeped in,"[33] gains won in the WTO in favor of certain export interests enjoy little popular support. Popular Indian self-perceptions remain closely bound with almost Nehruvian postcolonial ideals of self-sufficiency and resistance to neo-imperialism. In one of our earlier interviews, one Indian official offers an important insight along similar lines: "It is easier for our minister to come back home empty-handed as a wounded hero, rather than to come back with something after having had to make a compromise."[34] With such ideational leanings at home, India's resistance to reforming its behavior in the WTO becomes less surprising.

Third, what is clear when one traces India's trajectory in the WTO is that it is not straightforwardly a product of the size of its market or trade shares. Even with its 1991 program of liberalization, India's shares in world trade are small. In 2004, for instance, it ranked only twentieth among world exporters (1.1 percent of the total) and fifteenth among world importers of merchandise (1.4 percent of the total).[35] India's share of commercial services exports is higher, but still significantly smaller than that of the EU, the United States, or China. It ranks eighth as exporter of services and occupies a 2.6 percent share of the world market, in contrast to the EU, which ranks first and occupies 27.8 percent of the world market, or the United States, which ranks second with a share of 20.7 percent. Even in terms of services imports, India ranks seventh, with a share of 2.7 percent of imports of commercial services, a sum quite paltry in comparison to the EU's share of 25.7 percent of commercial services imports or the 17.1 share by the United States.[36]

These statistics suggest that India's bargaining power is limited—that it cannot easily hold its trading partners to ransom by denying them market access or disrupting large and well-entrenched trade patterns.[37] Rather, India has

---

32. Author's interview with a member of the Indian delegation, Geneva, May 20, 2003.

33. Author's interview with the head of a think tank, New Delhi, April 11, 2004.

34. Author's interview with a member of the Indian delegation, Geneva, May 20, 2003.

35. Data from World Trade Organization (www.wto.org/english/res_e/statis_e/its2005_e/section1_e/i06.xls); these figures exclude intra-EU trade.

36. Data from World Trade Organization (www.wto.org/english/res_e/statis_e/its2005_e/section1_e/i08.xls); these figures exclude intra-EU trade.

37. To these limitations one can add that the benefits of growth have bypassed the majority of India's population, the country's infrastructure is poor (with scarcity of such basic provisions as water and electricity even in large cities), growth is highly skewed, and

managed to acquire its position in the WTO because of its successful economic diplomacy, which itself is a product of years of learning and adaptation within the organization. This economic diplomacy has involved—critically—the reliance on coalitions that are seen to be "the voice of the voiceless," representing the world's poor and marginalized. Similarly India has appealed successfully to notions of fairness—of both process and substance—when using its distributive strategies, and thereby ensured not only that its demands have the backing of large number of developing countries, but also that they enjoy greater legitimacy. These strategies proved especially successful in the international context of the late 1990s and early 2000s, which saw the launch of the UN Millennium Development Goals and growing concern about the democratic deficit of international economic organizations. In this context India's formula of leading majoritarian coalitions of developing countries backed by demands framed in norms of fairness was a winning one, and played a significant role in getting it a place in different versions of the "New Quad." There is now little incentive for India to change the nature of its alliances, negotiation strategy, or framing, and thereby undermine the diplomatic source of its power.

What this analysis adds up to is that, in the WTO, despite the fact that the institution and its membership have proven amenable to adapting to India's rise, India has not responded with any reciprocal changes in its own behavior. Contrary to constructivist explanations, one sees no sign of its socialization within the institution. Contrary also to straightforward rationalist explanations, India has not abandoned its old allies as its power has risen, nor has it tempered the use of its distributive strategies (strategies which are clearly detrimental to the institution), even though its stakes within it have increased. What one sees instead is a form of revisionism at work of both balances of power and balances of norms.[38] India's pathway to power so far, along with certain domestic interests and even more powerful domestic ideas, means that accommodating India's rise, at least in the WTO, will not be as easy as some had hoped.[39]

---

communist insurgencies have erupted in several regions (see Pankaj Mishra, "The Myth of the New India," *International Herald Tribune*, July 6, 2006; and author's interviews, New Delhi, April 2006). Admittedly, even "weak states" can be strong negotiators, especially if aggregate national statistics indicate economic strength. However, it is difficult to imagine this strength continuing indefinitely, especially if there is a risk of a complete breakdown of infrastructure and governance, with attendant implications for foreign direct investment and trade flows.

38. A senior Indian foreign policy official, when asked about India's vision of international order, responded "revisionist, perhaps even revolutionary"; interview with the author, New Delhi, January 2006.

39. See, for example, Mohan (2003).

India and the Nuclear Nonproliferation Regime

The second regime in which institutional reform—indeed, complete restructuring—to accommodate India is already under way concerns nuclear nonproliferation. It began as an agreement in July 2005 between the United States and India and has evolved into the landmark *Henry J. Hyde United States-India Peaceful Atomic Energy Cooperation Act of 2006*, which promises to rewrite the rules of nuclear nonproliferation. After much controversy the agreement received the Indian Parliament's vote of confidence in July 2008. In August of that year the International Atomic Energy Administration (IAEA) cleared the India-specific safeguards agreement. Then, in September, the Nuclear Suppliers Group (NSG)—formed in the aftermath of India's first "peaceful nuclear explosion" in 1974 to set guidelines on the export of nuclear and dual-use technology to non-nuclear weapon states—was brought around after much lobbying by the United States to accept a waiver for the transfer of civilian technology to India. The agreement was finally approved by the U.S. Congress in October 2008. Together this package creates a major set of exceptions, anomalies, and distortions in the nonproliferation regime, directed entirely toward India's accommodation.

This case is of particular relevance for two reasons. First, it offers a very different route to regime change: it takes the shape of a bilateral accord that will generate major repercussions for the multilateral regime associated with the issue-area, in contrast to the WTO, where reform has been straightforwardly multilateral and within the institution. Second, institutional change thus far has produced different results in the two regimes. Unlike in the WTO, where there has been little change in India's negotiating behavior, the Indo-U.S. deal has produced at least some changes (however contested they may be). These differences, analyzed in the concluding section, shed light on India's aspirations as a new power on the one hand, and directions that institutional reform might take on the other.

From the NPT to the United States-India Nuclear Deal

Until very recently India's negotiating behavior with respect to nuclear nonproliferation bore striking similarities to its behavior in the GATT and WTO. Just as India fought for its own vision of a more equitable and fairer economic order in the GATT, it insisted on presenting its own vision on disarmament and nonproliferation. And akin to its strategy in the trade regime, India's nuclear diplomacy was also dressed in high-minded moral rhetoric.

With the exception of its signing the Partial Test Ban Treaty in 1963, India's resistance to joining the multilateral nuclear nonproliferation regime was consistent and strong. It played an important role in drafting the Nuclear

Non-Proliferation Treaty (NPT) as a member of the Eighteen Nations Committee on Disarmament, and was able to include in the treaty key principles that reflected the interests of the developing world: that peaceful nuclear energy would be made available to non-nuclear states, and that nonproliferation was not an end in itself but a step toward universal nuclear disarmament.[40] India not only refused to sign the NPT in 1968, it continued to berate and undermine the treaty on the grounds that, by recognizing only five nuclear weapons states and creating a separate category of non-nuclear weapons states for all other countries, the NPT discriminated between the nuclear haves and have-nots.

Having refused to make any concessions toward signing the NPT, India made another distributive move by conducting its first "peaceful nuclear explosion" at Pokhran in 1974. For this it incurred several costs—international condemnation and a end to nuclear technology transfers as well as foreign aid—suggesting India's taking an even more nonconformist role in security than in trade. Moreover, India, as a nonsignatory to the treaty, was not among the 177 countries that signed an extension of the NPT in 1995, and refused to sign the Comprehensive Test Ban Treaty (CTBT) in 1996 despite its near-isolation at the Conference on Disarmament. In 1998 Indian declared itself a nuclear weapons state after a series of tests.[41] International condemnation followed, with U.S. president Bill Clinton describing India as being on "the wrong side of history."

The Indo-U.S. nuclear agreement, however, turned this verdict on its head. The agreement, while placing some constraints on India, has triggered a substantive rewriting of some fundamental aspects of the existing nonproliferation regime.[42] For instance, by writing into the deal that India has both civilian and military facilities, it gives de facto recognition to India as a nuclear weapons state NWS, a reality that nonetheless is extremely difficult to square with the provisions of the NPT and that creates a major discrepancy for the regime. Further, the NSG has been persuaded to agree to exempt India from its guidelines—an irony, indeed, given the reason for the formation of the NSG in the first place and its explicit ban on exports of nuclear technologies to states that were not signatories to the NPT and that had not completed comprehensive safeguards agreements with the IAEA.[43]

---

40. See Ganguly (1999).

41. Pakistan then followed with its own series of tests. These events created some important ambiguities for the NPT, which does not allow for the creation or recognition of new nuclear weapons states. Both India and Pakistan claim that their emergence as nuclear weapons states does not violate the NPT as neither country actually signed the treaty.

42. For a debate on the implications of the deal for the nonproliferation regime, see Huntley and Sasikumar (2006).

43. For a critique of the NSG exception for India, see Arms Control Association (2008).

Some scholars argue that the reason why India has managed to secure this special status—and the fundamental redrawing of the nonproliferation regime to accommodate it—is that it has demonstrated its nature as a responsible nuclear power. India announced a voluntary moratorium on further testing after 1998, and it has shown a willingness to accept international controls and safeguards and has refrained from spreading nuclear material or technology to other states. It has also committed to the doctrine of "no first use."[44] An alternative reading of India's nuclear trajectory is also possible, however: prior to showing its willingness to bind itself through international controls and its voluntary moratorium on testing, India effectively violated several norms of non-proliferation (through its refusal to sign on to the NPT and CTBT and the nuclear tests it undertook at Pokhran. Indeed, despite the Indo-U.S. deal and NSG waiver, India is not legally bound to sign the CTBT. Its negotiation behavior has been strictly distributive (except for its signing of the Partial Test Ban Treaty) and its turn to somewhat integrative moves (via the concessions it has made as part of the Indo-U.S. deal) came only after it declared its status as a nuclear weapons state. If seen as India's reward for half a century of distributive strategies and some integrative moves after having achieved its nuclear ambitions, the Indo-U.S. agreement risks sending very mixed messages to the international community.[45]

Explaining India's Approval of the Deal

Insofar as the Indo-U.S. agreement was signed and approved from the Indian side, this case presents a contrast to India's negotiating behavior in trade. India agreed to be bound by at least some international controls—indeed, in the run-up to the deal, India bowed to U.S. pressure and broke ranks with other "nonaligned" countries in voting against Iran in the IAEA in 2005 on the question of referring that country's nuclear program to the UN Security Council, knowing it was jeopardizing its relationship with Iran and ongoing negotiations on an Iran-to-India natural gas pipeline.[46] These developments might indicate a fundamental transformation in India's foreign policy, but closer inspection reveals just how fraught was the process of getting the deal and how contested is India's foreign policy.

The Indo-U.S. strategic partnership was highly contested in India's domestic politics. In July 2008, when the cabinet gave its seal of approval to the nuclear deal, the left withdrew its support for Prime Minister Manmohan Singh's government, which narrowly survived a subsequent no-confidence motion against it only as a result of considerable horse trading. The reasons for popular and

44. See Huntley and Sasikumar (2006); and Paul and Shankar (2008).
45. For the mixed lessons the deal generates for other states with nuclear aspirations and its implications for the nonproliferation regime, see Ramana (2006).
46. See Huntley and Sasikumar (2006).

elite skepticism of the deal are similar to those that underlie India's recalcitrance in trade negotiations. First, ideological resistance to any international agreements that threaten India's autonomy is pervasive in all aspects of India's political life, not just in trade. For the political right, these autonomy costs stem from the required separation of India's civilian and military nuclear programs, which constrains India's ability to improve and expand its nuclear deterrent. For the political left, autonomy costs are an inevitable product of a deal that involves India's giving up its nonaligned stance and cozying up to the United States. Second, especially when posited against the limited gains that the deal allows in terms of meeting India's desperate energy requirements—only 3 percent of India's energy consumption—the costs of implementing the agreement seem too much of a luxury for a poor country.

That the deal went through at all on the Indian side can be attributed to three reasons. First, the Singh government's political investment in the deal was high and was backed by the Ministry of External Affairs—which, in contrast to the Ministry of Commerce, has shown a greater willingness in recent times to align with the Great Powers and tone down its third-worldist discourse. Second, even if the economic gains from the treaty are uncertain, its distributive costs are not as immediately obvious as those from a deal on agriculture. Third, the deal offers legitimacy to India as a nuclear weapons state and helps it escape the constraints placed on it by the existing nonproliferation regime. India's BATNA (Best Alternative to Negotiated Agreement) was considerably poorer: to remain outside the fold of recognized and legitimate nuclear powers and instead belong to a more dubious group of states that includes rogue and pariah states. Even if its domestic politics and ideology make it difficult for India to adhere to the deal for normative reasons, it is not surprising that India agreed to the deal for important strategic considerations. Some degree of regime conformity can be seen here, but it is conformity with a regime tailored specifically to India and based on a bilateral strategic relationship. Moreover the extent to which India actually adheres to the regime as it takes shape—including how India interprets the safeguards agreement and NSG guidelines, how it draws the distinction between civilian and military facilities, which civilian facilities it opens up for inspection, or indeed whether it is prepared to go beyond good-faith statements of nuclear responsibility and take on legally binding obligations—is still an open question.

Conclusion

In this paper I have investigated the extent to which institutional reform to accommodate India's rise has produced the intended results in terms of a greater acceptance, commitment, and leadership on India's part in the areas of trade and nuclear nonproliferation. Four conclusions emerge.

First, despite apparent differences in their outcomes so far, the two cases present an important similarity: the success with which India has used a distributive strategy to secure a place of considerable importance in both regimes. In the case of the WTO, India continues its distributive strategy even after having secured a place at the high table of multilateral trade negotiations and managing to set an effective agenda. India continues to act as the leader of coalitions of developing countries, as in the past, but it shows little sign of becoming a responsible leader willing to make concessions and broker compromises that stabilize and reinforce the gains from the regime. If anything, India's negotiation strategy, implemented now from a position of power, has heightened the proclivity of the system to deadlock and dented the legitimacy and sustainability of the multilateral trading regime. In nuclear nonproliferation, India has taken on the commitments required of it and signed a nuclear accord with the United States, but the many uncertainties involved in the reform of this regime mean that the deal's signing does not necessarily translate into regime conformity and leadership. If India's behavior in the WTO is any indication, it might continue to use distributive and disruptive strategies after institutional reform is complete.

Second, in both regimes, India's distributive behavior has been rewarded, which is one reason it continues to use such strategies in the WTO and might go on to use similar tactics in nonproliferation. Additionally, however, especially in multilateral trade, its high levels of income inequality, poverty, and indebtedness make it difficult for India to take on the role of a more responsible player that makes concessions, uses integrative moves, mediates, and contributes to the strengthening of the system. Further, India's commitment to a third-worldist ideology continues: in a culture where the "wounded hero" who has held his ground in an international negotiation is glorified over and above a conciliatory negotiator who comes back victorious after having made some concessions, there are added incentives to continue to use distributive strategies. This is the case even if the outcome goes against the overall interest of the country and is detrimental to the regime in which India's stake is high and its power rising.

Third, neither the multilateral nor the bilateral route to reform has resulted in increased Indian commitment to the regimes. In the multilateral case institutional reform might have contributed further to the tendency of the trading system to deadlock and dented its credibility. In the bilateral case of the Indo-U.S. nuclear deal, whether India will indeed conform to the norms of the new regime is still to be seen. But even in its early stages, this attempt to tailor the regime to accommodate India has created considerable discontent among other unrecognized nuclear weapons states as well as those that signed on to the NPT and gave up their nuclear options. This discontent may well turn out to be an additional source of instability for the evolving nonproliferation regime.[47] In other words institutional reform in both regimes has not generated the expected gains of accommodating India, but in fact has created new sources of instability.

Fourth, these pessimistic findings do not necessarily mean that all forms of institutional reform will fail to accommodate India effectively or help to reinforce the particular regime.[48] What they do show, however, is that certain features of India's domestic politics—particularly the scale of its poverty and high levels of corruption—make it especially difficult for India to assume the role that one might expect from a country with its pattern of national economic growth. In terms of policy prescription this means, first, that, if India is to negotiate more constructively in response to the institutional reforms undertaken to accommodate it—for instance, in trade negotiations—it will need to develop better welfare mechanisms that facilitate income transfers at the same time as it improves its domestic trade policy process. Second, in the WTO, institutional reforms may need to be more radical than they have been so far. Simply replacing old Quad members with new ones will not produce the acceptance even of the new powers that such reforms are trying to accommodate, let alone other developing countries that are still on the margins.[49] Depending on the range of difference that exists within the old and emerging core group of powers, more effective decisionmaking procedures will have to be found. Third, notions of fairness and legitimacy vary considerably depending on who one is, where one sits in the process, and how one perceives past treatment. In considerable measure some of the ideational peculiarities that one associates with India's worldview and that are further reflected in the use of its distributive strategies and alliances are very much a product of its colonial past and postcolonial reassertion. If new powers, including India, are to be accommodated effectively in international institutions, considerably more attention will have to be devoted to how their notions of fairness and legitimacy differ, why they negotiate the way they do, and what unique visions underlie their negotiation behavior.

47. Much will also depend on how the U.S.-Indian relationship evolves now that the Democrats are back in power in the United States, and particularly on how the Obama administration interprets the exceptions granted to India bilaterally within the context of greater commitment to multilateralism professed by the new president and his support for nonproliferation.

48. Note that India's inclusion in the G-5 Outreach Group as part of the G-8 reform has also failed to produce much socialization or regime conformity, as the recent L'Aquila Summit demonstrates; on India's suspicion of the "G-Groups" despite its inclusion in them, see Pramit Pal Chaudhuri, "G Groups Don't Work, Reform the UN: Manmohan," *Hindustan Times,* July 7, 2009.

49. This finding links up directly with the issue of evolving bargains that Ikenberry raises elsewhere in this volume.

References

Arms Control Association. 2008. "Text, Analysis, and Response to NSG 'Statement on Civil Nuclear Cooperation with India'." Washington (September 6) (www.armscontrol.org/node/3345).

Athreye, Suma. 2004. "Trade Policy, Industrialization and Growth in India." In *Making the International: Economic Interdependence and Political Order*, edited by Simon Bromley and others. London: Open University and Pluto Press.

Cooper, Andrew, and Kelly Jackson. 2007. "Regaining Legitimacy: The G8 and the "Heiligendamm Process." *International Insights* 4, no. 10: 1–4.

Ganguly, Sumit. 1999. "India's Pathway to Pokhran II: The Prospects and Sources of New Delhi's Nuclear Weapons Program." *International Security* 23, no. 4: 148–77.

Goldman Sachs. 2003. "Dreaming with BRICs: The Path to 2050." Global Economics Paper 99. New York: Goldman Sachs Global Research Center.

Hoekman, Bernard. 2003. "Cancdn: Crisis or Catharsis." Washington: World Bank (site resources.worldbank.org/INTRANETTRADE/Resources/Hoekman-Cancun Catharsis-092003.pdf).

Huntley, Wade, and Karthika Sasikumar. 2006. *Nuclear Cooperation with India: New Challenges, New Opportunities*, Vancouver: Simons Centre for Disarmament and Non-Proliferation Research.

Hurrell, Andrew, and Amrita Narlikar. 2006. "The New Politics of Confrontation: Developing Countries at Cancun and Beyond." *Global Society* 20, no. 4: 415–33.

International Centre for Trade and Sustainable Development. 2008. "Bridges Daily Update: WTO Mini-Ministerial." Geneva, July 29.

Ikenberry, G. John. 2008. "The Rise of China and the Future of the West." *Foreign Affairs* 87, no. 1: 23–37.

Jenkins, Rob. 1999. *Democratic Politics and Economic Reform in India*. Cambridge University Press.

———. 2004. "The Ideologically Embedded Market: Political Legitimation and Economic Reform in India." In *Markets in Historical Contexts: Ideas and Politics in the Modern World*, edited by Mark Bevir and Frank Trentmann. Cambridge University Press.

Kohli, Atul. 2004. *State-Directed Development: Political Power and Industrialization in the Global Periphery*. Cambridge University Press.

Kock, Karin. 1969. *International Trade Policy and the GATT: 1940–67*. Stockholm: Almqvist & Wiksell.

Mohan, C. Raja. 2003. *Crossing the Rubicon: The Shaping of India's Foreign Policy*. Delhi: Viking.

Narlikar, Amrita. 2003. *International Trade and Developing Countries: Bargaining Coalitions in the GATT and WTO*. London: Routledge.

———. 2009. "Theorizing on Bargaining Coalitions in the WTO." In *Leadership and Change in the Multilateral Trading System*, edited by Amrita Narlikar and Brendan Vickers. Leiden: Brill/Martinus Nijhoff.

Narlikar, Amrita, and John Odell. 2006. "The Strict Distributive Strategy for a Bargaining Coalition: The Like Minded Group in the World Trade Organization." In *Negotiating Trade: Developing Countries in the WTO and NAFTA*, edited by John Odell. Cambridge University Press.

Paul, T. V., and Mahesh Shankar. 2008. "Why the US-India Nuclear Accord Is a Good Deal." *Survival* 49, no. 4: 111–22.

Ramana, M. V. 2006. "Nuclear Power in India: Failed Past, Dubious Future." Paper presented at a workshop of the Nonproliferation Policy Education Centre, Washington, May 10 (www.npec-web.org/Essays/Ramana-NuclearPowerInIndia.pdf).

Ray, Amit Shovon, and Sabyasachi Saha. 2009. "Shifting Coordinates of India's Stance at the WTO." In *Leadership and Change in the Multilateral Trading System*, edited by Amrita Narlikar and Brendan Vickers. Leiden: Brill/Martinus Nijhoff.

World Trade Organization. 2001. "Doha Ministerial Declaration," adopted November 14, 2001 (WT/MIN(01)/DEC/1. 2001).

———. 2007a. *Trade Policy Review: India* (WT/TPR/S/182). Geneva: WTO Secretariat.

———. 2007b. *Trade Policy Review: Report by India* (WT/TPR/G/182). Geneva.

ANDREW HURRELL

6

Brazil: What Kind of Rising State in What Kind of Institutional Order?

Recent assessments of Brazil's role in the world have been increasingly upbeat—and with good reason. Brazil has indeed established itself as an important and influential player in world politics. Building on President Lula's extraordinary personal popularity, the country's continued economic stability, and the successes of its more assertive foreign policy, Brazil has undoubtedly acquired a new global prominence.

In this chapter I have two goals. First, I explore the evolution of Brazil's foreign policy ideas and of the attitudes and policies of recent Brazilian governments toward the existing global institutional order. Second, I argue that the structures of global order, the international political system, and the structures of global capitalism are in a state of extreme flux and uncertainty. In the 1990s much of the debate about emerging powers could be couched in terms of whether they were being integrated into Western-dominated order that styled itself as "liberal" and was widely viewed as both stable and hegemonic. This is no longer the case. In a relatively short time there has been a dramatic shift from the talk of a liberal moment in the early post–cold war period, to the focus on a U.S. empire in the early years of this century, to the analysis of emerging powers and evolving multipolarity. Most recently attention has naturally turned to the global financial crisis. But that crisis represents only one element in a broader set of changes that will shape the constraints of and opportunities for Brazilian diplomacy in the coming years. The world is witnessing the most serious challenge yet to the global order that the United States sought to construct within its own camp during the cold war and to globalize in the post–cold war

I would like to thank Leslie Armijo and the workshop participants for helpful comments on an earlier version of this chapter, and to acknowledge the research assistance of Arthur Bernardes and Daniel Hemel.

period. Brazil now faces opportunities, but also serious challenges and significant dangers.

Brazil as a Rising State

The idea of Brazil as a rising power is far from new. Inside the country predictions that Brazil was destined to play an influential role in world affairs have a
long history. Their intensity has varied across time: greatness often has been no
more than a vague aspiration, not tied to "practical political action";[1] at times
such ideas assumed a much more direct role in shaping foreign policy, as in the
1970s when the high growth rates of the so-called economic miracle seemed to
establish Brazil as an upwardly mobile middle power, if not one moving ineluc-
tably toward eventual Great Power status. As the Brazilian foreign minister put
it in 1970, "As we grow, and as we convert promises into reality, our participation in international relations will also widen and deepen. It falls to us to
demand, with simplicity but without hesitations, the recognition and respect
for the new dimensions of our interests."[2]

Outside Brazil such writing has come in waves. One occurred in the 1970s,
and it is worth recalling the sorts of claims being made at that time: for example, "Brazil possesses the will and resources to reach for, and possibly achieve,
the status of a major international power by the end of the 20th century";[3] and
"Brazil is plainly among the most likely candidates for great power status during the next two or three decades."[4] The success of economic stabilization in the
1990s, combined with a greater degree of international self-confidence, led to
a second wave and a revival of arguments about Brazil's increased importance,
often couched within the liberal globalization rhetoric that characterized that
decade. Thus outside commentators identified Brazil as one of the "Big Ten"
emerging markets, "countries like China, India, and Brazil—which are acquiring enough power to change the face of global politics and economics."[5] Others
saw the country as one of the "pivotal states" that were coming to dominate U.S.
policy toward the developing world.[6]

Recent assessments of Brazil's role and potential are still more positive. It
was common in the early years of this decade to focus exclusively on China and
India and to quip that there were only "two bric(k)s in the wall," a reference

---

1. de Carvalho (2000, p. 68).
2. Gibson Barbosa, Speech to Escola Superior de Guerra, Rio de Janiero, July 17, 1970.
3. Roett (1975, p. 139).
4. Perry (1976, p. 3).
5. Garten (1997, p. xxv).
6. Chase, Hill, and Kennedy (1999).

to the so-called BRIC countries: Brazil, Russia, India, and China. Now commentary increasingly uses titles such as "Brazil's Big Moment," "Brazil Joining the Front Rank of New Economic Powers," and "Sleeping Giant Awakens" to suggest that Brazil is finally moving to fulfill its long-unrealized potential as a global player.[7]

As in earlier periods, much of the recent writing on Brazil as a rising power looks at directly at capabilities and measurable indicators of power.[8] Material capabilities clearly matter and much of this writing is extremely valuable,[9] but it has its limits, particularly insofar as it downplays two of the basic lessons of social power analysis. The first is the importance of specifying the context within which an actor is said to be powerful. Hence when we hear that Brazil is becoming an increasingly influential power, we need to ask: influential over what actors, in which ways, and in respect to which matters? Set within that context, it is clear that Brazil does indeed matter and is becoming more influential. Nevertheless, the picture is complex and the constraints on Brazilian power and influence remain very real, both globally but also regionally. The second lesson is still more important: discussion of power and influence cannot be separated from analysis of motives and values—it might be true that all states seek power and security, but what sorts of power and for what purposes?

To find a partial answer to this question one needs to look, however briefly and schematically, at Brazilians' ideas about their foreign policy and the nature of the international system. A fuller account would need to say much more about how foreign policy ideas are related to the construction and institutionalization of interests and about processes of interest change.[10]

In 1967 James Joll famously suggested that we need to pay particular attention to the "unspoken assumptions" on which political leaders fall back, especially in times of change or crisis. He argued that much could be gained by drawing out the beliefs, rules, traditions, and modes of behavior that are taken for granted or that simply "go without saying," but that may not be immediately apparent from the documentary evidence.[11] Without trying to make everything or everyone fit a single mould, I think that we can indeed identify an orthodox framework for understanding the history of Brazilian foreign policy. It took the project of national developmentalism as its central organizing idea. It placed

7. See, for example, de Onis (2008); and Kingstone (2009).

8. For an influential but highly problematic example of this kind of analysis from the 1970s and 1980s, see Kline (1975); for a good 1990s list of reasons Brazil was seen as "mattering," see Krasno (1999).

9. For a valuable example, see Armijo (2007).

10. On the importance of purposes rather than abstract notions of power, see Legro (2007).

11. Reprinted in Joll (1986, pp. 6–7).

great emphasis on the external structures of both the international political system and the capitalist world economy. The core capitalist countries, first the United Kingdom and then the United States, were often viewed as natural obstacles to the achievement of both Brazilian development and to its upward mobility in the international power hierarchy. Perhaps above all the orthodox account took for granted the intrinsic value of national autonomy, of defending economic and political sovereignty, and of developing a more prominent international role for the country. It often took as axiomatic the idea that Brazil's position as a developing country involved a "natural" set of corresponding national interests.

This is a view of Brazilian foreign policy that reflects the close links between the academy and the foreign ministry (known as Itamaraty), and can be seen particularly in the writing of Brazilian diplomats, past and present. Two sets of theoretical ideas infuse this pattern of thought: a classical political realism (rather than neorealism) that stresses both the importance of power and the value of pragmatism; and the legacy of dependency theory, which stressed the dangers of the global capitalist system and external constraints on Brazilian development. Machiavelli and Marx were often in deep, if not always very consistent, conversation, and this nationalist and development tradition could draw support from both right and left on many (but certainly not all) core questions.

This autonomy-oriented, developmentalist ideology was institutionally firmly embedded within and around the state. Within the state it had been supported, especially in the post-1974 period, by a powerful coalition of economic technocrats, the development ministries and bodies (planning, industry and commerce, the development banks, and regional development), the senior military, and Itamaraty. Beyond the state it was supported by a powerful array of interest groups: the large public sector unions, the military establishment, the many economic interests created by the entrepreneurial role of the state and its extensive involvement in production, regulation, and distribution, the large sections of business that were dependent on state subsidized credit and access to state contracts; regional interests (given the widespread use of fiscal incentives and regional development packages), the mainstream political parties that were heavily reliant on the state and access to state spending, and, finally, the parties of the left, which looked to the state as a vehicle for tackling the huge social debt and inequalities accumulated during the country's rapid shift from a rural and agricultural to an urban and industrial society.

One needs to note a couple of further points here. First, through much of the post-1945 period, South America as a whole was viewed in ambiguous ways: on the one hand, the region was seen as a potential source of solidarity and support in the face of an uncertain and unwelcoming world; on the other the regional implications of Brazil's successful national development led to persistent tensions with neighbors—most notably, Argentina. Second, the particular combination of political realism and dependency theory to which I alluded above gave rise to a persistent conspiratorial view of the United States and of U.S. policy—a view that often overestimated the degree of coherence in U.S. cold war policy or the extent to which the United States has ever been seriously concerned with limiting or constraining Brazil's regional and international role. Examples include recurrent nationalist concern over U.S. interest in the Amazon and the view that Washington seeks to undermine the Mercosur trading bloc as an alternative to U.S.-led hemispheric integration.

Of course this picture of foreign policy thinking leaves out a great deal. But what I want to stress is the limited range of the historical debate in the period from roughly 1930 to the late 1980s. Consider alternative possibilities. If one thinks of economic liberalism, whether in terms of domestic development or of the global economy, the absence of a liberal economic tradition in Brazil is striking.[12] In terms of international political liberalism, it is true that Brazil forms part of the broad tradition of Latin American international law and that there are undoubtedly important elements of a broadly Grotian or legalist approach to international affairs that stresses Brazil's recurrent interest in seeking diplomatic and legal solutions to international problems.[13] But much of the legalist tradition (on sovereignty, the use of force, intervention, and so on) reflected strongly defensive imperatives, and legalism has been less influential than the legalist rhetoric of foreign policy would suggest.

Or consider the other end of the political spectrum. It is true that the so-called national security doctrine of the military years reflected the strongly geopolitical—indeed, Hobbesian—view of international relations that dominated the military mindset in the early 1960s. But much of this was driven by fears of domestic radicalization, rather than by anything to do with the international system, and by belief in the importance of a top-down, conservative, and exclusionary form of domestic modernization. In terms of foreign policy itself, it involved active alignment with the United States for only a very brief time after 1964, and subsequently remained important only in relation to particular issues (Cuba, Brazil's immediate neighbors to the south, China, and Angola). Moreover, absent the cold war overlay, there was a significant overlap between national developmentalism and military thinking both during and still more after the Cold War: inner-directed modernization, responding to domestic

12. See, for example, Bresser-Pereira (1982); and Loureiro and Lima (1994).
13. See, for example, both the policy and the academic writing of Brazil's former foreign minister, Celso Lafer (2001).

failures and aiming at integrating national territory, upholding domestic order, and promoting economic development. Finally, even during the years of military rule, there was a significant gap between the Hobbesian rhetoric of the military geopoliticians and the tendency to forsake or downplay hard-power projection, even within the region

What, then, happened to this dominant orthodoxy? The first point to note is that the end of authoritarian rule did *not* bring with it significant foreign policy change—there was little new thinking and policy exhibited significant continuity. The core premises of the national development model did not change under the Sarney government (1985–90). The real process of rethinking took place in the late 1980s and early 1990s, involving the cumulative pressures of economic instability, the multifaceted crisis of the state, and an emerging view of how the global system was changing and undermining existing strategies. There is not space here to delve deeper into this process of rethinking, but one should note the importance of a relative political outsider, in the form of President Collor, in breaking or unsettling the previous mould. Further, the complex process of ideational breakdown and adaptation was never simply about the wholesale dislodging of a prior set of foreign policy ideas and their replacement by a new set of liberal foreign and foreign policy beliefs.

I now look briefly at two sets of ideas of how Brazil should adapt to a changing world and changing notions of global order, first under President Cardoso and then under President Lula.

Great emphasis was given during the Cardoso years to the idea that Brazil needed to reestablish its "credentials" as a modern liberal democracy with an effective state and a coherent economic policy. Brazil's status was seen as flowing from its successful economic development and navigation of the transformed world of liberal globalization. Of course, there was a great deal of foreign policy activity, but, looking back, the greater sense is of what had to be achieved within Brazil rather than of the possibilities of changing the external world. On one side globalization was seen as a given against which one country could do little and where, as we shall see, the prospects for collective management were extremely limited. On the other side it was thought that external success must depend at the end of the day on successively implemented internal reforms.

In consequence the Cardoso administration tended to stress Brazil's need to accommodate itself to U.S. power and to liberal globalization—hence Brazil's growing willingness to accept the dominant norms of the post–cold war period, on missile technology, arms exports, and nuclear proliferation, for example. Similarly, in relation to the environment, Brazil moved sharply away from its defensiveness of the 1980s toward accepting the legitimacy of international environmental concerns and the activities of nongovernmental organizations (which had been previously often been denounced as subversive), and a more positive engagement in international negotiations. An important parallel shift was visible also in relation to human rights.

In part it seems that the reticence to assert Brazilian power during the Cardoso years was a matter of timing and contingent circumstance. Hence for Cardoso it was "too early" for Brazil to play a more interventionist and political role in South America; Brazil should develop a role as "organizer" of the region but it was "not yet" ready to play a more activist political role. In part the perceived "escassez do poder" [limits of power] was a function of continued economic vulnerability, especially against the background of the financial crises that engulfed emerging economies in the late 1990s. And yet the modesty of its aims and of what Brazilian power might achieve is striking. For example, the idea that Brazil should try to approximate to the G-7 "is mere illusion for a country like ours." Why this should be so was never fully explained; neither was the claim that it was always better to be off the U.S. radar screen and that "to provoke friction with the United States is always to lose."[14]

Nevertheless Cardoso's own views of the international system and of Brazilian development were never those of a straightforward neoliberal, and his foreign policy moved during his second term in a more critical and nationalist direction. Even if it had achieved its (important) initial purpose of reestablishing Brazil's international political and economic credibility, by the late 1990s the Cardoso foreign policy of "autonomy via participation" had come to face increasingly serious challenges. The relative optimism with which policymakers had viewed the post–cold war international environment was giving way to a greater emphasis on the country's continued international economic vulnerability and the difficulties of translating Brazil's adaptation to global liberal norms and its willingness to participate in international institutions into concrete and practical results.

Although his memoirs talk a great deal of his closeness with U.S. president Bill Clinton and other Western liberal leaders, and although many of his policies clearly consciously involved greater liberalization (and, correspondingly, increased external vulnerability), Cardoso did not share the liberal view that globalization could be managed easily by effective institutions. He felt that "the vocation of capitalism is its universal expansion, revolutionizing other systems" and "globalization is not a value, nor is it something that you want or don't want. It exists. And it is necessary to have controls because it is going in a dangerous direction."[15] Yet while there were niches and windows of opportunity

---

14. See *Folha de São Paulo*, August 4, 2004.
15. From a 1997 interview reproduced in Cardoso (1998, pp. 82, 87).

for individual countries, especially large countries in which the restructuring of capitalist production had moved forward, the effective regulation of globalization could only be international. The problem, however, was the lack of effective institutions. And, perhaps like many economic structuralists, Cardoso had a rather power-driven (and limited) view of existing institutions. Indeed he opposed the idea that Brazil should make UN Security Council reform a priority because "it does not help to have a permanent seat in the Security Council when what we need is an effective system of security."[16]

The Lula government that came into power in January 2003 sought to differentiate its own more assertively nationalist foreign policy from that of its predecessor, which it portrayed as insufficiently resolute in the defense of Brazilian interests and too accepting of the liberalizing and globalizing agenda of the 1990s. The new government's dominant view of foreign policy stressed both the dangers and instability of the international environment and the growing concentration of political and military power, wealth, and ideological power in the hands of the United States and its developed country allies. Reflecting many features of Brazil's traditional national developmentalism, the Lula government saw the global economy as containing far more constraints and snares than opportunities. Globalization was working to reinforce the power of the developed world, but it was also creating new sources of instability—especially recurrent and highly damaging financial crises—and politically dangerous and morally unacceptable inequalities, both within and among countries.

Within this harsher and more conflictual view of the international system, Brazil was seen as vulnerable because of its internal inequalities, social cleavages, and incomplete development, and because of its continued external weaknesses and its absence from international decisionmaking structures. But Brazil was not without options. Indeed one of the most interesting features of the early Lula years was its generally pessimistic view of the international system and belief that there was scope for an activist and assertive foreign policy. Hence there were repeated invocations of the idea that Brazil is neither small nor insignificant and that it has options in a world in which, despite the challenges, unipolarity is more apparent than real. Facing these "hegemonic structures of power," therefore, Brazil needed to reassert its national autonomy, form coalitions with other developing states to reduce its external vulnerability and increase its own bargaining power, and work, however modestly, toward a more balanced world order. It should seek "to increase, if only by a margin, the degree of multipolarity in the world," as the foreign minister, Celso Amorim, put it. For the Lula government, building up technological capacity remained a valid policy goal; it was also

16. Cardoso (2008, p. 87).

determined to protect the country's industrial base—which the FTAA negotiations of the 1990s had been seen as threatening but which the Lula government effectively ended—and to renew emphasis on the long-term goal of developing the country's nuclear capacity (but preserving industrial secrets while maintaining good relations with the global inspection regime).

From this general picture have followed the cornerstones of Brazil's foreign policy:[17] the drive to increase its presence in international institutions—as with its (so far unsuccessful) campaign for membership of the UN Security Council or its (successful) drive to join the core group of states negotiating the WTO Doha Round; the increased emphasis on expanding relations with other major developing countries (especially India, China, and South Africa) and the relaunch of a more activist policy toward Africa (and to a lesser extent, the Middle East); and the intensification of relations within South America involving attempts to deepen and broaden Mercosur and launch a South American Community of Nations.

A prominent theme of the Lula years has been the search for recognition, for securing "its sovereign presence" via an assertive and activist foreign policy. This does not mean direct confrontation in the style of Venezuela's Hugo Chávez but, rather, a more assertive policy pursued through engagement and negotiation: pressing for reform but operating very much within the system. Equally, reflecting both the ideological stance of those at the heart of its foreign policy and perhaps nature and limits of its material power, Brazil has followed a delicate and sometimes unstable path between aspirant Great Power status on the one hand and continuing to portray itself as representative of the developing world on the other.

Brazilian diplomacy under the Lula government has certainly achieved a good deal. It could build on the foundations laid during the Cardoso years, especially in restoring the country's international credibility. In keeping with both its self-perceived identity and its power-related interests, Brazil continues to foreswear the hard-power route in favor of heavy emphasis on multilateralism and exploiting what one diplomat has called the country's "diplomatic GNP": its capacity for effective coalition building and insider activism within international institutions, and its ability to frame its own interests in terms of arguments for greater justice. Thus mobilizing claims for greater representational fairness (as with membership of the UN Security Council) and distributional justice (as with promoting the 2004 Action against Hunger and Poverty) have been central tools of Brazilian foreign policy.[18]

17. For an initial assessment of Lula's foreign policy, see Hurrell (2008).
18. See Nina (2006).

Brazil has carved out an important role for itself in framing issues and set-ting agendas. Its leadership of the Trade G-20 coalition and its activism and assertiveness have changed the negotiating dynamics of the WTO system. Brazil has acquired something like veto-player status and has convinced many of its interlocutors that the country has to be part of any stable global trade regime for reasons of political legitimacy as much as for narrow economic logic. It is difficult to account for the role of Brazil in the WTO in material terms or in terms of economic or trade power. In part its success derives from successful coalitional politics combined with intensive "insider activism" and its capac-ity to work the informal norms of the WTO. In part Brazil has been able to frame its demands in terms of both the legitimacy deficit of the WTO and the importance of applying its supposed liberal values in a more even-handed way. But in part Brazil's status derives from a more old-fashioned notion of a club of powerful states that is able to provide effective leadership. In relation to cli-mate change it has helped to shift the focus of negotiations toward the North-South axis. Foreign policy has also proved a major domestic political success. In a situation where much of the original reform agenda and hopes for greater social justice at home of Lula's *Partido dos Trabalhadores* (PT, or Workers' Party) proved difficult to implement and where external economic vulnerability dic-tated an extremely orthodox macroeconomic and fiscal policy, an activist and assertive foreign policy proved highly popular in terms of domestic politics, both for the PT and for Lula personally.

Despite official statements to the contrary, the external environment for Bra-zil from early 2003 until the outbreak of the financial crisis in September 2008 was in fact extremely benign. For all its perversities "casino capitalism" favored Brazil with booming demand for commodities and raw materials, especially from China; buoyant markets of Brazilian exports in the developed world; and a growing position as a favored son of Wall Street investors (assisted by the gov-ernment's extremely orthodox domestic economic policies). At the same time Brazil was able to exploit an institutional environment that combined a signifi-cant role for multilateral governance with the growing importance of hierarchy and status built around the major states of the system and those deemed to be moving toward that status. Hence Brazil has both stressed the importance of formal multilateral institutions and concentrated much of its diplomacy on gaining entry into informal groupings, clubs, or networks of major states: for-mally, as in the case of the UN Security Council; informally, as in the case of the informal negotiating processes of the WTO or the emergence of ad hoc groups of "specially engaged states" on the issue of climate change.[19] Foreign policy was

---

19. See Hurrell and Narlikar (2006).

about reformism from within the system, with an emphasis on gaining influence within crucial sites of global decisionmaking. As Shogo Suzuki has argued in relation to Japan, Brazil has sought to persuade existing major powers that it is worthy of legitimate Great Power status through various forms of "recognition games."[20]

The crucial question is whether the current crisis is working to narrow the range of Brazil's international options and to challenge the established modalities of its diplomatic practice.

Brazil in a Changing Global Order and Evolving Institutional Structure

In the 1990s global order was widely understood through the lens of liberal internationalism or liberal solidarism. Globalization was rendering obsolete the old Westphalian world of Great Power rivalries, balance-of-power politics, and an old-fashioned international law built around state sovereignty and strict rules of nonintervention. Bumpy as it might be the road seemed to lead away from Westphalia—toward an expanded role for formal and informal multilateral institutions; a huge increase in the scope, density, and intrusiveness of rules and norms made at the international level but affecting how domestic societies are organized; ever-greater involvement of new actors in global governance; moves toward the coercive enforcement of global rules; and fundamental changes in political, legal, and moral understandings of state sovereignty and of the relationship between the state, the citizen, and the international community.

Academics, especially in the United States, told three kinds of liberal stories. Some stressed institutions. Institutions are needed to deal with the ever-more complex dilemmas of collective action that are emerging in a globalized world. As large states, including developing ones such as Brazil or India, expand their range of interests and integrate more fully into the global economy and world society, they naturally will be drawn by the functional benefits that institutions provide and pressed toward more cooperative and "responsible" patterns of behavior. Others stressed the Kantian idea of the gradual but progressive diffusion of liberal values, partly as a result of liberal economics and increased economic interdependence, partly as liberal legal order comes to sustain the autonomy of a global civil society, and partly as a result of the successful example set by the multifaceted liberal capitalist system of states. A third group told a U.S.-centered story. The United States was indeed the center of a unipolar world, but, true both to its own values and its rational self-interest, Washington

20. Suzuki (2008).

would continue to bind itself within the institutions it had created during the cold war to reassure smaller states and prevent balancing against U.S. power. In return for this self-binding and the procedural legitimacy it would create, and also in return for U.S.-supplied global public goods and the output legitimacy they would create, other states would acquiesce and accept the role of the United States as the owner and operator of the system. Through a mix of these three processes those states of the old "third world" that previously had challenged the Western order now would become increasingly enmeshed, socialized, and integrated.

Since well before George W. Bush, however, and certainly before the financial crisis, a compelling list of factors has been pushing in a very different direction: the renewed salience of security, the re-valorization of national security, and a renewed preoccupation with war fighting and counterinsurgency; the continued or renewed power of nationalism, no longer potentially containable politically or analytically in a box marked "ethnic conflict" but manifest in the identity politics and foreign policy actions of the major states in the system; the renewed importance of nuclear weapons as central to major power relations, to the structure of regional security complexes, and in the construction of Great Power hierarchies and the distribution of seats at top tables; and finally the renewed centrality of the balance of power as both a motivation for state policy (as with U.S. policies in Asia) and as an element in the foreign policy of all second-tier states.

Economic globalization has also fed back into the structures and dynamics of a Westphalian state system, rather than pointing toward its transcendence. The state as an economic actor has proved resilient in seeking to control economic flows and police borders and in exploiting and developing state-based and mercantilist modes of managing economic problems, especially in relation to resource competition and energy geopolitics. Successful liberal globalization has had a vital impact on the distribution of interstate political power. If the debate over power shifts in the 1990s concentrated on the shift of power from states to firms and nonstate actors, the "power shift" of the past decade has focused on rising and emerging powers, on state-directed economic activity, and on the mismatch between existing global economic governance arrangements and the distribution of power among those with the actual power of effective economic decision.

The importance of the global financial crisis is not related solely to its severely negative economic effects, but also to the challenge it represents to the idea of a stable, Western-led global order and to its reinforcement of the forces and factors outlined above, especially economic nationalism. High levels of uncertainty and unpredictability are pressing political and market actors to focus on the short term and will exacerbate zero-sum rivalries. Many are correctly warning about the dangers of protectionism. But protectionism is just one part of a broader phenomenon. Responses to the crisis are putting back into the realm of the political many of the decisions that the liberal economic orthodoxy of the 1990s had sought to consign to the market—as with the role of independent central banks domestically or of networks of financial regulators internationally. Economic decisionmaking now is being driven by unmediated politics, whether through government subsidies, direct state control, or increased regulatory supervision. The boundary between state and market is everywhere being redrawn, and that redrawing is likely to be heavily shaped by domestic constituencies, intensified interest-group politics, and demands for the protection and promotion of economic sovereignty.

International society therefore faces a series of classic Westphalian problems, especially to do with the rise of new powers and the reemergence of economic nationalism and resource mercantilism. But it faces these problems within a context that is clearly post-Westphalian. It is post-Westphalian, first, because of a structural change in the nature of the foreign policy and governance challenges that states face. Dealing with these challenges—climate change, stable trade rules, a credible system of global finance—necessarily involves not only cooperation but also rules that involve deep intervention in domestic affairs. As well as this structural change, the financial crisis pushes states toward economic nationalism, but also provides further graphic evidence of the limits of what a nation alone can achieve. As in other areas of globalization, technological and financial innovation will constantly challenge efforts to re-regulate and restabilize.

The context is post-Westphalian, second, because of the changing problem of legitimacy. All states and social orders need to gain the authority and legitimacy that the possession of crude power can never secure on its own. All major powers face the imperative of turning a capacity for crude coercion into legitimate authority. The Bush years marked the bankruptcy of hegemonic or top-down modes of governance. The financial crisis has exacerbated the already-evident decline in the idea that the legitimacy of international institutions could be grounded in claims to superior economic or technological knowledge. The inherited institutions of the Western-led international order have proved manifestly dysfunctional, and neither leading market actors nor technical specialists have ready ideas and answers. Legitimacy based on effective outputs and technical knowledge therefore is likely to be in short supply; taken together with the politicization of market transactions, this outcome is likely to place a premium on democratic forms of legitimacy. The dilemma, of course, is that such legitimacy is most securely established at the domestic level and weakest at the international level. Yet there is little alternative but to involve a growing range of major states within both formal and informal institutions, precisely to strengthen their claims to legitimacy and representative authority.

The third element of post-Westphalian context has to do with what one might call the "provincializing of Westphalia" and the shift of power away from the core Western industrialized world—historically first built around Europe and the European colonial order and then around the United States and the Greater West. It is increasingly difficult to see the Western, state-based order either as a universal model or as the stable core of a successful global system. The legitimacy of norms is never solely a matter of their intrinsic value; it is shaped by their provenance (where they come from) and by their practice (how are they used). In the 1990s many, including in Brazil, suspected that the new liberal norms concerned with human rights, democracy, and free markets were being used in selective ways to reflect narrow national interests. Today it is of immense significance for world politics that current instabilities of global capitalism are occurring at the core, rather than on the periphery, of the system. The most politically difficult aspects of power transitions are not to do with material power but with adjusting to the loss of what Abraham Lowenthal termed "hegemonic presumption" and the inherited belief that core bargains can be made on the West's terms and in institutions the West controls.[21]

The international system increasingly is characterized by a diffusion of power, to emerging and regional powers; a diffusion of preferences, with many more voices demanding to be heard both globally and within states as a result of globalization and democratization; and by a diffusion of ideas and values, with a reopening of the big questions of social, economic, and political organization that supposedly had been answered with the end of the Cold War and the liberal ascendancy. Within this context the inherited institutional structure is coming under severe stress and challenge, and it is far from clear what the "rising institutions" actually might be.

Challenges and Opportunities

Unlike India or China, Brazil does not have the hard-power resources to claim status within a more traditionally Great Power–centric concert or club. The more international society moves toward Westphalia, the more serious is the dilemma for Brazilian foreign policy. It is true that Brazil's natural resources and environmental goods are important in an age of geopolitical competition and neo-Malthusian resource conflicts. Notwithstanding the concentration on soft power, it is also worth noting that the past five years have seen the first glimmering of a more focused discussion of the links between foreign policy and

---

21. Lowenthal (1976).

military strategy, especially within the region. The reassessment of the importance of nuclear technology and plans to develop a nuclear-powered submarine also point in this direction. But it is precisely in such a world that the limits on Brazil's hard material power capabilities come sharply into focus. These limits apply both to the country's capacity to be a player in core major power relations and to its role as a regional power

What, then, of the region? A common view is that emerging global players will also be regional powers and that their status as regional leaders will be an important element of their global status. Historically, however, this view is incorrect. Some of the most successful major powers, the United Kingdom and the United States most obviously, were successful precisely because they avoided becoming ensnared in their regions but set the terms of their continental commitments or hemispheric involvement.

Brazil's own ambitions in South America have been complex, sometimes contradictory. Historically Brazil was in, but not of, South America, and its relations in the region, outside the Southern Cone, were often distant. The Latin Americanization of Brazil's foreign policy took place in the late 1970s, but it was under the Lula government that policies to develop a more prominent role in the region increased in salience and seriousness—during the first Lula government, especially, the body language of leadership became far more visible. Brazil also invested a good deal of rhetorical energy and high-level political time and effort in seeking to relaunch Mercosur. In addition Brasilia was prepared to assume a more assertive political role—political in the sense of an expansion of party-to-party relations, the creation of intense and dynamic relations among the president, his foreign policy advisors, and formal diplomatic channels, and involvement in floating politically charged ideas such as offering to mediate in Colombia. Moreover Brazil has been willing to pay a higher price to secure good relations with smaller neighbors—both literally (as with Paraguay in terms of energy prices) and metaphorically (in terms of a greater willingness to engage in regional institution building, even if mostly of a shallow kind).

However, even under the Lula government, the region represents only one part of the status to which the country has aspired. Brasilia's self-identification is of Brazil as a global player with global interests. More problematically, Brazil has found it difficult to secure acceptance of or even acquiescence in its status as a regional leader. Regional states failed to support its bid for UN Security Council reform and its candidates in other international bodies—Argentina, in particular, has rejected Brazil's increased political involvement in the region; Brazil has not been able to provide economic resources, regional public goods, or a distinctive political or economic model; Mercosur faces huge challenges; and Brazil has faced counterclaims on its leadership, most notably from Venezuela.

Brazil's regional policy has been the center of considerable criticism at home and is one area of foreign policy that could change after the 2010 elections, at least in terms of tone and rhetoric. But it is important to note the structural changes that have taken place in Brazil's relations with the region. The option of relative disengagement is no longer available; Brazil is now much more firmly enmeshed in the region and now must live with the spillovers and externalities that go with ever greater social, economic, and energy interdependence—including the protracted violence and the narco-economy of the Andean region, which have had profound effects on the patterns of violence in Brazil's cities. Equally, the political complexion of the region has changed dramatically in ways that make it difficult for Brazil to steer regional developments or to project its own model. The result is a delicate balance among three competing objectives: to promote its influence in order to stabilize a troubled region; to act defensively against the spillovers from instability; and to focus as much of its energy and attention on its global interests as possible.

Relations with Washington are always important to Brazil, and the Obama administration's accession undoubtedly has opened up new possibilities. But the Brasilia-Washington relationship is unlikely to become anything like the central axis of Brazilian foreign policy, reinforcing continuity rather than change. It is certainly the case that Brazil has welcomed Washington's greater willingness to engage in regional cooperative forums, and it hopes to assist the United States reintegrate Cuba into the hemisphere. Brazil is paying a great deal of attention to ethanol, biofuels, and cooperation in the fields of energy and the environment. Finally, Brazil has been viewed in Washington as a potentially moderating force in the region. Although formally rejecting the notion of "bridge builder," Brazilian diplomats themselves sometimes have stressed their country's moderating influence and fire-fighting role.

Against these factors the Obama administration has shown little sign it will make Latin America a high priority; to the extent it does, attention focuses on migration, Cuba, drug trafficking and organized crime, and Mexico. Energy cooperation is clearly important, but this is more likely to develop bilaterally and in the face of protectionist constraints. In relation to security, Brazil is reluctant to engage too deeply in any hemispheric initiatives that would complicate its own long-term preference for greater South American regional cooperation. And the idea of Brazil as a "regional manager," acting together with Washington, has no historical basis nor any present or likely future reality. Indeed Brazilian government expectations about changes in U.S. regional policy have been dented by what Brasilia sees as Washington's very limited moves on Cuba, as well as by significant differences over both the Honduran crisis and the issue of U.S. bases in Colombia.

The most important interactions between Brazil and the United States are likely to play out on broader-than-regional issues, including climate change, the management of the global trading and monetary systems, and the geopolitics of energy. For some in Washington the core task is to reassert the values and structures of the U.S.-led international order of the mid-1990s and to put the Bush years behind them as a damaging diversion from a clearly defined historical path.[22] Obama's choice of so many senior advisors from the Clinton years points potentially in this direction. Brazil does not fit easily into such a view, however, not because it is a radical challenger and certainly not because it could be seen as part of some illiberal autocratic revival, but because it has consistently stressed the limits of the Western-led system, for both its own aspirations and those of other developing countries.

For much of the cold war period Brazil did not view the Western-centered system as open, integrated, and rules-based, but as exclusionary and discriminating. Even under military governments Brazilian foreign policy was concerned with the dangers posed by superpower rivalry, especially in the third world, and by the gap between Washington's anticommunist struggle and Brazil's own imperatives as a developing country. Within its own region it has long experience of U.S. unilateralism, of Washington's deep unwillingness to commit to a meaningful set of binding institutions, and of Brazil's own difficulty in securing a voice in the councils and capitals of hegemonic power.

If we ask what the U.S.-led Western core was prepared to give during the 1990s to draw rising states into a stable structure of global governance, the answer surely is "not much": resistance throughout that era to the notion that liberalized global finance required effective regulation to avoid damaging financial crises; the assumption that the Western core could still set the terms of the WTO negotiating agenda; the claim as "global" a security agenda that reflected the West's own security concerns and those of its closest allies; and climate change negotiations that diluted the idea of common but differentiated responsibilities and increased resistance to the position, obvious at least to Brazilian policymakers, that the developed world clearly had both to take the lead in mitigation and underwrite the effective large-scale transfer of technology and finance to the developing world. Finally the Western core showed little sign of willingness to open up decisionmaking power within existing institutions or to give up its "hereditary claims" to the top posts at the International Monetary Fund (IMF) and the World Bank.[23]

22. See, for example, Ikenberry (2008).
23. See Biato (2008, p. 9).

As important as membership undoubtedly is, experience has taught Brazilian policymakers that membership alone does not in fact provide greater status or more effective influence. Indeed it has been a feature of multilateralism in the early years of this century that rising and emerging powers have disengaged themselves from existing institutions—for example, buffering themselves against dependence on the IMF by building up foreign exchange reserves and implementing far more effective banking regulation than exists even in most industrialized economies. Moreover one goal of the process of creating informal groupings has been to provide alternative forums for the discussion of shared global problems—both IBSA (the grouping of India, Brazil, and South Africa) and the meetings of the BRIC countries illustrate this (difficult) ambition.

Even before the financial crisis, Latin America provided some of the clearest lessons of how liberal prescriptions had been applied but found wanting. From a Brazilian perspective, therefore, the U.S.-centered "liberal" order is rather more tarnished and the institutional landscape looks more broken and problematic than the notion of "reasserting U.S. liberal leadership" would suggest.

What of the idea of building global governance around a club of liberal democracies? Again, Brazil illustrates the difficulties. For all its political and social problems, Brazil is a large and consolidated democracy and, with India, has a legitimate claim to a say in twenty-first century debates on the meaning and nature of democratic rule. But, first, Brazilian governments have long stressed the importance of universalist multilateral institutions, resisted coercive liberal interventionism, maintained the importance of national sovereignty, and consistently attacked what is seen as the politically driven selectivity of the United States in relation to both human rights and humanitarian intervention. Second, Brazil sees clear geopolitical and economic advantage in developing ties with nondemocracies, China most obviously, and its diplomatic soft power depends on the claim that it can act as interlocutor among many different kinds of states and political systems. Third, many (particularly on the left) sympathize with those democratic developments in Latin America to which Washington is least attracted and that either (on one view) reflect the weakness of narrow electoralism or (on another view) open up new forms of participatory democracy. Fourth, and however self-serving it might be, Brazil argues that the democratizing agenda should be about "democratizing" global governance, rather than reforming the power of the currently dominant. Finally, Brazil illustrates the degree to which views of the world and concrete foreign policy interests can vary greatly, even among states that are liberal, Western, and democratic.

During the cold war years there was a persistent and often highly politically charged debate about whether Brazil was part of the Western battle against communism and the Soviet Union or a member of the third world in its struggle for development and a greater role in international affairs. The developmentalist line was more often the dominant one, and relations with Washington were, if not conflictual, rarely close and harmonious. For long periods, including since 1990, Brazilian foreign policy toward the United States has aimed at prudent coexistence, possible collaboration, and minimal collision, but shied away from any kind of special relationship. Of course much depends on the criterion by which one evaluates alignments, but the historical record suggests skepticism of the view that "Brazil's future political alliances are significantly predetermined: It will be a Western power, closely linked to the United States and Western Europe."[24] Brazil is clearly a Western society, part of what Alain Rouquié calls "l'extrême occident," but only rarely has that identity been particularly significant in shaping either foreign policy ideas or foreign policy behavior.

More important still is the need to open up the debate on the nature of liberal order. One valid set of questions asks how the U.S.-led liberal order came to be challenged by the "autocratic and illiberal revival" of states such as Russia and China and by the "return of history." Another crucial dimension of the debate is to recognize that there are many versions of liberalism and that leading democratic emerging powers such as Brazil and India have a valid claim to shaping the character of the meaning of global liberalism and "global liberal order" in the twenty-first century. Potential change in the foreign policies of emerging powers might be captured along a spectrum from "autonomy and defensiveness" to "engagement and responsibility," but from Brazil's perspective the core capitalist countries have been highly "irresponsible" powers and the global economic crisis demands a much broader debate about who is responsible to whom and for what.

Conclusion

For Brazil the two greatest challenges—but also the two greatest opportunities—concern ideas and institutions. Crises naturally generate a great deal of policy improvisation and pragmatism. There is also a severe credibility gap in that so many of those who are in charge of managing the crisis in the United States and the United Kingdom were themselves deeply committed to the liberal orthodoxies of the 1990s and implicated in its excesses. But crises are an important catalyst for ideational change, and the intellectual landscape undoubtedly will become more open and contested. Brazil has the opportunity to contribute to restructuring liberal global order from within. Its contribution of course will be limited, but its position as an activist inside the structures of

24. Sotero and Armijo (2007, p. 44). On the U.S.-Brazilian relationship, see Hurrell (2005).

global governance gives it significant assets. The challenge is to look beyond the immediate and the current. In the WTO the challenge is not just to contain protectionism, but also to refashion global rules to reflect changes in the domestic role of the state and the balance between state and market. It is also to renegotiate those elements of earlier bargains that most stand in the way of effective responses to shared challenges—as, for example, when intellectual property norms work against the large-scale transfer of climate-change-related technology to developing countries. The global financial order will depend on developing a strengthened and legitimate system of monitoring and international insurance, with large increases in the resources of the IMF, a thorough reform of its governance structure, and a renewed mandate to tackle exchange rate policies.

Brazil would be damaged by the failure of the world economy to recover. But its options would also be constrained if the core economies recovered but without serious reform or rethinking. In such a situation market-liberal orthodoxies would remain dominant; the state would assume a much larger economic role but without effective regulatory structures either domestically or, still more, globally; and successful muddling through would involve a further concentration of financial, industrial, and technological power around a smaller number of giant global firms. After the initial flurry of calls for deeper and tighter regulation, there are already signs of such a "return to normal" attitude in both the United States and the United Kingdom.[25]

To be effective and sustainable, ideas have to be embodied in legitimate and effective institutions. The institutional challenge is greater and even more important for Brazil. The willingness of the Obama administration to re-engage with the world is extraordinarily important. Both in the United States and beyond there seems widespread acceptance of the need to reform international institutions to engage new centers of power—as the limits to U.S. influence and capabilities become more evident, as the balance of power becomes open to change, as the structure and stability of global capitalism once more become a matter of serious contestation, and as issues such as climate change and nonproliferation become more central and cannot be tackled without engaging the interests and capabilities of a wider set of regional powers.

The Obama administration professes a belief in multilateralism but many questions remain. Does the administration have the domestic political space to strike productive international bargains in areas such as climate change? What forms of multilateralism are the administration likely to favor? Is the United States willing to engage in serious institutional renewal and to accept the

25. See Crouch (2009).

inevitable constraints on political power and formal sovereignty that *all* multilateralism necessarily entails? Domestic political constraints, concern about effectiveness and capacity for action, and a straightforward interest in not wanting to accept reform that reduces its own power all press Washington toward foreign policy continuity and a form of "pragmatic multilateralism" in which flexible and informal groupings predominate, often with a traditional concert or major power focus and flavor.

Institutional incentives vary across regional powers and involve difficult trade-offs. China, for example, might relish the idea of a G-2, but such a visible and highly political arrangement would undercut its preference for "hiding" and ducking controversial positions in formal organizations. For its part Brazil has pressed strongly for the G-8 to be replaced by a broader grouping, whether in the form of the G-20 or some other "G-8 plus"—as Brazilian foreign minister Celso Amorim put it, "The G8 has died, I have not the slightest doubt about this, because it no longer represents anything."[26] Moreover Brazil's traditionally strong "sovereigntist" attitudes are resonant with similar views in China and India—and indeed in the United States. For example, its position on several human rights questions, including Darfur, underscores the continued attraction of more traditional pluralist or Westphalian views of sovereignty.

Yet far more than do other emerging powers, Brazil depends on formal institutions to provide the setting in which its institutional soft power can be most effective and where it can maximize its claims of "Southern" representativeness and its well-established coalitional strategies. It is partly for this reason that Brazil has put greater emphasis than has, say, India on reforming the UN Security Council, that it has been more willing to engage in institutional innovation (as with the creation of the Clean Development Mechanism in the late 1990s), and that, when push comes to shove (as at the July 2008 Geneva WTO Ministerial), it has been prepared to accept compromise within the WTO. Particularly in terms of informal groupings that are not tied to formal institutions (such as the G-20 finance ministers' meetings), the risk for Brazil is that membership brings shared responsibility and calls for shared burdens but without the effective capacity to influence decisionmaking and without the protections provided by the rules of formal institutionalization. Brazil's interests cannot therefore be reduced simply to gaining membership of whatever grouping of powerful states might be on offer.

The tone of Brazil's foreign policy could well change with the election of a new president in 2010, and there could well be a shift in emphasis—involving,

26. Quoted in "'G8 morreu, não tenho dúvida' diz Amorim," *Folha de São Paulo,* June 13, 2009.

for example, a less assertive policy in the region or a more restrained "Southern" rhetoric. But the structure of its economic interests (such as the importance of manufactured exports to other Latin American countries or of its agricultural trade within the WTO), the success of the Lula government's more assertive foreign policy, and, above all, its interest in both formal institutions and informal groupings all point broadly in the direction of continuity.

A striking contrast between debates on global governance in the 1990s and those on world order in the late 1940s concerns the nature of institutions. In the 1940s it was clear, in the security realm with the United Nations and in terms of global money and global trade, that the world needed strong and effective institutions. Keynes and White had the ideas and Washington had the power, but almost nobody questioned the view that the postwar order needed effective institutionalization. In the 1990s it was thought that an immensely more complex global and globalized system could be run on the back of relatively thin institutions, supplemented by networks and an increasing array of private and civil society-based governance mechanisms. This gap between ambition and action made sense only on the assumption that at the system's real political core would be U.S. hegemonic power. If one accepts that the material power and moral authority of the United States to set the terms of the new global bargains have declined, and adds the huge uncertainties in the global economic system and powerful Westphalian tendencies in the international political system, then the prospects for a successful combination of new ideas and strengthened institutions seem far from good. Of all the emerging powers Brazil potentially has the most to contribute to meeting this institutional challenge, but it is also likely to find the gap dangerous and discomforting.

References

Armijo, Leslie Elliott. 2007. "The BRICs Countries as Analytical Category: Mirage or Insight?" *Asian Perspectives* 31, no. 4: 7–42.

Biato, Marcel F. 2008. "Shaping Global Governance: A Brazilian Perspective." *CEBRI Artigos* 1 (January-March).

Bresser-Pereira, Luiz Carlos. 1982. "Seis interpretações sôbre o Brasil." *Dados* 5, no. 3: 269–306.

Chase, Robert, Emily Hill, and Paul Kennedy, eds. 1999. *The Pivotal States: A New Framework for U.S. Policy in the Developing World*. New York: Norton.

Cardoso, Fernando Henrique. 1998. *O Presidente Segundo o Sociólogo. Entrevista de Fernando Henrique Cardoso a Roberto Pompeu de Toledo*. São Paulo: Campanhia das Letras.

Crouch, Colin. 2009. "Privatised Keynesianism: An Unacknowledged Policy Regime." *British Journal of Political Science* 11, no. 3: 394–98.

de Carvalho, José Murilo. 2000. "Dreams Come Untrue." *Daedalus* 129 (Spring).

de Onis, Juan. 2008. "Brazil's Big Moment." *Foreign Affairs* 87, no. 6: 101–22.

Garten, Jeffrey. 1997. *The Big Ten: The Big Emerging Markets and How They Will Shape Our Lives.* New York: Basic Books.

Hurrell, Andrew. 2005. "The United States and Brazil: Comparative Reflections." In *The United States and Brazil: A Long Road of Unmet Expectations,* by Monica Hirst. New York: Routledge.

———. 2008. "Lula's Brazil: A Rising Power but Going Where?" *Current History* 107 (February): 51–57.

Hurrell, Andrew, and Amrita Narlikar. 2006. "A New Politics of Confrontation? Developing Countries at Cancun and Beyond." *Global Society* 20, no. 4: 415–33.

Ikenberry, G. John. 2008. "The Rise of China and the Future of the West." *Foreign Affairs* 87, no. 1: 23–37.

Joll, James. 1968. *1914: The Unspoken Assumptions.* Oxford: Clarendon Press.

Kingstone, Peter. 2009. "Brazil: The Sleeping Giant Awakens?" *World Politics Review* (January 12). (www.worldpoliticsreview.com/article.aspx?id=3145).

Kline, Ray S. 1975. *World Power Assessment: A Calculus of Strategic Drift.* Boulder, Colo.: Westview Press.

Krasno, Jean. 1999. "Brazil." In *The Pivotal States: A New Framework for U.S. Policy in the Developing World,* edited by Robert Chase, Emily Hill, and Paul Kennedy. New York: Norton.

Lafer, Celso. 2001. *A identidade internacional do Brasil e a política externa brasileira.* São Paulo: Editora Perspectiva.

Legro, Jeffrey W. 2007. "What Will China Want: The Future Intentions of a Rising Power." *Perspectives on Politics* 5, no. 3: 515–34.

Loureiro, Maria Rita, and Gilberto Tadeu Lima. 1994. "A internacionalização da ciência econômica no Brasil." *Revista de Economia Política* 14, no. 3: 31–50.

Lowenthal, Abraham. 1976. "The United States and Latin America Ending the Hegemonic Presumption," *Foreign Affairs* 55, no. 1: 199–213.

Nina, Alexandre. 2006. "Action against Hunger and Poverty: Brazilian Foreign Policy in Lula's First Term (2003–2006)." Working paper, Oxford University, Centre for Brazilian Studies.

Perry, William. 1976. *Contemporary Brazilian Foreign Policy: The International Strategy of an Emerging Power.* Beverly Hills, Calif.: Sage.

Roett, Riordan. 1975. "Brazil Ascendant: International Relations and Geopolitics in the late 20th Century." *Journal of International Affairs* 29, no. 2: 139–54.

Sotero, Paulo, and Leslie Elliott Armijo. 2007. "Brazil: To Be or Not to Be a BRIC?" *Asian Perspectives* 31, no. 4: 43–70.

Suzuki, Shogo. 2008. "Seeking 'Legitimate' Great Power Status in Post Cold War International Society: China and Japan's Participation in UNKPO." *International Relations* 22, no. 1: 45–68.

ANDREW MORAVCSIK

7

Europe: Rising Superpower in a Bipolar World

It has become fashionable to view the global system as dominated by the United States, China, and India. How often do we hear from leading politicians that "the most important relationship in the 21st century is that between Washington and Beijing"?[1] Or that the "rise of the rest" is the great phenomenon of our time?[2] Missing from the equation, however, is Europe. The "Old Continent's" reputation for sluggish economic and demographic growth, political disunity, and weak military force has convinced most foreign analysts that the future belongs to Asia and the United States.[3] Among scholars, commentators, and politicians alike the conventional view is that the contemporary world is "unipolar," with the United States standing alone as the sole "superpower." In their view, with the rise of China, India, and perhaps Brazil and Russia, the other two countries that make up the so-called BRICs, the world might become multipolar—if it is not already—but Europe's role in the geopolitical balance remains insignificant.

Such claims rest on demographic, economic, and military measures of power. European economic growth, it is believed, is sluggish and getting worse. The median age in Europe is predicted to increase from 37.7 in 2003 to 52.3 by 2050 (the median age of Americans, in contrast, is expected to rise only to 35.4 by 2050), with profoundly negative effects on Europe's productivity, growth, and fiscal stability.[4] According to this view Europe's low level of military spending

1. Richard Spencer, "Hillary Clinton: Chinese Human Rights Secondary to Economic Survival." Daily Telegraph [London], February 20, 2009.

2. Zakaria (2008).

3. For exceptions, with which I am in sympathy, see Reid (2004); Rifkin (2004); and Leonard (2005).

4. "Eurozone Economic Growth 'Will Halve by 2030' without Reforms," *Fund Strategy,* July 18, 2005 (www.highbeam.com/doc/1G1-134183745.html).

compared with that of the United States—which now accounts for close to half of global military spending—also condemns it to second-tier status.

Some analysts concede that Europe could rejoin the roster of future Great Powers, but only if it unifies so as to become something resembling a nation-state. As Henry Kissinger (probably apocryphally) is said to have asked over a quarter-century ago, "If I want to call Europe, what telephone number do I dial?" Yet most consider further centralization in Brussels unlikely. The U.S. National Intelligence Council Global Trends Report speculates that in 2050 Europe may well be "a hobbled giant distracted by internal bickering and competing national agendas and (even) less able to translate its economic clout into global influence."[5] Mark Leonard notes: "The conventional wisdom is that Europe's hour has come and gone. Its lack of visions, divisions, obsession with legal frameworks, unwillingness to project military power, and sclerotic economy are contrasted with a United States. We are told that if the American Empire is set to dominate the next fifty years, it is the Chinese and Indians who will take over the baton and dominate the second half of the century."[6] From Beijing to Washington—and even in Brussels—the "Old Continent" is widely viewed as a spent geopolitical force in the contemporary world.

This pessimistic prognosis of European decline is misguided. Today there are two global superpowers. One is the United States; the other is Europe. Europe is the only other region in the world today, besides the United States, to exert global influence across the full spectrum from "hard" to "soft" power. Europe is the only other region, besides the United States, that projects intercontinental military power. European countries possess, singly and collectively, a range of effective civilian instruments for projecting international influence unmatched by any country, even the United States. These include EU enlargement, neighborhood policy, trade, foreign aid, support for multilateral institutions and international law, and European values. Since the end of the cold war, as the world system, particularly relations among the Great Powers, has become more interdependent, networked, democratic, and freer of overt ideological rivalry, Europe's distinctive instruments of influence have become relatively more effective, leading to a rise in its power. Over the next three or four generations trends in the foundations of European power—high per capita income, sophisticated economic production, favorable social and cultural trends, and patterns of global consensus—are similarly likely to be favorable. If we view power in this multidimensional way, Europe is clearly the "second superpower" in a *bipolar* world.

5. National Intelligence Council (2008, p. 32).
6. Leonard (2005, p. 2).

In support of this general thesis, this paper advances five specific arguments.[7] First, the view that Europe is in decline rests on an anachronistic realist view of international power and influence based on nineteenth-century measures such as aggregate GNP, population, and military manpower. Instead power should be treated as multidimensional, focusing on the full spectrum of issue-specific military, economic, and cultural capabilities that constitute "smart power." Second, even judged by classic standards Europe is the world's second military power, possessing the great majority of non-U.S., globally deployable troops. Its efforts in low-intensity situations are more effective than those of the United States. Third, Europe is in most respects a preeminent power, superior even to the United States in mobilizing "civilian" and "soft" power instruments of international influence, including trade, institutional membership, economic aid, diplomatic pressure, and spreading values. In an era of multidimensional "smart power," Europe is the one region consistently able to deliver across the board. Fourth, Europe's civilian and military power capabilities have greatly increased since the end of the cold war because of its underlying per capita wealth, a shift toward democracy, capitalism, and compatible values among many of its states, and its advantageous alliance portfolio. As long as these trends continue Europe's position is likely to strengthen. Fifth, it is unnecessary for Europe to unify or centralize far beyond its current structure to reap the benefits of its power. In many ways Europe is optimally suited to project power in the contemporary global system.

Realist and Liberal Theories of International Power

The conclusion that Europe is in terminal decline as a force in Great Power politics rests on a traditional realist worldview. From this theoretical perspective sovereign nations engage in zero-sum competition by mobilizing coercive power resources—resources stemming ultimately from gross demographic and economic power—into relative military advantage. This global hierarchy of gross economic and military economic power is fungible: it permits countries to achieve their goals across a wide range of issues. Realists believe that nations adapt rationally to this environment of political-military competition. They husband coercive power resources carefully, constantly seeking a higher position in the hierarchy via military spending, shrewd alliances, and exploitation of the weaknesses of others. They maintain balance, exploiting concentrations in their favor to extract concessions from others, and opposing external concentrations of power to avoid relinquishing concessions to others. External

7. The author thanks Mareike Kleine and, in particular, Marina Henke for research assistance.

threats generate cooperation; the lack of immediate threats generates discord and disorder. Governments do not compromise their sovereignty in the name of international law and institutions, or lower their guard for any length of time due to democracy, economic interdependence, or compatible values.

From this realist perspective Europe's global influence—its ability to get what it wants—will decline proportionately with its percentage of aggregate global power resources. Most realists see the global system as unipolar, with the United States as the sole superpower, though they differ about the precise consequences of this fact.[8] It is trending toward a system where the largest sovereign states—the United States, China, India—will dominate an increasingly multipolar system. Immediately upon the collapse of the Soviet Union nearly twenty years ago, realists such as John Mearsheimer, Kenneth Waltz, Stephen Walt, and Charles Kupchan predicted that the decline of the common Soviet threat would undermine transatlantic and European cooperation, sow discord among Western powers, weaken NATO, and undermine European cooperation.[9] The Iraq crisis, with its illusion of "soft balancing" against the United States, seemed to confirm this prognosis. For slightly different reasons, having to do with new ideological challenges coming from autocracies such as Russia and China, as well as Islamic radicals, neoconservatives have predicted disorder, believing, in Robert Kagan's words, that "the 21st century will look like the 19th."[10] Neoconservatives like Kagan share the realist view that greater capability to project military power is the key for Europe to be taken seriously in the contemporary world. If Europe is to reestablish itself as a major global force, or simply to hedge against a wayward United States, many believe serious European defense cooperation and a European defense buildup are required.[11] This view is held in Washington and Beijing and among moderate European analysts such as Charles Grant: "These days few governments elsewhere view the EU as a rising power. They regard it as slow-moving, badly organized and often divided. They are particularly scornful of its lack of military muscle."[12] Some take the realist balancing theory even further, predicting the emergence of a Euro-Chinese alliance against the United States: two "multipolar" powers opposing the potentially "unilateralist" United States.[13] All this follows from realist theory.

---

8. See Ikenberry, Mastanduno, and Wohlforth (2009).

9. For variations on the realist view that the United States and Europe would drift apart, see Mearsheimer (1990); Walt (1998); Waltz (2000); and Kupchan (2002).

10. See Kagan (2002); and Robert Kagan "The End of the End of History: Why the Twenty-first Century Will Look Like the Nineteenth," *The New Republic,* April 23, 2008.

11. See Witney (2008).

12. Charles Grant, "How to Make Europe's Military Work," *Financial Times,* August 17, 2009.

13. Shimbaugh (2004).

Few short-term predictions in social science are as clear as these, and few have been so unambiguously disconfirmed. Since 1989 Europe, the EU, and transatlantic relations have enjoyed two decades of extraordinary amity, cooperation, and policy success. The continent has been pacified. The EU has enjoyed an extraordinarily successful run: it completed the single market; established a single currency; created the "Schengen" zone without internal frontiers; launched common defense, foreign, and internal security policies; promulgated a constitutional treaty; and, most important, expanded from twelve to twenty-seven increasingly multicultural members, with a half dozen more on the list. It has emerged as the most ambitious and successful international organization of all time, pioneering institutional practices far in advance of anything viewed elsewhere. At the same time, despite the lack of any military build-up, Europe has established itself unambiguously as the world's "second" military power, with 50,000 to 100,000 combat troops active throughout the globe. Military operations are conducted almost exclusively in close cooperation with the United States. No Euro-Chinese alliance has emerged; instead the United States and Europe have drawn closer together. The EU's distinctive instruments of civilian influence have seemed to gain in utility vis-à-vis hard military power. Enlargement of the EU by twelve new members, for example, might well have been the single most cost-effective instrument to spread peace and security that the West has deployed for the past twenty years.

To understand why realist predictions were disconfirmed, one needs to turn away from realism to a liberal theory of international relations.[14] By "liberal" I do not mean a theory that stresses the role of international law and institutions, nor left-of-center or utopian ideals, nor unbounded belief in *laissez-faire* economics. What I mean instead is a theoretical approach to analyzing international relations that privileges the varied underlying national interests—"state preferences"—that states bring to world politics, and that are transmitted from society to decisionmakers via domestic politics, societal interdependence, and globalization. In the liberal view these varied social pressures are the fundamental cause of foreign policy behavior. From this perspective (zero-sum) security rivalry, military force, and power balancing are not ubiquitous conditions but only a few of a number of possible circumstances, though indeed rather rare: many international interactions in fact are positive sum, where the rise of more than one country or region can be complementary.[15] From the liberal perspective interstate power relations are issue-specific, multidimensional, and dependent on the social preferences of states in the international system.

14. See, for example, Baldwin (1979); and Keohane and Nye (1989).
15. See Moravcsik (1997).

Liberal theory has important implications for the assessment of global power. Because nations cannot be assumed to be in zero-sum conflict, it cannot be assumed that every issue will be conflictual. Nor can it be assumed, even when there is disagreement that governments will draw down all their international power resources, including costly basic military force, to prevail in each conflict. Coercive military power is not fungible; most disputes involve positive-sum interactions and are solved by a peaceful process based on reciprocity: the negotiated exchange of concessions. The relevant power resources for this purpose are issue-specific, including from military, economic, and cultural power. The ways in which governments use power, or whether power resources are relevant at all, depend on the underlying distribution of national interests.

Liberals argue that, although the realist view of power—whereby global influence is grounded in population and aggregate national income, which then feeds into mass military mobilization and gross military spending—might not be entirely irrelevant, it is no longer central to most issues in world politics, if indeed it ever was. Instead most global influence today rests on various forms of "civilian" power: high per capita income; a central position in networks of trade, investment, and migration; an important role in international institutions; and the attractiveness of social and political values—all areas in which Europe is and will remain preeminent (even compared to the United States) for the foreseeable future. Even in military affairs European countries today have far more global reach than any except the United States; indeed in most important nonmilitary respects Europe possesses far more power projection capability than does the United States.

From the liberal perspective the biggest change wrought by the end of the cold war has been the underlying trend it encouraged by spreading democracy, deepening economic interdependence, diffusing the notion that states must take responsibility for the welfare of their citizens, and ushering in a marked decline in the number of interstate wars. These trends have reduced the underlying level of conflict of interest among the Great Powers and enhanced the relative value of civilian modes of influence in which Europe enjoys a comparative advantage vis-à-vis traditional military means. Europe's recent successes, notably the spread of integration in its region and of multilateral norms worldwide, are evidence of this. These beneficial trends help explain why—in contrast to realist predictions—Europe and the EU have *gained* influence over the past two decades and are likely to continue to do so, and why the end of cold war has encouraged, on balance, more peaceful relations among the Great Powers. To the extent current trends continue, Europe is likely to remain a rising superpower for the foreseeable future, whether or not Europe becomes more united.

Why Europe Is the World's Second Military Power

Europe's comparative advantage lies in its projection of influence via economic and civilian instruments. Yet it is also important to focus on the sources of its military power, which is far more formidable than most observers acknowledge. Military force, in the modern world, is a luxury that only countries with high per capita income, technological sophistication, and a legacy of military spending can afford. Europe enjoys unique advantages in this area. Even so, many observers write off European military power entirely. Robert Kagan has argued that Europe "lost [its] strategic centrality after the Cold War ended [because] outside of Europe . . . the ability of European powers, individually or collectively, to project decisive force into regions of conflict beyond the continent (is) negligible."[16] Comparisons with the United States, which accounts for 43 percent of global military spending, widespread criticism (much of it justified) of inefficiencies in Europe's decentralized military establishment, and Europe's disinclination to fund or deploy military force on the scale the United States does, give European militaries a bad reputation. Conservative criticism, pithily summarized in Kagan's oft-cited *bon mot* "Americans are from Mars, Europeans are from Venus," is often believed even in Europe.[17]

Yet rhetoric is misleading. We too easily forget that Europe accounts for 21 percent of the world's military spending—compared with 5 percent for China, 3 percent for Russia, 2 percent for India, and 1.5 percent for Brazil. France and Britain together spend 60 percent more on defense than China:[18] their forces are among the best equipped in the world, and their long-range strategic nuclear arsenals are substantially larger than those of China or India.[19] The combined European air forces are substantially larger and considerably more modern than their Chinese counterpart.[20] Four European nations possess aircraft

16. Kagan (2002, p. 4). What is most striking about this celebrated analysis is that it never takes seriously the possibility that nonmilitary power could be of use in dealing with the extra-European world. Kagan is explicit that only military power is of utility in this "modernist" enterprise. Moreover, he implies that the task of dealing with the "postmodern" world is a "happy benefit," overlooking that the surrender of sovereignty and difficult political challenges of integration are something Americans would find more difficult to contemplate than military engagement.

17. Kagan (2002, p. 1); see generally, Kagan (2003).

18. Even corrected for purchasing power parity, these numbers would show a substantial advantage for Europe.

19. Many other European nations have the capacity to construct nuclear weapons but have chosen not to do so.

20. France possesses 279 fighter aircraft and 122 transport aircraft; Germany 304 fighter and attack aircraft and 104 transports; the United Kingdom 322 attack and strike aircraft and 63 transport aircraft, with hundreds more on order.

carriers, while China and India possess one between them. The production of the world's most advanced weapons is dominated by U.S. and European firms.

Europeans do not just equip forces; they use them. European countries have had between 50,000 and 100,000 troops stationed in combat roles outside their home countries for most of the past decade. They provide the bulk of non-U.S. troops in global operations around the world. Criticism of Europeans for their failure to do more in Iraq and Afghanistan might give the impression that only the United States is engaged there. In fact twenty-four allied countries, of which twenty-one are European, are involved in Afghanistan's Operation Enduring Freedom, and 40 percent of the 1,327 military fatalities by August 2009 were non-U.S., with nearly a third European; some allies have suffered a higher casualty rate than the United States. Europeans not only fight and die, they lead, as in Sierra Leone, Lebanon, and Chad. Since the United States generally has refused to lead UN peacekeeping operations, this task often falls to Europeans. Over the past two decades European-led diplomacy or intervention has helped stabilize governments in disparate places in Africa and Asia, sometimes involving brief, high-intensity military activity, as in Iraq.[21] Europe also possesses significant regional high-intensity warfare capability, although it has had trouble swiftly and effectively deploying such forces abroad. European-led peacekeeping operations, moreover, are more efficiently and effectively run than U.S. operations.[22] No region or country save the United States possesses a portfolio of military capabilities and a willingness to use them comparable to those of Europe—nor is any likely to challenge European preeminence soon.

Why Europe Is the World's Preeminent Civilian Superpower

Although Europe possesses considerable hard military power, its unique geopolitical comparative advantage lies in deploying civilian instruments of international power. In contrast to the United States, Europe is a "quiet" superpower specializing in civilian power instruments based on economic influence, international law, and "smart" and "soft power."[23] Europe today is more effective at

21. Over the past two decades U.S.-led operations have taken place in: Panama (1989), Iraq (1991), Somalia (1992), Haiti (1994), Macedonia (1993-4), Bosnia (1995-6), Iraq (1998), Kosovo (1999), Afghanistan (2001), Iraq (2003). European-led operations have taken place in: Mozambique (1993), Rwanda (1994), Bosnia (1994), Albania (1997), Kosovo (1999), Sierra Leone (2000), Macedonia (2001), Ivory Coast (2002–04), Afghanistan (2001–present), Congo (2003), Chad (2005–present), Sudan (2005), Aceh (2005–06), Lebanon (2006), Georgia (2008–present), Somalia (2009–present).

22. Dobbins and others (2008).

23. See Cooper (2003); Kagan (2003); Nye (2004; 2008, p. 94).

projecting civilian power globally than any other state or nonstate actor. Europeans have demonstrated, contra realist claims, that such instruments of power can be extremely influential. Some are wielded by a unified Europe, some by European governments acting in loose coordination, some by European governments acting unilaterally.

EU Enlargement

Accession to the EU is the single most powerful policy instrument Europe possesses. Since 1989 Europe's "power of attraction" has helped to stabilize the polities and economies of over a dozen neighboring countries.[24] There is substantial evidence that enlargement creates a focal point and set of incentives around which moderate domestic forces organize.[25] The effects are visible well beyond the twelve members that have joined most recently. European diplomatic intervention clearly helped to avert recent war between Serbia and Montenegro. Sustained policy over generations of engaging Turkey has encouraged political transformation. EU enlargement has almost certainly had far more impact—and in a less provocative way—than NATO enlargement. European leaders continue to pursue EU enlargement courageously in the face of low—in some countries single-digit or low double-digit— public opinion support. The United States, China, India, Japan, and other major powers enjoy no comparable instruments for projecting regional influence.

Neighborhood Policy and Diplomatic Engagement

Europe pursues an active "neighborhood policy," intervening diplomatically to resolve conflicts and promote political and economic reform, or policy reversals, on the continent, backed by European economic, financial, legal, and military might. The EU has signed association and free trade arrangements with many countries in the region. European diplomats have taken successful diplomatic initiatives, not just with respect to countries that are candidates for membership, including Macedonia, Montenegro, Serbia, Croatia, and Turkey, but even those for which EU membership is only a distant possibility, as with Ukraine, Moldova, and Albania, or essentially nonexistent, as with Libya and Israel. In Morocco, quiet EU diplomacy, backed by trade, immigration, security, and human rights ties, has been credited with encouraging political and economic reform.

European diplomatic engagement extends beyond the scope of formal EU neighborhood policy. Compared to typical U.S. policies—one thinks of efforts

24. See Cooper (2003).
25. Vachudová (2005).

to extend NATO membership to Georgia or to democratize Iraq, both viewed
with some skepticism by European governments—Europe's policies are slower,
more incremental, more proactive than reactive. It might be argued that they
are also more realistic. Another example is the coordinated effort by individual European countries, notably the United Kingdom, France, and Germany,
with respect to Libya, whose policy toward the West has reversed over the past
15 years—a shift that predates 9/11 and any policy reversal on the part of the
United States. For most of the George W. Bush administration, the same European trio provided the only Western diplomatic link to the government in Tehe-
ran. Europeans have spearheaded various initiatives with regard to the Israeli-
Palestinian conflict, and European governments were recently active in helping
to resolve the Georgian crisis.

Multilateralism, International Law, and Functional Issues

European governments are the strongest and most consistent supporters of
international law and institutions. The EU is the single largest financial contributor to the UN system, funding 38 percent of its regular budget, more than
two-fifths of UN peacekeeping operations, and about one-half of all UN member states' contributions to UN funds and programs.[26] EU members are also
signatories of almost all international treaties currently in force.[27]

European countries are not only the primary funders and supporters of most
international organizations, in many they are also overrepresented in terms of
population. Those who favor institutional reform of highly symbolic elite international leadership bodies such as the UN Security Council and the G-x groups,
presumably with the aim of integrating and socializing some larger developing countries into responsible statecraft, are critical of European obstruction.
Yet Europeans did not block the evolution of the G-8 into the G-20, and have
favored integration of developing countries such as China into functional organizations such as the World Trade Organization (WTO). Many believe that, had
the United States acted accordingly in recent years, a deal would have been possible on Security Council reform as well.

Trade, Investment, and Finance

In trade and investment affairs Europe is unquestionably a genuine global economic superpower, larger than the United States and far ahead of countries such
as China or India. In some respects it is institutionally better able to exploit its

---

26. European Commission, "External Cooperation Programmes: International Organisa-
tions" (ec.europa.eu/europeaid/who/partners/international-organisations/index_en.htm).
27. See Laïdi (2008).

economic position. The motive force behind EU enlargement or neighborhood policy is not primarily an idealistic desire to be part of "Europe" but to take advantage of the enormous economic benefits of membership in (or association with) the EU. With the exception of Greece, member states that have joined since Spain and Portugal have grown between 6 and 10 percent in the first years after their accession. Europe dominates its neighborhood, trading more with Middle Eastern countries (except Jordan), and nearly all African countries than any other single trading partner.

Europe's continuing economic influence extends to the global level. Even excluding intraregional trade, the EU is the largest exporter and importer in the world. Of the top nine exporters in the world, five—Germany, France, Italy, the United Kingdom, and the Netherlands—are European.[28] Germany alone exports roughly as much every year as China and its goods have far more value added. Europe trades more with China than does the United States and its bilateral balance is stronger.[29] Yet trade statistics actually understate the importance of European centrality in the world economy.

Measured by intrafirm trade, investment, and research and development (R&D)—increasingly the drivers of modern international economic activity—Europe remains an order of magnitude more important than China or India. Trade statistics are often cited in the United States to illustrate a shift from Atlantic to Pacific economic activity, but if one looks not to trade but to investment, U.S. affiliate sales, foreign assets, and R&D, transatlantic economic exchange remains far more robust than transpacific exchange.[30] From 2000 to 2008, more than 57 percent of total U.S. foreign direct investment occurred in Europe, compared with 14 percent in *all* the BRICs—over the same period U.S. firms invested more than twice as much in Ireland as in China. In 2007 corporate Europe accounted for 71 percent of total foreign direct investment in the United States ($2.1 trillion), while in 2006 U.S. assets in the United Kingdom alone totaled $2.8 trillion, roughly a quarter of the global total and more than total U.S. assets in Asia, South America, Africa, and the Middle East combined. For U.S. companies Europe is far and away the most important global R&D destination accounting for nearly 65 percent of total R&D expenditures in 2006.

---

28. U.S. Central Intelligence Agency, "The World Factbook—Country Comparison: Exports" (www.cia.gov/library/publications/the-world-factbook/rankorder/2078rank.html).

29. In 2008 EU exports to China amounted to €78.4 billion and its imports to €247.6, while U.S. imports from China were worth US$69.7 billion and its exports US$337.8; see European Commission, "Trade: Countries" (ec.europa.eu/trade/issues/bilateral/countries/china/index_en.htm); and U.S. Bureau of the Census, "International Trade Statistics" (www.census.gov/foreign-trade/balance/c5700.html#2008.

30. Hamilton and Quinlan (2009).

U.S. companies deliver goods and services to various markets in Europe mainly via affiliate sales rather than exports—U.S. foreign affiliate sales in Europe totaled $2.1 trillion in 2006, *nine times* the value of U.S. exports to Europe and roughly double comparable sales in the Asia-Pacific region. U.S. affiliate sales in Belgium alone were on a par with those in China. Measured in these terms, Europe, not Asia, remains the global partner of choice for the United States.

The EU's common currency, the euro, is the only serious contemporary alternative to the dollar as a global reserve currency. Although the euro will not supplant the dollar any time soon, due primarily to the dollar's first-mover advantages and the greater depth of U.S. capital markets, it has established an important secondary position.[31] At the end of 2008 some 45 percent of international debt securities were denominated in dollars and 32 percent in euros, the dollar was used in 86 percent of foreign-exchange transactions and the euro in 38 percent, and 66 countries used the dollar as their exchange-rate anchor while 27 used the euro. The EU and the European Central Bank also play key roles in financial stabilization efforts outside the euro zone,[32] while the recent economic crisis might even have strengthened the euro's prospects as an international currency by emphasizing that the euro area can be a safe harbor in a financial storm.

Europe's unique economic position translates into political influence. European policy on tariffs and other basic trade issues is unified, due to the EU's status as a customs union, and the EU negotiates as a bloc at the WTO.[33] While it is true that developing countries are playing a stronger role and the trading world is slowly growing more multipolar, the EU and the United States remain dominant within the WTO. China, by contrast, has resigned itself to entering the trading system on Western terms.[34] For better or worse Europe's Common Agricultural Policy is probably the most influential single trade policy in the world today—and Europeans have been tenaciously successful in defending it. Trade also serves as a foundation for effective EU enlargement and neighborhood policies.

Aid

EU member states and the European Commission together dispense about 50 percent of the world's foreign aid, while the U.S. share amounts to about 20

31. See Eichengreen (2009).

32. Andrew Moravcsik, "Europe Defies the Skeptics: How Crisis Will Make the EU Stronger," *Newsweek,* August 1, 2009.

33. For a precise description of the circumstances under which this translates into effective political influence, see Meunier (2005).

34. See, for example, Eglin (1997).

percent. Contrary to popular belief, the EU even exceeds the United States in the disbursement of private aid flows, sending more than $170 million abroad in 2007 compared with $105 million from private U.S. sources.[35] Over the past five years, the EU and the United States have contributed a similar portion (about one-third) of all foreign aid delivered to Afghanistan, while most aid to Palestinians comes from Europe—indeed it is understood that no Middle East settlement would be viable without European aid to areas to which the United States is politically unwilling to provide resources.

Political and Social Values

The United States remains a salient symbol of democracy and capitalism in countries that have neither and in a handful of other countries such as India, Poland, and the Philippines, but both polling and practice suggest that European social and political models are more attractive than U.S. alternatives. Apparently publics around the world favor generous social welfare and health policies, parliamentary government, adherence to international human rights standards, and a smaller role for money in politics, all associated with Europe, rather than libertarian social policies and incomplete health coverage, the separation of powers, idiosyncratic national human rights definitions without international oversight, and a large role for money in politics, all of which are associated with the United States.[36] Few countries in the "third wave" of democracies have copied major elements of the U.S. Constitution, tending instead to model their work on the German, South African, or Canadian constitutions. An exception to this rule proves it. One distinctively U.S. practice has spread throughout the world since the end of World War II—namely, constitutional "judicial review" in accordance with a written bill of rights. Yet ironically the United States is now the leading developed-country opponent of the nearly universal form this institution has taken in the modern world: the incorporation of international standards of human rights and humanitarian law into national constitutions,[37] placing it alongside countries such as China, Somalia,

---

35. OECD, "Query Wizard for International Development Statistics" (stats.oecd.org/qwids/#?x=1&y=6&f=4:0,2:0,3:0,5:0,7:0&q=1:2+2:1+4:1+5:3+3:51+6:2003,2004,2005,2006,2007,2008+7:1). EU data do not include Bulgaria, Cyprus, Estonia, Latvia, Lithuania, Malta, Romania, or Slovenia. Widely cited studies argue that U.S. private aid makes the "United States the most generous country in the world" (see, for example, Adelman 2003). These studies are misleading, however, because they include private giving and remittances from foreign nationals residing in the United States but not such flows from foreign nationals residing in Europe. Moreover, it is questionable whether such giving constitutes a good example of U.S. generosity in the first place. If one equalizes giving at either level—public or private—European foreign aid is more generous.

36. See Andrew Moravcsik, "Washington Cries Wolf," *Newsweek,* March 31, 2008.

37. Moravcsik (2003).

Russia, and Saudi Arabia in debates over global legal values. In projecting most of these forms of civilian power, Europe enjoys a clear comparative advantage not just over China, India, and other middle powers, but also over the United States. Together with its military activities, it renders Europe a full-spectrum power, the world's "second superpower," wielding a wide range of instruments for regional and global influence.

Why Europe's Global Influence Is Rising

Of course Europe's military and civilian power derives ultimately from its highly developed economy, the byproducts of which are the informational, educational, and legal sophistication of European policies that are so attractive to others. Europe's economy also provides the funds to pay for aid, education, trade, the European social model, and other aspects of Europe's foreign policy portfolio. There are fears, however, that Europe is in decline, and that its sluggish demographic and economic growth rates might undermine its role in the world. This sort of conventional pessimism about Europe's future is misguided, for three main reasons.

First, *demographic and economic estimates of Europe's decline are greatly exaggerated.* Rising China, to which Europe is often compared, though it looks large on the map, is in most respects—military, economic, diplomatic—no more than a modest regional middle power, its geopolitical power resources those of a single larger European country. Its exports are roughly those of Germany *alone*, its strategic forces roughly those of France *alone*, its position in international organizations roughly that of the United Kingdom *alone*. Yet these nations are part of a bloc of twenty-seven countries that, explicitly coordinated or not, generally take similar positions. Europe's share of global economic activity is also quite stable over time. Even evaluated by the traditional measures of aggregate population and GDP, Europe's relative slice is declining only very slowly—even the most dire prognoses see its share declining only from 22 percent to 17 percent of global GDP over the next generation.[38] Moreover such scenarios rest on current BRIC and Asian growth rates continuing at a historically unprecedented 10 percent a year for the next thirty years—particularly unlikely given the demographic, environmental, and political hurdles these countries will face[39]—and even then per capita income in a country such as China would still be only a fraction of that in Europe or the United States, and it is per capita income that matters most.

38. Brown (2005, p. 4).
39. See Pei (2009)

Indeed the second reason the conventional view of European decline is misleading is that *aggregate population and GNP are the wrong measures of power.* The linear relationship between gross population and GDP aggregates and global power is an analytical anachronism of the nineteenth and twentieth centuries. Liberal theory, however, is highly suspicious of any such simple relationship, in part because the extent of underlying conflicts of interest among states is a variable rather than a constant: rivalries can occur, but zero-sum situations assumed by realism are relatively rare. To be sure, for much of human history, the simpler *Realpolitik* proposition might have held—though there is some reason to doubt even this. When most governments had few social welfare demands, could reliably control colonial territory, and planned for wartime mass mobilization, as during World Wars I and II or the cold war, population and aggregate GDP were perhaps plausible determinates of Great Power geopolitical influence. Yet this sort of simple calculation is increasingly passé. Governments today are unlikely to draw down their entire stock of potential resources for use in foreign policy, let alone coercive military activity. Rather the primary imperative for most governments—not least those in Beijing, New Delhi, Sao Paolo, and other major emerging country capitals—is to maintain legitimacy by providing adequate economic growth, social mobility, and public services. Interstate war of any kind, let alone total war decided by total commitment of population and thus aggregate GNP or demographics, has become exceedingly rare among Great Powers. Governments are thus severely constrained in how much wealth they can extract from the economy for military purposes. Nor, in contrast to times past, when armies were labor intensive, can a large population or a big aggregate GDP spread across a poor population be translated easily into military might or economic influence. Governments now need to assure internal stability and openness to prosper. Indeed, for poor countries, this dynamic can reverse the relationship between population and power: a large population can be as much a burden as a benefit.

Consider the case of China. One often reads alarming statistics about the sheer size of the Chinese population, economy, or military. In fact China would be far more capable internationally if not for the imperative of caring for 700 million poor in the hinterland—whose welfare is the paramount political issue for any Chinese leader.[40] Leaders of China (and India) face the additional headache of opposition from unruly national minorities across their vast multicultural spaces. The need to devote resources to internal priorities thus imposes a fundamental constraint on China's military spending and foreign policy

---

40. Shirk (2007).

adventurism—in contrast to cold war Soviet military spending rates of 15 to 20 percent of GDP, Beijing spends between 1 and 3 percent.

This is not to deny that Europe could face resource allocation difficulties in the future or that the relative sizes of the United States, China, and Europe count for something, but crude demographic and economic size is less important than high per capita income—and in this area the long-term structural trends still greatly favor Europe.[41] Per capita income not only measures the existence of a surplus that can be used to fund international power projection, but also indicates (in nonresource-based economies) a society's ability to use instruments of civilian power. Effective forms of global influence—not just advanced military technology, but also sophisticated legal mechanisms of cooperation, education, foreign aid, complex trade and investment arrangements, advanced political institutions, a favorable division of labor, diplomatic engagement, and inward immigration—all presuppose high per capita income. By these measures Europe's influence in areas such as trade, aid, education, international law, peacekeeping, and political values is considerable, and the long-term endurance of Europe's advantage in per capita income means that its economic and military advantages will not be eclipsed any time soon. High per capita income also generates cultural influence. Consider, for example, China's so-called charm offensive, aimed at the projection of Chinese civilian power in Asia.[42] Certainly Chinese economic influence is growing in East Asia and with it the number of people speaking Chinese, studying in China, and perhaps even appreciating things Chinese. But Chinese culture does not have the preponderant weight that Japanese or Korean culture enjoys in the region, let alone the extraordinary impact of EU legal norms or the English language or U.S. popular culture.[43]

The third and most important reason the conventional view of European decline is misleading is that *the underlying material and ideological conflict between Europe and other Great Powers is decreasing.* Governments increasingly interact on the basis of reciprocity—the peaceful negotiated exchange of concessions—unrelated to traditional material coercive capabilities of any

41. This is a historical generalization. The population and economy of the British Empire, or even of single portions of it such as India, were far larger than that of Britain itself, but what mattered was the disparity in per capita GDP, technology, administration, knowledge, finance, and allies.

42. See Kurlanznick (2008).

43. The cultural and linguistic influence of China in countries such as Vietnam, Cambodia, and Indonesia is greatly overstated. Most trade is done in a third language, usually English. In Vietnam, for example, the second most popular foreign language (after English) is not Chinese but Korean—due to the economic opportunities it offers; author's interview with Vietnamese official, February 2008.

kind. Europe is well placed to take advantage of this shift. The cold war is over. Fundamental ideological alternatives to regulated capitalism are disappearing. Democracy is spreading. Nationalist conflicts are disappearing, particularly in the immediate proximity of Europe. Europe is reaping advantages from all these trends, and the value of its portfolio of civilian power instruments is multiplying. This result is consistent with liberal international relations theory. Liberal theory treats the level of convergence and conflict of underlying social interests between nations as a variable that shapes both the likelihood of conflict and, via asymmetrical interdependence, relative power. Rivalries can arise, but the zero-sum situations assumed by realists to be ubiquitous—and expected to drive transatlantic and intra-European conflict—are in fact relatively rare. Specifically, such a post–cold war trend creates enormous global advantages for Europe: its enemies are disappearing. In contrast to realists' predictions Europe has been *rising* in regional and global influence over the past twenty years and is likely to continue to do so, not only because its civilian instruments of power projection have become more appropriate, but also because the extent to which any nation can project influence depends on how much its interests converge with those of other, particularly neighboring, Great Powers—the greater the level of consensus, the more slack resources a state will have.[44] Where underlying preferences converge due to the trends in trade, democracy, and ideological convergence that have been observed over the past two decades, widespread opportunities are created for cooperation with interdependent, democratic, modern states, such as those of Europe.

Looking to the future, three specific types of converging international interests are likely to be particularly advantageous for Europe, augmenting its relative global influence. First, the spread of democracy, trade, nationally satisfied states, and regional integration—in large part due to explicit Western and EU policies—has almost entirely pacified the European continent. This shift in state preferences means that European countries face ever-fewer regional security threats. Now that the Balkans have died down, the nearest threats are now in the Caucasus, the Middle East, or perhaps across the Mediterranean. This permits European governments to focus their efforts "out of area." By contrast, Asian powers face a far more hostile immediate environment, and even if they were to increase their military capability, they are less likely to be able to project it globally.

Second, Europe has seen a felicitous shift in the preferences of major governments around the world for European societal norms. Most European policy goals involve efforts to encourage long-term reform of countries toward

44. See Moravcsik (1997).

democracy, economic development, and cooperative international relations. Most Great Powers—notably, for all their problems, China and Russia—have made enormous strides in this direction since the end of the cold war. This trend reduces the useful range of (U.S.) high-intensity military capabilities while increasing the utility and efficacy of European civilian power instruments better suited to this environment. This is why policies such as European enlargement, neighborhood policy, a common trade policy, and support for multilateral organizations have been so cost effective. As more of the world becomes market oriented, democratic, and free of expansionist ideological claims, European countries' policies are well positioned to advance their regional and global interests as they find themselves closer to the consensus point of global bargains.[45]

Third, Europe's relationship with the United States, whatever tensions there may be, is less conflictual than at any time in recent memory. In general European and U.S. interests tend—in striking contrast to realist predictions—to be even more closely aligned than during the cold war. A world in which the United States and Europe can think of nothing more to argue about than international human rights law, fingerprint scanning at airports, subsidization of civilian aircraft, banking regulation, global warming, and, as ever, the subsidization of agricultural products—important though these topics may be on their own terms—is a geopolitical luxury of which cold war leaders could only dream. This is particularly true where realists and neoconservatives alike have predicted the least agreement—namely, military intervention "out of area." Far from becoming a source of transatlantic conflict, military intervention today is in fact a matter of near-total European-U.S. consensus. A broader range of European countries is fighting with the United States in peripheral conflicts than was ever the case during the cold war. Even more striking is the high level of current transatlantic consensus about the proper purposes of such intervention. Since the end of the cold war there have been more than a dozen major military interventions by Western powers, and fundamental disagreement has arisen in *only one case*: Iraq from 1998 to 2003. (I set aside tactical disagreements over the timing and mode of Balkans interventions, which, in any case, eventually were resolved.) An entire generation of debate—including over the consequences of unipolarity— has ignored the norm of transatlantic consensus and been sidetracked by the single exceptional case of Iraq. Europeans did not

---

45. Some view this as a "normative power" argument—indeed some have a ideational preference for Europe-like solutions; I claim here simply that the self-interest of an increasing number of countries is slowly converging with that of Europeans.

oppose the war in Iraq because it was unilateral; it was unilateral because they opposed it.[46]

Post–cold war transatlantic consensus on the use of force contrasts strikingly with relations during the last twenty-five years of the cold war, when the United States and Europe disagreed on *almost every major military unilateral intervention* after Korea.[47] Europeans often voted against their U.S. allies in the UN and even funded enemies of the United States—in Latin America, for example. Recent squabbles over Yugoslavia, Kosovo, or even Iraq pale in comparison to the sustained cold war battles over Suez, Algeria, Détente, Ostpolitik, Vietnam, Cuba, the construction of NATO and French withdrawal from it, Euromissiles, Eurocommunism, the bombing of Libya, Reagan's policies in Latin America and Africa, and many more. Post–cold war consensus on the use of force in fact flatly contradicts the explicit prediction of realist theory and provides the clearest possible confirmation of the liberal prediction of the importance of preferences.

Liberal theory's emphasis on the convergence of preferences as a precondition for cooperation, rather than the realist focus on power balancing, leads me to conclude that U.S.-EU cooperation is likely to persist. China scholar David Shambaugh, among others, argues that some sort of geopolitical realignment to offset U.S. "unipolarity" is likely to arise among states committed to a "multipolar" world order, leading to a "Europe-China axis."[48] No such trend has emerged. In fact when one considers such an alliance not in terms of an abstract notion like "multipolarity" but of concrete issues in need of management—trade, the appreciation and convertibility of Chinese currency, human rights, intellectual property, Tibet, North Korea, Burma, Darfur, the Olympics, Taiwan—one finds that Europe and the United States are closer to each other than either is to China. An axis against Europe's concrete interests in the service of a geopolitical abstraction has little appeal.

These trends explain why Europe has played an increasingly important global role over the past two decades, and why it is likely to do so for generations to come. They also explain why the particular instruments of global influence that Europe possesses—those of a civilian power *par excellence*—are likely to become more useful over time. In all these senses Europe is a rising power.

---

46. As Brooks and Wohlforth (2005) rightly argue, European policy in the case of Iraq cannot be interpreted as "soft balancing"—and this case itself is an anomaly. Indeed U.S. deployments are becoming more multilateral over time; see Kreps (2008–09).

47. The only consistent exceptions were the Western interventions in Lebanon.

48. Shambaugh (2004).

Why the EU's Decentralized Institutions Sometimes Might Be Optimal

Europe, it is often argued, must unify to remain a superpower. Proposals to achieve this include an expansion of majority voting, a centralized spokesperson, mandatory common policies, a common European military force, a European defense industrial policy and so on. Centralization is often taken to be the measure of effectiveness. If centralizing reforms fail, European defense and foreign policy fail as well.[49] Many important aspects of policy—trade, enlargement, regulation, UN policy, and much more— have already been centralized, but many others, particularly those "political-military" in nature, remain essentially decentralized. Is Europe destined to remain, as Henry Kissinger once said of Germany, an "economic giant and a political dwarf"?

The answer, I believe, is that it might not. Europe often functions more effectively when its governments work as a decentralized network than when they are more centralized.[50] Centralized institutions can generate international coordination and credibility through precommitment, but at the cost of flexibility and national sovereignty. If governments "undercommit" in advance, they might lack the means or legitimacy to act in a crisis; if they "overcommit," they might end up deadlocked or, even worse, might block decentralized action by individual states in a crisis. European governments have thus struck a prudent trade-off: the precise level of commitment shifts over time and across issues, depending on the potential collective gains and the possible risks from being overruled.

To illustrate the shifting considerations, compare cold war and post–cold war security institutions in Europe. During the cold war, European security policy was dominated by the task—which required a credible common position—of establishing a collective, visible institutional and ideological defense of potential Soviet intimidation or attack. It included a tight system of coordinated planning, tripwire defense, and coherent declaratory policy designed to enhance the credibility of commitment.[51] Considerable pressure was placed on any government that strayed from common NATO policy. If even a single NATO member did not support the alliance, the result could be disastrous for all.

---

49. See Andréani, Bertram, and Grant (2001); and Grant (2009).

50. See Slaughter (2004).

51. The NATO alliance against the Soviet Union can be modeled as something akin to an n-country prisoner's dilemma game in which individual governments have an incentive to defect by not contributing their full military effort to collective defense or by resisting controversial steps toward that defense, such as missile deployment. See, for instance, Sandler and Hartley (1999, pp. 225–26).

Post–cold war security challenges, by contrast, do not generally involve direct and immediate security threats to Europe, beyond homeland security concerns. The challenge rather is to encourage a subset of countries—a "coalition of the willing"—to deploy modest force against a smaller enemy in pursuit of a secondary security concern.[52] It is unrealistic to expect the EU or any international organization to precommit itself to act in such circumstances. Needless to say European governments are unlikely to relinquish sovereignty to form a common European army—they did not do so during the cold war, when the threat was more serious than it is today. Indeed such centralization might render policymaking even less effective by reducing flexibility without a corresponding increase in desired outcomes; governments would simply block effective collective action and preempt individual action. Given the smaller scale and less imperative nature of these operations, it is often unnecessary, and even counterproductive, for all nations to be involved in any given action. Europe's more decentralized, "coalition-of-the-willing" form thus might be more effective because it is more flexible.

Indeed flexible, rather than centralized, institutions might be not just adequate but advantageous. In the post–cold war era, the primary task of international organizations has not been so much to establish a credible commitment as to provide flexible coordination and legitimation to back such efforts. When governments prefer to act in their own name, they do so. When a "coalition of the willing" seeks to act, using an international institution as cover, it does so. When different international institutions offer different opportunities for domestic legitimation, the presence of multiple, redundant decisionmaking procedures can be advantageous. In such circumstances flexibility and ambiguity can be virtues. Consider the EU's recognition of Kosovo—a decision on which a number of members, including Spain, Cyprus, Romania, and Greece, were hesitant to act, fearing it would set a separatist precedent in their domestic politics. A compromise was reached whereby the EU recognized Kosovo and aid began to flow, but individual members were permitted to decide whether to accord bilateral recognition. Though widely criticized in the press as a "waffle," the compromise in fact marked a pragmatic turning point in Kosovo policy.[53] At the very least the European actions demonstrate that, under conditions of incomplete consensus, decentralized institutions are relatively effective and well suited to the challenges facing Europe.

52. Viewed ex ante, this is a problem more akin to a classic case of "collective security," where the objective is uncertain in advance and likely to be of relatively little concern to most members of the organization.

53. See, for example, Tansey and Zaum (2009).

Conclusion

The world of today and of the foreseeable future is bipolar. Only the two global superpowers, the United States and Europe, are consistently able to project the full spectrum of "smart" power internationally. In some respects, particularly the projection of high-intensity military force, the United States possesses instruments superior to those of European countries. Yet European countries possess an unmatched range and depth of civilian instruments for international influence. Moreover the post–cold war world is becoming more hospitable to the exercise of distinctively European forms of power, increasing Europe's influence accordingly. There is every reason to believe this trend will continue.

This is not to deny, however, that a number of other Great Powers—the United States, China, and India among them—are also on the rise. This might seem contradictory: how can most Great Powers be "rising" at once? Yet this is a puzzle only for realists, who assume that the aims of governments conflict in a zero-sum fashion. From a liberal perspective, the notion that more than one country gains influence at the same time is quite natural, as long as the environment is essentially positive sum and different Great Powers' aims are compatible. Since the end of the cold war such an environment has generally existed among the Great Powers—as even the George W. Bush administration came to see. This situation opens up a possibility for most Great Powers in the world system to increase their influence over global outcomes all at once—because their preferences converge more fully than they did previously, and because deepening interdependence generates greater potential for common problem solving. Yet even nonrealists can fall into anachronistic zero-sum habits of mind and assume that the rise of Chinese economic power must imply the decline of the United States or that the rise of U.S. military prowess must mean the decline of Europe.

Among the places where awareness of Europe's superpower status, and its unique civilian power assets, seems to have penetrated least is official Washington. Inside the Beltway, Europe is widely viewed as a declining region, barely able to take care of its own geopolitical interests and increasingly irrelevant unless it centralizes its policy. It is ironic that this should be so at a time when U.S. high officials have unanimously embraced the need for more "smart power"— the U.S. phrase for matching military with civilian forms of influence—yet the U.S. political system seems consistently unable or unwilling to generate the resources for such an effort. Rather than discussing the obvious possibilities for complementarity, the transatlantic debate remains mired, as it was ten, twenty, forty years ago, in discussions of military burden sharing. Today it takes the form of questions about who is providing troops to Afghanistan for a counterinsurgency mission that U.S. and European analysts agree will fail without a massive civilian surge. This is a failure to learn lessons not simply from current history but also from international relations theory.

References

Adelman, Carole. 2003. "The Privatization of Foreign Aid: Reassessing National Largesse." *Foreign Affairs* 82, no. 6: 9–14.

Baldwin, David A. 1979. "Power Analysis and World Politics: New Trends versus Old Tendencies," *World Politics* 31, no. 2: 161–94.

Andréani, Gilles, Christoph Bertram, and Charles Grant. 2001. *Europe's Military Revolution*. London: Centre for European Reform.

Brooks, Stephen G., and William C. Wohlforth. 2005. "Hard Times for Soft Balancing." *International Security* 30, no. 1: 72–108.

Brown, Gordon. 2005. *Global Europe: Full-employment Europe.* London: HM Treasury.

Cooper, Robert. 2003. *The Breaking of Nations: Order and Chaos in the Twenty-first Century.* London: Atlantic Books.

Dobbins, James, and others. 2008. *Europe's Role in Nation-Building: From the Balkans to the Congo.* Santa Monica, Calif.: RAND Corporation.

Eglin, Michaela. 1997. "China's Entry into the WTO with a Little Help from the EU." *International Affairs* 73, no. 3: 489–508.

Eichengreen, Barry. 2009. "The Dollar Dilemma: The World's Top Currency Faces Competition." *Foreign Affairs* 88, no. 5: 53–68.

Grant, Charles. 2009. "Is Europe Doomed to Fail as a Power?" London: Centre for European Reform.

Hamilton, Daniel, and Joseph Quinlan. 2009. The Transatlantic Economy 2009: Annual Survey of Jobs, Trade, and Investment between the United States and Europe. Washington: Johns Hopkins School of Advanced International Studies, Center for Transatlantic Relations.

Ikenberry, G. John, Michael Mastanduno, and William Wohlforth. 2009. "Unipolarity, State Behavior, and Systemic Consequences." *World Politics* 61, no. 1: 1–27.

Kagan, Robert. 2002. "Power and Weakness." *Policy Review* 113, nos. 3-4: 3–28.

———. 2003. *Of Paradise and Power: America and Europe in the New World Order.* New York: Alfred A. Knopf.

Keohane, Robert O., and Joseph S. Nye, Jr. 1989. *Power and Interdependence: World Politics in Transition*, 3rd ed. Boston: Little, Brown.

Kreps, Sarah E. 2008–09. "Multilateral Military Interventions: Theory and Practice." *Political Science Quarterly* 123, no. 4: 573–604.

Kupchan, Charles. 2002. *The End of the American Era: U.S. Foreign Policy and the Geopolitics of the Twenty-first Century.* New York: Alfred A. Knopf

Kurlanznick. Joshua. 2008. *Charm Offensive: How China's Soft Power Is Transforming the World.* Yale University Press.

Laïdi, Zaki. 2008. *Norms over Force: The Enigma of European Power.* New York: Palgrave Macmillan.

Leonard, Mark. 2005. *Why Europe Will Run the 21st Century.* London: Fourth Estate.

Mearsheimer, John. 1990. "Back to the Future: Instability in Europe after the Cold War." *International Security* 15, no. 1: 5–56.

Meunier, Sophie. 2005. *Trading Voices: The European Union in International Commercial Negotiations.* Princeton University Press.

Moravcsik, Andrew. 1997. "Taking Preferences Seriously: A Liberal Theory of International Politics." *International Organization* 51, no. 4: 513–53.

———. 2003. "The Paradox of American Human Rights Policy." In *American Exceptionalism and Human Rights,* edited by Michael Ignatieff. Princeton University Press.

National Intelligence Council. 2008. *Global Trends 2025: A Transformed World.* Washington: U.S. Government Printing Office.

Nye, Joseph S. 2004. *Soft Power: The Means to Success in World Politics.* New York: Public Affairs.

———. 2008. "Public Diplomacy and Soft Power." *Annals of the American Academy of Political and Social Science* 616, no. 1: 94–109.

Pei Meixin. 2009. "Think Again: Asia's Rise." *Foreign Policy* (July-August): 33–36.

Reid, T. R. 2004. *The United States of Europe: The New Superpower and the End of American Supremacy.* New York: Penguin Press.

Rifkin, Jeremy. 2004. *The European Dream: How Europe's Vision of the Future Is Quietly Eclipsing the American Dream.* New York: Jeremy P. Tarcher/Penguin.

Sandler, Todd, and Keith Hartley. 1999. *The Political Economy of NATO: Past, Present, and into the 21st Century.* Cambridge University Press.

Shambaugh, David. 2004. "China and Europe: The Emerging Axis." *Current History* 103 (684): 243–48.

Shirk, Susan L. 2007. *China: Fragile Superpower.* Oxford University Press.

Slaughter, Anne-Marie. 2004. *A New World Order.* Princeton University Press.

Tansey, Oisín, and Dominik Zaum. 2009. "Muddling Through in Kosovo." *Survival* 51, no. 1: 13–20.

Vachudová, Milada Anna. 2005. *Europe Undivided: Democracy, Leverage, and Integration after Communism.* Oxford University Press

Walt, Stephen M. 1998. "The Ties that Fray: Why Europe and America Are Drifting Apart." *The National Interest* 54 (Winter): 3–11.

Waltz, Kenneth. 2000. "Structural Realism after the Cold War." *International Security* 25, no. 1: 5–41.

Witney, Nick. 2008. *Re-energising Europe's Security and Defence Policy.* London: European Council on Foreign Relations

Zakaria, Fareed. 2008. *The Post-American World.* New York: Norton.

Rising Institutions

ALAN S. ALEXANDROFF *and* JOHN KIRTON

8

The "Great Recession" and the
Emergence of the G-20 Leaders' Summit

The week following the Group of Twenty (G-20) finance ministers' tenth annual autumn ministerial meeting in São Paulo, Brazil, the G-20 was suddenly transformed into a leaders-level club.[1] On November 14 and 15, 2008, the G-20 leaders gathered in Washington in a crisis atmosphere for a "Leaders' Summit on Financial Markets and the World Economy." The U.S.-turned-global financial crisis that had erupted earlier in the autumn had become so serious that it would take a meeting of leaders, not mere finance ministers and central bankers, to sort out. By calling and hosting the Summit, U.S. president George W. Bush appeared to acknowledge that the United States was not likely to solve the financial crisis unilaterally or with a hastily assembled "coalition of the willing." The creation of an expanded G-x process Leaders' Summit also suggested that solving the global financial crisis would require more than the formal Bretton Woods–UN institutions, especially the International Monetary Fund (IMF), could offer.

Most noticeably, however, the G-20 leaders' agreement to gather in Washington appeared to signal that a G-7/8 Summit—the gathering of the traditional powers, the so-called Club of the Rich that had been the core economic club since 1975—would also be inadequate to cope with the financial crisis. Rather, the large emerging powers, led by the Group of Five (G-5)—Brazil, India, China, South Africa, and Mexico—plus other developing countries, would have to be involved to tackle the crisis.

What would become the agenda of this new "economic crisis committee"? The Washington Summit focused on national and international financial matters, delved into domestic regulatory systems and even individual firms, and raised issues such as executive pay for bankers. The gathering of G-20 leaders

---

1. See Kirton (2008a, 2008b).

177

appeared to mark the possible creation of a permanent leaders-level club. At a minimum the economic crisis committee appeared to have assumed global economic and financial leadership. Within five months, on April 1–2, a second G-20 Leaders' Summit took place in London. A third, hosted by new U.S. president Barack Obama, was convened in Pittsburgh on September 24–25, 2009, at which the crisis committee was confirmed as a permanent Leaders' Summit. The leaders' statement from Pittsburgh noted that "Today, we designated the G-20 as the premier forum for our international economic cooperation." Some national leaders and many opinion-makers had long advocated such an enlarged leaders' club. Experts and officials had concluded that the G-7/8 failed to represent key players in the international system—such as emerging market powers China, India, and Brazil—and therefore lacked legitimacy. Pittsburgh confirmed, however, that the premier institution of global economic governance would be the expanded G-20 crisis committee. The G-20 Leaders' Summit thus reflects a world whose major powers and systemic structure go well beyond the old Atlantic-centered Westphalian world.[2]

In evaluations of the Washington Summit, the follow-on summits, and the G-x institution, experts disagree on the new forum's performance, prospects, and drivers. One school of thought sees the summit as a historic step backward. In abandoning the twentieth-century move to rules-based, hard-law multilateralism—through the League of Nations and then the UN and Bretton Woods institutions—in favor of a return to a nineteenth-century concert model, the G-20 Leaders' Summit raises all the possible defects and limitations that the concert model possessed.[3] A second school sees the G-20 Summit as a failure, pointing to its inability to deal with such fundamental issues as the need to replace the post-1971 experiment with floating exchange rates, to diagnose correctly the causes of the crisis, or to offer much that was new.[4] A third school sees the Summit as a good start to a process of reinvention whose benefits would appear when President Obama assumed the leadership role.[5] A fourth school sees the Summit as strong in direction setting and commitment, but lacking the

---

2. See Altman (2009).

3. See Anders Aslund, "The Group of 20 Must Be Stopped," *Financial Times,* November 27, 2009, p. 9.

4. See Richard Duncan, "Bring Back the Link between Gold and the Dollar," *Financial Times,* November 24, 2008, p. 15; and Mark Landler, "World Leaders Vow Joint Push to Aid Economy," *New York Times,* November 16, 2008, p. 1.

5. "Prudence Will Still Have a Role to Play," *Sunday Times,* November 16, 2008, p. 18; Min Zeng, "Support Seen for Dollar, Yen," *Wall Street Journal,* November 17, 2008, p. C6; Domenico Lombardi, "'Coping' with the G-20: Italy and the Challenge of Global Governance." *Up Front Blog,* October 16, 2009 (www.brookings.edu/opinions/2009/1016_Italy_g20_lombardi.aspx); and Weiss (2009, p. 268).

capacity to deliver and implement policy choices.[6] A fifth school highlights the Summit's green light for growth from leaders who needed it to secure international synergies and provide them political support back home for the collective international effort.[7] Finally, a sixth school sees the G-20 Leaders' Summit as a step toward creating the necessary global financial regime and ascribes its preeminence as a global governance institution to its wider membership, the severity of the crisis that gave it birth, its support from the G-20 finance ministers' forum, and its exclusive focus on economics, for which global cooperative policy can be crafted with relative ease.[8] As the first anniversary of the G-20 Leaders' Summit passes, however, little evaluation has been undertaken of what the process means for global governance. Accordingly this chapter presents an early analysis and evaluation of this new G-x institution.[9]

Overall the G-20 Leaders' Summit appears to have performed well on its initial, central task of economic stabilization and stimulus, given the magnitude of the crises and challenges it has confronted. The Summit also seems able to serve as a central hub of global governance across a wider range of issues because it operates in a manner designed to meet new vulnerabilities brought about by an uncertain, complex, and interconnected world. It is this ability that gives this leaders club a comparative advantage over the slow-moving, mandate-bound, organizationally inflexible Bretton Woods and UN institutions. The G-20 also has a comparative advantage over both the old G-7/8 and prospective new groupings because it incorporates rising, systemically significant powers as equals in a new informal club. Moreover the G-20 Leaders' Summit, which inherits the assets of the G-20 finance ministers' meetings, is dominated by leaders who value the openness of a globalized world. The G-20 Leaders' Summit thus appears to have at least two key dimensions of a successful global governance institution: legitimacy and equality. Still to be determined, however, is whether the Summit also has the dimensions of

6. See, for example, "No Time to Waste," *The Economist,* November 20, 2008, p. 18; "Where's Angela?" *The Economist,* November 20, 2008, pp. 18–19; "The Coddle and Protect Policy," *The Economist,* November 22, 2008, p. 65; "Miss World Goes Missing," *The Economist,* November 22, 2008, pp. 61–62; Bergsten (2009); Jha (2009); Layton and Smith (2009); and Edwin Truman, "Globalization Goes into Reverse?" *Realtime Economic Issues Watch,* January 30, 2009 (www.petersoninstitute.org/realtime/?p=453).

7. See David Smith and Jonathan Oliver, "Fighting the Financial Inferno," *Sunday Times,* November 16, 2008, p. 5

8. See Walter Mattli and Ngaire Woods, "A New Architecture for Global Financial Regulation," *Financial Times,* November 19, 2008, p. 20; and Gideon Rachman, "A Modern Guide to G-ology," *The World in 2010* (London: The Economist, 2009), pp. 73–74.

9. We gratefully acknowledge the research assistance of Jenilee Guebert, Sandra Larmour, Anton Malkin, Zaria Shaw, and Ting Xu.

effectiveness, informality, and like-mindedness, without which this global governance club could well be doomed.

The Washington Summit, November 14–15, 2008

In response to the financial crisis that erupted in September 2008 with the collapse of Lehman Brothers, French president Nicolas Sarkozy called for a summit to be held.[10] He suggested a gathering in New York of the G-7 or G-8, perhaps with additional members such as China, India, and Brazil. Canada's prime minister Stephen Harper endorsed the call when he met with Sarkozy at the Francophone Summit in Quebec City on October 17, 2008. UN secretary-general Ban Ki-moon offered his New York headquarters as a site.

On October 18, immediately following the Francophone Summit, Sarkozy met Bush in Washington. Following their discussion, it was announced that a special summit would be held in the United States before the end of November. On October 22 the United States announced it would host the event. The announcement also stated that the G-20 leaders would be invited to this crisis meeting,[11] that the meeting would take place in the Washington area on November 15, and that a dinner at the White House would initiate the Summit with the working sessions coming the following day. Participants initially identified were the G-20 leaders, the managing director of the IMF, the president of the World Bank, the chair of the Financial Stability Forum (FSF), and the UN secretary-general.

The name of the "Summit on Financial Markets and the World Economy" indicated what would occupy the leaders' time.[12] Participants, it was hoped, would identify the underlying causes of the spreading global financial crisis, agree on a set of principles for reforming regulatory and institutional regimes in the global financial arena, review progress in addressing the financial crisis, and erect the framework for future action, details of which could be left to the G-20 finance ministers.

The agenda of the regularly scheduled G-20 finance ministers' meeting on November 8– 9, in fact, included many of the same issues that the G-20 Leaders' Summit likely would face, including currencies, financial regulation, and institutional reform. But the leaders were likely to extend their sights to trade, investment, and the importance of open economies in the face of the growing

10. See Kirton and Koch (2008); President Sarkozy was a strong advocate of expanding the G-7/8 by adding the G-5 to create a G-13.

11. See Price (2009). Australians have an alternate view that it was Prime Minister Kevin Rudd who convinced President Bush to convene a G-20 Leaders' Summit.

12. See Brookings Institution (2008), Eichengreen and Baldwin (2008), and Kirton (2008a).

financial crisis.[13] Australia, Germany, and the World Bank indicated early on that they would like the leaders to discuss the Doha Development Agenda. Participants, it was hoped, would also review proposals put forward by several countries on how best to tackle the financial crisis. Some, such as the United Kingdom's Gordon Brown, even predicted that the meeting would be a "Bretton Woods II." But IMF managing director Dominique Strauss-Kahn, among others, argued it was unlikely that such drastic reforms would result from the Leaders' Summit.

The two major Summit founders, France and the United States, had competing conceptions of what it should do. President Sarkozy, backed by other continental Europeans, sought quick, ambitious action with immediate but far-reaching results. The French goal was a comprehensive new international financial architecture, relying heavily on international-level regulation. In sharp contrast the U.S. administration, supported by Canada, saw the Summit as the first step in a process meant to prepare the ground for future action aimed at stronger intergovernmental cooperation.

Several G-20 leaders—those of Australia, Brazil, Canada, India, Italy, Japan, Saudi Arabia, South Africa, and South Korea—quickly confirmed that they would attend. China and Brazil suggested that they would participate as leading voices for the developmental and "Southern" perspective, viewing the Summit as an opportunity to help protect the South from being hurt by the "Northern-created" financial crisis and to obtain a greater role for emerging and developing countries in international financial institutions.

Demands to be invited soon came from a variety of countries. In response, President Sarkozy declared that France would give up its self-proclaimed "second seat" as the rotating president of the European Council so that Spain's leader could attend. Sarkozy also apparently invited the Czech Republic's finance minister to participate, as that country would take over the EU presidency from France in January 2009. With the last-minute addition of the Dutch leader, however, the Summit, to the annoyance of many Asian countries, became notably more Eurocentric than were the G-20 finance ministers' meetings.[14] It also put more consumers rather than producers of financial and economic security at the table, even if it also strengthened the number of democratic states in the club. Organizers turned down the many demands of African countries to attend.

Several meetings were scheduled to take place before the Summit to feed into the preparatory process. British prime minister Brown met with his French

<hr />

13. Kirton and Koch (2008).
14. Price (2009).

counterpart at the end of October to establish a common European front for the EU and G-20 Summits. Brown and German chancellor Angela Merkel met to discuss the world economy and financial market reforms. Russian president Dmitry Medvedev talked with both Australian prime minister Kevin Rudd and Italian prime minister Silvio Berlusconi to discuss the economic situation. Japan's prime minister Taro Aso dispatched emissaries to the G-20 countries, particularly the G-8 and emerging countries such as Indonesia, to prepare for the event. An EU-Russia summit led by Medvedev, Sarkozy, and European Commission head José Barroso was also scheduled before the G-20 meeting. The Asia-Europe Meeting in Beijing in October highlighted several issues on the proposed G-20 Summit's agenda. At the EU Summit on November 7, European countries completed a proposal to be tabled at the G-20 meeting.

The November 14–15 gathering was expected from the start to be the first in a series of crisis summits. The Europeans declared they wanted to reconvene within a hundred days, establishing a date for the next Summit immediately after the inauguration of the new U.S. president, Barack Obama. Leaders hoped that the principles that would emerge out of the November 14–15 gathering would be developed further by working groups for consideration at future gatherings that might well continue until the global financial crisis was "contained." At a minimum the leaders needed to show their continued concern over the crisis and their commitment to seeing new directions and decisions put into effect.

One week before the Summit, the leaders' G-8 sherpas and G-20 finance deputies agreed on most of the draft communiqué. But only on November 13, the day before the Summit, did an agreement take shape on a college of supervisors for the world's biggest international banks, and only after FSF chair Mario Draghi and IMF managing director Strauss-Kahn resolved their disagreement about the role and relationship of their respective institutions in the new global financial architecture.[15] The two agreed that a lightly institutionalized FSF would set the new standards, but the organizationally powerful IMF would then monitor and enforce compliance with them. On November 14, beginning in the early afternoon, the deputies together hammered out the final communiqué and action plan. The IMF was heavily involved in the deputies' drafting session—much of communiqué reads like a work plan for the IMF.

The Summit itself began with the dinner, the working portion of which was led by five-minute statements from the IMF's Strauss-Kahn, the World Bank's Robert Zoellick, the UN's Ban Ki-moon, and the FSF's Draghi. The following day the working sessions commenced in the morning and continued until early afternoon.

15. Engelen (2008).

The Results

Opinion-makers and experts judged this first G-20 Summit a success. Indeed, the Summit acted ambitiously to produce immediate decisions in areas directly controlled by government: fiscal stimulus, trade, and international institutional reform. The Summit simultaneously left the subject of private sector–driven finance, which the leaders poorly understood, to principles and a process where experts from the public and private sectors could devise solutions that would work in the new complex, uncertain, crisis-driven world.

Many of the G-20 leaders used the Summit to help manage their domestic politics. Their very presence in Washington showed domestic audiences that leaders were personally and directly concerned with the financial crisis and efforts to solve it. Simply being at the Washington Summit was a matter of prestige for some countries. Spanish politicians, with their country reeling from a housing collapse, benefited from their attendance, as did Dutch leaders faced with collapsing banks that needed bailing out with taxpayers' money to survive.

The Summit also allowed a number of leaders to alter previous positions, especially with respect to fiscal stimulus. The United Kingdom's Brown was able to set aside his long-standing "golden rules" of fiscal sustainability and introduce a major stimulus package, using the G-20 consensus, as well as an earlier G-7 one as justification for the move. Brown's Summit performance earned him, at least for a short time, a badly needed boost in public opinion at home. Similarly Canada's Harper, who had just won a federal election on October 14 after a campaign in which he (and indeed his opponents) had promised never to put Canada into a fiscal deficit, used the Summit to justify his deliberate post-election move to do just that.

The Summit's deliberations also seemed to go well. While it was held in half the time and with more than double the number of participants as the G-8 Summit, the Summit displayed a substantial degree of personal involvement, passion, and even spontaneous discussion among the leaders. On trade, for example, a wide range of leaders intervened during both the morning session and at lunch to warn of the dangers of protectionism. This caused the communiqué passages on trade to be made stronger and more detailed than the draft declaration had been.

The Summit's two concluding documents compared favorably with the first G-7 Summit's declaration in 1975. The G-20 Summit documents focused on finance, the economy, trade, development, and reform of international financial institutions. The leaders also declared that "We remain committed to addressing other critical challenges such as energy security and climate change, food security, the rule of law, and the fight against terrorism, poverty, and disease."

The Summit thus extended its declaration into the global-transnational and political security domains.[16]

The G-20 Summit also set new principled and normative directions. Most significantly it suggested guidelines for decisionmaking still to come on financial stability, regulation, and economic growth. The Summit declaration arbitrated between government regulation and open markets by highlighting the benefits these markets bring. It extended this emphasis on openness into the political domain. The Summit also made ninety-five specific, future-oriented commitments, largely dealing with macroeconomics and finance but with several on trade and one on development.

The G-20 leaders, well aware of the importance of implementation to their credibility, chose to demonstrate their personal commitment by agreeing to hold another Summit by the end of April—a short three-and-a-half months later. The leaders also set a tight schedule—a deadline of March 31, 2009—to implement many of the short-term decisions announced at the Washington Summit.

Some of the commitments—for example, the pledge to hold the next Summit by April 30, 2009— were complied with quickly, but others were violated almost immediately. Notwithstanding the G-20 leaders' "Standstill Provision" not to raise trade barriers, Russia and India soon raised import duties on automobiles; France changed its plans for the Common Agriculture Policy; and the United States imposed labeling requirements on meat imported from Canada. The commitment to secure a modalities agreement for the Doha Development Round—a major effort to reach a final successful agreement by December 31, 2008—failed to gain traction, with trade ministers unable even to agree to hold a meeting by that time. So a mixed picture emerged on the delivery of Summit decisions.

The Summit also developed the institutions of global economic governance "inside" and "outside" the G-20. "Inside" the G-20, countries agreed to hold a second Summit and encouraged a new gathering of G-20 trade ministers. This action signaled the G-20's desire to replace the G-7's old trade Quadrilateral (the United States, Canada, Japan, and the EU) and to extend beyond the World Trade Organization's Mini-Ministerials and the several other "G-20" developing states trade clubs. Working groups to deal with the global financial crisis were also formed to take on the tasks identified in the leaders' statement.

"Outside" the G-20, the leaders gave clear instructions to the G-8–created FSF to expand its membership. The leaders also signaled their desire to reform the Bretton Woods bodies. The G-20 called for action from several other international governmental and nongovernmental supervisory bodies, including the

16. G-20 Leaders (2008).

International Organization of Securities Commissions and the International Accounting Standards Board. The net result was that G-20 leaders reached out from their global governance perch to deal directly with the private sector and to define new components and connections in an expanding multistakeholder network for global economic governance.

The London Summit, April 1–2, 2009

The G-20's second Summit took place in London on April 1 and 2, 2009, with Prime Minister Brown as chair and host.[17] Going into the Summit, there were several significant disagreements among the members, both within the established G-7 and between the G-7 and the major emerging market members.

A divide over priorities appeared between a new U.S. president who wished to secure early fiscal stimulus and a continental Europe, led by France's Sarkozy and Germany's Merkel, that emphasized the need for strong, even supranational, financial regulation. A further divide emerged between the traditional powers, with their emphasis on stimulus and financial regulation, and the emerging powers that continued to focus on trade openness, trade finance, development, and reform of international financial institutions. A final divide appeared between the United Kingdom and some other G-7 members that sought to add climate change to the London agenda, and the large emerging economies that had resisted raising the topic at the Washington Summit.

The Results

Notwithstanding concerns during the lead-up that it would fail, in retrospect the London Summit, like its predecessor, was viewed as a success, if only because of the collective sense of relief that a second Summit had occurred. The Summit signaled once again the G-20 leaders' commitment to tackle the global financial crisis, and mobilized an unprecedented $1.1 trillion in new money for global development and stimulus.

The Summit deliberations began with a reception with the Queen and a leaders-only dinner on April 1, followed by working sessions from breakfast to mid-afternoon on April 2. The leaders produced collective documents covering macroeconomic stimulus, financial regulation, reform of international financial institutions, trade, social inclusion, and climate change. Several key agreements were reached. The Summit also developed several new G-20–related institutions, most notably expanding the membership and strength of the FSF and renaming it the Financial Stability Board (FSB).

17. Kirton and Koch (2009b).

On macroeconomic policy, G-20 leaders promised to provide whatever future fiscal and monetary stimulus was necessary to restore growth, to have the IMF assess what more was needed, to refrain from competitive currency devaluation, and to support IMF surveillance of G-20 economies and financial sectors.

On regulatory reform the leaders endorsed high-standard, internationally consistent and cooperative regimes aimed at reducing macroprudential risks. These covered all systemically important institutions, instruments, and territories, with the details to be defined by the new FSB, the IMF, and the Financial Action Task Force at the next G-20 finance ministers' meeting scheduled for Scotland in November 2009.

On the resources and reform of international financial institutions, the G-20 leaders mobilized $1.1 trillion in new funds, including a new $250 million allocation of Special Drawing Rights (SDRs). In addition, the Summit set a firm deadline of January 2011 for the IMF and spring 2010 for the World Bank to advance their "quota and voice" reform.

On trade and investment the leaders extended the "Standstill Provision"— their antiprotectionist trade and investment pledge—to the end of 2010, and added further promises concerning remedial action, avoidance of fiscal and financial protectionism, notification of and monitoring by the WTO and other institutions of national measures, and at least $250 million for trade finance.

On social support and cohesion the Summit endorsed the UN's Millennium Development Goals (MDGs), pledges for official development assistance (ODA), and earlier G-8 commitments to sub-Saharan Africa to mobilize money for food security and for the poorest countries. The leaders also promised to create employment and income support in a gender-balanced way.

On climate change the leaders endorsed the principle of intergenerational equity, sustainability, and a green stimulus, recovery, future economy, technologies, and infrastructure. They approved a framework for common but differentiated responsibilities. They also called for a successful conclusion of the UN Climate Change Conference set for Copenhagen in December 2009.

At the London Summit the United States was represented by a new president who had come, he said, to London largely to listen and learn. The United States secured a promise of future, rather than immediate, stimulus, relatively light financial regulation, substantial results on trade and investment, but little on climate change. It led a successful push for $500 billion in new loans to and from the IMF, and welcomed the $1.1 trillion in global stimulus that the overall package would bring. The United States also emerged as a mediator between Europe and China on one issue: tax havens.

Japan, despite its deep domestic economic and political difficulties, provided leadership as well. While Japan, like the United States, failed to secure

the immediate stimulus package it had sought, it did obtain the light financial regulation it preferred. Japan's leadership in offering $100 billion for the
international financial institutions was followed by similar-sized pledges by the
United States and the European Union—a burden-sharing formula that made
Japan their equal in providing this critical global public good. Japan also gained
support for climate change as a priority, building on the emphasis of the G-8
Summit it had hosted in 2008.

Among the large emerging powers China began to show it was prepared to
bear the burden of global leadership. On the eve of the Summit the governor
of its central bank, the People's Bank of China, had publicly offered a rather
aggressive proposal to move away from reliance on the U.S. dollar.[18] This SDR
proposal was in China's interest, given its massive U.S.-dollar-denominated foreign exchange assets and worries about the prospect of a U.S. currency devaluation. It was arguably China's first major policy proposal for global governance
reform. The G-20 Summit's approval of a $250 billion SDR allocation—
amounting to an almost eightfold increase in the stock of SDRs—represented
an initial and partial acceptance of China's proposal, which other emerging
powers had backed.

China also defended its sovereignty-sensitive position on financial regulation by having the strengthened G-20–driven tax haven regime leave Hong
Kong and Macau untouched. Elsewhere China escaped supranational intrusion
into its financial supervision, while securing in its own right full membership
in the expanded new FSB. It was similarly successful on climate change, where
the "common but differentiated" principle and UN location for the "beyond-
Kyoto" negotiations were approved. China also secured a reasonable result on
stimulus and trade. Perhaps most important was China's apparent willingness
to contribute at least $40 billion to the IMF's $500 billion package. While not
equal to the U.S., Japanese, or European shares, the contribution suggested that
a fully integrated China might be willing to put its global responsibilities before
its international rights and benefits.[19] Although China would lend the money
immediately, the G-20 leaders agreed that the emerging powers would secure a
greater role in the IMF only in 2011.

Another major emerging power, India, similarly did well. With its established identity as the defender of the developing world, India was able to use the
$1.1 trillion global stimulus package to good effect abroad and at home, where
Prime Minister Manmohan Singh was about to face a hard-fought general election campaign. Even more than China, India welcomed the UN-centric result

18. See Fratianni and Alessandrini (2009).
19. Deudney and Ikenberry (2009).

on climate change, the light touch on regulation, and membership in the FSB. Only on fiscal stimulus, where India supported the U.S. and Japanese desire for more spending, were results less than India's leadership had hoped. Nonetheless, his London performance helped propel Singh to an unexpectedly strong victory in the polls.

The Pittsburgh Summit, September 24–25, 2009

Six months after their London Summit the G-20 leaders gathered yet again, in Pittsburgh on September 24 and 25, 2009.[20] This was President Obama's first opportunity to host a global Summit and perhaps to make history on the world stage.

The Pittsburgh Summit addressed a broad agenda, building on the achievements of Gordon Brown's successful London Summit in several ways. The Summit's results, however, would depend on the state of the global financial system and the national political contexts of the assembled leaders, several of whom faced elections. Japan, in fact, had just held an election on August 30 that had resulted in a historic change in political leadership, while Germany was to go to the polls on September 27, just days after the Summit.

Pittsburgh's agenda spanned the financial and economic, the global and transnational, and even, at a side event, the Iranian nuclear program. Pride of place went to macroeconomic stimulus, responsible bankers' bonuses, a framework for balanced growth, international financial institution reform, climate change, and G-20 architecture. Most domestic financial regulations, antiprotectionism, and development, including food and health, took a significantly lesser stage.

On fiscal stimulus the Germans and French, encouraged by their growing economies, wanted the Summit to direct its political energies to winding down the massive fiscal and monetary stimulus that, by then, seemed to be working. But the U.S., U.K., and Canadian economies still showed only anemic growth. These countries' leaders argued that the stimulus was needed until the private sector began to invest and hire again. They had the backing of most other G-20 leaders, so the "keep the stimulus" view prevailed. But the leaders also put in place firmer plans to design careful, coordinated exit strategies that would be activated during the following year if the global economy continued to improve. The Leaders recognized the need for action on global imbalances and exchange rates, but decided that the matter should be postponed for future Summit agendas.

20. See Kirton and Koch (2009c).

On domestic financial regulatory reform most of the difficult details were left to technically more proficient G-20 finance ministers to work out at their regular meeting in November. On multilateral trade the leaders repeated their antiprotectionist pledge and reiterated the move by the July 2009 G-8 Summit in L'Aquila, Italy, to conclude the Doha Round in 2010. Nevertheless most G-20 countries were succumbing to various national initiatives—state aid and subsidy policies, in particular—to protect jobs.[21]

The Summit addressed development in its own right with a push to deliver the targets for ODA that the developed countries had promised for 2010 and to meet the much bigger MDGs due in 2015. The leaders pledged to implement the $1.1 trillion London commitments and to ensure that the new resources would be used effectively to combat food and health crises that were then arising. Microfinance was added to the agenda.

The Pittsburgh Summit also focused on reforming international financial institutions to give the emerging economies the expanded voice and vote they sought. With the 2010 and 2011 deadlines for a revision of quota shares in the World Bank and the IMF looming, much depended on whether the Europeans in particular would give up some of their privileged positions.

One of Pittsburgh's challenges was to deliver an acceptable framework for financing climate change mitigation and adaptation to help the UN's still-deadlocked negotiations succeed at the Copenhagen conference in December. The Pittsburgh Summit also looked to advance energy subsidy reduction, green stimulus and investment, and clean technology development.

On the question of process and indirectly on global governance architecture, the Pittsburgh Summit leaders also had to decide about whether, when, and where to hold the next Summit. As President Obama had observed at London in April, "I'm pleased that the G-20 has agreed to meet again this fall, because I believe that this is just the beginning. Our problems are not going to be solved in one meeting; they're not going to be solved in two meetings. We're going to have to be proactive in shaping events."[22]

The Results of the Pittsburgh Summit

The G-20 Leaders' Summit in Pittsburgh was a gathering of significant success. Pittsburgh saw the leaders take up a broad agenda, covering key economic and

---

21. See the Global Trade Alert Project's efforts to identify discriminatory measures in the major trading countries, including violations of the G-20's own "Standstill Provision" (www. globaltradealert.org).

22. As cited in Kirton (2009b).

development issues, as well as adding microfinance and environmental issues such as climate finance, energy efficiency, and food security.

Pittsburgh established a unified message on stimulus, but the leaders also agreed it was time to design exit strategies that could be implemented over the following year in ways appropriate to unfolding economic conditions. They further agreed to put in place a framework to encourage a more balanced foundation for the newly growing global economy. The leaders also moved to strengthen and coordinate domestic financial regulations, starting with the core issue of improving banking capital and liquidity. Finally, the leaders took a major step forward on the reform of international financial institutions, specifying that by 2011 there would be a shift of at least 5 percent of the quota share and resulting votes in the IMF from the established powers to the rapidly emerging powers.

To be sure, there were disappointments. The Pittsburgh Summit did little on trade beyond repeating past pledges. The leaders did little to ensure that the current economic recovery would soon create the good, clean, green jobs that many had discussed—indeed the Copenhagen climate change conference in December underlined the difficulties of cutting a collaborative climate change deal. The lack of progress at the Major Economies Forum and in the bilateral encounters between China and the United States in particular foreshadowed the limited possibilities for success in this large UN forum. Finally, the Summit as a whole did little, relative to the G-20 Summit in London or the G-8 at L'Aquila, to mobilize new money to help the struggling developing and least-developed countries. While still acknowledged as successful, the Pittsburgh Summit left much on the table unresolved.

Prospects for G-20 Summitry in 2010 and Beyond

Arguably the most consequential decision emerging from the Pittsburgh Summit was the agreement to institutionalize the G-20 as the premier economic global governance institution. This achievement was all the more remarkable given that the financial and economic crisis, which had stimulated the G-20 process, was abating. The Summit seemed focused principally on traditional macroeconomic imbalances, and there were little examination by leaders of the microeconomic agenda such as jobs—in contrast to the agenda of the G-7 in its early years. There were signs, however, that the abating crisis had had a performance-restricting effect, and that it would be up to the newly institutionalized G-20 to develop in a way to take up these economic global governance issues, and potentially other global tasks.

By deciding to hold the next G-20 Summit, in June 2010, under the joint chair of Canadian prime minister Harper and South Korean president Lee Myung-bak, in Canada, where the G-8 Summit had already been scheduled, the leaders affirmed the equality between traditional and emerging market powers. What was left unclear on leaving Pittsburgh was how, or if, the G-8 would fit with the new G-20 Leaders' Summit. Would the G-8 and G-20 cooperate or compete? Would these G-x processes continue to have separate but linked futures?[23]

Also left unclear was how a gathering of a group of more than thirty leaders for less than a day could meet the many challenges facing global governance. Though more diverse than the G-7/8, the G-20 plus leaders' group was also more Eurocentric than the evolving configuration of economic capability and power performance in the world, which increasingly pointed toward Asia. As the G-20 moved from the relatively easy tasks of stimulus to designing and delivering smart exit strategies, and as leaders looked to having fewer than three summits a year, doubts arose about the likelihood that the G-20 Summit could meet these challenges without continuing leadership from the G-8. The G-20 itself seemed to recognize this difficulty in its choice of hosts and chairs of five of the first six Summits: the G-7/8 powers of the United States in 2008 and 2009, the United Kingdom in 2009, Canada in 2010, and France in 2011.

An additional task, it seemed, for the institutionalized G-20 Summit was to forge a productive relationship with the ongoing G-8. Constructing such a relationship began with the practical physical and policy tasks of deciding just how to hold two summits in temporal and geographic proximity in June 2010. It appeared logistically easier—at least to the Canadian host—for the G-20 Summit to follow the long-arranged G-8 meeting. Powerful Asian voices led by China and Indonesia, as well as Brazil, felt strongly, however, that the G-20 Summit should convene first; they were concerned that the order of summits should avoid any appearance of G-8 leaders' arriving at decisions that G-20 leaders somehow would be asked to endorse.

A second process issue was to establish the exact relationship shared between the June G-20 Summit in Canada and the stand-alone November G-20 Summit in Seoul. There was good reason to think that each Summit should have a distinct theme, the first possibly focusing on smart, job-generating, climate-enhancing exit strategies, and the second in Korea taking up global imbalances and global green technologies.

A final process concern for the new G-20 Summit was to establish the relationship between the G-7 finance ministers, due to meet in February 2010,

---

23. See Kirton (2008c, 2009a).

and the G-20 finance ministers, who needed to gather either in Canada or in South Korea (the 2010 chair of the G-20 finance ministers) to prepare for the co-chaired G-20 Summit.

Solving these complicated process questions likely would determine the initial path of development for the G-20 Leaders' Summit. Starting at L'Aquila it was agreed that France would host the G-8 Summit, the G-20 Summit and the G-20 finance ministers in 2011.[24] Yet even with this trilateral alignment it remained unclear how many summits the French would hold, with what number of participants, and when. Uncertainty was compounded by speculation that President Sarkozy might like to do away with the G-8 Summit altogether, despite his agreeing at L'Aquila to host it. He had made it clear—before the Pittsburgh Leaders' Statement—that his preference was to replace both the G-8 and G-20 Summits with a G-14 consisting of the G-8 and the G-5 (Brazil, China, India, South Africa, and Mexico) plus a Muslim nation. It was even less clear what Barack Obama might do about the G-8, considering that the United States, if it followed the traditional G-8 sequence, was due to host the G-20 in the immediate lead-up to Obama's re-election bid in 2012. U.S. officials strongly hinted at the time of the G-20 announcement in Pittsburgh that the United States favored a G-20 Summit alone. In any event the presidency of the G-20 Leaders' Summit for 2012 had not been determined as of this writing. The G-20 finance ministers' meeting is similarly unsettled. Mexican officials have suggested that their country host the 2012 G-20 Summit—there is some logic to having an emerging power assume the host position after France, and the United States likely would favor Mexico as a rising power that was additionally a member of the OECD. But as yet the decision has not been taken.

Yet with such rapid G-20 institutionalization, it is clear the governance by plurilateral informal institutions continues to win out over the old formal multilateral organizations.[25] To be sure the G-x process gave the IMF the resources and reforms it could not secure from these states on its own. G-x has also created new international organizations, such as the FSB, that are separate from the IMF and born in plurilateral form to lead on designated tasks. This seems a sensible approach, as G-8 experience showed that its commitments were more likely to be met when the lead multilateral organization in the field helped in the delivery task.[26] While emerging powers sought to use the G-20 to secure a greater voice and vote in the IMF and World Bank, none argued that the formal multilateral organizations should replace or direct the G-20.

24. Kirton and Koch (2009a).
25. Schneckener (2009).
26. Kirton, Larionova, and Savona (2010).

Conclusion

As leaders set their sights on the G-20 Summit as the permanent premier international economic institution in 2010, it appeared that the new forum had become the hub of a global governance club and network, beginning with finance. It seemed possible that the Summit's apparent effectiveness and legitimacy could establish far-reaching principles, rules, and resources for the global economy. The advent of the G-20 Leaders' Summit also appeared to mark the transition from the traditional focus on the United States and the G-8 to a wider set of actors. The broad range of financial and economic issues identified in the Summit statements suggested that the forum was assuming a major global governance role.

Two major questions remain. The first is architectural: is the G-20 Summit now a permanent feature of, at least, economic global governance or will it fade away once the "Great Recession" has passed? The second question is functional: is the G-20 Leaders' Summit an effective decisionmaking organization capable of directing policy change in the global economy? From this question flow others: Will the G-20 Summit be able to direct the Bretton Woods institutions? Will the UN and the broader "192 Club" accept this implicit global executive committee? If the wider global community accepts its legitimacy, if only grudgingly, will the G-20 policy domain expand to include key matters not yet well embedded in this club and network, such as the environment, food, health, and human and global security?

The current G-x process has spawned a variety of club and network institutions. Both the traditional and the rising powers seem willing to participate in various of these global governance institutions. But participation in these institutions depends on the relative attractiveness of their different dimensions. For legitimacy and equality, the G-20 Leaders' Summit appears to be the natural setting. For informality, however, the G-20 might be too large (especially with the European add-ons), and the G-8, G-8+, G-13, or even the seventeen of the Major Economies Forum might be preferred. And if effectiveness—including both commitment and "like-mindedness"[27]—are valuable aspects of a

---

27. The lack of like-mindedness was much in evidence at the Copenhagen Conference, where China strenuously resisted the U.S. call for transparency—international verification that countries were meeting their agreed emission cuts. The Chinese insisted that such verification breached national sovereignty and interfered in the domestic affairs of states. While both the United States and China could agree on the outcome—a global reduction in greenhouse gas emissions—a wide gulf opened up over these values and principles. Though Europe and the United States could easily disagree on goals, they seldom disagree on values in the way the United States and China do. These international values determine whether countries are in fact like-minded or not.

leadership club, then the preference might be for a smaller or different grouping than the G-20. The G-x process likely will create several ongoing forums. The G-20 Leaders' Summit might hand much policy direction and technical financial work back to the G-20 finance ministers. And climate change and energy could be lodged in the Major Economies Forum, with decisionmaking and ratification left to a much larger setting—perhaps the UN Copenhagen process. In short, numerous possibilities remain.

The Pittsburgh G-20 Leaders' Summit might well prove to be significant, both in contemporary global governance politics and policy and in defining the overall architecture of the twenty-first-century world. But the architecture of the G-20 process itself is still taking shape.

References

Altman, Roger. 2009. "The Great Crash, 2008: A Geopolitical Setback for the West." *Foreign Affairs* 88, no. 1: 2–14.

Bergsten, C. Fred. 2009. "Obama's 500–Day Report Card." *International Economy* (Spring): 11.

Brookings Institution. 2008. *The G20 Financial Summit: Seven Issues at Stake.* Brookings.

Deudney, Daniel, and G. John Ikenberry. 2009. "The Myth of the Autocratic Revival." *Foreign Affairs* 88, no. 1: 77-93.

Eichengreen, Barry, and Richard Baldwin, eds. 2008. *What G20 Leaders Must Do to Stabilize Our Economy and Fix the Financial System.* London: Centre for Economic Policy Research.

Engelen, Klaus. 2008. "Rift Barely Avoided: Letter from the G20 Summit." *International Economy* 22 (Fall): 10–11.

Fratianni, Michelle, and Pietro Alessandrini. 2009. "The Common Purse." In *G8 2009: From La Maddalena to L'Aquila*, edited by John Kirton and Madeline Koch. London: Newsdesk.

G-20 Leaders. 2008. "Declaration of the Summit on Financial Markets and the World Economy." Washington, November 15 <www.g20.utoronto.ca/2008-leaders-declaration-081115.html> (January 2010).

Jha, Prem Shankar. 2009. "Globe in a State." *The World Today* 65, no. 3: 4–7.

Kirton, John, ed. 2008a. *The G20 Leaders Summit on Financial Markets and the World Economy.* G20 Research Group. <www.g20.utoronto.ca/g20leadersbook> (January 2010).

———. 2008b. "The G20 Takes Centre Stage," in *Growth, Innovation, Inclusion: The G20 at Ten*, edited by John Kirton and Madeline Koch. London: Newsdesk.

———. 2008c. "A Governanca Global do G8," *Cadernos Adenauer* 9 (3): 39–60.

———. 2009a. "Coexistence, Cooperation, Competition: G Summits," *Aspenia* 14 (43-44): 156– 162.

———. 2009b. "Prospects for the Pittsburgh Summit," in *The G20 Pittsburgh Summit 2009*, edited by John Kirton and Madeline Koch. London: Newsdesk.

Kirton, John, and Madeline Koch, eds. 2008. *Growth, Innovation, Inclusion: The G20 at Ten*. London: Newsdesk.

———, eds. 2009a. *G8 2009: From La Maddalena to L'Aquila*. London: Newsdesk.

———, eds. 2009b. *The G20 London Summit: Growth, Stability, Jobs*. London: Newsdesk.

———, eds. 2009c. *The G20 Pittsburgh Summit 2009*. London: Newsdesk.

Kirton, John, Marina Larionova, and Paolo Savona, eds. 2010. *Making Global Economic Governance Effective: Hard and Soft Law Institutions in a Crowded World*. Farnham, U.K.: Ashgate.

Layton, Duane, and Tiffany Smith. 2009. "Ditching Doha?" *International Economy* 23 (Spring): 21–23.

Price, Daniel. 2009. "Recovery and Reform." In *The G8 2009: From La Maddalena to L'Aquila*, edited by John Kirton and Madeline Koch. London: Newsdesk.

Schneckener, Ulrich. 2009. "The Opportunities and Limits of Global Governance by Clubs." *SWP Comments* 22 (September).

Weiss, Thomas G. 2009. "What Happened to the Idea of World Government?" *International Studies Quarterly* 53, no. 2: 253–71.

JOHN KIRTON

9

The G-20 Finance Ministers: Network Governance

At first glance, the Group of Twenty (G-20), founded at the level of finance ministers and central bankers in 1999, is a conventional intergovernmental institution. Its twenty members, largely the world's leading countries, are long-established sovereign states. As the twenty are full, equal members, the G-20 affirms in its composition and decisionmaking procedures the sovereign equality of states to a greater degree than do the United Nations or Bretton Woods bodies, with their stratified governance arrangements, or even the G-7/8, which still leaves Russia out of select ministerial forums. And after more than a decade in operation the G-20 finance ministers have no institutionalized civil society participants in their annual gatherings or in their special meetings that started in October 2008.

The G-20 has affected the otherwise unconstrained behavior of its members, the international institutions they control, and even some of the world beyond.[2] The international relations literature offers a debate primarily about who leads and benefits from the G-20's effective governance—the established G-7 powers,[3] the emerging economies,[4] the developing world and its key regions,[5] or the global community as a whole.[6] In exploring the causes of this form of global governance,

For the purposes of this chapter, the G-20 refers to the finance ministers and central bank governors of the countries in the group. For a discussion of the G-20 at the leaders level, see the chapter by Alexandroff and Kirton in this volume. I gratefully acknowledge the research assistance of Jenilee Guebert, Sandra Larmour, Anton Malkin, Zaria Shaw, and Xu Ting.

2. See Helleiner (2001a); and Sohn (2005).

3. See, for example, Porter (2000); Soederberg (2002); Taylor (2005); Baker (2006); and Martinez-Diaz (2007).

4. See, for example, Bergsten (2004); Boyer and Truman (2005); Yu Yongding (2005a, 2005b); and Beeson and Bell (2009).

5. See de Brouwer (2007); and Fues (2007).

6. See Kirton (2000, 2001a, 2001b, 2001c, 2005a, 2005b); Germain (2001b); Parkinson (2006); de Brouwer and Yeaman (2007); G-20 (2007); and Samans, Uzan, and Lopez-Carlos (2007).

experts rely heavily on classic realist, liberal-institutionalist, and political economy concepts, rather than starting with constructivist insights on the demand for, and dynamics of, a new form of network governance to address the shocks and new vulnerabilities that a complex, adaptive globalized system breeds.

Yet the G-20 operates in practice as such a global governance network appropriate for a tightly wired, twenty-first-century world.[7] While founded by the established G-8 countries and dominated by them in its early years, the G-20's Ministerial and Deputy meetings increasingly serve as the hub for influential relationships that spread out horizontally to embrace all geographic regions and many policy areas in an increasingly interconnected, coherent, consensual manner, rather than in a centrally controlled way. The G-20 has more easily absorbed as equals rising powers—led by China and India—and then reflected their perspectives in G-20 governance outcomes.

The G-20 combines as equals the world's "systemically significant" countries in a network devoted to global financial stability. Its raison d'être is not to constrain competition among the world's highly capable rival states or old intergovernmental organizations or prevent them from playing a classic game whose rules all states understand and employ; rather it is to search for innovative solutions and to provide global public goods "starting with stability" for a densely interconnected, uncertain, complex system that no one state can control. To fulfill this systemic mission in a world of new, nonstate-controlled vulnerability, the G-20 offers global predominance in collective capabilities; great diversity in wealth, political systems, historical experience, legal tradition, language, and religion, and a global reach. Within its network, finance ministers, central bankers, and their officials are induced to listen, learn, innovate, and initiate together. The G-20 finance ministers collectively confront complex systemic crises and issues rather than allowing the traditional powers to dictate decisions. The finance ministers and central bankers who directly deliver G-20 governance increasingly are agents adept at acting in the post-Westphalian networked way that the twenty-first-century global system demands. In so doing the G-20 has reached out to involve additional intergovernmental organizations in its governance network, and reached up to educate, advise, and lead the G-8 and now G-20 Summits. The G-20 also has reached "down" to be informed by civil society experts, professionals, business, and empowered individuals. Finally the G-20 finance ministers have reached in to develop their own informal institution as the hub of a global network to which others are attracted and to which the G-20 institutionally adapts.

Six forces have driven the emergence of the G-20's network governance. One is the spreading succession of shocks that have activated a new sense of

7. See Slaughter (2004, 2009).

vulnerability in an interconnected, uncertain, complex, adaptive global system. The Asian-turned-global financial crisis of 1997–99 catalyzed the creation of the G-20 finance ministers' forum in 1999; and the U.S.-turned-global financial crisis of 2008 caused it to add several special meetings and to support the new leaders-level G-20 Summits that started in November 2008.

A second force spurring G-20 success is the failure of the old Westphalian multilateral organizations of the Bretton Woods–UN architecture with their reliance on entrenched hegemonic power, hierarchy, formal legalized purposes, procedures, and self-contained bureaucracies and expertise to control and comprehend the complex new world.[8]

A third force is the rising relative capability of the large emerging powers led by China, India, and Brazil, which, through the G-20, have obtained the institutional rights, offered the resources, and accepted the global responsibilities that the Bretton Woods and UN organizations and even the G-7/8 institutions had largely denied them.[9]

A fourth force is the increasing, if still incomplete, devotion of the G-20 to principles of economic and political openness. Members fear that financial shocks and economic instability could engender social instability that would imperil the economic growth and political openness of the emerging and even established nations in the group.

A fifth force acting on the G-20 is the political control, capital, commitment, and continuity of the finance ministers and central bankers, individuals with a systemic perspective and with the incentive, experience, and intellectual openness to listen, learn, and look into the future. These members then collectively invent responses through the G-20 network.

A final force is the constrained and controlled participation—and resulting intimacy, trust, and social construction of new interests and identities—in a network. The G-20 has contained the same twenty core members since 1999; none has been added or expelled.

An Overview of the G-20's Performance, 1999–2009

Scholars generally agree that the G-20 finance ministers have been effective in domestic political management, deliberation, and direction setting, but less effective in decisionmaking, delivery, and the development of global governance. The G-20 was initially constructed for domestic political management and reassurance, open discussion, and deliberation, and for creating consensus

---

8. See Alexandroff (2008).
9. See Cooper and Antkiewicz (2008).

on new principles and normative directions. But it quickly and increasingly made concrete decisional commitments, catalyzed compliance with them, and developed global governance as a whole. In this process, the initial G-8 leadership in the G-20 has given way to the equal influence of the emerging economy members, to the benefit of the latter, emerging market countries, and the global community as a whole.

Domestic Political Management through International Compliments

The first task of the G-20 was to manage domestic politics and policy at home, primarily by reassurances that finance ministers' publics were being protected from crises from abroad and their preferences heard and understood on the international stage. This was done by encoding compliments, or favorable references, to individual countries in communiqués that their ministers could refer to back home as a sign of importance or an international seal of approval. The G-20 started awarding them in 2000 when Canada's then finance minister Paul Martin hosted the meeting in Montreal. The practice emerged even more strongly in 2004, 2005, and 2006, but dropped sharply after that, as G-20 governors moved from domestic worries about finance and globalization to other concerns.[10]

The sheer fact of hosting a G-20 Ministerial bolsters the host's prestige, political standing, and domestic policy influence, especially if the network approves of what the host is doing or wants done at home. This has been the case especially for the emerging powers, which are absent from most of the relevant first-tier clubs—among such host countries have been India (2002), Mexico (2003), China (2005),[11] South Africa (2006), and Brazil (2008), with South Korea scheduled for 2010. South Africa initially doubted it had the capacity to host, but did so successfully with help from its G-20 partners. All appeared as being in the top tier, capable of operating as equals. South Korea's desire to host all the stand-alone Ministerials to prepare for the two G-20 Leaders' Summits in 2010 shows how important is the status of hosting to the non–G-8 states.

Deliberation through Conversation

As a deliberative forum designed for open, frank, freewheeling dialogue aimed at education and discovery, the G-20 has engendered transparency, understanding, and trust on key issues and an emerging group identity overall. While it remains grounded in an annual two-day gathering of finance ministers and

10. From a slender start at Berlin in 1999, with only six paragraphs, the communiqué-encoded record of the annual Ministerial discussions soared the next year at Montreal to fourteen paragraphs and kept increasing thereafter.

11. See G-20 (2005a, 2005b); Dan Zhihui (2005); and Jiao Yan (2005).

central bankers, the onset of crisis in mid-September 2008 added a brief ad hoc gathering on the margins of the meetings of the International Monetary Fund (IMF) and World Bank in October 2008 and April 2009. It also added full-scale but separate meetings to help prepare, guide, and implement the directions of the new G-20 Leaders' Summit at Horsham, England, in March 2009 and in London in September 2009. The crisis-induced leap to the leader level has thus intensified the G-20 finance ministers' conversation. It has also, vastly increased virtual and direct meetings among the finance deputies, making for nearly continuous contact in the network.

Almost from the start the G-20 has embraced financial and economic issues, global-transnational issues, social policy, and security issues of a "new security" sort.[12] The agenda has slowly shifted toward global-transnational social issues, until the 2008 financial-economic crisis brought attention sharply back to this foundational field in full force. The continuous core agenda consists of global economic growth, trade liberalization, and international financial regulation, with financial system vulnerability and crisis response and prevention arising in almost every annual meeting. To this core the Montreal meeting in 2000 added poverty reduction and development assistance, 2001 added terrorist finance, and the 2003 meeting the UN Millennium Development Goals (MDGs).

Direction Setting through Consensus

In its principled and normative direction setting through consensus, the G-20 started with a mission of financial stability alone.[13] But this was increasingly accompanied by principles of equity—for instance, 1999's general affirmation of "growth that benefits all" became in 2000 growth that brings income inequality, poverty reduction, and benefits to the poorest countries, most vulnerable groups of society, and all members as individuals.[14] In 2002 there came a specific attachment to the MDGs, and the 2003 Summit introduced a "fairness" norm.[15]

A second expansion in principles brought "embedded liberalism" under conditions of globalization.[16] International openness has been a constant value, starting with trade liberalization and in 2000 adding globalization and appropriately sequenced capital account opening.[17] A strong emphasis on domestic protections by national governments started in 1999 with sound economic and

12. See Kirton (1993).
13. Kirton (2005a, 2005b).
14. G-20 (1999, 2000).
15. G-20 (2002, 2003).
16. See Ruggie (1983).
17. G-20 (2000).

financial policies that could differ by country, and extended in 2001 to domestic government's important role in producing policies that spread benefits to all and in promoting social safety nets to protect the vulnerable.[18] Later came strong institutions, sound social policies, investments in infrastructure and human capital, and appropriate management of the process of reform. The communiqué from the 2009 Ministerial in St. Andrews, Scotland, opened by noting that high unemployment was a major concern, and proceeded to identify as its reigning values the pentarchy of "sustainable growth, stability, job creation, development and poverty reduction." It added embedded ecologism, by affirming its commitment to tackling the "threat" of climate change.[19]

The third expansion brought the principles of open democracy, individual liberty, human rights, and the rule of law. The G-20 has continuously affirmed such values, with particular bursts in 2001, immediately after the September 11 terrorist attacks, and in 2004, when the meeting was held in a united Germany for the second time.[20] Since 1999 the G-20 has discussed "transparency;" in 2000 the G-20 added international mobility and citizens' access to outside ideas; and since the 2001 meeting "good governance" has formed the new core. At India's Ministerial in 2002 the Summit added accountability, worldwide surveillance, the rule of law, support for the New Plan for Africa's Development (NEPAD), and information and knowledge exchange.[21]

Such internally interventionist, anti-sovereignty and thus anti-Westphalian principles started early, with "no safe haven" for terrorists in 2001 and internal access to combat financial abuse in 2003.[22] In 2009 the recovery of stolen assets was added. The 2008 crisis brought a concern with domestic financial regulation and the principle of intervention in the economic domain. Indeed at the 2009 Ministerial in St. Andrews the G-20 presented principles about compensation for senior executives within their countries' private sector firms.[23]

The G-20 has progressively linked its political and economic principles in an ever-tighter causal net. The G-20 in 2006 noted how the economy could affect political security through energy, security, and conflict links.[24] But the primacy of the political has stood out. Starting in 2001 the G-20 affirmed the essential role of governments in reaping the full benefits of globalization, and linked open markets to growth, equity, and well-being for its peoples. In 2002

18. G-20 (1999, 2001).
19. G-20 (2009).
20. G-20 (2001, 2004a).
21. G-20 (1999, 2000, 2001, 2002).
22. G-20 (2001, 2003).
23. G-20 (2008, 2009).
24. G-20 (2006).

the group proclaimed that strong institutions, transparency, the rule of law, and investments in infrastructure and human capital in developing countries were essential for growth and poverty reduction. The 2003 communiqué added the links among aid, good governance, financing, and trade.[25] These outcomes reflected the domestic values the G-8 traditional powers, but also those of all the G-20's emerging members save China and Saudi Arabia.

Decisionmaking through Commitments and Delivery through Compliance

The G-20 was formed as a deliberative and direction-setting network, where the horizontal dynamics of open mutual adjustment through learning and consensus would dominate the hierarchical process of making hard, law-like decisional commitments.[26] Nonetheless the G-20 has been a decisional forum from the start, with its regular and rising performance in the number, breadth, and ambition of its commitments showing notable spikes.

On the dimension of delivery the group's official history has concluded that "G-20 support for global initiatives has had only a modest effect on members' behavior, and even less impact on the behavior of non-member countries."[27] The available outside evidence also suggests that compliance has been in the modestly positive range.

The 2009 November Ministerial featured a lengthy appendix that tracked progress in implementing all the commitments made by the G-20 leaders and their finance ministers. Internal mechanisms for self-binding suggest that members are consciously seeking to improve their compliance performance. But those few catalysts that have been effective in increasing compliance with the G-8 finance and development commitments——setting a one-year timetable, relying on core international organizations, and not involving other international organizations—have seldom been in evidence in the G-20 finance ministers' commitments.[28] Only as the financial crisis approached and then hit in 2007–08 did G-20 ministers adopt them in full force.

The limited direct evidence available suggests the G-20 has complied adequately with its commitments during its first ten years. It has a mixed record in implementing the far more ambitious commitments of G-20 leaders since November 2008. It has done well on stimulus, international financial institutional reform, and tax havens. But it has done poorly on trade, exit strategies, and most important aspects of domestic financial system reform. It has yet to confront the challenge of delivering on its boldest commitments to deliver an

25. G-20 (2002, 2003).
26. See Kokotsis (1999); and Abbot and others (2000).
27. G-20 Study Group (2008, p. 53).
28. See Kirton (2006); and Kirton, Larionova, and Savona (2010).

effective framework for balanced growth and the agreed voting reform of the World Bank and IMF by deadlines in 2010 and 2011.

The Development of Global Governance through International Construction

In the development of global governance the G-20 has done much institutionally to thicken itself through "in-reach," to offer support, direction, and limited participation to countries and other international institutions through "outreach" to involve civil society, through "down-reach" in a limited if not major, multistakeholder way, and, finally, to exert influence through "up-reach" to the leaders level.

In its internal in-reach the G-20 immediately established the convention of an annual two-day autumn meeting at the Ministerial level that begins with a dinner and continues for the full next day. Initially, at the end of the meeting the host and chair of the next gathering were announced, but this "shadow of the future" was extended to two years in 2003 and later to three years through a governing troika of past, present, and future presidencies. Hosting choices quickly acquired G-8-emerging country and geographical regional balance characteristics—indeed the two most powerful G-8 members, the United States and Japan, have not yet hosted at the finance level, while the most powerful G-5 emerging powers all have.

Since 2004 the G-20 has relied in a well-defined manner on its experts' workshops, with an average of three a year with specified themes. In 2008 it accepted a Canadian initiative to turn itself into a more robust and reliable decisionmaking forum. Due to the 2008 financial and economic crisis it also began to meet more frequently at the levels of ministers, deputies, and lower officials and to involve trade and energy ministers as well.

In outreach the G-20 has issued a large and expanding array of instructions and endorsements to other international institutions. Driven in part by its changing agenda, since 2005 the G-20 has moved from the G-7–centered, plurilateral, informal finance-focused institutions, such as the Financial Stability Forum (FSF), the Financial Action Task Force (FATF), and the Organization for Economic Cooperation and Development (OECD), to broadly multilateral, organized, more comprehensively focused ones—above all the IMF and the World Bank. Yet the G-20 has done virtually nothing at the Ministerial level to include outside countries in its highly self-contained regular annual forum. Nonetheless as the IMF and the World Bank, along with the EU, have been members since the start, the G-20 has institutionally embraced virtually the entire global community.

In its down-reach to civil society, the G-20 has conducted workshops and conferences, and involved the private sector and experts, on specified subjects. In 2000 Canada's then-finance minister Paul Martin felt strongly that civil society groups should be involved in the Ministerial but other members prevented such a move. The G-20's civil society outreach, while expanding, remains largely oriented toward experts and exists largely at the national level.In its up-reach the G20 network's influence on national leaders is growing. Finance ministers, on average, are the most influential ministers in national governments, due to their comprehensive concern with issues in their domestic and international dimensions and their predominant control of the macroeconomy (along with central bankers) and the fiscal purse.

The strong performance of the G-20 finance ministers' forum led U.S. president George W. Bush to choose it, rather than France's preferred G-8–centered model, as the group to respond at the leaders' level to the 2008 financial crisis, and also led to the creation of the G-20 Leaders' Summit.[29] Even as the G-20 finance ministers have been guided by their leaders since November 2008, they still take the lead on issues, notably domestic financial regulations, where they have the expertise but few leaders do.

Critical Cases in G-20 Finance Governance

These broad trends in G-20 network governance are confirmed by a detailed look at a number of cases on which most G-20 experts base their conclusions about G-20 effectiveness.

Creation and Construction, 1999–

The first case is the creation of the G-20 from 1997 to 1999.[30] Most generally the G-20 was born from Canada's traditional position—and resulting instinct—as one of the most well-connected countries in the world through its extensive membership in plurilateral institutions of global relevance with both traditional and developing countries.[31] The Clinton administration's Treasury Department joined with Canada in adopting a "proliferate-the-fora" approach, involving emerging and developing countries through "APEC [Asia-Pacific Economic Cooperation] and Latin American Finance Ministers meetings, the New Arrangements to Borrow, and the various G-22, G-33, and ultimately G-20 groups."[32]

---

29. See Price (2009).

30. See Kirton (2000, 2001a, 2001b, 2001c); Martin (2005, 2008); Amato (2008); Kirton and Koch (2008); Sautter (2008); and Summers (2008).

31. Kirton (2007).

32. Summers (2007, p. 13).

President Clinton and some G-8 colleagues also sought a more effective, inclusive, flexible forum to respond to the challenges of the rapidly globalizing world and to mobilize the rising capabilities of emerging countries, particularly in Asia.[33] The emergence of the Asian-turned-global financial crisis in July 1997 led Clinton, at the Canadian-hosted APEC leaders' meeting in November 1997, to mount a short-lived Group of Twenty-Two (G-22). Soon thereafter the FSF, New Arrangements to Borrow, and the International Monetary and Finance Committee (with the United Kingdom's chancellor of the exchequer Gordon Brown as the first chair) were formed.

Formally created by the G-7 finance ministers in September 1999, the G-20 arose from the steady succession of ever more severe shocks that escalated through Asia in 1997, consumed Russia, immobilized U.S. markets (with the collapse of Long-Term Capital Management) in 1998, and then spread to the Americas and elsewhere.[34] The response to these crises by the established, hierarchical, hard-law, multilateral organizations—above all the IMF—was inadequate, a failure first evident in the 1994 Mexican peso crisis and then in the overall failure of the 1995 Halifax G-7 Summit to reform the Bretton Woods–UN bodies for the twenty-first-century world. The crises created a unifying desire to restore financial stability, so that the growth bred by the globalization of the 1990s could continue for the benefit of all. Behind these actions lay a desire by G-7 countries to protect hard-hit South Korea's recent democratic revolution and to promote badly afflicted Indonesia's embryonic one.

President Clinton, then-treasury secretary Larry Summers, Canada's finance minister Martin, and their German colleagues were brought together in the plurilateral institutional nest of APEC and then caucused in the G-7/8 to take action. Martin, along with Summers, took the lead in designing the forum. The 1999 G-8 Cologne Summit had agreed "to work together to establish an informal mechanism for dialogue among systemically important countries, within the framework of the Bretton Woods institutional system."[35] On September 25, 1999, the G-7 finance ministers and central bank governors formally created the G-20 "as a new mechanism for informal dialogue in the framework of the Bretton Woods institutional system, to broaden the dialogue on key economic and financial policy issues among systemically significant economies and promote cooperation to achieve stable and sustainable world economic growth that benefits all."[36] The agenda and principles thus expanded from financial stability in a Bretton Woods framework to economic issues aimed at "world growth" that

33. Kirton (2005a).
34. See Kirton (2000).
35. G-8 (1999).
36. G-7 (1999).

was stable, "sustainable," and would "benefit all." The membership moved from "systemically important" countries to those from "regions around the world" as well as representatives of the EU, the IMF, and the World Bank.

Summers and Martin chose the membership.[37] All G-8 countries plus China and India were clear admits; Australia, Saudi Arabia, South Korea, and Turkey were not so obvious but nevertheless were chosen.[38] The Europeans secured a place, uniquely among regional organizations, for both the EU and the European Central Bank. Canadian candidates Thailand and Chile were left out.

China's decision to join was critical. Weighty, financially invulnerable, and responsible through the crisis, China had long been internationally unengaged and saw itself as standing between the North and South rather than as a member of either group.[39] Martin's desire to use the G-20 to promote better supervisory and self-regulation arrangements helped China chose to join.

Democratic values also mattered. Turkey, although a consumer rather than a producer of financial security, was admitted to sustain its character as a stable Muslim democracy in an unstable, nondemocratic Middle East. Indonesia had a place reserved for it once it proved that its embryonic, crisis-catalyzed democratic revolution and the respect for human rights and anti-corruption commitment that came with it were real. Malaysia was excluded because its leader's autocratic treatment of its well-respected finance minister defied the rule of law cherished by Martin, a lawyer and close colleague of his Malaysian counterpart in the Commonwealth. Similarly, Nigeria's admittance would be deferred until it had solved internal political problems. But once it had done so it faced competition for membership from authoritarian Egypt; democratic South Africa thus remains the only African member of the club.

At their first meeting, in Berlin in December 1999, the G-20 ministers, through an open, free-flowing dialogue, came to consensus on a core agenda, an identification of the problem, and an agreement to work by cooperation on standards and rules, if not regulations, on international and domestic banking and private sector involvement in government bailouts. The Montreal G-20 meeting in 2000 brought an agreement to have two deputies' meetings and one Ministerial meeting in the following year, helping ensure the G-20's permanence once the crisis that had catalyzed it had passed. It was agreed that private sector representatives would be involved, as they had been when G-20 deputies had met in Toronto.

37. See Kirton (2000); Martin (2008); and Summers (2008).

38. Economic (especially financial) capability, geographic location, the G-8 memory of earlier energy shocks, and U.S. energy dependence on imported oil favored Saudi Arabia's inclusion.

39. Kirton (2001b); Medeiros and Fravel (2003).

Financial Crisis and Stability

These early years saw the creation of the G-20, the defining of its core mission, and the focusing of its work agenda. Initial judgments that the G-20 promised "tremendous progress if it worked as intended" have been largely supported by its record since.[40]

The economic crisis of the late 1990s had been largely contained by 1999, due mainly to the effective response of the G-7.[41] The G-20 confirmed and rendered more comprehensive and durable the G-7's response, preventing aggrieved regions—Asia in particular—from retreating to new regional ideas and institutions such as an "Asian way" or an Asian Monetary Fund. G-20 governance then helped contain the debt crisis in emerging markets and allowed emerging powers to grow rapidly.[42] But the G-20's focus was on preventing future crises, rather than on remedying the deep damage done by the one of 1997–99.[43]

In November 2007, ten months before the collapse of Lehman Brothers, the G-20 presciently expressed concern over the growing downside risks from financial market disturbances, the difficulty of prediction, and the need for better financial supervision. It acknowledged that "the nature of the recent turbulence also suggests that there may be important new lessons for understanding the origins of crises; the way financial shocks are transmitted; and the respective roles of regulators, rating agencies, the private sector and the international financial community."[44] Less than a month earlier the G-7 finance ministers had merely called for a full analysis of the causes of the turbulence and asked the FSF to undertake the required analytic work. The G-20 thus did better than the G-7 and the IMF in anticipating and addressing the coming crisis. But its enduring concern with now-stable emerging markets, its focus on Africa at its 2007 meeting, and its character as a consensus-oriented forum inhibited it from taking the bold action that was required to prevent the global financial 2008 crisis. Not surprisingly, over the next year Canada sought to turn the club into a stronger decisionmaking forum.

Reform of the IMF and the Architecture
of International Financial Institutions

The G-20 also dealt with reform of the IMF and the architecture of international financial institutions, including issues of voice, vote, and senior management

40. Germain (2001b); Taylor (2005).

41. Kirton and Kokotsis (1997/98); Kirton (2000).

42. Bergsten (2004).

43. Helleiner (2001a, 2001b).

selection. This case involved the constitutional challenge of changing an order that had been in place since 1944.[45] Here the IMF and the G-7 had proven unable to bring change, despite a major push by G-7 leaders at their 1995 Halifax Summit. The ongoing failure to reform the UN Security Council shows how difficult change in such constitutional issues can be.[46]

Virtually all experts agree that the G-20 deliberations led to the consensus generating the first stage of IMF voice and vote reform and its effective implementation by the IMF.[47] Critics concede that the G-20 decision to change the voting structure of the IMF led to exogenous institutional pressures that generated ad hoc quota increases for China, Mexico, South Korea, and Turkey in September 2006, even if this move brought only modest benefits.[48] These incremental increases were the first such first changes since the 1960s.[49] The G-20 also created the momentum for the second stage of much larger voice and vote reform, a process hastened when the 2008 global financial crisis struck.[50]

In 2005 Australian treasury minister Peter Costello had noted the problem of Asian representation within the IMF—a cause taken up by Canada, the United Kingdom, and Japan but opposed by the Europeans. The G-20's sustained advocacy of IMF reform and its capacity to break logjams in hard-law institutions, backed by changing relative economic capability, led to a successful realignment.[51]

At the November 2006 meeting in Melbourne the G-20 reaffirmed its commitment to deliver the second stage of reform.[52] A G-20 working group on IMF reform argued that, despite criticism that the quota increases were inadequate, the reforms were an essential first step. At Kleinmond, South Africa, in 2007, the G-20 reported further progress, noting that the "forum's efforts in 2007 have contributed to a convergence of views among the IMF's members."[53] In April 2008, before the global financial crisis struck in the autumn, the IMF board of governors approved quota increases for 54 members and an increase in voting shares for 135 (IMF 2009).

44. G-20 (2007).

45. See Ikenberry (2001).

46. Ikenberry (2008).

47. See O'Neill (2006); Parkinson (2006); de Broewer and Yeaman (2007); and Beeson and Bell (2009).

48. Martinez-Diaz (2007, p. 15).

49. Parkinson (2006).

50. See G-20 (2004b).

51. Parkinson (2006); Beeson and Bell (2009).

52. See G-20 (2006); and de Brouwer and Yeaman (2007).

53. G-20 (2007).

On the broader architecture of international financial institutions, including the mission, mandate, resources, coverage, competition, and coordination of the Bretton Woods's twins and newer entrants such as the regional development banks and the FSF, a broad consensus affirms G-20 effectiveness. Nevertheless most experts note that emerging and developing country issues, such as the conditionality voiced by the G-24, were not addressed in 2003 or later they argue that the maintenance of global integration and surveillance reflects the interests of the G-7 and represents an intrusion into the domestic financial systems of non-G-7 members.[54]

Since the start, the G-20 has addressed global financial governance as a whole, with key founders Paul Martin and Gordon Brown recognizing that developing countries needed to be involved in the process and buy into its result.[55] To be sure the G-20 ignored, until the 2008 crisis, the G-24's call for a more expansive forum than the G-7–dominated FSF. The G-20 also did not deal seriously with sharing the adjustment burdens among international lenders and borrowers.[56] And the G-20 failed to increase substantially the resources available to the international financial institutions. It concentrated on policy errors by individual governments more than on the global structure. Such defects of omission were also true of other international institutions at work in the field.

Energy, Environment, and Climate Change

Experts maintain that the G-20 created a consensus that efficiency in energy markets provides better security than locking in supply and demand and that energy and minerals security "need not be a zero sum game."[57] Progress was also made on energy and climate change starting in 2006.[58] Some observers say the finance ministers' focus on market efficiency and concern over fiscal deficits give them a natural interest and advantage on this issue.

The G-20 identified environmental issues as early as 2000, but only much later did it devote serious attention to them and to the central component of climate change. The 2006 Melbourne meeting specified ways to strengthen energy and mineral markets, including reducing fiscal subsidies for resources and more transparency on extractive firms and resource-rich countries.[59] The G-20 presciently warned that "global demand for energy and minerals commodities is

---

54. See Soederberg (2002); Sohn (2005); Taylor (2005); and Martinez-Diaz (2007). The G-24 is the joint ministerial committee of the World Bank and the IMF.

55. Germain (2001a).

56. Sohn (2005).

57. Parkinson (2006).

58. See de Brouwer and Yeaman (2007); and Samans, Uzan, and Lopez-Carlos (2007).

59. de Brouwer and Yeaman (2007).

set to increase significantly over coming decades driven by a strong world economy, rising incomes, and ongoing industrialization and urbanization in many economies." Participants agreed that "enhancing global trade by strengthening markets, and ensuring sustainability by promoting investment and encouraging efficiency, are the best ways to deliver lasting resource security."[60] The G-20 agreed that "the most sustainable way to address resource security is to make sure that markets work as well as they can," with the implication that large investments would have to be made on the supply side.[61] As one analyst notes, "The recognition that the solution to securing a stable and predictable supply of energy and minerals need not be a zero-sum strategic game" showcased a growing consensus about the need for finding collective solutions, rather than national ones, to these multidimensional problems.[62]

On climate change, the G-20 at Melbourne endorsed international policy frameworks and actions, well-functioning markets, clear price signals, open trade and investment, market transparency, good governance, effective competition among firms, investment in new supply, efficiencies and new technologies, the use of alternative and renewable energy sources, and knowledge and resources flowing across borders.[63] Yet the G-20 found it difficult to extend its climate governance into the decisional domain. This may be because the success of the G-20 inspired the U.S.-led creation in 2007 of a very similar forum—the Major Economies Meeting, later changed to the Major Economies Forum—devoted to energy and climate change, but without Saudi Arabia included to drag progress down. It was later due to the insistence of the emerging members that climate change be dealt with in the fully multilateral, developing country–dominated United Nations Framework Convention on Climate Change (UNFCCC), rather than the plurilateral G-20, where emerging economies were evenly balanced by established ones.

At the November 2009 G-20 at St. Andrews, Scotland, held just before the UNFCCC's Copenhagen Conference in December, climate finance was the most divisive issue of all. With China and India insisting on their standard, public, hard-line, UN-approved positions, all the efforts at compromise—led by the United Kingdom, the host, and emerging Mexico—were to no avail. As the communiqué moved from draft to final version, climate finance dropped from the top to the bottom; the document recognized only "the need to increase significantly and urgently the scale and predictability of finance" and promised weakly to take further work to define options for financing and institutional

60. G-20 (2006).
61. de Brouwer and Yeaman (2007).
62. Parkinson (2006).
63. G-20 (2006).

arrangements.[64] Thus forum shopping by emerging economies and the loom-ing presence of the Copenhagen Conference led to the G-20's failure to advance decisionmaking on climate change.

Forces Driving G-20 Governance

Six forces acting on the global economy have driven the G-20 to achieve more effective performance as a global governance network. The first is "shock-activated" vulnerability. The Asian-turned-global crisis that attacked Asia, spread to Russia and Brazil, and almost engulfed the United States by fall 1998 led to the meetings of G-20 finance ministers. Then the September 11 terrorist shock on a newly vulnerable United States inspired the G-20 to develop new and effective work on terrorist financing, expanding G-20 governance into the core security realm.

Within a decade came a second, much bigger financial shock. By the first quarter of 2009, the financial system crisis, which originated in the United States, had extended to the United Kingdom, Russia, Germany, France, and Italy, leaving intact only the banking systems of Japan and Canada within the G-8. The scale, speed, functional scope, geographic spread, and severity of this shock created the worst contraction in global economic growth since the Great Depression. The shock was made all the worse by transmission mechanisms that no country could confidently comprehend or control. Unlike the 1997–99 crisis, no country could be counted on to provide the financial and economic security to extricate financially troubled countries from the global meltdown. To discuss the challenge the G-20 finance ministers added emergency meetings, gathering seven times in the year from October 2008.

A second force is the failure of established multilateral organizations to respond adequately to such shocks on their own. This failure started with the IMF during the 1997–99 period and continued with the UN in 2001 on terror-ism and the IMF again in 2008.[65] More broadly the G-20 has prevailed amid intense competition from obsolete or inadequate G-x institutions, including the G-7/8 and even newer ones.

A third force is the strong equalization of capability between the established and emerging economies and among those within the G-7. The first-ranked United States was afflicted by the collapse of Long-Term Capital Management in 1998, the terrorist attacks of September 11, and the global financial crisis of 2007–09. In contrast to the United States' slowly diminishing relative capability,

64. G-20 (2009).
65. Weiss (2009).

seen in its declining dollar and mounting deficits and debts, the leading rising powers of China and India emerged relatively unscathed from these economic crises. But even the emerging economies have not been powerful enough to protect themselves from the new systemic threats, let alone prevent them.

On the specific capabilities related to demography and migration, for example, the G-20 included key financial markets and population centers and countries from the two poles of the demographic problem: the advanced industrialized states with aging and largely declining populations and emerging economies with young populations and growing workforces. This enabled the G-20, in a specialized supply-demand match, to "play a crucial role in highlighting how to improve the policy environment and in ensuring that policies are in place to facilitate, at least cost, the economic adjustment required by demographic change."[66]

A fourth identifiable force is the G-20 members' common commitment to political stability and, for all but China and Saudi Arabia, to political openness and democracy, which some had only recently won. The EU in particular and its G-7 partners in general were concerned about the recent democracies in its many new and prospective members in eastern and central Europe. The emerging economies of Indonesia, Mexico, and South Korea aroused similar concerns throughout the G-7 and among the G-20 as a whole.

A fifth force is the considerable political control, capital, commitment, and continuity of the G-20 finance ministers and central bankers. As most are appointed, rather than elected, their ranks have enjoyed exceptional continuity, which allows them to take a longer-term perspective and to develop understanding and trust as well as a group identity and a sense of responsibility with their peers. During the G-20's first decade, for example, South Africa and Saudi Arabia sent only three different individuals as finance ministers or central bankers, Mexico, Australia, Russia, and the United Kingdom have sent only four. Indeed this advantage of continuity has an equalizing impact, as the two most powerful members in the club, the United States and Japan, do not benefit from continuity.

A last force is the constricted and controlled membership of the G-20: the network added no additional members or participants during its first decade. At the same time the G-20 collectively constitutes the hub of a global network that extends horizontally through all globally consequential, plurilateral institutions of trans-regional reach, containing established and emerging countries alike. While the G-7 members remain the most well connected, emerging economy members are adequately and increasingly linked too, especially as the G-7/8 finance ministers' forum has begun to invite key emerging country colleagues to its meetings.

66. Parkinson (2006).

Conclusion

The G-20 has served for more than a decade as an effective club for domestic political management, deliberation, direction setting, and, increasingly, decisionmaking, delivery, and the development of global governance. Under the G-x process this network has emerged with equal numbers of established and emerging powers and is governed by consensus rather than by formal, legally entrenched, weighted voting or unit vetoes under a unanimity rule. Its direct delivery by finance ministers and central bankers and the equity element in its mission help the G-20 to focus on the needs of the global system as a whole. The 2007–09 crisis drove it to move well beyond governments and intergovernmental organizations to deal with private sector standards and individual firms. The 2007–09 crisis also forced any G-7 members that had started with a sense of one-formula-fits-all triumphalism in 1999 to set such an attitude aside.

The unprecedented speed, scale, and scope of the 2007–09 global financial crisis led the G-20 both to meet more intensively and then to leap to the leaders level, much as the 1997–99 crisis had caused the finance ministers' G-20 to arise.[67] And much as the G-7 finance ministers and G-8 Summit had led to the G-20 finance ministers' meeting in 1999, the G-20 finance ministers were crucial in creating the G-20 Leaders' Summit. The fact that the Summit-level response to the 2007–09 crisis came in the form of an elevated G-20, rather than on a G-8 foundation or a U.S.-defined "coalition of the willing" confirms the success of the G-20 finance ministers' governance network.

References

Abbott, Kenneth W., and others. 2000. "The Concept of Legalization." *International Organization* 54, no. 3: 401–20.

Alexandroff, Alan S., ed. 2008. *Can the World Be Governed? Possibilities for Effective Multilateralism.* Wilfrid Laurier University Press.

Amato, Giuliano. 2008. "From Bretton Woods to the G20." In Growth, Innovation, Inclusion: The G20 at Ten, edited by John Kirton and Madeline Koch. London: Newsdesk.

Baker, Andrew. 2006. *The Group of Seven: Finance Ministries, Central Banks and Global Financial Governance.* London: Routledge.

Beeson, Mark, and Stephen Bell. 2009. "The G20 and International Economic Governance: Hegemony, Collectivism, or Both?" *Global Governance* 15, no. 1: 67–86.

Bergsten, C. Fred. 2004. "The G20 and the World Economy." Speech to the Deputies of the G20, Leipzig, Germany. March 4 (www.iie.com/publications/papers/paper.cfm?ResearchID=196).

---

67. Kirton (2008a, 2008b, 2008c).

Boyer, Jan E., and Edwin M. Truman. 2005. "The United States and the Large Emerging-Market Economies: Competitors or Partners?" In *The United States and the World Economy: Foreign Economic Policy for the Next Decade*, edited by C. Fred Bergsten and the Institute for International Economics. Washington: Institute for International Economics.

Cooper, Andrew F., and Agata Antkiewicz, eds. 2008. *Emerging Powers in Global Governance: Lessons from the Heiligendamm Process*. Wilfrid Laurier University Press.

Dan Zhihui. 2005. "The G20 Came to China to Find the Answer for Global Economic Imbalance." *Data* 11: 22–24.

de Brouwer, Gordon. 2007. "Institutions to Promote Financial Stability: Reflections on East Asia and an Asian Monetary Fund." In *The International Monetary System, the IMF, and the G20: A Great Transformation in the Making?* edited by Richard Samans, Marc Uzan, and Augusto Lopez-Carlos. Houndmills, U.K.: Palgrave Macmillan.

de Brouwer, Gordon, and Luke Yeaman. 2007. *Australia's G20 Host Year: A Treasury Perspective*. Canberra: Treasury (www.treasury.gov.au/documents/1268/PDF/03_G-20_Article.pdf).

Fues, Thomas. 2007. "Global Governance Beyond the G8: Reform Prospects for the Summit Architecture." *International Politik und Gesellschaft* 2: 11–24 (www.fes.de/ipg/arc_07_set/set_02_07e.htm).

G-8. 1999. "Communiqué." June 20, Cologne (www.g8.utoronto.ca/summit/1999koln/finalcom.htm).

G-7 (G-7 Finance Ministers and Central Bank Governors). 1999. "Statement." Washington, September 25. (www.g8.utoronto.ca/finance/fm992509state.htm).

G-20 (G-20 Finance Ministers and Central Bank Governors). 1999. "Communiqué." Berlin, December 16 (www.g20.utoronto.ca/1999/1999communique.htm).

———. 2000. "Communiqué." Montreal, October 25 (www.g20.utoronto.ca/2000/2000communique.html).

———. 2001. "Communiqué." Ottawa, November 17 (www.g20.utoronto.ca/2001/2001communique.html).

———. 2002. "Communiqué." Delhi, November 23 (www.g20.utoronto.ca/2002/2002communique.html).

———. 2003. "Communiqué." Morelia, Mexico, October 27 (www.g20.utoronto.ca/2003/2003communique.html).

———. 2004a. "Communiqué." Berlin, November 24 (www.g20.utoronto.ca/2004/2004communique.html).

———. 2004b. "G-20 Accord for Sustained Growth." Berlin, November 24 (www.g20.utoronto.ca/2004/2004growth.html).

———. 2005a. "Communiqué." Xianghe, Hebei, China, October 16 (www.g20.utoronto.ca/2005/2005communique.html).

———. (2005b. "G-20 Statement on Reforming the Bretton Woods Institutions." Xianghe, Hebei, China, October 16 (www.g20.utoronto.ca/2005/2005bwi.html).

———. 2006. "Communiqué." Melbourne, November 19 (www.g20.utoronto.ca/2006/2006communique.html).

———. 2007. "Communiqué." Kleinmond, South Africa, November 18 (www.g20. utoronto.ca/2007/2007communique.html).

———. 2008. "Communiqué." Sno Paulo, November 9 (www.g20.utoronto. ca/2008/2008communique1109.html).

———. 2009. "Communiqué." St. Andrews, Scotland, November 7 (www.g20.utoronto. ca/2009/2009communique1107.html).

G-20 Study Group. 2008. "The Group of Twenty: A History" (www.g20.utoronto.ca/ docs/g20history.pdf).

Germain, Randall D. 2001a. "Global Financial Governance and the Problem of Inclusion." *Global Governance* 7, no. 4: 411–26.

———. 2001b. "Reforming the International Financial Architecture: The New Political Agenda." Paper presented at the International Studies Association convention, Chicago, February 20–24 (www.g8.utoronto.ca/scholar/germain2001/Germain_G20.pdf).

Helleiner, Gerry. 2001a. "Developing Countries, Global Financial Governance and the Group of Twenty: A Note." University of Toronto (www.globaleconomicgovernance. org/wp-content/uploads/Helleiner%20on%20G20.PDF).

———. 2001b. "Markets, Politics and Globalization: Can the Global Economy Be Civilized?" *Global Governance* 2, no. 1: 243–63.

Ikenberry, G. John. 2001. *After Victory: Institutions, Strategic Restraint, and the Rebuilding of Order after Major Wars.* Princeton University Press.

———. 2008. "The Rise of China and the Future of the West." *Foreign Affairs* 87, no. 1: 23–37.

Jiao Yan. 2005. "G20 New Chapter for China's Financial Diplomacy." *China Economy and Trade* 11.

Kirton, John. 1993. "The Seven-Power Summit and the New Security Agenda." In *Building a New Global Order: Emerging Trends in International Relations*, edited by David Dewitt, David Haglund, and John Kirton. Oxford University Press.

———. 2000. "The Dynamics of G7 Leadership in Crisis Response and System Reconstruction." In *Shaping a New International Financial System: Challenges of Governance in a Globalizing World*, edited by Karl Kaiser, John Kirton, and Joseph Daniels. Aldershot, U.K.: Ashgate.

———. 2001a. "The G20: Representativeness, Effectiveness and Leadership in Global Governance." In *Guiding Global Order: G8 Governance in the Twenty-First Century*, edited by John Kirton, Joseph Daniels, and Andreas Freytag. Aldershot, U.K.: Ashgate.

———. 2001b. "The G7/8 and China: Toward a Close Association." In *Guiding Global Order: G8 Governance in the Twenty-First Century*, edited by John Kirton, Joseph Daniels, and Andreas Freytag. Aldershot, U.K.: Ashgate.

———. 2001c. "Guiding Global Economic Governance: The G20, the G7 and the International Monetary Fund at Century's Dawn." In *New Directions in Global Economic Governance: Managing Globalization in the Twenty-First Century*, edited by John Kirton and George von Furstenberg. Aldershot, U.K.: Ashgate.

———. 2005a. "From G7 to G20: Capacity, Leadership, and Normative Diffusion in Global Financial Governance." Paper presented at the International Studies

Association convention, Honolulu, March 1–5 (www.g8.utoronto.ca/scholar/kirton 2005/kirton_isa2005.pdf).

———. 2005b. "Toward Multilateral Reform: The G20's Contribution." In *Reforming from the Top: A Leaders' 20 Summit*, edited by John English, Ramesh Thakur, and Andrew F. Cooper. Tokyo: United Nations University Press.

———. 2006. "Explaining Compliance with G8 Finance Commitments: Agency, Institutionalization and Structure." *Open Economies Review* 17, nos. 4–5: 459–75.

———. 2007. *Canadian Foreign Policy in a Changing World*. Toronto: Thomson Nelson.

———. 2008a. "The G20 Takes Centre Stage." In *Growth, Innovation, Inclusion: The G20 at Ten*, edited by John Kirton and Madeline Koch. London: Newsdesk.

———. 2008b. "The Performance of the Meeting of the G20 Finance Ministers and Central Bank Governors, November 8–9, Sao Paulo, Brazil" (www.g20.utoronto.ca/ analysis/2008performance1109.html).

———. 2008c. "Planning for the Future." In *Growth, Innovation, Inclusion: The G20 at Ten*, edited by John Kirton and Madeline Koch. London: Newsdesk.

Kirton, John, and Madeline Koch, eds. 2008. *Growth, Innovation, Inclusion: The G20 at Ten*. London: Newsdesk.

Kirton, John, and Ella Kokotsis. 1997/98.. "Revitalizing the G7: Prospects for the 1998 Birmingham Summit of the Eight." *International Journal* 53, no. 1: 38–56 (www. g8.utoronto.ca/scholar/kirton199801).

Kirton, John, Marina Larionova, and Paolo Savona, eds. 2010. *Making Global Economic Governance Effective: Hard and Soft Law Institutions in a Crowded World*. Farnham, U.K.: Ashgate.

Kokotsis, Eleanore. 1999. *Keeping International Commitments: Compliance, Credibility, and the G7, 1988–1995*. New York: Garland.

Martin, Paul. 2005. "A Global Answer to Global Problems: The Case for a New Leaders' Forum." *Foreign Affairs* 84, no. 3: 2–6.

———. 2008. "Time for the G20 to Take the Mantle from the G8." In *Growth, Innovation, Inclusion: The G20 at Ten*, edited by John Kirton and Madeline Koch. London: Newsdesk.

Martinez-Diaz, Leonardo. 2007. "The G20 after Eight Years: How Effective a Vehicle for Developing-Country Influence?" Global Economy and Development Working Paper 12. Brookings (www.brookings.edu/papers/2007/1017development.aspx).

Medeiros, Evan S., and M. Taylor Fravel. 2003. "China's New Diplomacy." *Foreign Affairs* 82, no. 6: 22–35.

O'Neill, Jim. 2006. "Will India Steal China's Thunder?" *International Economy* 20, no. 2: 8–21.

Parkinson, Martin. 2006. "The G20: Addressing Global Challenges." Presentation to the Australian Business Economists Luncheon, Sydney, November 8 (www.treasury.gov. au/documents/1185/HTML/docshell.asp?URL=ABE_nov2006.htm).

Porter, Tony. 2000. "The G7, the Financial Stability Forum, the G20, and the Politics of International Financial Regulation." Paper presented at the annual convention of the International Studies Association, Los Angeles, March 15 (www.g8.utoronto.ca/g20/ biblio/porter-isa-2000.pdf).

Price, Dan. 2009. "Recovery and Reform." In *The G8 2009: From La Maddalena to L'Aquila*, edited by John Kirton and Madeline Koch. London: Newsdesk.

Ruggie, John. 1983. "International Regimes, Transactions, and Change: Embedded Liberalism in the Postwar Economic Order." In *International Regimes*, edited by Stephen Krasner. Cornell University Press.

Samans, Richard, Marc Uzan, and Augusto Lopez-Carlos. 2007. "The International Monetary Convention Project: A Public-Private Exploration of the Future of the International Monetary System." In *The International Monetary System, the IMF, and the G20: A Great Transformation in the Making?* edited by Richard Samans, Marc Uzan, and Augusto Lopez-Carlos. Houndmills, U.K.: Palgrave Macmillan.

Sautter, Christian. 2008. "Fundamental Principles for Global Financial Governance." In *Growth, Innovation, Inclusion: The G20 at Ten*, edited by John Kirton and Madeline Koch. London: Newsdesk.

Slaughter, Anne-Marie. 2004. *A New World Order*. Princeton University Press.

———. 2009. "America's Edge." *Foreign Affairs* 88, no. 1: 94–113.

Soederberg, Susanne. 2002. "On the Contradictions of the New International Financial Architecture: Another Procrustean Bed for Emerging Market Economies?" *Third World Quarterly* 23, no. 4: 607–20.

Sohn, Injoo. 2005. "Asian Financial Cooperation: The Problem of Legitimacy in Global Financial Governance." *Global Governance* 11, no. 4: 487–504.

Summers, Lawrence. 2007. "Summers Speaks." *International Economy* 21, no. 4:12–17 (www.international-economy.com/TIE_F07_Summers.pdf).

———. 2008. "The Birth of the G20." In *Growth, Innovation, Inclusion: The G20 at Ten*, edited by John Kirton and Madeline Koch. London: Newsdesk.

Taylor, Ian. 2005. "South Africa: Beyond the Impasse in Global Governance." In *Reforming from the Top: A Leaders' 20 Summit*, edited by John English, Ramesh Thakur, and Andrew F. Cooper. United Nations University Press.

Weiss, Thomas. 2009. "What Happened to the Idea of World Government?" *International Studies Quarterly* 53, no. 2: 253–71.

Yu Yongding. 2005a. "China's Evolving Global View." In *Reforming from the Top: A Leaders' 20 Summit*, edited by John English, Ramesh Thakur, and Andrew F. Cooper. United Nations University Press.

———. 2005b. "The G20 and China: A Chinese Perspective." *China and World Economy* 13, no. 1: 3–14.

DANIEL W. DREZNER

10

BRIC by BRIC: The Emergent Regime for Sovereign Wealth Funds

Sovereign wealth funds (SWFs) sit at the intersection of high finance and high politics. In summer 2008 their net worth was estimated to exceed $3 trillion—more than the value of all private equity or hedge funds.[1] SWFs were responsible for 35 percent of total mergers and acquisitions activity in 2007. Between March 2007 and June 2008 these actors injected $59 billion into Western financial institutions, including high-profile equity purchases of Barclays, Citigroup, Credit Suisse, Merrill Lynch, Morgan Stanley, and UBS.[2] In January 2008 the deputy secretary of the U.S. treasury wrote that "SWFs are already large enough to be systematically significant . . . . They are likely to grow larger over time, in both absolute and relative terms."[3] Eighteen months into the Great Recession SWFs are bloodied but unbowed—they are projected to increase dramatically in size over the next decade. Indeed the global financial crisis has led many of these funds to come under even more direct control of their home governments.[4]

The explosive growth of SWFs triggered regulatory and geopolitical concerns. Market analysts and regulators were concerned about the transparency of

I am grateful to Alan Alexandroff, Charles Bralver, John Ikenberry, Eliot Kalter, Jonathan Kirshner, Doug Rediker, Nick Schulz, and Brad Setser for their thoughts and reflections. Portions of this paper were presented previously at the National Intelligence Council. Jen Weedon provided invaluable research assistance during the drafting of this paper. The usual caveat applies.

1. These categories are not mutually exclusive; by one estimate (Johnson 2007), SWFs account for 10 percent of private equity investments globally.

2. Farrell, Lund, and Sadan (2008, pp. 9–10).

3. Kimmitt (2008, p. 121).

4. See Jamil Anderlini and others, "CIC Makes Food Security a Priority," *Financial Times*, September 23, 2009.

these funds, while free market enthusiasts fretted about their ideological implications—and the protectionist backlash they could create.[5] Prominent leaders such as Germany's Angela Merkel and France's Nikolas Sarkozy worried that SWFs possessed bargaining leverage over the economic and political futures of major economies.

Many policy analysts argued that the rise of SWFs was symptomatic of shifts in the global distribution of power away from the members of the Organization for Economic Cooperation and Development (OECD) and toward the large emerging powers and energy exporters (or, using a different lens, from liberal democratic states to capitalist authoritarian states).[6] A senior OECD economist acknowledged: "What is clear is that at the present moment, [SWFs] certainly have a lot of bargaining power."[7] Brad Setser blogged, "One thing is clear: the world's biggest financial powers are no longer the world's large democracies."[8]

This chapter examines the quasi-voluntary international regime created in 2008 to regulate sovereign wealth funds, to see whether and how existing governance structures have coped with the phenomenon. The divergence of interests between recipient and host countries suggests that the regulatory outcome could signal whether power genuinely has shifted from established to rising powers. The global policy response to SWFs therefore represents an ideal test case to see whether rising states and established powers can interact within existing power structures.

The international regime for SWFs remains in chrysalis at the time of writing—emergent, rather than fully established. Nevertheless one can draw some tentative conclusions from examining the governance process to date. First, the established powers in global financial governance—the United States, the European Union, and other G-7 members—retain considerable influence in determining global economic governance. Contrary to popular perception, market power resides with the large capital importers, not the large capital exporters. This is consistent with the argument that large consumers have more bargaining leverage than do large producers over global regulatory outcomes.[10] Second, this market power in global finance is nevertheless in slow decline, which will affect the implementation of international regimes over time.

5. See Cox (2007); Truman (2007); and Markheim (2008a).

6. Lyons (2007); Behrendt (2008).

7. Quoted in Thao Hua, "Sovereign Wealth Funds Offer a Vigorous Defense," *Pensions and Investments*, March 17, 2008.

8. Brad Setser, "The Changing Balance of Global Financial Power," August 14, 2008 (blogs.cfr. org/setser/2008/08/14/the-changing-balance-of-global-financial-power/).

10. Drezner (2007).

This chapter is divided into six sections. The next section provides a brief primer on SWF. The third section details the policy concerns—at the core of which are transparency and sovereignty—that SWFs have raised. The fourth section reviews ongoing efforts to establish a global regulatory framework for SWFs. The fifth section interprets the governance process to date. The final section concludes with some speculation about the future.

A Primer on SWFs

There are as almost as many definitions of "sovereign wealth fund" are there are sovereign wealth funds.[11] I define them as *government investment vehicles that acquire international financial assets to earn a higher-than-risk-free rate of return.* This definition distinguishes SWFs from central banks that hold traditional currency reserves exclusively,[12] or state-owned enterprises that own or acquire sector-relevant affiliates overseas, or public pension funds that invest overwhelmingly in domestic assets. This definition nevertheless encompasses a variety of government investment vehicles, including stabilization funds and many pension funds.

SWFs are not a recent invention—Kuwait created the first modern fund in 1953, eight years before its independence. Nor are SWFs alien to the advanced industrialized states. Alaska, New Mexico, and Wyoming have set up SWFs designed to manage the revenues that emanate from energy booms.[13] Norway's central bank controls the Government Pension Fund-Global (GPFG), one of the largest SWFs in existence. Australia, Canada, Mexico, New Zealand, and South Korea also have funds. In total, the advanced industrialized states hold more than 40 percent of all SWF international assets.[14]

What is new about SWFs is their size, anticipated rate of growth, recent investment trends, and countries of origin. The combined heft of SWFs is currently estimated to be between $3 trillion and $3.5 trillion—or between 1 and 1.5 percent of global asset markets.[15] Randolph estimates their annual growth

11. The term was coined by Rozanov (2005). For collections and debates of these definitions, see Balding (2008); International Monetary Fund (2008); and Truman (2008a).

12. It does, however, include institutions such as China's State Administration of Foreign Exchange, the Hong Kong Monetary Authority, and the Saudi Arabian Monetary Authority, which do hold higher-risk investments. In his original definition, Rozanov (2005) observed that central banks that split reserves into separate funds for separate purposes qualified as SWFs.

13. One could also argue that the California Public Employees' Retirement System (CalPERS) also qualifies as an SWF; see Benn Steil, "California's Sovereign Wealth Fund," *Wall Street Journal*, March 7, 2008.

14. Truman (2008a).

15. Kern (2009).

rate at 24 percent between 2002 and 2007.[16] The inelastic demand for oil, combined with the persistence of global macroeconomic imbalances, led many analysts to predict an annual 20 percent growth rate over the next decade.[17] Even given the Great Recession private sector analysts have projected that the total valuation of SWFs could reach $8 trillion—or close to 4 percent of global asset markets—by 2015.[18]

Before the turn of the century most SWFs were content to keep most of their cross-border investments confined to safe assets—that is, bonds and index funds. Furthermore SWFs outsourced investment decisions to external money managers for close to half their assets.[19] In recent years, however, both trends were partially reversed. Seeking higher rates of return, SWFs shifted from portfolio investments to foreign direct investment: SWF cross-border mergers and acquisitions more than doubled between 2006 and 2007.[20] They were also increasingly attracted to "alternatives" such as hedge funds, derivatives, leveraged buyout firms, and real estate, and to commodity futures markets.[21] This affected the political calculus—controlling investments in firms triggered greater political backlash in recipient countries than did passive investments in bonds.[22] Long-established SWFs also began to manage a greater share of their assets in-house.[23] Norway's GPFG, for example, has shifted over the past eight years from having external managers handle a majority of its assets to managing most of them directly.

Although the concept of an SWF is not new, close to half the top forty funds have been created since 2000.[24] The most prominent come from manufacturing and energy powerhouses in the developing world, with the larger Middle Eastern and East Asian economies responsible for most of the world's large SWFs—of the top twenty SWFs measured by asset size, seven are based in the Middle East and nine in Pacific Rim economies. Since 2007 Brazil, China, Russia, and Saudi Arabia have all created large SWFs.

16. Randolph (2008).

17. See Jen (2007); Brad Setser and Rachel Ziemba, "Understanding the New Financial Superpower: The Management of GCC Official Foreign Assets," *RGE Monitor*, December 2007; and Randolph (2008). For a dissenting view, see Afnab Das, "SWF Growth Set to Slow," *Financial Times*, July 22, 2008.

18. "Sovereign Fund Assets to Hit $8 Trillion by 2015—Report," *Reuters*, November 16, 2009.

19. See "Managers Run 44 percent of Sovereign Wealth Assets," *Pensions and Investments*, March 7, 2008.

20. Maslakovic (2008).

21. David Cho, "Sovereign Funds Become Big Speculators," *Washington Post*, August 12, 2008.

22. See Drezner (2008a, p. 61); Miracky and others (2008, p. 12).

23. International Monetary Fund (2008, p. 9).

24. Maslakovic (2008).

Two kinds of governments pump money into sovereign wealth funds: commodity exporters and countries running fiscal and trade surpluses, with the former holding approximately two-thirds of total SWF assets.[25] For the oil exporters the incentive to create an SWF is threefold. First, these economies want to create assets that ensure a long-term stream of revenue to cushion themselves against the roller coaster of commodity booms and busts. As many economists have observed, these countries are simply converting assets extracted from the earth into a more liquid form.[26] Second, many of these governments are trying to build up reserve funds for the day when all the oil is extracted. Third, by focusing on foreign investments, these governments are attempting to forestall the "Dutch disease" of rapidly appreciating currencies. Overseas investment via sovereign wealth funds can accomplish all of these tasks.

Export engines such as China also use SWFs to keep their currencies fixed to the U.S. dollar at a low par value.[27] By 2007, for example, China had accumulated more than $1.8 trillion in foreign assets to prevent the renminbi from appreciating too rapidly and to keep Chinese exports competitive in the United States. More than 80 percent of these assets were foreign exchange reserves—safe investments with very low rates of return. As these reserves accumulated, the Chinese government debated the opportunity cost of holding dollars in such low-yield investments and expressed a willingness to diversify its holdings into higher-risk investments. This explains the equity investments made by China's State Administration of Foreign Exchange, as well as the creation of the China Investment Corporation (CIC) in 2007.[28]

The Public Policy Concerns about SWFs

As the capabilities of SWFs have increased, policymakers have focused on their intentions in global capital markets and recipient countries,[29] with three core concerns in mind. First, most SWFs lack transparency in their objectives and actions. Second, since the funds are government actors, their inherent sovereignty causes both market participants and government officials to question their motivation. Third, policymakers in recipient countries are concerned that the uncertainty surrounding SWFs' intentions could trigger the financial equivalent of the security dilemma in capital markets. If they took steps to alleviate

25. Fernandez and Eschweiler (2008, p. 8).

26. Reisen (2008).

27. Dooley, Folkerts-Landau, and Garber (2003); Summers (2006).

28. Amadan International (2008); Cognato (2008); Martin (2008).

29. See Cox (2007); Kimmitt (2008); and Truman (2008a) for overviews of the concerns discussed in this section.

security concerns about SWFs, they could trigger even greater financial insecurity from SWFs, leading to greater levels of financial protectionism.

Compared to mutual funds or pension funds, the transparency of most SWFs ranges from bad to worse.[30] For example, the largest fund, the Abu Dhabi Investment Authority (ADIA), has never revealed its size, portfolio structure, performance, or investment objectives.[31] Until early 2008, despite the fund's having been in existence for more than thirty years, ADIA's official website was confined to a single page containing no financial information; it has since been expanded to several pages, but still contains no financial information.[32] According to a 2008 survey of SWFs by the International Monetary Fund (IMF), more than a fifth are not required to report any information about their activities to their national legislatures.[33] Not all funds are as opaque as ADIA. Norway's GPFG is quite open about its objectives, ownership structure, and pattern of investment.[34] Nonetheless there is a strong positive correlation between SWF transparency and a country's democratic accountability and the quality of its legal system.[35] Not surprisingly, SWFs headquartered in the OECD countries are much more transparent than those headquartered in the so-called BRICSAM countries: Brazil, Russia, India, China, South Africa, and Mexico.[36]

Because of the lack of transparency, analysts argued that the unanticipated actions of SWFs could roil financial markets.[37] SWFs responded by pointing out that peer actors—central banks, hedge funds, and private equity—also lacked transparency. But central banks, particularly in the aftermath of the Asian financial crisis, have moved in recent years toward more public disclosure, while hedge funds and private equity firms have faced calls from public officials to open their operations to outside observers and to demands that they adhere to voluntary codes of conduct.[38] As Edwin Truman has observed, "The days of

30. Lyons (2007); Truman (2008a).

31. Fernandez and Eschweiler (2008, p. 23).

32. Bob David, "U.S. Pushes Sovereign Funds to Open to Outside Scrutiny," *Wall Street Journal,* February 26, 2008. On ADIA, see also Landon Thomas Jr., "Cash-Rich, Publicity-Shy, Abu Dhabi Fund Draws Scrutiny," *New York Times,* February 28, 2008; Emily Thornton and Stanley Reed, "Inside the Abu Dhabi Investment Authority," *Business Week,* June 6, 2008.

33. International Working Group Secretariat (2008).

34. Truman (2008a); Velculescu (2008).

35. See Beck and Firdora (2008, p. 13); Mitchell, Piggott and Kumru (2008).

36. The correlation coefficient is .64; transparency data accessed August 2008 from SWF Institute (www.swfinstitute.org/research.php).

37. Kimmitt (2008).

38. On central banks, see Geraats (2002); and Hoguet, Nugée, and Razanov (2008). On hedge funds, see Hedge Fund Working Group (2008); and President's Working Group (2008). On private equity, see Financial Stability Forum (2007); and Walker Working Group (2007).

cozy undisclosed financial arrangements by large players including hedge and private-equity funds are, and should be, drawing to a close, and that prescription applies to SWFs as well when they invest in international markets."[39]

The second source of concern about SWFs is that, by definition, they are extensions of the state and therefore their main goal is seen as maximizing their country's strategic interests rather than maximizing profit. Even defenders of SWFs as responsible financial actors acknowledge that some might have strategic objectives in their acquisitions.[40] The SWFs themselves insist that they merely seek to maximize their rate of return, but a recent survey of global financial institutions revealed that private actors believed otherwise.[41]

The sovereign backing of these wealth funds triggers a variety of policy issues. The most obvious concern is whether national governments will use their SWFs to exercise political leverage over recipient countries. This could happen through the manipulation of domestic interests—by co-opting financial actors eager to do business with SWFs.[42] It could happen through the strategic manipulation of assets owned in another country.[43] Leverage also could be exercised through the implicit or explicit threat of investment withdrawal. Indeed, in response to U.S. criticism of its activity the CIC's president warned in 2008 that "there are more than 200 countries in the world. And, fortunately, there are many countries who are happy with us."[44] The director of U.S. national intelligence declared in early 2008 that "concerns about the financial capabilities of Russia, China, and OPEC countries and the potential use of market access to exert financial leverage to achieve political ends represents a major national security issue."[45]

39. Edwin Truman, "Do Pick on Sovereign Wealth," *Wall Street Journal,* July 23, 2008.

40. Butt and others (2007, p. 75); Fernandez and Eschweiler (2008, p. 6); and Miracky and others (2008). Lyons (2007) classifies several of the large sovereign wealth funds as having "strategic" investment approaches.

41. Norton Rose (2008).

42. Andy Mukherjee, "Sovereign Wealth Funds a Boon for Asset Managers," *Bloomberg News,* October 23, 2007; Chris Larson, "Managers Eye Asian SWF Billions," *Financial Times,* August 3, 2008; Miracky and others (2008, pp. 28–29).

43. See Luft (2008); Peter Navarro, Testimony before the U.S. China Economic and Security Review Commission hearing on the Implications of Sovereign Wealth Fund Investments for National Security, Washington, February 9, 2008 (www.uscc.gov/hearings/2008hearings/written_testimonies/08_02_07_wrts/08_02_07_navarro_statement.pdf).

44. Quoted in Jamil Anderlini, "China Fund Shuns Guns and Gambling," *Financial Times,* June 13, 2008.

45. John McConnell, testimony before the U.S. Senate Select Committee on Intelligence, Washington, February 5, 2008.

Beyond political leverage, some recipient countries are concerned that SWFs tilt the playing field in mergers and acquisitions, acting to boost "national champions" in global markets.[46] A related concern is the maintenance of a level playing field in financial markets: if SWFs are an extension of the state, they might profit from exploiting other organs of the state—intelligence agencies, central banks, justice ministries—to gain an unfair advantage in acquiring assets.[47]

The final policy concern is not about SWFs per se, but about the political response to them in recipient countries. SWFs exacerbate suspicions of foreign investment because the investors are foreign governments. Indeed public hostility to such investment threatens to lead to protectionist overreaction in OECD countries. In polling, Americans are overwhelmingly opposed to SWF investment, with opposition particularly pronounced with respect to investment in high-tech or financial firms and by SWFs headquartered in the Middle East or East Asia. In the past decade alone public hysteria in the United States helped to block Dubai Ports World's acquisition of port facilities and China National Offshore Oil Corporation's attempt to acquire Unocal.[48] Politicians have responded to this public distrust in hearings and public statements hostile to SWFs, but could find themselves forced by their own public rhetoric to implement adverse economic policies.[49] As the co-chairs of the Congressional Working Group on Sovereign Wealth Funds warned, "Strong-arm tactics by our government can be counterproductive given the fact that SWFs can and will take their money elsewhere if the political risk premium for U.S. investment grows too high."[50] It should be stressed, however, that many of these concerns are still "in the realm of the hypothetical," as Truman puts it.[51]

There is in fact little evidence that SWFs have acted in any way other than as profit-maximizing actors.[52] The general consensus among financial analysts is that such funds have taken a long-term, passive approach to their overseas investments.[53] There have been, it is true, a few attempts to use SWFs as a tool of economic statecraft—though most of these efforts came from funds based in the OECD—but these efforts yielded little in the way of tangible policy

46. Truman (2008a, p. 3).

47. Cox (2007); Kimmitt (2008).

48. Bob Davis, "Americans See Little to Like in Sovereign-Wealth Funds," *Wall Street Journal*, February 21, 2008

49. See Snyder (1991, pp. 41–42).

50. James Moran and Thomas Davis, "Sovereign Good," *Wall Street Journal*, August 6, 2008.

51. Truman (2008a, p. 3).

52. Balding (2008); Miracky and others (2008).

53. For a dissenting view, see Brad Setser, "Just How Stabilizing?" July 30, 2008 (blogs.cfr.org/setser/2008/07/30/just-how-stabilizing/).

concessions and have not imposed any actual costs on targeted firms or states.[54] These results are consistent with the general consensus in international relations: threats of economic exit work only under a limited set of circumstances.[55]

From an international relations perspective, however, these concerns are not surprising. Opaque actors holding billions of dollars are inconsequential in a $200 trillion asset market. Furthermore a realist approach would argue that past evidence of good behavior is no guarantee of future behavior: As one analyst put it, "who knows what the governments of countries such as China, Russia, and Saudi Arabia may look like a decade from now, and what their political motivations might be?"[56] Given the uncertain political alignments between the home countries of significant SWFs and the primary recipient countries of SWF investment to date, it is hardly surprising that the latter would want to create governance structures that require sovereign financial actors to signal their intentions.

The Emergent Regime for SWFs

Momentum for some kind of international regime to address concerns about SWFs began in early 2007. The topic was first raised as a global governance question at an April "outreach dinner" between the G-7 finance ministers and officials from Russia, Saudi Arabia, and the United Arab Emirates. (A follow-up dinner was held in October.) SWFs were also discussed at a May meeting of the G-20 finance ministers to discuss financial stability. In June Acting Undersecretary of the Treasury for International Affairs Clay Lowery publicly stated that SWFs raised "broad, strategic issues for the international financial system" and called for the IMF and World Bank to draft best practices to address these issues.[57]

By the fall the issue had moved to the front of the queue of financial governance issues. SWF investments in preeminent financial institutions heightened public anxiety, and policy analysts began to propose concrete regulatory

54. See Beck and Fidora (2008); and Drezner (2008b). The one undeniable example of a sovereign investor's using its resources to achieve a policy concession is the purchase by China's State Administration of Foreign Exchange of $300 million in Costa Rica bonds—and $150 million in untied aid—in exchange for that country's switching its recognition from Taiwan to the government in Beijing; see Jamil Anderlini, "Beijing Uses Forex Reserves to Target Taiwan," *Financial Times*, September 11, 2008.

55. See, for example, Knorr (1975); Keohane and Nye (1978); Wagner (1988); Kirshner (1995); Drezner (1999, 2009); Crescenzi (2003); and Steil and Litan (2006).

56. Jeffrey Garten, "We Need Rules for Sovereign Funds," *Financial Times*, August 8, 2007; see also Mearsheimer (2001).

57. Clay Lowery, "Remarks on Sovereign Wealth Funds and the International Financial System." San Francisco, June 21, 2007.

responses.[58] At the urging of both the United States and France, the G-7 finance ministers called on the international financial institutions to devise a code of conduct for the SWFs and for the OECD to design best practices for recipient countries.[59]

The home countries of SWFs reacted coolly to the G-7 pronouncement. An early draft of the G-7 statement explicitly demanded that SWFs not invest with political motivations in mind, but G-7 officials were worried that this would upset Russia, China, and Saudi Arabia.[60] At the G-20 finance ministers' meeting a month later, developing country representatives were wary about the G-7 request for standards. The G-20 communiqué praised the virtues of SWFs, then merely stated that finance ministers "noted the work" of the international financial institutions, without any positive affirmation.[61] At the Davos Economic Forum in January 2008, SWF representatives rejected criticisms of their activities across the board. Muhammad Al-Jasser, the vice governor of the Saudi Arabian Monetary Agency, complained, "it's like the sovereign wealth funds are guilty until proven innocent." Some SWF representatives began to highlight their financial bargaining power. At one point Norway's finance minister Kristin Halvorsen said, "It seems you don't like us, but you need our money."[62]

In contrast the OECD process to develop recipient country guidelines generated few ripples or complaints by participants. Following open consultation with SWFs, the OECD Investment Committee issued a report concluding that "the OECD's existing investment instruments already contain fundamental principles for recipient country policies needed for the required guidance."[63] Those principles included nondiscrimination, transparency, and progressive liberalization. After the report was released, Angel Gurría, the president of the OECD, wrote, "Sovereign wealth funds, welcome! OECD markets are open for your investments . . . . [N]ational security should not be a cover for protectionism, and OECD countries have agreed to use the security argument with

58. See, for example, Rediker and Rediker (2007); and Truman (2007). Intriguingly many of these analysts had reversed course by 2008, warning against excessive action; see Jeffrey Garten, "Keep Your Rich Rivals Close," *Newsweek,* August 18, 2008.

59. See G-7 Finance Ministers and Central Bankers (2007); and Badian and Harrrington (2008, p. 53).

60. Steven Weisman, "Rules Urged to Govern Investing by Nations," *New York Times,* October 20, 2007; see also Sean O'Grady, "G7 Compromises over Calls to Reform Sovereign Wealth Funds," *The Independent,* October 20, 2007.

61. G-20 Finance Ministers and Central Bankers (2007).

62. Al-Jasser quoted in Natsuko Waki and Clara Ferreira-Marques, "Wealth Funds Bristle at Rich Country Wariness," *Reuters,* January 24, 2008; Halverson quoted in Daniel Gross, "SWF Seeks Loving American Man," *Slate,* January 24, 2008.

63. OECD (2008, p. 3).

restraint."[64] OECD members and SWFs greeted the report favorably,[65] but it also linked the response of members to the willingness of SWFs adhere to more stringent standards: "Although the OECD work focuses on host country policies, observance by SWFs of high standards of transparency, risk management, disclosure and accountability can affect the political and policy environment in which recipient countries act."[66] This was consistent with prior OECD calls for transparency in SWFs.[67]

The IMF effort was a more contentious process. The initial steps were unremarkable. The Fund's director of research wrote in September 2007 that he saw no need for "dramatic action" in response to SWFs.[68] Consultations began in November, with the first meeting described as "very successful" by the head of the IMF working group.[69] The Fund asked representatives from Singapore, Norway, and Abu Dhabi to develop benchmarks for best practices.[70] As the global credit crunch deepened, however, IMF officials reported pushback from some SWF officials at the very idea of voluntary best practices. Beyond the public complaints aired at Davos in January, officials expressed their opposition directly to Fund officials involved in drafting a work agenda.[71]

At the end of February 2008 the IMF issued a paper concurring with SWFs that many of the stated concerns about such funds were exaggerated.[72] The paper also argued, however, that there were valid regulatory concerns with regard to financial stability and transparency, justifying IMF involvement. In suggesting a work agenda the IMF proposed that an International Working Group draft a set of best practices by August, with a view to receiving approval at the meetings of the IMF and World Bank in October. The paper also called for the application of preexisting Fund standards on governance and institutional arrangements. The biggest issue was transparency on a variety of dimensions. The report argued that if SWFs were more explicit about their objectives, organizational structure, and investment portfolio, it would assuage anxieties

64. Angel Gurría, "Sovereign Wealth Funds an Opportunity, not a Threat," *The Guardian*, April 9, 2008.

65. Steve Schifferes, "Lifting the Lid on Sovereign Wealth Funds," *BBC News*, June 3, 2008; and OECD (2008). Indeed the chair's summary praised the "rapidity" with which the report had been written and accepted.

66. OECD (2008, p. 6).

67. OECD (2007, p. 40).

68. Johnson (2007).

69. Quoted in David Francis, "Will Sovereign Wealth Funds Rule the World?" *Christian Science Monitor*, November 26, 2007.

70. John Burton, "IMF urges action on sovereign wealth," *Financial Times*, January 24, 2008.

71. Steven Weisman, "Sovereign Wealth Funds Resist IMF Attempts to Draft Code of Conduct," *International Herald-Tribune*, February 9, 2008.

about their cross-border investments. The paper acknowledged that transparency on the last point was "likely to generate considerable discussion."[72] Sovereign fund officials argued that there were sound financial reasons for keeping their portfolio composition a secret.

The advanced industrialized states also took steps outside the OECD–IMF–G-7 process. Australia and the European Union issued their own voluntary guidelines for a code of conduct. The content of the EU's voluntary guidelines mirrored the IMF work agenda, stressing governance, accountability, and transparency. While the guidelines were voluntary, the president of the European Commission stated that legislation was still a possibility. He warned: "We cannot allow non-European funds to be run in an opaque manner or used as an implement of geopolitical strategy."[73]

The United States began formulating guidelines in response to the 2007 Foreign Investment and National Security Act (FINSA), which passed in response to the Dubai Ports World fiasco. FINSA toughened the national security review process investments by foreign government investment vehicles, which include SWFs. At the same time, the treasury department also worked on gaining SWF acceptance of a voluntary code of conduct. Treasury representatives consulted with SWF host officials at the Davos Forum.[74] Treasury secretary Henry Paulson met with more than thirty SWF representatives in the first quarter of 2008. As a way of signaling the desired outcome of the IMF process, the United States persuaded the ADIA and the Government of Singapore Investment Corporation jointly to issue a set of policy principles regarding SWFs and recipient countries, including commitments to governance and transparency standards and a pledge to use commercial, not political, criteria in determining investments.[75] This was significant for two reasons. First, these two funds ranked near the bottom of transparency scores on sovereign wealth funds,[76] and their commitment signaled a clear change of tack. Second, with these pledges, the G-7 by then had obtained de facto or de jure commitments to transparency from funds controlling more than half of all assets of SWFs.

72. International Monetary Fund (2008).

72. International Monetary Fund (2008, p. 26).

73. José Manuel Barroso, Statement, February 25, 2008; Tony Barber, "Brussels Pushes Wealth Funds to Sign Code," *Financial Times*, February 27, 2008.

74. Gillian Tett, "SWFs Face Growing U.S. Pressure," *Financial Times*, January 23, 2008.

75. Bob Davis, "U.S. Pushes Sovereign Funds to Open to Outside Scrutiny," *Wall Street Journal*, March 3, 2008; for the policy principles, see U.S. Department of the Treasury, "Treasury Reaches Agreement on Principles for Sovereign Wealth Fund Investment with Singapore and Abu Dhabi," Press release HP-881, Washington, March 20, 2008 (treas.gov/press/releases/hp881.htm).

76. Truman (2008a).

Other SWFs, however, responded to these steps on two parallel tracks. On one track they continued to resist any effort to craft a set of best practices within the IMF process. Russia and China in particular expressed skepticism about the IMF work agenda even before the Board of Governors had approved it. The first meetings of the International Working Group in April 2008 made little headway. In June, EU trade commissioner Peter Mandelson characterized the International Working Group negotiations as "prickly."[77] In the spring individual SWF officials were surprisingly outspoken in arguing against any code of conduct. In April the managing director of the Kuwait Investment Authority said, "Recipient countries are placing handcuffs on Sovereign Wealth Funds in the form of regulations, termed in the best tradition of George Orwell's Newspeak, by calling them code of conduct or principles of operations or best practices . . . . [T]here should be limits placed on transparency. Complete transparency would raise more questions than answers."[78] That same month Gao Xiqing, president of the CIC, told *60 Minutes* that an IMF code would "only hurt feelings" and characterized the idea as "politically stupid." In June he was more blunt, characterizing the process as "political bullshit."[79]

Outside the IMF process, however, SWFs demonstrated receptivity to greater openness. As part of a concerted effort by the CIC to tell the media that its sole concern was maximizing its rate of return on overseas investments, Gao pledged in the *60 Minutes* interview that the CIC would be as transparent as Norway's SWF. Even skeptics like Edwin Truman acknowledged that, in response to public pressure, SWFs had taken steps toward greater transparency.[80]

Despite resistance to the IMF process, the G-7 continued to push the issue. In the bilateral Strategic Economic Dialogue in June 2008, U.S. treasury secretary Paulson indicated to his Chinese counterparts that a successful IMF process would help keep barriers to investment relatively low in the United States and Europe.[81] SWF host countries increasingly understood the linkage between accepting a code of conduct and maintaining access to OECD markets. The IMF process also received encouragement in the communiqué from the G-8 meeting

77. Peter Mandelson, "The Politics of Sovereign Wealth," *Wall Street Journal*, June 7, 2008.

78. Al Sa'ad (2008).

79. *60 Minutes* (www.cbsnews.com); Jamil Anderlini, "China Fund Shuns Guns and Gambling," *Financial Times*, June 13, 2008.

80. Bruce Stokes, "New Moves on Wealth Funds," *National Journal*, March 15, 2008, p. 54. Fernandez and Eschweiler (2008, p. 6) observe that newly created SWFs were actually more transparent than older funds.

81. U.S. Department of the Treasury, "Transcript of U.S. Delegation Press Conference at the Fourth Meeting of the U.S. China Strategic Economic Dialogue," Press release HP-1048, Washington, June 18, 2008. (www.treas.gov/press/releases/hp1048.htm).

in Toyako, Japan, in early July—which meant Russia had publicly signed on to the idea of the IMF code of conduct.[82]

These G-7 efforts appeared to yield progress. The July working session of the International Working Group working session, in contrast to the previous one, constructively drafted a set of Generally Accepted Principles and Practices (GAPP). Participants agreed on institutional and governance issues, leaving transparency as the remaining sticking point;[83] they also reiterated the goal of codifying the GAPP by the October meetings of the IMF and the World Bank, although IMF officials voiced doubts that this target would be met.[84]

At the September meeting of the International Working Group in Santiago, Chile, according to a co-chair, "there was a very frank exchange between the sovereign wealth funds and the recipient countries on a whole host of topics." The primary drafter of the GAPP code noted that "there were many people in our group who did not think it was possible for us to get to the point where we could move to consultation with our governments."[85] Despite these frictions, participants reached consensus on 24 "Santiago Principles" addressing the legal framework, the institutional framework, governance issues, and risk management.[86] The head of the drafting group concluded that the Santiago Principles precisely matched the IMF's terms of reference.[87] Pledges of transparency, compliance, and profit maximization were made explicit. Principle 15, for example, stated that "SWF operations and activities in host countries should be conducted in compliance with all applicable regulatory and disclosure requirements of the countries in which they operate." Principle 19 stated that "The SWF's investment decisions should aim to maximize risk-adjusted financial returns in a manner consistent with its investment policy, and based on economic and financial grounds." Press reports characterized the outcome as "a rare triumph for IMF financial diplomacy."[88] The IMF approved the Santiago

82. G-8 (2008).

83. John Jannarone, "Sovereign Wealth Group Aims to Improve Transparency," *Dow Jones,* July 10, 2008.

84. "Sovereign Funds May not Agree to Code of Conduct," *Reuters,* July 28, 2008.

85. International Working Group of Sovereign Wealth Funds, "Press Conference Call: International Working Group of Sovereign Wealth Funds," Transcript 08/01, September 2, 2008 (www.iwg-swf.org/tr/swftr0801.htm).

86. International Working Group of Sovereign Wealth Funds, "Sovereign Wealth Funds: Generally Accepted Principles and Practices—'Santiago Principles,'" October 2008 (www.iwg-swf. org/pubs/eng/santiagoprinciples.pdf).

87. International Monetary Fund (2008).

88. Bob Davis, "Foreign Funds Agree to Set of Guiding Principles," *Wall Street Journal,* September 3, 2008

Principles at its October 2008 meeting. In April 2009 came the creation of an International Forum of Sovereign Wealth Funds to "facilitate an understanding of the Santiago Principles and SWF activities."[89]

Interpretations of the Emergent Regime

Contrary to perceptions about the enhanced bargaining power of SWFs, the established powers of global financial governance appear to have had their way. The most important SWFs have agreed in principle to greater transparency but the IMF and the G-7 remain the policy drivers on this issue. Despite the extreme reluctance of key BRICSAM countries, the most powerful SWFs have pledged to adopt the Santiago Principles.

There are two competing interpretations of this turn of events. One possibility is that the governance process will produce a "sham standards" outcome in which principles are vaguely articulated but not codified or implemented. In February 2008 an official involved in the IMF negotiations predicted the GAPP would be "toothless and devoid of anything other than motherhood and apple pie,"[90] while a financial publication characterized the International Working Group process as "pointless."[91] Nine months after the Santiago Principles were adopted, one analyst acknowledged that "authorized information on asset sizes, asset allocation, funding, investment strategies and investment transactions of SWFs is still very scarce."[92] One could also argue that the OECD's guidelines for recipient countries already resemble a sham standard. A study of the inward foreign direct investment policies of eight OECD members found a drift toward investor protectionism that was attributed explicitly to the rise of state-owned enterprises and SWFs engaging in cross-border mergers and acquisitions.[93] If OECD and IMF guidelines are promulgated but honored only in the breach, then the outcome will be a hypocritical regime in which sham standards are created.[94] If the Santiago Principles are not honored, the OECD response likely will be to block a greater number of SWF investments.[95]

89. International Working Group of Sovereign Wealth Funds, "Working Group Announces Creation of International Forum of Sovereign Wealth Funds," Press release, April 6, 2009 (www.iwg-swf.org/pr.htm).

90. Quoted in Steven Weisman, "Sovereign Wealth Funds Resist IMF Attempts to Draft Code of Conduct," *International Herald-Tribune*, February 9, 2008.

91. "IMF Persists with Pointless Sovereign Wealth 'Code'," *International Financial Law Review*, September 1, 2008.

92. Kern (2009, p. 2).

93. Marchick and Slaughter (2008).

94. Drezner (2007, pp. 81–85).

95. Marchick and Slaughter (2008).

The more likely possibility is that the code of conduct eventually becomes widely accepted. The depth of opposition from SWFs suggests they interpreted the IMF's involvement as a significant policy step, perhaps because compliance with the standards the OECD and the IMF proposed on transparency and governance would be relatively easy for private and public sector officials to observe and monitor. The consensus among financial analysts and regulators is that the Santiago Principles would address all the concerns of recipient country concerns.[96] Indeed, to date the effect of greater transparency is being felt in both home and host countries alike.[97]

What explains this outcome? The preferences of capital importers matter more than those of capital exporters, and the principal markets for inward investment remain the OECD economies. In this situation, agreement by the largest markets can trigger a cascade effect of cooperation by other market participants.[98] The United States and the EU articulated very similar preferences on SWF standards in early 2008, in sharp contrast to the heterogeneous preferences of SWF home countries—countries that housed older funds were upset with *arriviste* SWFs from the BRICSAM countries that attracted unwanted attention to their activities.[99] In the end the combined market size of the OECD economies will induce most recalcitrant states to shift their standards.

The decision by the Abu Dhabi and Singapore funds to comply with U.S. requests for transparency is consistent with this argument: they did so to prevent further strictures on cross-border investment. The Singapore fund's deputy chairman explained, "The greatest danger is if this is not addressed directly, then some form of financial protectionism will arise and barriers will be raised to hinder the flow of funds."[100] A few days before the policy principles were articulated, Abu Dhabi's director of international affairs wrote an open letter to the *Wall Street Journal* stressing the importance of an open investment climate.[101] At the Santiago meeting, the more established SWFs, combined with recipient countries, were able to apply sufficient pressure on new capital exporters to ensure agreement.[102]

96. Deloitte Touche Tohmatsu (2008); Kern (2008); Markheim (2008b); Truman (2008b); and "Perceptions GAPP," *Oxford Analytica*, October 17, 2008.

97. Natsuko Waki, "Push for Open SWFs Risks Investment Shift," *Reuters*, September 15, 2009.

98. Simmons (2001); Drezner (2007, chap. 5).

99. Krishna Guha, "Sovereign Funds Back Code," *Financial Times*, September 3, 2008.

100. Peter Thal Larsen and Martin Dickson, "Singapore Fund Pledges Greater Transparency," *Financial Times*, January 27, 2008.

101. Yousef al Otaiba, "Our Sovereign Wealth Plans," *Wall Street Journal*, March 19, 2008.

102. Krishna Guha, "Sovereign Funds Back Code," *Financial Times*, September 3, 2008.

The threat by SWFs to withdraw from OECD markets is largely hollow in the short term. It is true that many OECD economies, and prominent firms within these jurisdictions, would like SWF investment—indeed, during the depths of the credit crunch in fall 2008, several OECD countries appealed for greater SWF investments.[103] It is equally true, however, that capital exporters need the United States and Europe to keep their jurisdictions open to capital inflows—three-quarters of foreign direct investment by SWFs is concentrated in the developed world, particularly in Germany, the United States, and the United Kingdom.[104] Most other asset markets are neither big enough nor open enough to cater to large-scale sovereign wealth investments. Large market jurisdictions—the Japan, United States, and the EU—remain the only ones deep and liquid enough to absorb inflows in the trillions of dollars.[105]

A Warning Note

The emergent regime on sovereign wealth funds suggests that the established powers and institutions in global financial governance are far from dead. On the financial dimension, the rise of the BRICSAM countries does not appear to presage a serious disruption in the global political economy. The home countries of SWFs have not balanced or organized against the G-7's effort to create a regime to govern their behavior. The emergent regime lends some credence to John Ikenberry's argument that existing global governance structures can accommodate the rise of the non-West.[106]

The 2007–08 global financial crisis also exposed some of the weaknesses of sovereign wealth funds.[107] The crisis devastated the balance sheets of many, with paper losses of up to 25 percent estimated for 2008, and a 15 percent reduction in long-term growth.[108] In 2008, Norway's fund reported a negative return of 23 percent, Singapore's Temasek lost more than 30 percent of its holdings, and Deutsche Bank projected a 45 percent loss in the equity investment of

---

103. "Spain wants sovereign wealth funds to help cover its debt," *Reuters*, October 20, 2008.

104. UNCTAD (2008).

105. Johnson (2007) notes that the total value of all traded securities in Latin America, Africa, and the Middle East is less than $8 trillion.

106. Ikenberry (forthcoming).

107. Heather Connon, "Sovereign Funds Lose $1bn in Western Banks," *The Guardian*, September 28, 2008; Rachel Ziemba, "Sovereign Wealth Funds: Tallying the Losses (Again)," *RGE Monitor*, November 25, 2008; Stanley Reed, "Sovereign Wealth Funds Taste Bitter Losses," *Business Week*, December 11, 2008; Natsuko Waki, "Sovereign Wealth Funds May Be Net Sellers of World," *Reuters*, December 15, 2008.

108. Jen and Andreopoulos (2008).

SWFs over the previous eighteen months.[109] The subsequent flight of private capital back to the OECD economies encouraged all governments with SWFs to redirect their investments inward to bolster sagging equity markets.[110] The rapid decline in oil prices and global export volumes led to immense pressure on SWFs to invest in their home economies to boost domestic growth.[111] These trends reduced anxieties in the OECD economies about SWF investment practices. By the end of 2009 the SWF issue had largely faded into the political background.

A note of caution, however, should be sounded about the future. This emergent regime rests on a traditional source of power: market size. But what happens once other countries develop capital markets equal in size to those of the OECD economies?[112] From 2008 onwards, a number of sizable funds announced intentions to increase their investments in East Asia and other emerging markets. The head of Dubai International Capital explained, "The world is changing fast. When we think about where the real growth will be in the years ahead, we are very much looking to Asia."[113] As economists point out, this trend is consistent with efforts by these funds to increase their rate of return from exposure to greater risk.[114]

The more that sovereign wealth funds bypass OECD markets, the more "go-it-alone" power they possess[115]—indeed non-OECD economies are developing ever-greater economic linkages that do not rely on the advanced industrialized states.[116] In the long run, the more that SWFs diversify away from Western markets, the less they need to adhere to Western rules.

Ironically, the policy responses to the Great Recession have also mitigated concerns. The greater degree of state intervention in the economy, in the form of bailouts and quantitative easing, has made it intellectually more problematic for OECD countries to object to active state investors, including SWFs.[117]

---

109. "Singapore Wealth Fund Loses Steam," *BBC News*, February 10, 2009; Robert Anderson, "Norway Reviews €75bn Loss in Wealth Fund," *Financial Times*, April 3, 2009; Kern (2009, p. 8).

110. Miracky and Bortolotti (2009, p. 17).

111. Andrew England and Robin Wigglesworth, "Mideast States Urged to Prop Up Stocks," *Financial Times*, September 16, 2008; Landon Thomas Jr., "Sovereign Wealth Funds Seek Safety," *International Herald Tribune*, October 12, 2008; David Ibison, "Norway to Dip into $332bn Oil Fund," *Financial Times*, December 15, 2008.

112. See Drezner (2007, 2008b).

113. Quoted in William Pesek, "Chrysler Building May be Aberration," *Bloomberg*, July 23, 2008.

114. See Beck and Fidora (2008); International Monetary Fund (2008).

115. Gruber (2000).

116. Barma, Ratner, and Weber (2007).

117. Grennes (2009).

Over time, perhaps, the governance structures and practices of sovereign wealth funds and OECD governments will converge.

References

Al Sa'ad, Bader M. 2008. "Overview on the Kuwait Investment Authority and Issues Related to Sovereign Wealth Funds." Keynote address at the First Luxembourg Foreign Trade Conference, Luxembourg, April 9 (www.kia.gov.kw/En/About_KIA/Overview_of_KIA/Pages/default.aspx).

Amadan International. 2008. "The Creation of the China Investment Corporation." Washington, January.

Badian, Laura, and Gregory Harrington. 2008. "The Politics of Sovereign Wealth." *The International Economy* 22, no. 1: 52–84.

Balding, Christopher. 2008. "A Portfolio Analysis of Sovereign Wealth Funds." HSBC School of Business, Shenzhen, China (ssrn.com/abstract=1141531).

Barma, Naazneen, Ely Ratner, and Steven Weber. 2007. "A World without the West." *The National Interest* 90 (July-August): 23–30.

Beck, Roland, and Michael Fidora. 2008. "The Impact of Sovereign Wealth Funds on Global Financial Markets." Occasional Paper Series 91. Frankfurt-am-Main: European Central Bank (July).

Behrendt, Sven. 2008. "When Money Talks: Arab Sovereign Wealth Funds in the Global Public Policy Discourse." *Carnegie Papers* 12 (October).

Butt, Shams, and others. 2007. "Sovereign Wealth Funds: A Growing Global Force in Corporate Finance." *Journal of Applied Corporate Finance* 19 (Winter): 73–83.

Cognato, Michael. 2008. "China Investment Corporation: Threat or Opportunity?" *NBR Analysis* 19 (June): 9–36.

Cox, Christopher. 2007. "The Rise of Sovereign Business." Gauer Distinguished Lecture in Law and Public Policy, American Enterprise Institute, Washington, December 5.

Crescenzi, Mark. 2003. "Economic Exit, Interdependence, and Conflict." *Journal of Politics* 65 (August): 809–32.

Deloitte Touche Tohmatsu. 2008. *Minding the GAPP: Sovereign Wealth, Transparency, and the "Santiago Principles."* October.

Dooley, Michael, David Folkerts-Landau, and Peter Garber. 2003. "An Essay on the Revived Bretton Woods System." NBER Working Paper W9971. Cambridge, Mass.: National Bureau of Economic Research.

Drezner, Daniel W. 1999. *The Sanctions Paradox: Economic Statecraft and International Relations.* Cambridge University Press.

———. 2007. *All Politics Is Global: Explaining International Regulatory Regimes.* Princeton University Press.

———. 2008a. "The Realist Tradition in American Public Opinion." *Perspectives on Politics* 6 (March): 51–70.

———. 2008b. "Sovereign Wealth Funds and the (In)Security of Global Finance." *Journal of International Affairs* 62 (Fall/Winter): 115–30.

———. 2009. "Bad Debts: Assessing China's Financial Influence in Great Power Poli-tics." *International Security* 34, no. 2: 7–45.

Farrell, Diana, Susan Lind, and Koby Sadan. 2008. "The New Power Brokers: Gaining Clout in Turbulent Markets." McKinsey Global Institute (July).

Fernandez, David, and Bernhard Eschweiler. 2008. *Sovereign Wealth Funds: A Bottom-Up Primer.* Singapore: JPMorgan Research.

G-8. 2008. "Communiqué on the World Economy." Hokkaido Toyako, Japan, Summit, July 8 (www.g8.utoronto.ca/summit/2008hokkaido/2008-economy.html).

G-7 Finance Ministers and Central Bankers. 2007. "Statement." Washington, October 19 (www.g8.utoronto.ca/finance/fm071019.htm).

G-20 Finance Ministers and Central Bankers. 2007. "Statement." Kleinmond, South Africa, November 18 (www.g8.utoronto.ca/g20/g20-071118.html).

Geraats, Petra. 2002. "Central Bank Transparency." *Economic Journal* 112 (November): F532–65.

Grennes, Thomas. 2009. "The Volatility of Sovereign Wealth Funds." *Global Economy Journal* 9, no. 3, article 7.

Gruber, Lloyd. 2000. *Ruling the World: Power Politics and the Rise of Supranational Insti-tutions.* Princeton University Press.

Hoguet, George, John Nugée, and Andrew Rozanov. 2008. *Sovereign Wealth Funds: Assessing the Impact.* State Street Global Advisors Vision Report (July).

Ikenberry, G. John. Forthcoming. *Liberal Leviathan: The Origins, Crisis, and Transforma-tion of the American System.* Princeton University Press.

International Monetary Fund. 2008. "Sovereign Wealth Funds—A Work Agenda." Wash-ington, February 29 (www.imf.org/external/np/pp/eng/2008/022908.pdf).

International Working Group Secretariat. 2008. "Sovereign Wealth Funds: Current Institutional and Operational Practices." International Working Group of Sovereign Wealth Funds, September 15 (www.iwg-swf.org/pubs/eng/swfsurvey.pdf).

Jen, Stephen. 2007. "How Big Could Sovereign Wealth Funds be by 2015?" Morgan Stan-ley Research Global (May 3).

Jen, Stephen, and Spyros Andreopoulos. 2008. "SWFs: Growth Tempered—US$10 Tril-lion by 2015." Morgan Stanley Research Global (November 10).

Johnson, Simon. 2007. "The Rise of Sovereign Wealth Funds." *Finance and Development* 44, no. 3: 56–57.

Keohane, Robert, and Joseph Nye. 1978. *Power and Interdependence.* Boston: Scott Foresman.

Kern, Steffen. 2008. "SWFs and Foreign Investment Policies—An Update." Frankfurt-am-Main: Deutsche Bank Research (October 22).

———. 2009. "Sovereign Wealth Funds—State Investments during the Financial Crisis." Frankfurt-am-Main: Deutsche Bank Research (July 15).

Kimmitt, Robert. 2008. "Public Footprints in Private Markets." *Foreign Affairs* 87 (Janu-ary-February): 119–30.

Kirshner, Jonathan. 1995. *Currencies and Coercion.* Princeton University Press.

Knorr, Klaus. 1975. *The Power of Nations.* New York: Basic Books.

Luft, Gal. 2008. "Selling Out: Sovereign Wealth Funds and Economic Security." *The American Interest* 3 (July-August): 53–56.

Lyons, Gerald. 2007. "State Capitalism: The Rise of Sovereign Wealth Funds." Standard Chartered (October).

Marchick, David, and Matthew Slaughter. 2008. "Global FDI Policy: Correcting a Protectionist Drift." Special Report 34. New York: Council on Foreign Relations (June).

Markheim, Daniella. 2008a. "Sovereign Wealth Funds and U.S. National Security." Heritage Lecture 1063. Washington: Heritage Foundation (February 7).

———. 2008b. "Sovereign Wealth Funds: New Voluntary Principles a Step in the Right Direction." Heritage WebMemo 2175. Washington: Heritage Foundation (December 18).

Martin, Michael. 2008. "China's Sovereign Wealth Fund." Washington: Congressional Research Service Report (January 22).

Maslakovic, Marko. 2008. "Sovereign Wealth Funds 2008." London: International Financial Services (April).

Mearsheimer, John. 2001. *The Tragedy of Great Power Politics.* New York: Norton.

Miracky, William, and others. 2008. *Assessing the Risks: The Behaviors of Sovereign Wealth Funds in the Global Economy.* Cambridge: Monitor Group.

Miracky, William, and Bernardo Bortolotti, eds. 2009. *Weathering the Storm: Sovereign Wealth Funds in the Global Economic Crisis of 2008.* Cambridge: Monitor Group.

Mitchell, Olivia, John Piggott, and Cagri Kumru. 2008. "Managing Public Investment Funds: Best Practices and New Challenges." NBER Working Paper 14078. Cambridge, Mass.: National Bureau of Economic Research (June).

Norton Rose. 2008. "Sovereign Wealth Funds and the Global Private Equity Landscape." (www.nortonrose.com/knowledge/publications/2008/pub15287.aspx?page=all&lang=eng-gb).

OECD. 2007. *OECD Economic Outlook* 82. Paris: Organization for Economic Cooperation and Development (December).

———. 2008. *Sovereign Wealth Funds and Recipient Country Policies.* Paris: OECD (April).

Randolph, Jen. 2008. *Sovereign Wealth Fund Tracker.* Global Insight, April.

Rediker, Douglas, and Heidi Crebo-Rediker. 2007. "Foreign Investment and Sovereign Wealth Funds." Working Paper 1. Washington: New America Foundation Global Strategic Finance Initiative (September 25).

Reisen, Helmut. 2008. "Commodity and Non-commodity Sovereign Wealth Funds." Frankfurt-am-Main: Deutsche Bank Research (July).

Rozanov, Andrew. 2005. "Who Holds the Wealth of Nations?" *Central Banking Journal* 15 (November): 52–57.

Simmons, Beth. 2001. "The International Politics of Harmonization: The Case of Capital Market Integration." *International Organization* 55, no. 3: 589–620.

Steil, Benn, and Robert Litan. 2006. *Financial Statecraft.* Yale University Press.

Summers, Lawrence. 2006. "Reflections on Global Account Imbalances and Emerging Markets Reserve Accumulation." L. K. Jha Memorial Lecture, Reserve Bank of India, Mumbai, March 24 (www.president.harvard.edu/speeches/2006/0324_rbi.html).

Truman, Edwin. 2007. "Sovereign Wealth Funds: The Need for Greater Transparency and Accountability." Policy Brief 07-6. Washington: Peterson Institute for International Economics (August).

———. 2008a. "A Blueprint for Sovereign Wealth Fund Best Practices." Policy Brief PB08-3. Washington: Peterson Institute for International Economics (April).

———. 2008b. "Making the World Safe for Sovereign Wealth Funds." Washington: Peterson Institute for International Economics, October 14 (www.iie.com/realtime/?p=105).

UNCTAD. 2008. *World Investment Report: Transnational Corporations and the Infrastructure Challenge*. New York: United Nations Conference on Trade and Development.

Velculescu, Delia. 2008. "Norway's Oil Fund Shows the Way for Wealth Funds." *IMF Survey* 37 (July): 110–11.

Wagner, R. Harrison. 1988. "Economic Interdependence, Bargaining Power, and Political Influence." *International Organization* 42 (Summer): 461–83.

FLYNT LEVERETT

11

Consuming Energy: Rising Powers, the International Energy Agency, and the Global Energy Architecture

For the past thirty years or so, international markets for crude oil and its increasingly important companion, natural gas, have operated under discernible "rules of the game" and accompanying institutional frameworks. These rules and framework were established largely as a consequence of policy initiatives launched by the United States in cooperation with other advanced industrial nations. These initiatives were undertaken in response to the ascendance of the Organization of the Petroleum Exporting Countries (OPEC) as a major force in the production and marketing of crude oil during the 1970s. Collectively the rules and frameworks that emerged from these initiatives—including the liberalization of upstream oil and gas sectors in much of the non-OPEC world, the cultivation of a single integrated market for international oil trading, and the creation of the International Energy Agency (IEA) as a formal oil consumers' "regime"—may be said to constitute a global energy "architecture." This architecture consists of an interconnected set of market norms and practices and formal and informal institutions intended to enhance energy security for major consumer states.[1]

This U.S.-sponsored global energy architecture seems to have been quite successful during the late 1980s and 1990s in "pushing back" against OPEC's prior assertion of market power in the 1970s. Since the turn of the millennium, however, ongoing structural shifts in international energy markets have put various pillars of the global energy architecture under increasing strain, manifested most

The author is grateful to Hillary Mann Leverett for her comments on successive drafts of this chapter as well as her inestimable contributions to his understanding and analysis of the issues treated here. He is also grateful for the comments of Alan Alexandroff, Steven Bernstein, Gregory Chin, Miles Kahler, Andrew Moravcsik, Amrita Narlikar, and others.
1. See Leverett (2008b).

prominently in sharply rising oil and gas prices from 1999 through the first half of 2008.[2] Even with the downturn in energy prices in the second half of 2008, ongoing structural shifts in international energy markets (and a partial recovery of energy prices during 2009) are prompting serious questions about the adequacy of existing governance arrangements for international energy markets.

Structural shifts in international energy markets, on both the demand side and the supply side, are inextricably bound up with the rise of new power centers in international affairs. Among the "rising states" singled out for consideration in this volume, China and India have emerged as new demand centers for hydrocarbon-based energy at the same time as they are establishing themselves as increasingly influential players in the global economy and international politics more broadly. In coming years and decades, promoting global energy security will require the effective renovation of the existing international energy architecture to incorporate rising power centers into the structures and mechanisms of energy governance.[3] In particular, the rise of China and India as new demand centers for hydrocarbon-based energy holds potentially profound implications for the composition and functioning of the IEA, the part of the current global energy architecture that is most directly affected by the emergence of new powers in the international order.

Unless it incorporates the rising powers, I argue, the IEA will become ever less able to contribute positively to effective global energy governance. Bringing China and India into the IEA, however, will take, in essence, a "re-invention" of the agency, including a thoroughgoing redistribution of decisionmaking power within it. At present there is no consensus among IEA members in favor of such

2. The trend toward higher oil prices can be dated to March 1999, when OPEC, for the first time since 1985, successfully increased market prices by limiting member states' production. Between March 1999 and September 2000 oil prices roughly tripled—albeit from a low base—as a result of OPEC's actions. In September 2000 OPEC publicly stated that it would work to keep its "basket" price for crude oil within a $22–$28 a barrel price range. In keeping with that commitment, oil prices remained relatively stable from September 2000 until November 2003, when rising demand from Asia began to drive prices steadily upward. Then, from November 2003 until the first half of 2008, oil prices effectively quadrupled. With the onset of the global financial crisis in the summer of 2008, oil prices declined substantially in the second half of the year, but recovered significantly in 2009. Notwithstanding the decline in prices from their historic highs in the first half of 2008, they remain noticeably higher than in the 2000–03 period. Moreover, prices are very likely to rise more in the longer term.

3. Another important aspect of renovating the global energy architecture is likely to be the alignment of governance structures for international oil and gas markets with emerging governance structures in separate but related issue areas—for example, the investment activities of sovereign wealth funds, as considered in Daniel Drezner's chapter in this volume, and, of course, climate change.

a redistribution of power. Whether established powers are prepared to share decisionmaking authority with rising states such as China and India is shaping up to be a fundamental challenge of effective global governance in the twenty-first century.

This chapter develops arguments concerning the IEA and global energy governance in four sections. The first section examines the origins and evolution of the existing global energy architecture, including the emergence and evolution of the IEA, as an exercise in international leadership by the United States. The second section looks more specifically at the IEA's place in the current energy architecture and its evolving role in global energy governance. The third section looks at ongoing structural shifts on both the demand side and the supply side of international oil and gas markets, and at the strains these shifts are exerting on the existing global energy architecture. Finally, the chapter explores what it would mean for the IEA to accommodate rising power centers such as China and India.

Designing the Current Architecture

The new institutional economics reminds us that real-world markets—as opposed to the approaches presented in microeconomics textbooks—are historically evolved social constructs. To use the language of new institutional economics, markets and economies more broadly are shaped by the continuous interaction of "organizations" (the "players of the game," including both political and economic actors) and "institutions" (the humanly constructed "rules of the game" that structure interactions under conditions of scarcity and competition).[5] The new institutional economics also teaches that institutions are themselves the products of "political markets" in which the relative balance of bargaining power among various actors exerts determinative influence on institutions' origins and subsequent evolution.[6]

In the real world, therefore, markets are always "governed"—that is, they operate within systems of norms, rules, and, at least potentially, instruments and procedures to enforce the rules. Furthermore these structures of market governance are themselves the products of political bargaining and exchange. Of course, the notion of socially constructed markets operating under politically generated modes of governance applies to transnational markets as well as to purely domestic markets.

5. The definitions of organizations and institutions are adapted from Alexandra Benham, "Brief Glossary of New Institutional Economics" St. Louis, Mo.: Ronald Coase Institute (www.coase.org/nieglossary.htm).

6. For an overview, see North (1993).

A focus on market governance is especially appropriate with regard to international energy markets. In the real world, oil and gas markets have never come close to the paradigms of microeconomic theory; among other things, the operation of these markets has always entailed the generation and capture of "rents" and the internalization of significant transaction costs. Furthermore, to a greater extent than most industries, the energy business has always been intensely political, and outcomes in international energy markets have always carried strategic implications going far beyond purely commercial considerations.

For much of the twentieth century, international energy markets operated within institutional frameworks defined largely by the United States. The legacy of the United States' hegemonic influence is clearly manifest in the current array of formal and informal principles, norms, rules, and decisionmaking procedures that shape actors' calculations regarding international energy markets. It is these structures of global energy governance—including the operation of formal international organizations like the IEA—that constitute the global energy architecture.

Employing the standard definition of an international regime as "principles, norms, rules, and decision-making procedures around which actor expectations converge in a given issue-area,"[7] it is difficult to argue that there is a single regime addressing international interdependence with respect to hydrocarbon-based energy resources. There is a set of norms, rules, and decisionmaking procedures, formally embodied in the IEA, to coordinate the maintenance and use of strategic petroleum reserves by industrialized consumer states belonging to the Organization for Economic Cooperation and Development (OECD). But there are also other discrete sets of norms, rules, and decisionmaking procedures, each of them dealing with a different aspect of the production and international marketing of crude oil and natural gas.

In some respects the interaction of various energy-related international regimes has had a perceptible impact on real-world outcomes with regard to energy security and global energy governance: in another context the term "regime complex" has been suggested to describe situations in which multiple formal regimes intersect in the governance of a particular issue area.[8] In other respects, though, global energy governance is characterized by what could be described as "regime fragmentation," especially as ongoing structural shifts in international energy markets put existing governance mechanisms under increasing strain.[9] What is needed, under these circumstances, is an efficient

7. Krasner (1983, p. 1).
8. See Raustiala and Victor (2004).
9. The author is grateful to Steve Bernstein for this point.

rubric that captures the array of market rules and practices and formal and informal institutions involved in governing international energy markets. The phrase "the global energy architecture" seems to fit well.

The existing global energy architecture took shape in response to OPEC's dramatic assertion of market power in the 1970s.[10] During the 1960s OPEC members consolidated effective national control over their oil and gas sectors by revising Western oil companies' concessions via equity participation and, in many cases, outright nationalization. By the early 1970s OPEC production represented a significant enough portion of global oil supply that members could leverage substantially higher prices on the international oil market by adjusting their production levels under the group's quota system—a classic expression of market power.[11] Through the 1970s and the first half of the 1980s, OPEC oil ministers set not only member states' production quotas but also world oil prices, using Arabian Light as a benchmark crude and defining reference prices for member states' oil exports.[12]

For some analysts, the rise of OPEC and its subsequent assertion of market power was an early indicator of decline in the status of the United States as the world's economic hegemon.[13] These assessments notwithstanding, the subsequent design and construction of a new global energy architecture in response to OPEC's assertion of market power were intimately bound up with the continuing exercise of international leadership by the United States.[14] It should hardly be surprising that the architecture that took shape under U.S. leadership strongly reflects both U.S. ideological preferences—in particular, an emphasis

10. In microeconomic theory, market power is normally defined as the ability of a market actor—producer or consumer—to alter the market price of a good or service

11. Overall, world oil prices increased by more than 500 percent during the 1970s. Largely as a result of collective decisions and actions by Arab members of OPEC in the last quarter of 1973, world prices for crude oil more than tripled in the space of three months, going from roughly $3 per barrel to over $11. From 1974 through 1978, world oil prices were relatively flat, ranging between $12 and $14 a barrel. However, at the end of the 1970s and beginning of the 1980s— through the combined effects of the Iranian revolution, actions by some OPEC member states (most notably Saudi Arabia), and the outbreak of the Iran-Iraq war—oil prices once again more than doubled, rising from roughly $14 a barrel to roughly $35 a barrel in 1981.

12. For discussion, see Skeet (1988, pp. 99–177); Parra (2004); and Mabro (2005).

13. Thus, Robert Keohane, writing in 1984, summarized his account of the "collapse" of the post-World War II petroleum "regime" by arguing that "the transformation of oil politics between the mid-1960s and the mid-1980s reflected a decline in the ability of the United States, acting in conjunction with Britain and the major oil companies, to make the rules and support the regime" (Keohane 1984, pp. 202–03).

14. For an insightful discussion of the U.S. role in forging a post-1973 global energy architecture, see Noël (2004).

on market-oriented tools and approaches—and an interest in preserving U.S. hegemony over international energy affairs to the greatest extent possible.

At least three pillars of the current global energy architecture warrant consideration as products of international leadership by the United States: upstream liberalization, market integration, and—of most immediate relevance to this chapter—creation of the IEA. In addition, the United States' provision of physical security for the world's oil flows, especially from the Persian Gulf, has reinforced U.S. influence over the global energy architecture.

Upstream Liberalization

For more than a quarter of a century, the United States has encouraged the opening of upstream oil and gas sectors around the world to foreign investment. This effort, inaugurated during the Reagan administration, represents U.S. policymakers' most direct resort to market-based approaches to push back against OPEC's market power. Specifically, upstream liberalization was aimed at boosting both non-OPEC oil production and the production of natural gas, which began to emerge in the 1980s as an increasingly attractive alternative to oil as a fuel for power generation.[15]

In practical terms, of course, there was not going to be a return to a "pre-OPEC" environment, with international energy companies based in the United States or western Europe holding oil and gas concessions throughout the developing world's most important hydrocarbon provinces. But, as an alternative to restoration of a concession-based *ancien regime,* the United States began during the 1980s to promote the adoption of investment regimes by energy-producing states that would offer Western energy companies the prospect of "risked" investment contracts, best exemplified in so-called production sharing agreements (PSAs).[16]

For the most part the Reagan administration and its successors promoted the liberalization and internationalization of upstream sectors around the world through bilateral engagement with individual energy producers in the Middle East, Latin America, Africa, and Asia. After the breakup of the Soviet Union, the Clinton administration extended U.S. promotion of upstream liberalization to Russia and former Soviet republics in the Caspian Basin. Although PSAs had originated in the 1960s, U.S.-encouraged upstream liberalization led to the diffusion of PSAs and similar instruments across literally dozens of countries during the 1980s and 1990s.

---

15. On the growing role of natural gas in the global energy balance since the 1973 oil embargo, see Barnes and others (2006, pp. 6–9).

16. For useful introductions to PSAs, see, *inter alia,* Johnston (1994); and Bindermann (1999).

Market Integration

Along with its promotion of upstream liberalization, the United States provided critical support to the creation of a single, integrated, and truly global market for trading crude oil and refined products, with prices based on spot transactions and the U.S. dollar serving as the currency in which oil is priced. Apart from a relatively brief episode during Henry Kissinger's tenure as secretary of state, the United States has resisted proposals to "manage" international energy markets through producer-consumer dialogues—particularly proposals for producer-consumer dialogues that would address the question of oil and gas prices. Instead, successive U.S. administrations have sought to bolster the role of market-oriented approaches to structuring and operating international energy markets.[17]

An important early step down this road was the Carter administration's decision, in April 1979, to decontrol domestic oil prices in the United States. Following domestic deregulation successive U.S. administrations and cooperative OECD partners have sought to steer more of the world's oil trade into the spot market or into contracts based on spot prices, rather than the long-term supply contracts favored by OPEC producers. As more and more non-OPEC oil production began to enter the international market in the late 1970s and early 1980s, exchanges in New York and London began to handle an ever-expanding portion of the world's oil trade. By the late 1980s the spot, futures, and options markets on the New York Mercantile Exchange (NYMEX, using West Texas Intermediate as its principal benchmark crude) and the International Petroleum Exchange in London (now the Intercontinental Exchange, or ICE, using Brent Crude as its principal benchmark) had consolidated their standing as the international oil market's principal arenas for price formation.[18]

The Creation of the IEA

The United States played a key role in establishing the IEA, as both the formal embodiment of a new oil consumers' "regime" and the rallying point for marshalling support among OECD states on behalf of market-based approaches to energy security. In this latter role the IEA became, in effect, a multilateral forum for building support among industrialized energy consumers for upstream liberalization and market integration.

---

17. Goldthau and Witte (2009, pp. 375–77) also identify the creation of a "liquid, competitive, and truly liquid" oil market as an important step in forging the existing institutional framework governing international energy markets, but without addressing the political factors conditioning this step.

18. For a useful overview and analysis, see Mabro (2005).

The IEA was founded in 1974 largely at the instigation of the United States as an autonomous agency of the OECD. Originally, the United States—under the Nixon and Ford administrations, with Secretary of State Henry Kissinger playing a dominant policymaking role—envisioned the IEA as an authoritative forum for multidimensional cooperation among OECD countries to limit their oil imports and stimulate non-OPEC oil production. On this basis the IEA would then serve as the consumer states' platform for negotiating with OPEC over production levels and prices. In Kissinger's original vision, the IEA was to be the spearhead that the United States and its allies would use to "roll back" the dramatic increases in oil prices OPEC had wrought.[19]

In the end the IEA did not take on such an encompassing set of strategic tasks, largely because the United States and other key industrial countries had different views of the oil supply challenges of the 1970s. The United States interpreted the crises of the 1970s primarily in terms of "price risk"—that is, volatility in and upward pressure on the prices of crude oil and refined products. Other OECD states, most notably France (which did not initially join the IEA) and Japan, interpreted the oil supply problem during the 1970s in terms of "volume risk"—the prospective inadequacy of oil supplies available on the international market. On top of these analytic differences with some of its OECD partners, the United States never consistently or effectively pursued policies that would have enabled it to meet serious targets in reducing its overall oil demand. This failure helped to undermine the plausibility of U.S. ambitions that the IEA define and enforce limits on oil imports for other OECD states.

The failure to realize Kissinger's original ambitions for the IEA led some early commentators, such as G. John Ikenberry, to conclude that the agency's contributions to global energy governance would not be particularly significant.[20] But the IEA's record in the years since its founding suggests that the agency has indeed become an important pillar of the global energy architecture.[21]

The Military Dimension

Beyond exercising leadership in the creation of these three pillars of the global energy architecture, U.S. influence in international energy affairs has been

19. See Ikenberry (1988). For Kissinger's account of this episode, see his *Years of Upheaval* (1982, chaps. 19, 20); and *Years of Renewal* (1999, chap. 22).

20. In this regard, Ikenberry argues that, with the abandonment of Kissinger's original ambitions for the IEA, the organization "became a modest mechanism for contingency oil-sharing agreements and the exchange of information . . . . As a device by which to recapture the erstwhile petroleum order, however, the IEA fell far short of American hopes" (1988, p. 10).

21. On the origins and evolution of the IEA, see Scott (1994, 1995, 1996); and Bamberger (2004).

ed by the United States' commitment to provide physical security for the
oil flows, particularly from the Persian Gulf.[22] Since the promulgation
Carter Doctrine in 1980 and the "Reagan corollary" in 1981, the United
has publicly committed to use force to defend the security of Persian Gulf
rves and the free flow of oil exports from the region as vital U.S. interests. Spurred by these commitments, the United States has built up operational capabilities that have turned the Persian Gulf, in military terms, into an
"American lake."

The IEA Regime

A first step is to look at the IEA's place within the global energy architecture. At
one level the IEA might be described as a formal energy consumers' regime; at
another level it might be evaluated in terms of the functions it performs that
contribute to the broader project of global energy governance. The IEA is the
organizational embodiment of a formal regime for industrialized consumers of
hydrocarbon-based energy, from which it is possible to break out four constitu-
ent elements.[24]

The first element is its *principles*. In the literature on international regimes,
principles are commonly defined as statements of fundamental belief about
causation or rectitude that define a regime's purpose. The underlying principle
of the IEA-centered regime can be stated as: the advanced industrial democracies (until recently, a category embracing the world's most important consumers of hydrocarbon-based energy) should commit themselves to and prepare

22. This discussion is adapted from Leverett (2008b, p. 229).

23. From the 1940s through the 1970s, in an accumulating collection of public statements
and policy documents, successive U.S. administrations defined the security of Persian Gulf oil
reserves and the free flow of oil exports from the region as vital interests of the United States. But
the United States did not commit itself, in either its formal declaratory posture or its operational
posture, to project substantial military power into the region, until the 1980s. After the Iranian
revolution in 1979 and the Soviet invasion and occupation of Afghanistan later that year, President Jimmy Carter declared in his January 1980 State of the Union address that the presence of
Soviet military forces in Afghanistan posed "a grave threat to the free movement of Middle East
oil," pledging that "an attempt by any outside force to gain control of the Persian Gulf region
will be regarded as an assault on the vital interests of the United States of America, and such an
assault will be repelled by any means necessary, including military force." In October 1981, following the outbreak of the Iran-Iraq war, President Ronald Reagan extended the Carter Doctrine
by explicitly committing the United States to defend the Saudi monarchy.

24. The definitions of principles, norms, rules, and decisionmaking procedures employed in
this discussion are adapted from Krasner (1983, pp. 1–2); and Keohane (1984, pp. 57–59). The
application of these definitions to the IEA-centered energy consumers' regime is the author's own.

for collective action to mitigate the economic and strategic impact of significant disruptions in the world's oil supply.

The second element is the regime's *norms*, commonly described as standards of behavior defined in terms of regime members' rights and obligations. These standards seek to operationalize a regime's underlying principles through broad statements about members' legitimate and illegitimate behavior. In this regard one can identify two important norms for the IEA-centered regime: first, energy consumers should maintain strategic reserves of crude oil and refined products and commit to coordinate releases from these reserves with one another; and, second, the accumulation of national petroleum stockpiles and any releases from them should be carried out in ways that do not distort market outcomes.

The third element is *rules*. Rules are often seen as "fleshing out" norms regarding regime members' rights and obligations by providing more specific prescriptions and proscriptions of members' behavior. Thus rules are derivative of norms and, by extension, may be changed more easily than norms. One can identify at least four IEA rules that have been essential to the operation of the existing energy consumers' regime. First, IEA members should maintain strategic petroleum reserves equivalent to at least 90 days of their oil consumption. Second, regime members should submit the management of their national stockpiles to the IEA's intergovernmental authority. Third, releases from national stockpiles should be undertaken solely mitigate the impact of significant supply disruptions, not to lower oil prices. Finally, IEA members should be prior members of the OECD.[25] (This rule reflects the IEA's founding assumption that advanced industrial democracies were, and would continue to be, the world's major energy consumers.)

The final element is the regime's *decisionmaking procedures,* its members' prevailing or established practices for making and implementing collective choices. The IEA was established under the authority of the Governing Board, consisting of one or more ministers or their delegates from all member states. The agency's executive director and secretariat report to the Board. The Board meets more frequently at the subministerial than at the ministerial level. Within the Governing Board, two formally codified decisionmaking procedures stand out. The first is weighted voting, which regime members accept on all decisions that would be legally binding on them regarding releases from national stockpiles. (The formula for allocating voting power among IEA members is discussed below.) Additionally, members accept weighted voting on all decisions regarding policy matters, such as changes in the IEA's rules and the acceptance

25. Of course, the IEA and its member states have, over the years, developed sets of more specific regulations to operationalize these four "macro-level" rules.

of new members. The second decisionmaking procedure is the committed participation of members in coordinated planning and preparation for stockpile releases in response to major supply disruptions.

The IEA and Global Energy Governance

In the years since its founding the IEA has consolidated its position as the authoritative forum for coordinating OECD states' policies regarding the maintenance of petroleum stockpiles and emergency oil sharing.[26] To be sure, the IEA has moved along a distinctive "learning curve" concerning the optimal management of member states' petroleum reserves, particularly in times of actual or potential crisis. In 1979 shortfalls in oil supply caused by the disruptive impact of the Iranian revolution did not meet the levels specified in the IEA's International Energy Program as triggers for member states to release oil from their strategic stockpiles. At the same time the uncoordinated responses of member states to the loss of Iranian production—in particular, the decisions of some members to purchase additional oil volumes for their stockpiles when the market was already in turmoil—actually reinforced upward pressure on oil prices. By contrast, when the Iran-Iraq war broke out in 1980, the IEA was far more effective in coordinating the actions of member states—including drawdowns from strategic stockpiles—and preventing individual members from taking steps that could have bid up prices.[27]

On the basis of this experience, the IEA's Governing Board took a decision in 1981 to institutionalize the agency's policies and procedures for coordinating member states' management of their stockpiles. This process of institutionalization culminated with the Board's adoption in 1984 of a set of "Co-ordinated Emergency Response Measures" (CERM) and its formal endorsement by member states at the ministerial level the following year. With the CERM system in place, the IEA took the lead in organizing consumer countries' responses to the oil market turmoil engendered by Iraq's invasion of Kuwait in August 1990. During this period, oil prices spiked in the immediate aftermath of the Iraqi invasion and again, very briefly, in the immediate run-up to Operation Desert Storm. However, the IEA's efforts to reassure markets by drawing down stocks, sharing information, and encouraging transparency helped to maintain what,

26. In this regard, Keohane notes that the formal provisions of the IEA's International Energy Program, focused on the coordinated use of member states' strategic petroleum reserves in response to a reduction in global oil supply, constitute "a remarkable delegation of authority to an international organization" (1984, p. 225).

27. For discussion, see Martin and Harrje (2005, pp. 101–03). Keohane (1984, pp. 224–37) makes a similar point in comparing the IEA's lack of effectiveness in 1979 with its far more positive impact in 1980 and 1981

under the circumstances, seemed a remarkable degree of market stability and set the stage for a rapid return to lower and less volatile prices in the first quarter of 1991.[28]

The IEA's now-demonstrated capacity to limit the effects of supply-side disruptions on the global oil market subsequently helped to mitigate the potential impact of the 2003 Iraq war on world oil prices.[29] In the months preceding the launch of Operation Iraqi Freedom, the IEA's dialogue with OPEC—especially with Saudi Arabia—was at least as important as the George W. Bush administration's bilateral representations to the Saudis in eliciting the necessary decisions by producer states to bring spare productive capacity online before hostilities started. In its dialogue with OPEC, the IEA's credibility was enhanced significantly by its publicly and privately expressed willingness to use coordinated drawdowns from member states' oil stocks to keep the market well supplied. As a consequence of these efforts, oil prices remained remarkably steady in the months immediately preceding and following the Iraq war. The IEA also coordinated releases from member states' stockpiles in 2005 in response to the disruptive effects of Hurricane Katrina on production and refining activities in the United States in and near the Gulf of Mexico.

Thus the IEA regime—through its coordination of member states' management of their petroleum stockpiles—bolstered the market-based approach to energy security long favored by the United States by functioning as a kind of "insurance policy" against supply-side disruptions in the international oil market. In the language of the new institutional economics, the international regime anchored in the IEA is an institution embodying important "rules of the game" for energy consumers. One can analyze the creation and evolution of this institution through a liberal prism, emphasizing the economic efficiency gains generated by the IEA's role in correcting "market failures" resulting from disruptions in international flows of crude oil and refined products.[30] In keeping with the logic of new institutional economics, however—and more power-oriented approaches to the study of international regimes—it is also important to understand the political factors influencing the IEA's origins and evolution.

---

28. See Martin and Harrje (2005, pp. 105–06). Former U.S. officials say that, for five months after the Iraqi invasion, the IEA worked closely with the George H. W. Bush administration to prevent market players around the world from panicking, by keeping markets informed about the true state of oil supplies and inventories and encouraging increased oil production. Then, in January 1991, as the United States and its Coalition partners commenced military operations to expel Iraqi forces from Kuwait, the IEA coordinated the release of oil from national stockpiles in the United States, Germany, and Japan.

29. Martin and Harrje (2005, p. 107).

30. Goldthau and Witte (2009).

These factors include most particularly the leading role of the United States, with its particular policy preferences and strategic interests.

In addition to its role as the authoritative forum for coordinating OECD states' policies regarding the maintenance of petroleum stockpiles and emergency oil sharing, the IEA has contributed to the broader project of global energy governance by serving as the outstanding official organizational forum for information sharing and analysis on international energy matters. IEA publications indicate that the agency's contributions to the international sharing of information and analysis on energy matters extend well beyond the oil market to encompass natural gas, renewable energy, downstream markets for refined products and electricity, and (more recently), the relationship between energy use and the management and mitigation of climate change.

In the course of discharging these informational and analytic functions, the IEA has assumed an increasingly important "soft power" role in global energy governance, serving as a proactive policy adviser to its member states and contributing quietly but significantly to building international support for market-oriented approaches to energy security.[31] During the 1980s, for example, the IEA effectively encouraged policy decisions in a number of member states to decontrol oil and natural gas prices, reduce energy subsidies, deregulate national electricity markets, and—in the case of Japan—open previously closed products markets to imports.[32] As part of its informational and analytic functions, the IEA regularly scrutinizes the energy policies of its member states through individual country reviews. These reviews reinforce the agency's advocacy of market-based approaches to energy security.

Writing in 1984, Robert Keohane argued that the IEA represented a new model of "post-hegemonic" cooperation among advanced industrial economies.[33] This assessment of the IEA's importance was challenged by later scholars such as G. John Ikenberry, who concluded in 1988 that the IEA could not be that important for global energy governance, given that its efforts at rules making and enforcement outside the specific issue area of emergency oil sharing

31. This point is also made in Van de Graaf and Lesage (2009).

32. Martin and Harrje (2005, p. 105). In the context of the agency's efforts to promote more liberal approaches to energy security, France's decision to join the IEA in 1992 was an important indicator of how much Paris had realigned its energy policy to be more compatible with the market-based approaches championed by the United States.

33. In Keohane's model of post-hegemonic cooperation, "What international regimes can accomplish depends not merely on their legal authority, but on the patterns of informal negotiation that develop within them. Rules can be important as symbols that legitimize cooperation or guidelines for it. But cooperation, which involves mutual adjustment of the policies of independent actors, is not enforced by hierarchical authority. The International Energy Agency illustrates these points in an exemplary way." See Keohane (1984, p. 237).

had been symbolic at best.[34] But the evolution of international energy markets over the past two and a half decades has validated, to a significant degree, the thrust of Keohane's observations about the IEA's potential contributions to global energy governance.

An Edifice under Strain: Implications for the IEA

During the 1980s and 1990s, the U.S.-sponsored global energy architecture seemed quite successful in dealing with OPEC's dramatic assertion of market power. Upstream liberalization helped pave the way for major new "plays" by the international energy industry in the 1980s and 1990s—in the North Sea, the North Slope, the deepwater Gulf of Mexico, the Gulf of Guinea, and the Caspian Basin following the Soviet Union's collapse—and a significant worldwide expansion of installed productive capacity. During the 1980s the resulting surge in non-OPEC production helped drive oil prices down from the dizzying heights they had reached during the 1970s; prices remained low through the 1990s.[35]

During the same period, consolidation of a single, integrated market for crude oil generated efficiency gains in international oil trading that reinforced downward pressure on prices.[36] By 1984 OPEC's "administered price" system had become unsustainable in the face of increased non-OPEC production and decreased worldwide demand. By 1986 OPEC countries, led by Saudi Arabia,

34. Thus, Ikenberry (1988, p. 10) argues that, with the abandonment of Kissinger's original ambitions for the IEA, the organization "became a modest mechanism for contingency oil-sharing agreements and the exchange of information . . . . As a device by which to recapture the erstwhile petroleum order, however, the IEA fell far short of American hopes."

35. Between 1980 and 1986, for example, non-OPEC production grew by 10 million barrels a day. In 1982 world oil prices started a slow decline, as ever larger volumes of non-OPEC production came onto the market and worldwide oil demand dropped. Price declines accelerated in 1985, with oil prices falling below $10 a barrel in 1986 before stabilizing between roughly $15 and $18 for the remainder of the decade. Oil prices spiked to more than $30 a barrel in summer and fall 1990 as a consequence of Iraq's invasion of Kuwait, but stabilized again around $20 during 1991. Prices then started another slow decline, reaching roughly $15 to $16 a barrel by the mid-1990s; in inflation-adjusted terms, oil prices in 1994 were at their lowest levels since the first half of 1973. Prices began to recover in 1996 and 1997, rising above $20 a barrel before falling sharply in 1998 as a result of the Asian financial crisis and concomitant demand destruction. By the end of 1998, oil prices had dropped below $10 a barrel again, and did not start to recover until March 1999, when OPEC successfully increased market prices by limiting member states' production for the first time since 1995.

36. Not coincidentally, the use of the U.S. dollar as the universal transactional currency for oil trading helped to bolster its standing as the world's leading transactional and reserve currency, thereby reinforcing U.S. hegemony more generally. On this point, see Noreng (2004); and "The Case for Euro Oil Trading," *OPEC Review* 32 (March 2008); see also Leverett (2008a).

had dropped this system and begun linking prices for their oil exports to the spot market.[37] Additionally, openness to international energy companies in gas-producing countries such as Algeria, Australia, Indonesia, Malaysia, and Qatar paved the way for the launch of liquefied natural gas (LNG) production, which—in theory, at least—promises to create a more globalized and efficient market for natural gas.[38]

In the 1990s, as the cold war was coming to a close, the United States and its European partners began to explore the possibility of using a multilateral convention to consolidate international endorsement of liberal treatment for energy-related foreign direct investment. They also wanted to use a multilateral convention to codify a set of rules for energy trade and transit across national boundaries, including natural gas and crude oil and refined products, based on the principles embodied in the General Agreement on Trade and Tariffs (GATT) and, later, the World Trade Organization (WTO).[39] To these ends, in 1991 a group of European countries, working through the European Council and with the support of the United States, launched the so-called Energy Charter initiative, followed in 1994 by the signing of an Energy Charter Treaty (ECT) and the creation of an Energy Charter Secretariat in Brussels.[40]

37. For discussion, see Skeet (1988, pp. 178–221); Parra (2004, pp. 276-292); and Mabro (2005).

38. This point is also made by Goldthau and Witte (2009, p. 377). On the development of the LNG business, see Barnes and others (2006, pp. 9–15). For more detailed treatments, see von der Mehden and Lewis (2006); Hashimoto, Elass, and Eller (2006); and Shepherd and Ball (2006).

39. This development constituted a striking shift in Western governments' perspectives about the place of oil and gas in multilateral trade arrangements. In effect, hydrocarbons had been left out of the GATT in 1947 and the eight rounds of negotiations conducted under GATT auspices before creation of the WTO in 1995. The de facto omission of energy resources from the international trade regime was rooted in the prevailing institutional framework governing international oil and gas markets at the time GATT was originally negotiated and for the first two decades that the agreement was in force—namely, that, from the end of World War II until the mid-1960s, Western international energy companies controlled the entire oil and gas value chain in most of the world's hydrocarbon provinces. (This institutional framework, of course, also reflected important geopolitical realities.) Under these circumstances, the tariffs the United States and its allies imposed on imported hydrocarbons were low or non-existent, and Western governments had no interest in subjecting international oil and gas trade to broad multilateral scrutiny. Starting in the mid-1960s, though, the "OPEC revolution" re-established states' ownership rights over hydrocarbon reserves within their national boundaries. This transformation of the institutional framework governing international oil and gas markets converted the United States and other Western governments to supporting not just the implementation of more market-oriented approaches to structuring and operating those markets, but also the creation and application of liberal, rules-based trade regimes for international oil and gas trade.

40. For a general discussion, see, *inter alia*, Dore and De Bauw (1995); Wälde (1996); and Energy Charter Secretariat (2002). The ECT formally came into force in 1998.

To be sure, since 1994, the United States has declined to sign the ECT, in part, according to former officials of the Energy Charter Secretariat, because it believes that the investment protections in U.S. bilateral investment treaties with individual energy-producing countries are superior to those in the ECT. In addition Washington sees a potential conflict between the ECT's rather unconditional provisions on most-favored-nation treatment and the Jackson-Vanik Amendment to the U.S. Trade Act of 1970.[41] Nevertheless, the adoption of the ECT by most of the United States' OECD partners—and the energy-related provisions of the North American Free Trade Agreement—reflected OECD countries' growing acceptance of the market-based approach to energy security championed by Washington.[42]

Since the turn of the millennium, however, the elements of the existing global energy architecture have come under increasing strain. The driving forces for such strain include ongoing structural shifts in international oil and gas markets on both the demand side and the supply side. On the demand side of international energy markets, there has been a substantial expansion of demand for crude oil, refined products, and natural gas. Among OECD countries the United States continues to account for the bulk of incremental demand for hydrocarbons, but energy demand has also expanded dramatically in the developing world—a phenomenon highlighted by the emergence of China and India as the world's most important incremental demand centers.[43] As Daniel Yergin has pointed out, the explosion of energy demand in China, India, and elsewhere in the developing world should be considered a globalization "success story." The sustained economic growth in these countries has lifted hundreds of millions out of poverty and, as a consequence, created ever greater demands for energy.[44] At the same time, though, rising energy demand creates new challenges to worldwide energy security. The recent economic downturn caused demand for crude oil to drop almost everywhere in the world, but any

41. Personal communication with the author. The Jackson-Vanik Amendment is a cold war legislative measure that continues to condition U.S. trade policy toward Russia.

42. On the investment-related aspects of the ECT, see, *inter alia*, Wälde (1995); Tucker (1998); Ribeiro (2006); and Coop and Ribeiro (2008). On the energy-related provisions of NAFTA, see, *inter alia*, Hufbauer and Schott (2005, chap. 7); and Selivanova (2007, p. 9–10). For a comparative discussion of the investment-related provisions of the ECT and NAFTA, see Wälde (2000).

43. On the growth of Chinese and Indian energy demand, both historically and prospectively, see, *inter alia*, International Energy Agency (2007, pp. 117–34, 165–81, 243–82, and 425–87). Of course, the phenomenon of exploding energy demand in the developing world extends well beyond China and India; in recent years the pressures of rising demand for oil and natural gas have been felt throughout the developing world, in Africa, Asia, Latin America, and the Middle East.

44. Daniel Yergin, "Energy's Challenges," *Forbes*, April 23, 2007.

reasonable projection anticipates substantial growth in primary energy demand over the next quarter century.[45]

Like their analogues on the demand side, structural shifts on the supply side of international oil and gas markets exert their own pressures on the existing global energy architecture and pose new challenges to global energy security. The potential to expand upstream productive capacity is conditioned by the ever-increasing concentration of the world's hydrocarbon reserves under the control of national governments and national energy companies, particularly in the Middle East and the former Soviet Union.

The confluence of an expansion of worldwide demand for hydrocarbon-based energy with structural shifts on the supply side of international energy markets is prompting serious doubts about the adequacy of the existing energy architecture to forestall potential long-term market failures and ensure global energy security. In this context, the emergence of new demand centers for hydrocarbon-based energy in the developing world poses significant and direct challenges to the IEA-centered energy consumers' regime. Certainly the exclusion of China and India from the regime raises pressing questions about the agency's capacity to discharge its functions effectively. Most immediately, leaving China and India outside the existing network of petroleum stockpiles and associated decisionmaking procedures for the management of those stockpiles could fundamentally undermine the IEA's future effectiveness as a "buffer" against the effects of major disruptions in oil supplies.

Taking a broader perspective, Chinese and Indian energy security strategies in themselves pose challenges to the IEA regime and to market-based approaches to energy security. Like their French and Japanese counterparts in the 1970s and 1980s, Chinese and Indian officials today seem to be at least as concerned about volume risk in international energy markets as about price risk. As a consequence, Beijing and New Delhi are pursuing energy security, at least in part, through what can be described as "resource mercantilism"—that is, the use of economic and foreign policy instruments by national governments to help their state-owned national energy companies secure access to overseas hydrocarbon resources on more privileged bases than simple supply contracts.[46] These mercantilist strategies of competing for access to hydrocarbon resources

45. Even after the downturn hit, the IEA (2008, p. 38) still projected worldwide primary energy demand to grow at an average annual rate of 1.6 percent between 2006 and 2030, an increase of 45 percent in the aggregate.

46. The phrase "resource mercantilism" was coined by this author in "The Geopolitics of Oil and America's International Standing," testimony to the U.S. Senate Committee on Energy and Natural Resources, Washington, January 10, 2007. For more detailed discussion of resource mercantilism in the Chinese and Indian cases, see Leverett (2008b).

contradict, in some respects, the longstanding interest of the United States and many of its OECD partners in fostering a more liberal, rules-based order governing transnational trade and investment in hydrocarbon-based energy.[47]

To be sure, how best to achieve energy security is an increasingly contested issue in both China and India. In Beijing and New Delhi, advocates of market-based approaches are competing for influence over policy with advocates of statist and mercantilist strategies. Remarkably, some of the strongest advocates of more liberal approaches to energy security in both China and India are these countries' national energy companies, which are increasingly market oriented and profit driven in their own strategic outlook. Under these circumstances building support for more market-oriented approaches to energy security within decisionmaking circles in Beijing and New Delhi and encouraging the "internationalization" of their national energy companies should be important longer-term objectives for the reform of global energy governance.[48] Integrating China and India into the IEA is vital to achieving these longer-term goals.

Taking an even broader perspective, reconstituting the IEA through the inclusion of China and India is essential if the agency is to play a strategically significant role in addressing the challenges to global energy governance emanating from structural shifts on the supply side of international oil and gas markets. The increasingly dominant role of national energy companies in upstream oil and gas sectors, along with geopolitical risk factors (such as U.S. policies that have severely circumscribed the ability of Iran and Iraq to contribute to the expansion of worldwide productive capacity), mean that there is a prospective gap between anticipated levels of demand and supply for crude oil and natural gas over the course of the next quarter-century. For example, the IEA predicts that almost 65 million barrels of crude oil a day of additional productive capacity will be needed by 2030 to accommodate demand growth—the equivalent of six times Saudi Arabia's current productive capacity—but questions whether, because of "above ground" barriers and risks, the massive investments required to expand upstream capacity on this scale will actually be undertaken.[49]

In the face of these challenges the traditional pillars of the existing global energy architecture are less and less able to forestall potentially serious market failures in the long term and ensure global energy security well into the future. From a strategic perspective, the outer limits of upstream liberalization and market integration have been reached.

47. On this point, see Leverett and Noël (2006, pp. 66–68).

48. For further discussion of these objectives, see Leverett and Bader (2005–06); and Leverett (2008b).

49. International Energy Agency (2008, pp. 221–78, 303–30).

Limits on a state's enthusiasm for upstream liberalization can characterize the policies of democratic energy-producing states—for example, Australia, Canada, and Norway, which have declined to sign and ratify the ECT—as well as those of nondemocratic energy producers. Russia signed the treaty in 2006 but declined to ratify it, and in August 2009 Russian prime minister Vladimir Putin signed an executive order formally rejecting Russia's participation in the ECT.[50]

As a consequence there are no new, large upstream "plays" freely available to international energy companies comparable to the opportunities they enjoyed in the 1980s and 1990s. In the first half of the twenty-first century, the United States and its partners no longer have a credible option for responding to a looming supply "crunch" in the future by reflexively (and futilely) pushing for further upstream liberalization in established hydrocarbon provinces.

Overall, structural shifts on the supply side of international energy markets are generating profound changes in the relative balance of bargaining power in international energy markets, as the "OPEC Five" (Saudi Arabia, Iran, Iraq, Kuwait, and the United Arab Emirates), Qatar (the world's leading producer and exporter of LNG), Russia, and other major energy-producing states are becoming increasingly influential "market makers." Eliciting from these states the kinds of decisions that are needed to ensure adequate long-term growth in oil and gas supplies requires something other than continued exhortations to further upstream liberalization from the United States and its OECD partners. More specifically, it is likely to require a far more robust dialogue with producers than the consuming countries have heretofore been willing to pursue. Only a refurbished IEA potentially would be able to organize the interests of consumer countries for such a dialogue.

Reinventing the IEA

The institutional, organizational, and political challenges associated with renovating the global energy architecture to cope with ongoing structural shifts in international oil and gas markets are multifaceted. Before the start of his tenure as the agency's executive director, Nobuo Tanaka urged the IEA to "move up the ladder of energy security, to natural gas, nuclear power, and renewable energy." In this regard Tanaka has voiced an aspiration for the IEA to become for global energy security what the International Monetary Fund is supposed to be for global financial security or the United Nations for humanitarian security.[51]

---

50. For a review of Russian concerns about ratifying the ECT, see Konoplyanik (2009, p. 23).

51. David Pilling, "Energy Agency Must Engage China, India to Maintain Relevance," *The Australian*, January 8, 2007.

One of the more self-evidently necessary steps in renovating the global energy architecture is the integration of China and India into the IEA. As Tanaka noted publicly, "without engaging these big non-member consuming countries, the relevance of the IEA could be undermined."[52]

To be sure, in recent years the IEA has launched outreach initiatives to China and India—as well as to other non-OECD countries—through its Standing Group on Global Energy Dialogue. In the course of these initiatives the IEA has brought China and India into agency-sponsored discussions on developing alternative energy sources and improving energy efficiency as well as on energy policy and regulatory reform; IEA experts are also providing Beijing and New Delhi with technical advice on the development and management of strategic petroleum reserves.[53] The IEA also includes the two countries as observers at the agency's specialized committees and working groups, and in 2008 China and India agreed to participate, on a voluntary basis, in the IEA's periodic Emergency Response Reviews, through which member states seek to improve their readiness to undertake collective actions in the event of a major disruption in global oil supplies.[54] China and India were also invited to participate in the IEA Governing Board's October 2009 Ministerial meeting.

Notwithstanding these steps, adding China and India to the roster of the IEA's twenty-seven full members remains a distant prospect. Little progress was made at the October 2009 Ministerial toward advancing formal membership for the two rising powers, according to senior agency and member state officials.[55]

Officials from Western states frequently point to the internal "deficiencies" of China and India—their lack of both membership in the OECD and petroleum stockpiles as specified by IEA guidelines for member states—to justify their exclusion from the IEA. In fact, however, discussions of OECD membership and stockpiles provide rhetorical cover for the actual motives for the resistance

52. "IEA Must Do More to Engage China, India, Says Next Chief," *Agence France-Presse*, January 5, 2007.

53. Personal communications with the author by IEA officials. Formally, the IEA concluded its first memorandum of understanding (MOU) with China's State Development and Planning Commission (previously, the State Planning Commission; subsequently, the National Development and Reform Commission; and now, for energy matters, the National Energy Bureau) in 1996, and an MOU with China's Ministry of Science and Technology in 2001. The IEA concluded an MOU with India's Ministry of Power in 1998.

54. This decision was formalized at a meeting of the energy ministers of China, India, Japan, and South Korea in advance of a meeting of G-8 energy ministers in June 2008 as part of the run-up to the 2008 G-8 Summit in Hokkaido, Japan. See "Joint Statement by Energy Ministers of the G8, the People's Republic of China, India, and the Republic of Korea," Aomori, Japan, June 8, 2008; see also "China, India Praised for Oil Preparedness," *Xinhua*, June 8, 2008.

55. Personal communications with the author.

of several member states to Chinese and Indian membership, which is rooted in basic concerns about politics and power.

OECD Membership

IEA membership currently requires prior OECD membership, but since neither China nor India is likely to be taken into the OECD over the next several years,[56] IEA membership rules would need to be modified to bring these two rising powers into the agency in a timely way. A recent analysis of institutional change in the IEA notes the importance of entrepreneurial initiative by the executive director and secretary and the impulses of member states (in particular, the impulses of its G-7/8 members).[57] Under Tanaka's leadership, there is clear support from the agency's executive bureau for institutional flexibility in extending membership to China and India,[58] but, over the past few years, working-level discussions among IEA members on relaxing the rule have failed.

On this issue, the United States has been more forward leaning than have the European members and Japan. The George W. Bush administration, in its waning days, was relatively forthcoming on the importance of bringing China and India into the IEA and on the need for flexibility in defining membership requirements for rising economic powers. In particular, in December 2008, at the fifth and final iteration of the Bush administration's U.S.-China Strategic Economic Dialogue, the United States publicly declared its support for China's joining the IEA.[59] While the Obama administration is still defining its policy on this issue, it is difficult to imagine that it would be less forthcoming than its predecessor. In this regard, Hillary Clinton—in hearings preceding her Senate confirmation to serve as secretary of state—argued that "the IEA should be laying the groundwork now for eventual Chinese and Indian membership. . . . If its membership does not change to reflect who those nations are today, its authority and effectiveness will erode."[60]

56. In 2007 the OECD Council invited several countries to open discussions on formal membership in the OECD, but offered only "enhanced engagement" with a view to possible membership in the future, to China, India, and three other emerging economies (Brazil, Indonesia, and South Africa).

57. See Van de Graaf and Lesage (2009).

58. A former senior European Commission official points out that "nothing prevents the OECD from turning the IEA into a separate institution with a membership that may no longer fully coincide with OECD membership"; see Eberhard Rhein, "China, India, and Russia Should Join IEA," *Rhein on Energy and Climate,* August 6, 2008 (rhein.blogactiv.eu/2008/06/08/china-india-and-russia-should-join-iea/).

59. See U.S. Embassy, "Energy and Environment Accomplishments at the Fifth Cabinet-Level Meeting of the U.S.-China Strategic Economic Dialogue," Beijing, December 4, 2008.

60. Senator Hillary Clinton, in response to written questions from Senator Richard Lugar (R-Indiana), the ranking member of the Senate Foreign Relations Committee.

In contrast to the U.S. position, a number of European countries continue to resist relaxing the requirement of prior membership in the OECD. According to diplomats from a range of IEA member states, some European states—including smaller western European countries and "new" ones that emerged out of the Soviet bloc—argue that it is important not to dilute the democratic character of IEA members, in keeping with the OECD's mandate to espouse democratic government and human rights in addition to market economics. Other European countries with close relations with Russia—including Germany and Italy—have reportedly argued against singling out China and India for "special treatment" while, in effect, excluding Russia, the IEA's third major "outreach" country.[61]

Ninety-Day Stockpiles

The prospect of IEA membership for China and India is also complicated by the current requirement that member states maintain crude oil stockpiles equivalent to ninety days of their oil consumption. Neither China nor India has yet met this requirement, although Beijing is much closer to doing so than New Delhi.

As with the question of prior OECD membership, the IEA's executive secretariat and the United States have been more flexible on the stockpile requirement than have most other IEA members. In this regard, Secretary of State Clinton noted during her confirmation hearings that "both [China and India are] building strategic petroleum reserves. Given their growing weight in international energy markets it is in our interest to include them as members of the International Energy Agency and to coordinate closely with them on usage of strategic petroleum reserves in case of an oil supply emergency."[62]

Redistributing Voting Power

Discussions of OECD membership and stockpiles, however, deflect attention from the real motivation for some IEA members' resistance to China and India's full integration into the agency. For Chinese and Indian membership in the IEA to become plausible, current member states would have to accept fundamental changes in the agency's decisionmaking rules and procedures—in particular, the allocation of weighted voting power. Specifically, under the IEA's current rules, as defined in the International Agreement on an International Energy Program (the IEA's founding document), new members are allocated weighted voting power on the Governing Board based on their oil consumption in 1974, the year of the agency's founding. This is hardly an attractive prospect for China or India, which have seen their energy demand (and reliance on imported

61. Personal communications with the author.
62. Senator Hillary Clinton, in response to written questions from Senator Lugar.

hydrocarbons) increase by orders of magnitude over the past quarter-century.

IEA membership would entail considerable costs for China and India—both the direct costs of developing and maintaining large strategic oil reserves and the "opportunity costs" associated with increasing the transparency of their energy sectors to the outside world.[63] As they weigh these prospective costs against the presumptive benefits of IEA membership, China and India are also clear that they will not accept on terms that would make them, in effect, "second-class citizens" of the agency. Thus, the full integration of China and India into the IEA will require a thoroughgoing redistribution of decisionmaking power within the agency, with OECD states giving up decisionmaking power in favor of prospective new members from continental Asia. The International Agreement on an International Energy Program authorizes IEA member states to review established allocations of voting power and revise them. Nevertheless, serious discussion among IEA members about the necessity of reforming the agency's decisionmaking structure to accommodate China and India is just beginning, and member states are sharply divided on the issue.

In keeping with its relatively flexible position on prior membership in the OECD as a requirement for Chinese and Indian membership in the IEA, the Bush administration took a comparatively forward-leaning approach to the question of adjusting and reallocating decisionmaking authority within the agency to accommodate China and India as new members. The Obama administration has yet to define its policy on this issue. Secretary Clinton, however, noted during her confirmation hearings that "full membership would likely require the modification of the original 1974 International Energy Program treaty agreement that created the International Energy Agency (IEA) . . . . The IEA makes decisions by consensus among the member states, and consensus can and will reached on how to prepare the IEA for eventual Chinese and Indian membership, even as China and India must also commit themselves to and prepared for IEA membership. The State Department will support these efforts, up to and including revision of the International Energy Program."[64]

Many IEA members are not nearly so open to the prospect of Chinese and Indian membership in the agency. In the aggregate European states have the most to lose in any reallocation of voting power within the IEA. Not surprisingly there is no common European view on the issue as it relates to prospective membership in the IEA for China and India—but some European states are clearly focused on guarding their current measure of voting power within the

63. For a discussion of these issues from a Chinese perspective, see Zhu Xiaolei, "A Slippery Proposition," *Beijing Review,* June 21, 2008.

64. Senator Hillary Clinton, in response to written questions from Senator Lugar.

agency. At this stage even stronger resistance to the prospect of reforming the IEA's decisionmaking structures and processes to accommodate China comes from Japan.

With member states so far from consensus, it is hard not to be pessimistic about the prospects for Chinese and Indian membership, at least in the near to medium term. Some current and former IEA officials suggest that, for the foreseeable future, the agency will be able to build up the formal basis for its cooperation with Beijing and New Delhi only through the negotiation of ad hoc treaties.[65] While this approach might facilitate improved Chinese and Indian cooperation with the agency in some areas, it is unlikely to help address more consequential challenges to effective global energy governance.

References

Bamberger, Craig. 2004. *History of the IEA*, vol. 4, *Supplement to Volumes I, II and III*. Paris: International Energy Agency.

Barnes, Joe, and others. 2006. "Introduction to the Study." In *Natural Gas and Geopolitics: From 1970 to 2040*, edited by David G. Victor, Amy M. Jaffe, and Mark H. Hayes. Cambridge University Press.

Bindemann, Kirsten. 1999. *Production-Sharing Agreements: An Economic Analysis*. Oxford: Oxford Institute for Energy Studies.

Coop, Graham, and Clarisse Ribeiro. 2008. *Investment Protection and the Energy Charter Treaty*. Huntington, N.Y.: JurisNet, LLC.

Dore, Julia, and Robert De Bauw. 1995. *The Energy Charter Treaty: Origins, Aims, and Prospects*. Brookings.

Energy Charter Secretariat. 2002. *The Energy Charter Treaty: A Reader's Guide*. Brussels.

Goldthau, Andreas, and Jan Martin Witte. 2009. "Back to the Future or Forward to the Past? Strengthening Markets and Rules for Effective Global Energy Governance." *International Affairs* 85, no. 2: 375–77.

Hashimoto, Kohei, Jareer Elass, and Stacy Eller. 2006. "Liquefied Natural Gas from Qatar: The Qatargas Project." In *Natural Gas and Geopolitics: From 1970 to 2040*, edited by David G. Victor, Amy M. Jaffe, and Mark H. Hayes. Cambridge University Press.

Hufbauer, Gary, and Jeffrey Schott. 2005. *NAFTA Revisited: Achievements and Challenges*. Washington: Peterson Institute for International Economics.

Ikenberry, G. John. 1988. *Reasons of State: Oil Politics and the Capacities of American Government*. Cornell University Press.

International Energy Agency. 2007. *World Energy Outlook 2007*. Paris.

———. 2008. *World Energy Outlook 2008*. Paris.

Johnston, Daniel. 1994. *Production Sharing Agreements*. University of Dundee, Centre for Petroleum and Mineral Law and Policy.

65. Personal communications with the author.

Keohane, Robert O. 1984. *After Hegemony: Cooperation and Discord in the World Political Economy*. Princeton University Press.

Kissinger, Henry. 1982. *Years of Upheaval*. Boston: Little, Brown.

———. 1999. *Years of Renewal*. New York: Simon and Schuster.

Konoplyanik, Andrey. 2009. "Russia: Don't Oppose the Energy Charter, Help to Adapt It." *Petroleum Economist* 76, no. 7: 22–23.

Krasner, Stephen. 1983. "Structural Causes and Regime Consequences: Regimes as Intervening Variables." In *International Regimes*, edited by Stephen Krasner. Cornell University Press.

Leverett, Flynt. 2008a. "Black Is the New Green." *National Interest* 93 (January/February): 37–45.

———. 2008b. "Resource Mercantilism and the Militarization of Resource Management: Rising Asia and the Future of American Primacy in the Persian Gulf." In *Energy Security and Global Politics: The Militarization of Resource Management*, edited by Daniel Moran and James Russell. Oxford: Routledge.

Leverett, Flynt, and Jeffrey Bader. 2005–06. "Managing China-U.S. Energy Competition in the Middle East." *Washington Quarterly* 29, no. 1: 187–201.

Leverett, Flynt, and Pierre Noël. 2006. "The New Axis of Oil." *National Interest* 84 (Summer): 62–70.

Mabro, Robert. 2005. "The International Oil Price Regime: Origins, Rationale, and Assessment." *Journal of Energy Literature* 11, no. 1: 3–20.

Martin, William, and Evan Harrje. 2005. "The International Energy Agency." In *Energy and Security: Toward a New Foreign Policy Strategy*, edited by Jan Kalicki and David Goldwyn. Johns Hopkins University Press.

Noël, Pierre. 2004. "Les États-Unis et la sécurité pétrolière mondial: politique pétrolière américaine et production d'un bien collectif global." CFE working paper. Paris: Centre français sur les États-Unis, Institut français des Relations internationales.

Noreng, Øystein. 2004. "Oil, the Euro, and the Dollar." *Journal of Energy and Development* 30, no. 1: 53–80.

North, Douglass. 1993. "The New Institutional Economics and Development." Working Paper, Washington University.

Parra, Francisco. 2004. *Oil Politics: A Modern History of Petroleum*. London: I. B. Tauris.

Raustiala, Kal, and David Victor. 2004. "The Regime Complex for Plant Genetic Resources." *International Organization* 32, no. 2: 277–309.

Ribeiro, Clarisse. 2006. *Investment Arbitration and the Energy Charter Treaty*. Huntington, N.Y.: JurisNet, LLC.

Scott, Richard. 1994. *History of the IEA: The First 20 Years*, vol. I, *Origins and Structure*. Paris: International Energy Agency.

———. 1995. *History of the IEA: The First 20 Years*, vol. II, *Major Policies and Actions*. Paris: International Energy Agency.

———. 1996. *History of the IEA: The First 20 Years*, vol. III, *Principal Documents*. Paris: International Energy Agency.

Selivanova, Yulia. 2007. "The WTO and Energy: WTO Rules and Agreements of Relevance to the Energy Sector." Trade and Sustainable Energy Series, Issue Paper 1. Geneva: International Centre for Trade and Sustainable Development (August).

Shepherd, Rob, and James Ball. 2006. "Liquefied Natural Gas from Trinidad & Tobago." In *Natural Gas and Geopolitics: From 1970 to 2040*, edited by David G. Victor, Amy M. Jaffe, and Mark H. Hayes. Cambridge University Press.

Skeet, Ian. 1988. *OPEC: Twenty-Five Years of Prices and Politics*. Cambridge University Press.

Tucker, Andrew. 1998. "The Energy Charter Treaty and 'Compulsory' International State/Investor Arbitration." *Leiden Journal of International Law* 11, no. 3: 513–26.

Van de Graaf, Thijs, and Dries Lesage. 2009. "The International Energy Agency after 35 Years: Reform Needs and Institutional Adaptability." *Review of International Organizations* 4 (July 11). (www.springerlink.com/content/n742546n25681531/).

von der Mehden, Fred, and Steven Lewis. 2006. "Liquefied Natural Gas from Indonesia: The Arun Project." In *Natural Gas and Geopolitics: From 1970 to 2040*, edited by David G. Victor, Amy M. Jaffe, and Mark H. Hayes. Cambridge University Press.

Wälde, Thomas. 1995. "International Investments under the 1994 Energy Charter: Legal, Negotiating, and Policy Implications for International Investors within Western and CIS/Eastern European Countries." CMPLP Professional Paper 17. University of Dundee, Center for Petroleum and Mineral Law and Policy.

———, ed. 1996. *The Energy Charter Treaty: An East-West Gateway for Investment and Trade*. The Hague: Kluwer Law International.

———. 2000. "International Law of Foreign Investment: Towards Regulation by Multilateral Treaties." CEPMLP Paper CP1/2000. University of Dundee, Center for Petroleum and Mineral Law and Policy.

STEVEN E. MILLER

12

The War on Terror and International Order: Strategic Choice and Global Governance

There are two parallel if sometimes overlapping stories to tell about the impact of 9/11 on the international order. The dominant tale—high profile, controversial, and mostly damaging to the cause of global governance—is one in which a wounded but angry, willful, and extraordinarily powerful state launches an aggressive, self-proclaimed global war on terror, resolved to do "whatever it takes" to eradicate the newly understood grave threat to U.S. security.[1] Though the United States was happy to accept international support for its policies and was willing to conform to international laws and norms when this was convenient or advantageous, it was also unambiguously clear that Washington would not deviate from its chosen paths even in the absence of international blessing. Nor was the George W. Bush administration prepared to be inhibited by international legal constraints when these interfered with the courses of action it deemed necessary for effective response to 9/11. According to this mindset, the United States' security is too important to be "turned over" to international institutions or jeopardized by international legal niceties.

The second tale—less publicly visible, less well known, and with less immediate impact on the character of international politics—involves the remarkable degree to which 9/11 was not simply a U.S. experience but a global phenomenon that rippled dramatically through the instruments of global governance. The world's global and regional institutions, no less than the United States, responded in significant ways to the attacks of September 11, 2001. Across a surprising array of international institutions, high-level meetings were convened, resolutions were passed, policies adopted, commitments made, cooperation promised. Counterterrorism became a central preoccupation not only in

1. The phrase is attributed to President George W. Bush, his response to warnings about the potential costs and difficulties of the war on terrorism; see Mayer (2008, p. 31).

Washington but also in the world's institutions of global governance. Cynics of international order might suggest that all this multilateral activity was much ado about nothing, but there was certainly much ado. Moreover, the decisions taken and the agreements reached laid the legal foundation for future counter-terrorism actions and provided frameworks within which coordinated international efforts to combat terrorism could take place. But whereas the Bush administration's response to 9/11 safeguarded unilateral freedom of action and emphasized the use of force, the international reactions promoted collaborative approaches to coping with transnational threats and sought to strengthen legal remedies to the terrorism challenge.

These two tales unfolded simultaneously, similarly impelled by the horrors of 9/11. One is a cautionary tale about the limits of global governance, the durability of the self-help instinct in the face of grave perceived threats, the unrestrained willfulness of Great Powers when provoked, and the frailty of legal constraints when the forces of war are unleashed. The other tale reveals a powerful habit of global governance among many leading governments, and illustrates their instinct to build and rely upon multilateral mechanisms for coping with transnational threats. In this frame global governance is desirable, necessary, perhaps even unavoidable. The global governance saga privileges cooperation over unilateralism, diplomacy over force, law over policy freedom of choice. Though these stories are in part contradictory, each captures a portion of the complex international reality that emerged after 9/11. And while it was the forceful and impulsive U.S. reactions to 9/11 that have dominated since—Washington's military responses commanded the international agenda in these years—the steps the United Nations and other international institutions have taken to strengthen collaborative capacities for combating terrorism and to enlarge the legal frameworks addressing terrorism could be both lasting and consequential.

Choosing Force over Order: The Bush Administration's War on Terrorism

Given the vast power of the United States, its response to 9/11 was bound to have wide international repercussions. But how would the United States respond? Would it marshal the instruments of international order against the terrorist attackers? Would it mobilize existing laws and institutions as central elements of its counterterrorism strategy? Would it build upon its long-time role as the primary provider of international public goods to strengthen the antiterrorism capacities of international organizations and legal frameworks? In fact, more than is often recognized, the United States did do many of these things. It operated through various international institutions in pushing its counterter-rorism agenda, supported the expansion of the antiterrorism legal framework, and pressed states to fulfill their counterterrorism obligations in various international institutions and under various international conventions.[2] Such steps were not incompatible with the Bush administration's broader war on terrorism. It was to this record that the Bush administration would draw attention when rebutting the widespread criticism that it was retreating from multilateralism and global governance and instead forging a unilateral path.

Nevertheless this is only part of the story of Washington's reactions to 9/11. The Bush administration's reputation for unilateralism and hostility to global governance derives from several other considerations. First, Washington regarded laws and institutions not as rules to be followed or regimes to be respected but as instruments in its campaign against terrorism—to be embraced and used when this advantaged the U.S. cause and to be ignored, discarded, or unilaterally reinterpreted when it served U.S. interests. This is not surprising behavior on the part of a threatened and mobilized Great Power but it was disappointing to those championing the evolution of a rules-based order—and particularly to those advanced democratic friends and allies of the United States who looked to Washington for leadership and support in building what most regarded as a U.S.-inspired international order.

Second, the United States was unambiguously clear that, while it welcomed international support and would prefer to have the legal blessings and backing of international institutions, it would take action unilaterally if necessary to defeat the terrorist threat. Particularly in its assertion of the controversial "preemption policy," widely regarded as an illegal and extremely undesirable precedent, Washington showed that it would not be bound by the rules if the security of the United States required it to act otherwise. As viewed from many quarters around the world, the preemption policy did not advance the cause of a rules-based order; rather, the world's leading power had become, in effect, an avowed rules breaker.

Third, and most important, the global governance theme of Washington's response to 9/11 was the subordinate dimension of the Bush administration's counterterrorism policy. It was real but secondary—and greatly overshadowed by the dominant components of the strategy. Far more central, visible, and immediately consequential were unilateral choices the Bush administration made about U.S. security policy in the aftermath of 9/11. These strategic choices were crucial in determining the subsequent course of events, in shaping

2. See, for example, *National Strategy for Combating Terrorism* (Washington, 2003, p. 11), which calls on states to live up to the many UN conventions and resolutions on counterterrorism.

the Bush administration's approach to questions of global governance, in coloring the world's reaction to Washington's war on terror, and in influencing the international order. Washington declared global war only to discover that much of the world was not with it. As historian John Lewis Gaddis explains, "If Washington could go against the wishes of the United Nations and most of its own allies in invading Iraq, what could it *not* do? What were to be, henceforth, the constraints on its power? . . . Within a little more than a year and a half, the United States exchanged its long-established reputation as the principal *stabilizer* of the international system for one as its chief *destabilizer*."[3]

The Bush administration saw itself as engaged in a worldwide war of indefinite duration against a huge, ominous, elusive, multiheaded, and extremely dangerous adversary. This conception emerged almost instantly with the 9/11 attacks and served as the foundation of all that was to come. President Bush never deviated in the slightest from this initial conception of threat and response. In his speech to the Veterans of Foreign Wars Convention on August 20, 2008, his message was identical to that voiced in September 2001: the United States is in a multifront global war "defending America in our nation's first war in the twenty-first century. That war reached our shores on September 11, 2001 . . . . We're at war against determined enemies and we must not rest until that war is won."[4] And in a war so vast against an enemy so dangerous, the United States would not allow itself to be hamstrung by the shackles of global governance.

Bush's War and Global Governance

The first move in the U.S. global war on terror was the attack on Afghanistan in fall 2001 to remove the Taliban regime. Though the invasion was widely accepted as justified in view of the apparent close connection of the Taliban government with the perpetrators of the 9/11 attacks, it was questioned from a legal point of view. Washington argued that it was an act of self-defense in response to an attack on the territory of the United States, and made a formal representation to this effect to the UN Security Council on October 7, 2001, with claims that Taliban support had made possible the al Qaeda attack. International lawyer Hisakazu Fujita writes, however, that "these reasonings are not certainly sufficient for the justification of self-defense because they do not prove that Afghanistan or the Taliban regime had full responsibility for the acts of the

---

3. Gaddis (2004, p. 101).

4. White House, Office of the Press Secretary, "President Bush Attends Veterans of Foreign Wars National Convention, Discusses Global War on Terror," Washington, August 20, 2008.

al Qaeda organization. Only the actual armed attack and not the ongoing threat
. . . would justify the use of armed force by an individual state."[5]

Though the intervention in Afghanistan did not attract much international
criticism, a debate opened up almost immediately after 9/11, which continues
to this day, about what responses to terrorist attacks are permitted under international law and, conversely, what are the implications for international law of
the transnational terrorist threat.[6]

In Washington it was widely accepted by a large bipartisan coalition that the
war on terror was both necessary and appropriate in response to 9/11. At the
heart of that war as defined by the Bush administration was an embrace of the
concept of preventive war that explicitly called for U.S. attacks against mounting threats abroad. Many outside the United States, however, saw war as the
wrong paradigm; to them, it seemed obviously undesirable to alter the international legal regime so that recourse to force might become both legal and
commonplace. The U.S. doctrine of preventive war—of which Afghanistan was
the first exemplar—represented, as one international lawyer put it in 2002, "a
fundamental challenge to international legality."[7]

This same set of issues arose in much more dramatic and spectacularly public fashion in the period leading up to the invasion of Iraq in March 2003. In
this instance there was no evidence of Iraq's involvement in the 9/11 attack.
Nor was there ever any genuine and convincing evidence of a meaningful or
operational link between Iraq and al Qaeda—as the Bush administration later
acknowledged. Nor was Saddam Hussein's Iraq threatening, nor had it ever
threatened, to attack the United States. Hence the war was difficult to justify
as a legal act of self-defense as defined in the UN Charter. Rather, it was a pure
application of the Bush doctrine of preventive war: acting to remove a potential
threat that was seen as too dangerous to leave unaddressed.

What seemed necessary and justified to the Bush administration, however,
seemed objectionable and problematic to much of the world, including to
many of the United States' long-standing allies. When Bush reluctantly took

---

5. Fujita (2003, p. 61). Fujita also cautions (p. 62) that, legally, the so-called war on terror
"does not always produce a situation of armed conflict. The U.S. Department of Defense has
extended the concept of armed conflict to include single hostile acts or attempted acts, or con-
spiracy which carries out such acts. This definition is so broad that it could encompass many acts
that would normally fall under the jurisdiction of the normal criminal justice system."

6. See, for example, Charney (2001); and Franck (2001). A particularly extensive discussion
of the legality of preventive war can be found in Mueller and others (2006, pp. 43–90). An excellent discussion of the need to adapt legal frameworks to new forms of conflict can be found in
De Nevers (2006).

7. An-Na'im (2002, p. 162).

his case for war against Iraq to the United Nations in fall 2002, he encountered the criticism and opposition that many in his administration had feared. Months of intense and bruising diplomatic battles ensued, to the frustration and fury of Bush and his lieutenants. Seeking UN blessing for his forthcoming war, Bush discovered that the majority on the Security Council would neither accept the U.S. position that war against Iraq was justified by earlier UN resolutions (related to the termination of the 1991 war against Iraq in Kuwait) nor provide new and explicit Security Council authorization for the use of force against Iraq.

The Bush administration viewed the matter simply in terms of the desirability of ridding the world of Saddam Hussein, and regarded the choice for other states as a clear-cut question of supporting Washington or supporting Baghdad. But for many other governments, including some close allies, the prospect of war with Iraq represented, in much starker terms than did Afghanistan, a test of the rules-based international order. At stake was a fundamental issue of global governance: did the rules apply to everyone? To many governments, though not to the Bush administration – this issue was more consequential than the fate of Saddam Hussein. Washington's apparent appetite for war with Iraq consequently elicited extensive opposition, particularly as the Bush administration made clear its intention to have its war no matter what laws or institutions it contravened along the way.

In the end Washington failed to gain the authorization it sought from the UN Security Council for the use of force against Iraq. Indeed, despite strenuous diplomatic exertions by the Bush administration in favor of the appropriateness and legality of the war, there was little support for the U.S. position even from its friends and allies. Able to garner no more than four of fifteen votes on the Security Council, and with allies France and Germany as well as permanent members Russia and China all strongly opposed, the United States withdrew its proposed resolution legitimizing the war with Iraq. Explaining the wide and unshakeable resistance that Washington met at the UN, a French diplomat described the stakes of the dispute as viewed from outside Washington: "This is about the rules of the game in the world today. About putting the Security Council in the center of international life. And not permitting a nation, whatever nation it may be, to do what it wants, when it wants, where it wants."[8]

Another core component of the Bush war on terror, pursued with vigor from the earliest days after 9/11, was a campaign—sometimes labeled "the great

---

8. As quoted in Maggie Farley and Doyle McManus, "To Some, Real Threat is US," *Los Angeles Times*, October 30, 2002.

global manhunt"—to "bring to justice" key leaders of the al Qaeda high command. Insofar as this entailed finding and apprehending terrorists, it did not raise any concerns about respecting the laws governing the use of force (though, as noted below, it did raise other legal issues related to the laws of war and international human rights law). However, here too the Bush administration was willing to employ violence in its campaign to eliminate individuals it deemed threatening. This involved both limited use of force—such as cruise missile and Predator attacks—and targeted assassinations by military or intelligence operatives.[9] The full extent of these efforts remains shrouded in mystery and controversy, but there is no question that a number of such attacks have taken place in Yemen, Somalia, Pakistan, Afghanistan, and Iraq.

The U.S. urge to eliminate terrorists and decapitate terrorist organizations is understandable (and echoes similar policies on the part of Israel) and has its defenders.[10] The United States, of course, has defended its practice, arguing that these are acts of war that flow from the country's right to defend itself and are undertaken in the context of an ongoing war. But an international order that accepts and legitimizes self-generated and self-justified campaigns of targeted assassination is widely regarded as neither desirable nor compatible with existing legal constraints. Moreover the Bush administration insisted that the global war on terror was of unlimited duration, implying an open-ended right to engage in targeted assassination—how many years or decades of this practice does the morning of September 11, 2001 justify? The United States does not accept targeted killings as legitimate when its adversaries conduct them, as in Iraq; it is hard to believe that Washington will find congenial a world in which states are thought to have a right to engage in targeted killings on foreign soil of those they regard as hostile and threatening.

As in other instances where the United States has used force, the policy of targeted assassination bumps up against legal and normative constraints already established in the international order.[11] In the U.S. debate there is a tendency to be dismissive of such concerns when the issue at play is the elimination of a violent and lawless terrorist. And it should be acknowledged that there are difficult judgments and trade-offs to be made when considering whether or when

---

9. There are also reports of an unsuccessful CIA program to form assassination teams; see Mark Mazzetti and Scott Shane, "After 9/11, CIA Had Plan to Kill Qaeda's Leaders," *New York Times,* July 14, 2009.

10. For the argument that targeted assassinations are "legal and necessary," see Corn (2009).

11. For an extensive discussion of the norm against international assassinations, see Thomas (2000).

targeted assassination is justified.[12] Nevertheless the policy is questionable and attracts considerable criticism on the world stage—perhaps more than would otherwise be the case because it appears to be part of a pattern of aggressive unilateral use of force by the United States regardless of the rules governing the use of force.

Then there is the question of torture. Though the full facts of the situation are almost surely not yet public, its seems reasonably established that the United States engaged in a systematic program—authorized at the highest levels of the U.S. government—of torture of prisoners it thought might provide valuable information or have knowledge of future attacks.[13] This was a reflection of the Bush administration's perceptions of the ruthlessness and dangerousness of the terrorist enemy. The reigning philosophy was clear: in this dangerous new environment, with this dangerous new enemy, U.S. security must be protected at all costs, even if this meant breaking some rules. As Mark Danner explains, "For many in the United States, torture still stands as a marker of political com-mitment—of a willingness to 'do anything to protect the American people,' a manly readiness to know when to abstain from 'coddling terrorists and do what needs to be done.'"[14] Hence the United States employed practices that have long been accepted as torture, that Washington itself in the past condemned as torture, and that again put the Bush administration at odds with international law, which bans such practices under the UN Convention on Torture and other Cruel, Inhuman, or Degrading Treatment or Punishment. The United States is not only a signatory of this convention, but in the past had been a champion of it. Refusing to be constrained by this legal instrument the Bush administration launched into a remarkable saga involving convoluted and bizarre legal justi-fications by friendly Bush-appointed lawyers. When in 2008 the House Com-mittee on Foreign Affairs investigated the dramatic decline in the United States' international reputation, it found that one of the explanations was "torture and abuse of prisoners in violation of treaty obligations."[15]

Washington's overweening commitment to ensuring security after 9/11 thus resulted in a cavalier attitude toward international law and international order.

---

12. For a particularly thoughtful assessment of these tradeoffs from a strong advocate of assassinating Osama Bin Laden, see Richard A. Clarke, "Targeting Terrorists," *Wall Street Journal*, July 18, 2009.

13. For an extensive overview of recent developments, see Mark Danner, "The Red Cross Tor-ture Report: What It Means," *New York Review of Books*, April 30, 2009, pp. 48–56. The authorita-tive account to date of the origins and character of U.S. torture policy is Mayer (2008).

14. Danner, "The Red Cross Torture Report," p. 48.

15. U.S. House of Representatives (2008, p. 4).

The central thrust of the Bush war on terrorism was security at all costs, and instruments of global governance were accorded neither priority nor authority. This was not the only relationship the Bush administration had with the rules-based order, but it was the most significant one.

The World Responds to 9/11: Law, Cooperation, and Global Governance

On October 12, 2001, a little-known regional institution, the Caribbean Community (CARICOM), meeting in the Bahamas, adopted the "Nassau Declaration on International Terrorism." Though the 9/11 attacks had had nothing to do with the Caribbean and though there was little likelihood that CARICOM would figure centrally in the U.S. retaliation against its extremist enemies in the remote reaches of southwest Asia, CARICOM was stirred to address the terrorism challenge and to pledge more effective action against that threat. No doubt this was in part a reflection of the dramatic events of 9/11. Perhaps it was also in part an expression of solidarity with the United States in the context of a horrible attack on its soil. The CARICOM declaration also might say something about the phenomenon of globalization—the sense of the interconnectedness of events and of shared vulnerability in an era of technology, mobility, and transnational actors. But without question CARICOM's impulse to tackle terrorism was symptomatic of the extent to which, in the aftermath of the September 11 attacks, not only the U.S. government but also the world's multilateral institutions were seized with the problem of terrorism.

The multilateral urge to respond to 9/11 in some meaningful way was pervasive. The Organization of American States (OAS), for example, passed no fewer than five terrorism-related resolutions in the months after 9/11, including a document on "Strengthening Hemispheric Cooperation to Prevent, Combat, and Eliminate Terrorism." Similarly, the core institutions of the industrial world—NATO, the European Union, and the G-8—raised terrorism to the top of their agendas and swung into action to fashion new and improved counterterrorism policies. And at the United Nations, 9/11 provoked a veritable blizzard of activity in the Security Council, the General Assembly, and the Secretariat. More than a dozen resolutions were passed, committees were convened, an action plan was created and adopted, and the long-standing effort to fashion an international convention against terrorism was revived.

To a remarkable extent the world shared the Bush administration's obsession with the counterterrorism mission. The character of the global response, however, was significantly different in emphasis (though not completely or inherently incompatible with) the approach chosen in Washington. To be sure, some of the post-9/11 commotion was rhetoric, but at least some of the global governance activity represented genuine efforts to build institutions, expand the legal framework for fighting terrorism, and facilitate counterterrorism cooperation in areas such as financing and policing.[16]

The United Nations Responds to the Attacks of September 11

The United Nations responded to 9/11 with immediate steps, and with efforts over a period of years to strengthen the UN-based international regime against terrorism. These exertions almost surely were inspired in part by the horrors of 9/11. No doubt they were also in part a reaction to the powerful drive by the Bush administration to put terrorism at the top of the international agenda. And it seems likely that they also were motivated to demonstrate the relevance and the utility, if not the centrality, of the UN.[17] Terrorism represented a serious global threat to international peace and security and, hence, as UN secretary-general Kofi Annan insisted, "of course the United Nations must be at the forefront in fighting against it."[18] The main lines of activity fell in four areas.

New Security Council Resolutions: The Primacy of 1373 and 1540

In the four years after 9/11 the UN Security Council passed at least ten terrorism-related resolutions, of which two stand out as particularly important. The first, UN Security Council Resolution (UNSCR) 1373, passed unanimously on September 28, 2001, authorizes and requires a sweeping array of antiterrorism measures.[19] It is widely described as the "cornerstone" of post-9/11 UN counterterrorism efforts, and virtually all subsequent UN resolutions that bear on terrorism contain exhortations that UNSCR 1373 be fully implemented by member states.[20] One set of provisions in 1373 aims at disrupting terrorist financing. It calls on states to prevent the transfer of funds to terrorists by freezing assets

16. This multilateral response to 9/11 and the substantial intergovernmental cooperation it facilitated has been little noted, but for an exception, see Slaughter (2004). She begins with a description of post-9/11 international arrangements for collaboratively combating terrorism and suggests that international cooperation is necessary to cope effectively with such threats: "Networked threats require a networked response" (p. 3).

17. See, for example, Frum and Perle (2003), in which they argue that the United States should not be blamed if, as they expected, the United Nations failed the test of utility in relation to the greatest issue of the day as they saw it.

18. Annan (2005).

19. For a summary and the text of UNSCR 1373, see United Nations, "Security Council Adopts Wide-Ranging Anti-Terrorism Resolution: Calls for Suppressing Financing, Improving International Cooperation," Press Release SC/7158, New York, September 28, 2001.

20. See, for example, Mariner (2007).

of anyone directly or indirectly connected, criminalizing any intentional support of terrorist acts or groups, and prohibiting the use of national territory for financial transactions or financial services associated with terrorism. Another set of provisions is intended to deny terrorists any state support and to make it as difficult as possible for them to operate. UNSCR 1373 thus proposes that states deny safe haven to terrorists and prevent any other use of their national territory for terrorist purposes. A third set of provisions calls for greater international cooperation in fighting terrorism and for, "intensifying and accelerating the exchange of operational information."

None of these initiatives is dramatically new. Indeed, as UNSCR 1373 itself reiterates, as early as 1970 the UN General Assembly had established the principle that "every State has the duty to refrain from organizing, instigating, assisting or participating in terrorist acts in another State or acquiescing in organized activities within its territory directed towards the commission of such acts."[21] Furthermore, there was considerable overlap with the pre-existing UN conventions on terrorism. In several respects, however, UNSCR 1373 was new. First, Security Council resolutions adopted under Chapter VII of the UN Charter, as 1373 was, are binding on all member states regardless of whether they are signatories of the various relevant UN conventions; moreover, this was the first time that the Security Council had invoked its Chapter VII powers. Second, UNSCR 1373 created a Counter-Terrorism Committee (CTC) whose principal purpose was to monitor implementation of the resolution. This oversight mechanism set UNSCR 1373 apart from many other resolutions that typically exhort states to take action but lack the capability to assess fulfillment. Finally, UNSCR 1373 created a reporting requirement that calls on all member states to provide information to the CTC on their progress in meeting the counterterrorism objectives.[22] Under UNSCR 1373 the UN would be in a stronger position to gather information, assess performance, and provide assistance to member states in improving counterterrorism laws and capabilities.

Compliance with UNSCR 1373, of course, has been uneven. Moreover, there have been complaints about the weakness of the CTC, the absence of enforcement mechanisms, the difficulties of coordinating the UN with other international institutions, and reliance on self-reporting as the source of information about the performance of member states. The impact of UNSCR 1373 should not be overstated, but to a surprising degree it has provided an omnibus

21. UN General Assembly Resolution 2625 (XXV), October 1970, reaffirmed in the preamble to UNSCR 1373.

22. The first such report was due within ninety days of the adoption of the resolution. See, for example, European Union (2001).

framework for counterterrorism activity, establishing priorities and structuring counterterrorism policy in other institutions as well as in UN member states. Some institutions not only have attempted to monitor fulfillment but have also found extensive compliance on the part of member states. This was the conclusion of the G-20, for example, when it assessed the efforts of its members to take steps to combat terrorist financing.[23] Any net assessment of UNSCR 1373 is thus inevitably a mixed picture. In some groups of states, within certain regions, and with respect to some substantive areas, compliance with 1373 has been incomplete, imperfect, or even absent. Imposing a broad agenda of steps on the entire membership of the United Nations is bound to be flawed in execution. Over the longer term, however, the priorities and the frameworks for improving states' capabilities and level of cooperation on counterterrorism activities are likely to prove valuable.[24]

The second particularly noteworthy resolution is UNSCR 1540, adopted on April 28, 2004, and intended to address the threat of terrorism using nuclear or other "weapons of mass destruction" (WMD). As with many other UN measures, UNSCR 1540 was in part a response to an immediate crisis. In this instance the catalyst was revelations in fall 2003 of the existence of a network—the so-called A. Q. Khan network—specialized in the illicit trafficking of sensitive nuclear technology and willing to assist states, and perhaps terrorists, in the covert pursuit of nuclear weapons. It was widely recognized that a substantial nuclear black market posed a potentially catastrophic threat to the international nonproliferation regime. The A. Q. Khan saga highlighted the threat posed by nonstate actors (as both suppliers and seekers of sensitive nuclear technology) and drew attention to the existing legal framework's failure to address this challenge.

Memories of 9/11 were fresh, evidence of al Qaeda interest in acquiring nuclear weapons had been discovered in caves in Afghanistan, and the threat of nuclear terrorism seemed all too real. UNSCR 1540 was meant to fill this gap; its broad purpose was to deny nonstate actors access to technology and materials associated with weapons of mass destruction and to prevent illicit trafficking in such technology and materials. It called on states to avoid any support or assistance to any WMD-related activities by nonstate actors. It required the comprehensive criminalization of such activities and established that states "shall adopt and enforce" measures that make it illegal for nonstate actors "to manufacture,

---

23. See, for example, G-20, "Measures to Combat the Financing of Terrorism: Summary of Country Measures" (http://www.g20.org/Documents/measures_to_combat_the_financing_of_terrorism.xls), which finds that all G-20 members have complied with at least some of the obligations under 1373.

24. For a more extensive discussion of this issue, see Heupel (2008).

acquire, possess, develop, transport, transfer or use nuclear, chemical or biological weapons and their means of delivery."[25] In a series of provisions regarded as particularly significant by the international nonproliferation community, UNSCR 1540 required states to take "appropriate effective" steps to inventory and secure materials and technologies, provide physical protection of sensitive materials, technologies, and facilities, strengthen border controls in order to impede illicit trafficking, and establish and enforce strong export and transshipment controls. In effect, this potentially far-reaching resolution provides the basis for establishing a stronger international regime for preventing WMD terrorism. Like 1373, UNSCR 1540 was adopted under Chapter VII of the UN Charter, establishes a committee to monitor compliance, and requires states to report on their efforts to fulfill their requirements. As with 1373, 1540 envisions that the UN should provide assistance to member states to help them meet the objectives of the resolution.

The impact of UNSCR 1540 will depend on how it is interpreted and implemented. The document does not provide clear definitions of key phrases. For example, it calls for "appropriate effective measures" in a number of areas but nowhere specifies what these should be.[26] It imposes an ambitious agenda of obligations on states that might have little motivation to act—particularly given the resistance of some states to the imposition of requirements by the Security Council, the lack of a deadline for compliance, and the absence of penalties for failure to comply.[27] Even states that are inclined to comply might find implementation a challenge given the sweep of the obligations and the difficulty of substantially reforming legal frameworks and export control mechanisms. Moreover, given the vagueness of the resolution, states might have little understanding of what fulfilling their 1540 commitments entails. Yet if 1540's implementation is limited substantively and incomplete geographically, its potential benefits will not be fully realized.[28]

By May 2009 148 states had submitted reports to the 1540 Committee, but some 50 had not and the quality of the submitted reports was uneven.[29] Just

25. Language from UN Security Council, Article II of UNSCR 1540, S/Res/1540 (2004), April 28, 2004.

26. For an excellent discussion of this point, see Bunn (2008).

27. On criticism of the Security Council and the uneven implementation of UNSCR 1540, see Ahlstrom (2008).

28. As a consequence, there is a modest cottage industry of work focusing on implementation of UNSCR 1540. Examples include Crail (2006); and Heupel (2007).

29. Nuclear Threat Initiative, "United Nations Security Council Resolution 1540 Database," June 2009 (www.nti.org/db/1540/index.html). The national reports are available on the website of the 1540 Committee (www.un.org/sc/1540/nationalreports.shtml).

reading through the accumulated submissions is a large chore, but verifying their accuracy is an altogether major undertaking. The impact of UNSCR 1540 depends not so much on the adequacy and accuracy of reporting, though, or even on the adoption of appropriate legal frameworks, as on changes in state behavior that derive from the fulfillment of the resolution. The indications so far are not heartening. Roger Crail notes, for example, "no state has fulfilled all of 1540's obligations and the vast majority has only a few of the resolution's domestic legal requirements in place."[30] UNSCR 1540 may be exemplary in design, it seems clear that it has been disappointing in terms of execution. Despite these limitations, UNSCR 1540 is regarded as "a major new nonproliferation tool" because it contains an ambitious, comprehensive, and binding agenda of counterterrorism steps and provides grounds for pressing states to take the necessary actions.

Boosting the Comprehensive Convention on International Terrorism

Terrorism has been on the UN agenda for decades, but agreement has failed to be achieved on a small but fundamental set of issues. At the most basic level there is disagreement on how to define terrorism.[31] Some states hold that it is necessary to distinguish between terrorism and the legitimate use of violence by stateless peoples seeking self-determination and independence. Should violence by states against their own peoples or against civilians on foreign soil be regarded as terrorism? Should the armed forces of states be addressed by a comprehensive convention—as the agents of state terrorism—or should their behavior be exempt? These questions have deeply divided the international community.[32] Years of diplomatic effort have produced little progress.

In the aftermath of 9/11, it was anticipated that perhaps the time had come when these divisions could be surmounted. UN secretary-general Kofi Annan took up this cause and repeatedly urged that the convention be completed as rapidly as possible. The United States, now preoccupied to the point of obsession with the problem of terrorism, pushed strongly in support of the convention. The international political environment seemed more sympathetic, and in fact in the period immediately after 9/11 rapid progress was made in negotiating a draft treaty and completing the text. But basic definitional disagreements remained, and a comprehensive convention on terrorism was not achieved. The convention remains on the UN agenda and a UN ad hoc committee

---

30. Crail (2006, p. 356).

31. For an extensive discussion of the difficulties of defining terrorism, see Meisels (2008, pp. 7–29), who emphasizes that definitions of terrorism routinely reflect political agendas.

32. For useful surveys of the disputes related to the comprehensive convention on terrorism, see Arpad and Silek (2002); and Hmoud (2006).

continues to meet with the objective of bringing the negotiations to a successful conclusion.[33]

Developing the UN Global Counterterrorism Strategy

The UN moved ahead after 9/11 with new resolutions and efforts to achieve a comprehensive convention, but this was not the entirety of its work on terrorism. There was also the matter of improving the UN's own capacities to combat terrorism—something it was being urged to do from multiple directions. The UN's High-level Panel on Threats, Challenges and Change, for example, recommended in 2004 that the organization adopt a more effective strategy for marshalling its capacities against terrorism. Similarly, the Outcome Document of the 2005 UN World Summit urged the UN secretary-general to offer proposals for strengthening the ability of the UN to assist in the fight against terrorism. Secretary-General Kofi Annan took this issue to heart and led a process that produced an unprecedented outcome: on September 6, 2006, the General Assembly adopted the United Nations Global Counter-Terrorism Strategy, the first time that the member states (then 191 of them) had agreed on a common framework for fighting terrorism.

The strategy document includes a remarkably extensive "Plan of Action" to which states have committed themselves. The dozens of proposed actions are clustered under four broad headings:[34] measures to address the conditions conducive to the spread of terrorism; measures to prevent and combat terrorism (in eighteen diverse areas of activity); measures to build states' capacity to prevent and combat terrorism and to strengthen the role of the United Nations in this regard; and measures to ensure respect for human rights for all and the rule of law as the fundamental basis of the fight against terrorism. The overall aim of the global strategy is to serve as "the common platform that brings together the counterterrorism efforts of the various UN entities into a common, coherent, and more focused framework."[35] Viewed as a whole, the strategy represents a sweeping, ambitious, comprehensive agenda of items aimed at confronting the threat of international terrorism.

33. For details on the evolution of the negotiations on the comprehensive convention, see Nuclear Threat Initiative, "Draft Comprehensive Convention on International Terrorism," May 27, 2009 (www.nti.org).

34. The text of UN General Assembly Resolution A/RES/60/288 and associated Plan of Action, from which this brief précis is drawn, can be found in "United National General Assembly Adopts Global Counter-Terrorism Strategy" (www.un.org/terrorism/strategy-counter-terrorism).

35. United Nations, "Coordinating Counter-Terrorism Actions within and beyond the UN System" (www.un.org/terrorsim/cttaskforce).

Adopting the strategy was a significant step, but it is not easy to assess the extent to which it has been converted into meaningful action, particularly given an agenda that is so vast in the number of measures it seeks to push forward and so broad and diffuse in the goals it seeks to advance. Nevertheless there are indications that concrete steps are being taken in some areas. Some of this activity might well have occurred in any case at the initiative of specific UN agencies, but it seems likely that the priority and spotlight associated with this high-profile UN effort has produced more and better coordinated effort. Implementation can be seen in a number of areas.[36] For example, the UN Office of Legal Affairs has developed programs to promote "universal counter-terrorism instruments" and to encourage universal adherence to all relevant conventions and treaty regimes. The Counter-Terrorism Committee created by UNSCR 1373 has consulted with more than ninety states about their technical assistance needs and has sought to find donors to provide needed assistance. The CTC has also created a best-practices directory and established standards for implementing 1373. The UN Office of Disarmament Affairs has launched a Bio-Incident Database. The International Civil Aviation Organization has conducted security audits of the airports and aviation-related facilities of 159 states. The International Maritime Organization has adopted a mandatory International Ship and Port Facility Security Code, which has been put in place by 158 states. The World Bank and the International Monetary Fund have done extensive work with more than 150 states on the elimination of money laundering and the suppression of terrorist financing.

The net effect of all these steps still needs to be assessed but it appears that many useful actions are flowing from the UN's embrace of a universal and comprehensive global counterterrorism strategy.

Creating the Counterterrorism Implementation Task Force

The UN has also engaged in some institutional innovation, creating several bodies intended to augment its own ability to advance the counterterrorism agenda. One is the CTC Executive Directorate, a standing organization intended to provide greater capacity to carry out the CTC's decisions and to improve the UN's ability to assess the needs of states and to provide assistance. In 2005 the UN formed what has become the central coordinating body and clearinghouse

---

36. Because of the diverse nature of the elements of the UN Global Strategy, relevant material is scattered around the UN website. However, a very useful overview, on which I draw here, is "Implementing the Global Counter-Terrorism Strategy," UN Fact Sheet, May 2007 (www. UN.org).

for its counterterrorism activities: the Counter-Terrorism Implementation Task Force (CTITF). The CTITF is designed to link disparate organizations and programs, coordinate their activities, and generally facilitate the implementation of the UN Global Counter-Terrorism Strategy.[37] The CTITF also regularly reports on and assesses progress in implementing the strategy.[38] The responsibility of the task force and associated committees and directorates to monitor and facilitate implementation means there is some oversight and follow-through— that the UN's role does not end when a resolution is passed or a strategy adopted. This does not guarantee full, rapid, or effective implementation—many areas require clarifying obligations, standards need to be established, greater efforts are needed to promote wide if not universal compliance. Still, the UN system has built greater counterterrorism capacity and now has in place organizations with which to undertake the task.

Since 9/11, the United Nations has been impressively active in the field of counterterrorism. It has worked to enlarge the legal framework covering terrorism, to adopt a strategy that defines a substantial role for the UN in assisting states to build counterterrorism capacity, and to build organizational structures within the UN system to enhance its ability to play a constructive counterterrorism role. Critics note the limits and imperfections of the UN's actions, but there can be no question that it has made a considerable effort to adapt to the post-9/11 world.

Institutions against Terrorism

Although the UN has played a central role in efforts to combat terrorism, a similar tale of post-9/11 preoccupation and adaptation can be told about nearly all of the world's leading institutions. Terrorism has been high on the agendas of meeting after meeting, summit after summit. New counterterrorism strategies have been accepted, new committees and institutions created, and new commitments made.

The G-8 Tackles Terrorism

On July 8, 2009, at its Summit in L'Aquila, Italy, the Group of Eight major industrialized countries issued a declaration calling for strengthening international

---

37. United Nations, "Implementing the Global Counter-Terrorism Strategy," UN Fact Sheet, March 2009 (www.un.org/terrorism/pdfs/CT_factsheet_March2009).

38. For a recent example of one of these regular documents, see "United Nations Global Counter-Terrorism Strategy: Activities of the United Nations System in Implementing the Strategy," UN General Assembly, A/62/898, July 7, 2008.

cooperation and intensifying efforts to thwart terrorism—the latest commitment of the G-8's sustained attention to the terrorism threat since 9/11.[39]

As with nearly every other international institution, the G-8 became intensely preoccupied with counterterrorism in the period immediately after 9/11 and made a number of moves to address the terrorism threat, which was now an issue of "highest importance" on its agenda. Its first step was to revise its set of "Recommendations on Counter-Terrorism"; the new document was issued at the meeting of G-8 foreign ministers in Canada in June 2002. Its purpose was specified in its preamble: "The following revised G8 Recommendations on Counter-Terrorism comprise standards, principles, best practices, actions and relationships that the G8 views as providing improvements to the mechanisms, procedures, and networks that exist to protect our societies from terrorist threats. They are intended as commitments by the G-8, which we commend as guiding principles to all states. . . . We urge all states to join the G-8 in the implementation of the following measures."[40] There follows a list of measures that resembles that found in UNSCR 1373 along with exhortations that all states should pursue "rapid implementation of existing counter-terrorism instruments," including all terrorism-related UN conventions—particularly UNSCR 1373.

Beyond establishing its counterterrorism principles, the G-8 took a number of concrete steps.[41] It was particularly and immediately active in the area of disrupting terrorist financing. In October 2001, the finance ministers of the G-7 and Russia adopted an action plan aimed at freezing assets, sanctioning individuals and entities, and strengthening the global financial system against abuse. They also successfully pressed the intergovernmental Financial Action Task Force on Money Laundering to recommend attacking terrorism financing by criminalizing such behavior and foreclosing common methods of funding terrorism.[42]

At its Summit in Evian, France, in June 2003, the G-8 adopted a counterterrorism action plan.[43] This exercise was conceived to buttress the UN's efforts to improve the counterterrorism capacities of member states—indeed it was explicitly identified as in support of UNSCR 1373's Counter-Terrorism

39. G-8 (2009).

40. G-8 (2002).

41. A very useful survey of these early steps, on which I draw here, is "G8 Counter-Terrorism Cooperation since September 11, June 27, 2002 (www.mofa.go.jp/policy/economy/summit/2002/coop_terro).

42. See Financial Action Task Force on Money Laundering, "9 Special Recommendations on Terrorist Financing" (www.fatf-gafi.org/document/9/0,3343,en_32250379_32236920_3403 2073_1_1_1,00.html).

43. For the official document, see G-8 (2003).

Committee. To promote this agenda, the G-8 simultaneously established a Counterterrorism Action Group (CTAG) to coordinate counterterrorism assistance from the group; establish priorities among potential actions and recipients; stimulate funding for needed programs; report regularly on progress and shortfalls; facilitate joint initiatives; and expedite the exchange of information about best practices. Unfortunately the CTAG has been hampered by the lack of consistent leadership due to the rotating chairmanship of the G-8, difficulties in establishing effective ties with UN units, the bureaucratic overload caused by the profusion of new terrorism-related institutions, and the overlap of its agenda with that of other entities.[44] Counterterrorism nevertheless remains high on the agenda of the G-8—further galvanized by the dramatic terrorist attack on London on July 7, 2005, in the midst of the G-8 Summit in Gleneagles, Scotland.

NATO Goes Nonstate

Although its creation goes back to the origins of the cold war, NATO remains a powerful military alliance of twenty-eight member states, which together account for more than 70 percent of global defense spending, and a further twenty-two formal partners. Its decisionmaking can be cumbersome, but NATO, more than most international organizations, commands resources. Since September 11, 2001, NATO has echoed Washington in its preoccupation with the terrorism threat.

As a defensive alliance led by the United States, NATO swung into action almost immediately in the aftermath of 9/11.[45] On September 12, for the first time, it invoked the famous Article V of the North Atlantic Treaty: an attack on one is an attack on all. On October 4, 2001, NATO approved a roster of eight measures meant to assist the United States in its responses to 9/11. These included such essential operational items as "blanket over flight clearances" for U.S. and allied aircraft, access to ports and airfields, increased security for NATO and U.S. facilities, and use of NATO air assets for early warning missions. NATO members also committed to increase resources devoted to the counterterrorism mission, to share intelligence, and to deploy NATO military assets for counterterrorism purposes if and when this would be useful. In

44. For a critical assessment, see Rosand (2009), who suggests that the establishment of the CTAG was a reflection of dissatisfaction with the pace and progress of UN counterterrorism efforts.

45. A convenient overview, on which I have relied, is NATO, "NATO and the Fight against Terrorism: Response to 11 September" (www.NATO.int/issues/terrorism/evolve02). Also extremely useful is NATO, "NATO and the Fight against Terrorism: Chronology of Events Following 11 Sept. 2001" (www.nato.int/issues/terrorism/chronology).

Operation Eagle Assist, NATO airborne early warning aircraft patrolled U.S. airspace for seven months after 9/11, seeking to protect U.S. cities from further attacks involving aircraft—an unprecedented use of NATO military capability under Article V. In Operation Active Endeavor, NATO Standing Naval Forces were assigned to the antiterrorism role in the Mediterranean, with the goal of preventing illegal trafficking and other terrorist-related activity. And with respect to the primary initial U.S. response to 9/11—the intervention in Afghanistan—fourteen NATO members contributed to the campaign. In 2003 NATO took responsibility for Afghanistan and now leads the International Security Assistance Force in that country.

The immediate and improvised responses to the 9/11 attacks are significant NATO initiatives. More fundamental over the long run, however, might be NATO's efforts to refashion itself as a counterterrorism instrument. Given the U.S. obsession with terrorism, NATO leaders were keen to show the alliance's responsiveness and relevance to the greatly altered security agenda.

A signature moment in this effort to "retool" the alliance came at the NATO Summit in Prague on November 21 and 22, 2002, where members adopted the "Prague Package," which focused on "adapting NATO to the challenge of terrorism."[46] The centerpiece of the new approach was the approval of a new "Military Concept for Defence against Terrorism."[47] As with parallel efforts in other institutions, NATO sought to craft an ambitious and comprehensive program that would guide and enhance its efforts to address the terrorism threat. NATO's "Military Concept" for counterterrorism envisions a role for NATO military operations in defensive measures to protect against terrorist attacks, offensive measures to disrupt, damage, or destroy terrorist groups, and in measures to mitigate the consequences of terrorist attacks. It also concluded that NATO should be prepared, on a case-by-case basis, to participate in counterterrorist operations by other international institutions, such as the EU or the UN. At Prague, NATO members also committed to acquire additional or improved capabilities for carrying out the counterterrorism mission—including efforts to improve intelligence, upgrade the timely deployability of forces, augment precision strike capabilities, and strengthen force protection.

In conjunction with the Military Concept, the Prague Package launched a series of related initiatives. NATO adopted a "Partnership Action Plan on Terrorism" to draw its twenty-two partners into its counterterrorism program. It initiated a set of five programs aimed at detecting and mitigating the consequences

46. See, for example, NATO, "Prague Summit: Adapting to the Threat of Terrorism" (www.nato.int/issues/terrrorism/evolve04).

47. See NATO (2003).

of WMD terrorist attacks. It adopted a Civil Emergency Planning Action Plan intended to develop greater capacity to respond effectively to terrorist incidents. It called for studies on missile and cyber defense.

At its subsequent Summit in Istanbul in June 2004, NATO members adopted an "enhanced package" of counterterrorism measures that included institutionalizing a Terrorist Threat Intelligence Unit at NATO headquarters, promoting the development of high-technology equipment for counterterrorism, and highlighting NATO's willingness to help member states to cope with terrorist threats or attacks.[48]

There had been a long debate in the period after the collapse of the Warsaw Pact and the demise of the Soviet Union about what NATO's role and purpose should be in the post–cold war era. The rise of the terrorism threat after 9/11 seemed to provide one clear and compelling answer to that question. This did indeed give NATO new roles to play, as certain of its counterterrorism activities—such as naval patrols in the Mediterranean or its intervention in Afghanistan—became protracted or even institutionalized. NATO did not, however, come to play a central role in the war on terror as it was prosecuted during the course of this decade.[49] In part this was because Washington often preferred to decide unilaterally and to act with "coalitions of the willing" rather than through existing formal alliance structures. The Bush administration also seemed more inclined to deal with allies bilaterally than to engage through the cumbersome mechanisms of the formal alliance. The war in Iraq was definitively not a NATO operation and there were real limits on what many NATO allies were willing and able to contribute. Moreover NATO as a military alliance was not the natural lead institution in those many domains of counterterrorism policy that were not military in nature.

The EU Embraces the Counterterrorism Business

Terrorism might not seem like an obvious topic to occupy a prominent place on the agenda of the European Union, but like every other significant international institution the EU found itself grappling with the issue of counterterrorism in the post-9/11 era. In the initial phase of its response, the EU was oriented toward the United Nations and focused on UNSCR 1373. As it reported to the UN in 2002, "the implementation of Resolution 1373 has been a central priority for the EU since the adoption of the Resolution."[50]

48. On the results of the Istanbul Summit, see NATO (2004).

49. For an excellent detailed analysis that emphasizes NATO's limited role, see de Nevers (2007).

50. See "EU Presidency: Counter-Terrorism—Resolution 1373," European Union@United Nations, April 23, 2002 (www.europe-eu-un.org/articles/en/article_1323_en.htm). For background on the EU's terrorism policies, see Keohane (2005).

For the EU, however, shocks closer to home provided further and perhaps decisive impetus to develop and embrace an overall counterterrorism strategy. The catalytic event was the terrorist attack in Madrid on March 11, 2004, in which 191 people were killed. The impact of "3/11" was reinforced by the terrorist bombing of the London subway and bus system in July 2005, killing 52 people (followed two weeks later by another thwarted but frightening attempted attack in London). After Madrid and London, the transnational terrorist threat was no longer distant and hypothetical but real and immediate.

The Madrid attack was followed immediately by the appointment, on March 25, 2004, of the EU's first counter-terrorism coordinator. Reporting to the EU's high representative for common foreign and security policy, the mission of the counter-terrorism coordinator was "to streamline, organize, and coordinate the EU's fight against terrorism," and to monitor member state implementation of EU counterterrorism initiatives.[51] "Very importantly," EU high representative Javier Solana said in announcing the new position, "we must make sure that every country, once a decision has been made collectively by the European Union, implements it at the national level."[52] The counter-terrorism coordinator is not a powerful position but the creation of this post reflects the elevation of terrorism on the EU agenda and the desire to develop more effective counterterrorism policies. And EU documents insist that the coordinator has been "playing an influential role in pressuring member states to rectify their failure to adopt or implement measures adopted at the EU level."[53]

If the appointment of the EU counter-terrorism coordinator was a first tangible if modest innovation after Madrid, other notable steps soon followed. In June 2005 the EU Council endorsed a remarkably comprehensive and detailed "Revised EU Plan of Action on Combating Terrorism" encompassing literally dozens of specific "actions and measures" to be undertaken by EU units or member states.[54] The plan identifies the "competent bodies" relevant to the implementation of each measure, specifies deadlines where they exist, and often includes information about the status of the measure in question. Perhaps inevitably, implementation of the plan has been uneven—particularly because not

51. "Interview—Gijs de Vries: EU Counter-Terrorism Coordinator," *NATO Review*, Autumn 2005 (www.nato.int/docu/review/2005/issue3/english/interview.html).

52. "Summary Transcript of Joint Press Briefing: Javier Solana, EU High Representative for the CFSP, and Gijs de Vries, EU Counter-Terrorism Coordinator," S0090/04, Brussels, March 30, 3004.

53. European Commission, "Counter-Terrorism Coordinator" (ec.europa.eu/justice_home/fsj/terrorism/institutions/fsj_terrorism_institutions_counter_terrorism_coordinator_en.htm).

54. See Council of the European Union (2005).

all EU members are equally gripped by the terrorism threat—but in design this scheme is coherent, ambitious, and impressive.

The EU's counterterrorism efforts were further codified in December 2005, when EU heads of state adopted "The European Union Counter-Terrorism Strategy," built around four "pillars": prevent, protect, pursue, and respond. This document provided, in effect, a broad conceptual rationale for the plethora of actions already called for under the EU action plan, and identified key priorities in each area of focus.

In short, by the end of 2005, goaded by 9/11, 3/11, and 7/7, the EU had developed a counterterrorism strategy, created a detailed action plan, and introduced a counterterrorism coordinator.

An Assessment of the Institutional Response to 9/11

This brief sketch of the responses of just a few key institutions to 9/11 does not begin to convey accurately the profusion of activity. Much of the effort is overlapping, much is mutually reinforcing, and virtually all of it is viewed as responding to the dictates of UN Security Council Resolution 1373 of September 28, 2001. Many institutions, for example, are preoccupied with finding ways to disrupt the financing of terrorism; in this there seems to be nearly universal agreement with the G-8 principle that "Money is the lifeblood of the terrorists" and hence suppression of terrorist financing must be "a central focus" of counterterrorism.[55] Similarly there is wide agreement on the need to take steps to prevent WMD terrorism.

In the end, however, the crucial question is what all this activity and effort add up to. If this complicated web of institutional approaches and arrangements can be conceived as an international counterterrorism regime, then the crux of the matter becomes: how effective is this regime? It turns out to be surprisingly difficult to judge.[56] In all likelihood, more states have taken more actions to combat terrorism than would have occurred without the commitments, the action plans, the prodding, the obligations, and the assistance associated with the counterterrorism efforts of the world's international institutions. Though in many realms not enough has been done, steps have been taken to make the international system more resilient to terrorist challenges and to create an environment in which it is more difficult for terrorists to operate. And not least, the foundation has been laid for more effective international action against terrorism if states and institutions only followed through on the rules that have been

---

55. "G8 Counter-Terrorism Cooperation since September 11," June 27, 2002 (www.mofa.go.jp/policy/economy/summit/2002/coop_terro).

56. See the extended discussion of this issue in Young (1999, pp. 108–32).

established and the programs that have been created. As with earlier phases of law making and institution building in the counterterrorism context, the post-9/11 responses of the UN and other international organizations are likely to become lasting features of the international landscape—part of the global governance assets in place to deal with the next crisis.

Conclusion

The terrorist attacks on 9/11 nearly a decade ago provoked extraordinary reactions both by the United States and by the international community. The Bush administration's response commanded wide support in Washington at first. In time, however, the costs and difficulties of this approach became increasingly obvious. Many came to believe that the unilateralist impulses evident in the Bush approach were neither good foreign policy nor sound counterterrorism strategy.

Not surprisingly, with the arrival of a new administration in Washington in January 2009 a substantial change followed in the tone and apparent direction of U.S. policy. President Obama had said in his Berlin speech during the 2008 campaign, "Partnership and cooperation among nations is not a choice; it is the one way, the only way, to protect our common security."[57] This was a striking assertion of the necessity of multilateral approaches to security. The new secretary of state, Hillary Clinton, called for "stronger mechanisms of cooperation" with multilateral institutions and argued that an intelligent American policy would contribute to "building the architecture of global cooperation."[58] The Obama administration even abandoned the notion of a "global war on terror" with its emphasis on force, its open-endedness, and polarizing "with-us-or-against-us" strictures.

The al Qaeda threat and the broader challenge of violent extremism is still taken seriously in Washington but the strategy chosen focuses more narrowly on disrupting al Qaeda and its affiliates while also tackling the broader social, political, and economic factors that undergird the long-term terrorism problem.[59] Not every policy has changed—Predator missile attacks still occur, for example. But in a number of areas that have raised so much international concern over recent years—whether on Iraq, torture, Guantanamo, detainee

---

57. "Transcript: Obama's Speech In Berlin," *New York Times,* July 24, 2008 (www.nytimes.com/2008/07/24/us/politics/24text-obama.html).

58. These excerpts are drawn from "Council on Foreign Relations Address by Secretary of State Hillary Clinton," July 15, 2009 (www.cfr.org/publication/19840/).

59. The essential text on the Obama administration's counterterrorism strategy is a speech by Obama's counterterrorism advisor, John Brennan (2009).

policies, and so on—the Obama administration is moving in a different direction. Thus it seems as if the Bush approach will not be enduring; instead a new administration is advancing a philosophy more sympathetic to global governance and is intent on pursuing policies that will produce less conflict between U.S. preferences and international rules.

After 9/11 there were also extraordinary efforts by the UN and other global governance institutions to adapt to the transnational terrorism threat. This impulse to strengthen instruments of global governance was pursued in parallel with the Bush administration's war on terror, sometimes with the administration's support, perhaps even provoked, as some argue, by Washington's unilateralism.[60] Earlier terrorism crises left a lasting mark on the international order in the form of UN resolutions and other measures that gradually cumulated in a considerable long-lived infrastructure of counterterrorism instruments embedded in institutions of global governance. The same seems to be true of 9/11.

How much do the counterterrorism efforts of international institutions matter? Most international institutions acknowledge that states are the pivotal players in combating terrorism. Nevertheless the record suggests global governance institutions play four constructive roles in the struggle against terrorism. First, they provide the legal infrastructure that criminalizes varieties of terrorist behavior and legitimizes international action against terrorism. Second, they establish the rules that should constrain state reactions to terrorism, such as the provisions that govern the use of force, that forbid torture, and that establish protections for human rights. Third, they support, encourage, mandate, and assist states' efforts to improve their counterterrorism capabilities. In virtually every institutional context, international institutions have pushed member states to adopt desirable counterterrorism measures such as UNSCR 1373, NATO's Prague commitments, and the EU action plan. Finally, international institutions can facilitate cooperation among states, which is essential when combating a transnational threat.

There is a plausible argument to be made that, by virtue of all the efforts—national, international, unilateral, multilateral—since 9/11, the world has been made more resistant to the terrorist threat and an environment has been created in which it is more difficult for terrorists to operate. Yet it is clear that not enough has been done and that neither the unilateral efforts of the Bush administration, nor global governance initiatives, nor the two together have been sufficient to eliminate the transnational terrorist threat. If the true test of the effectiveness of the counterterrorism regime that has been created since

---

60. See, for example, Dryzek (2006, p. 233), who argues that Bush's policies provoked a "multilateral reaction."

9/11 is its impact on the level of terrorism, then the facts are disheartening: while the world has been working urgently to augment counterterrorism capabilities, there have been dozens of al Qaeda attacks. Indeed since the vulnerability of modern societies to terrorist attack is at some level inescapable, no initiative can make the world truly safe from terrorism.

References

Ahlstrom, Christer. 2008. "United Nations Security Council Resolution 1540: Nonproliferation by Means of International Legislation." In *SIPRI Yearbook 2007*. Oxford University Press.

An-Na'im, Abdullahi Ahmed. 2002. "Upholding International Legality against Islamic and American Jihad." In *Worlds in Collision: Terror and the Future of Global Order*, edited by Ken Booth and Tim Dunnes. London: Palgrave.

Annan, Kofi. 2005. "A Global Strategy for Fighting Terrorism." Keynote address to the International Summit on Democracy, Terrorism, and Security, Madrid, March 10 (summit.clubmadrid.org/keynotes/a-global-strategy-for-fighting-terrorism.html).

Prandler, and Rita Silek. 2002. "United Nations and Measures to Eliminate International Terrorism." *European Integration Studies* 1: 96–102.

Brennan, John. 2009. "A New Approach to Safeguarding Americans." Remarks to the Center for Strategic and International Studies, Washington, August 6 (www.whitehouse.gov/the_press_office/Remarks-by-John-Brennan-at-the-Center-for-Strategic-and-International-Studies/).

Bunn, Matthew. 2008. "Appropriate Effective Nuclear Security and Accounting: What Is It?" Presentation to Joint Global Initiative/UNSCR Workshop, Nashville, Tenn., July 18 (www.managingtheatom.org).

Charney, Jonathan I. 2001. "The Use of Force against Terrorism and International Law." *American Journal of International Law* 95, no. 4: 835–39.

Corn, Geoffrey. 2009. "Clean Kills." *Foreign Policy Online*, July 17 (www.foreignpolicy.com/articles/2009/07/17/clean_kills?obref=obinsite).

Council of the European Union. 2005. "Revised EU Action Plan on Combating Terrorism." Brussels, June 10 (register.consilium.eu.int/pdf/en/05/st09/st09809-re01ad01.en05.pdf).

Crail, Peter. 2006. "Implementing UN Security Council Resolution 1540: A Risk-Based Approach." *Nonproliferation Review* 13, no. 2: 355–99.

de Nevers, Renée. 2006. "Modernizing the Geneva Conventions." *Washington Quarterly* 29, no. 2: 99–113.

———. 2007. "NATO's International Security Role in the Terrorist Era." *International Security* 31, no. 4: 34–66.

Dryzek, John S. 2006. *Deliberative Global Politics*. Cambridge, U.K.: Polity Press.

European Union. 2001. "Report of the European Union to the Security Council Committee Established Pursuant to Resolution 1373 (2001) Concerning Counterterrorism." S/2001/1297. New York: UN Security Council (December 28).

Franck, Thomas M. 2001. "Terrorism and the Right of Self Defense." *American Journal of International Law* 95, no. 4: 839–43.

Frum, David, and Richard Perle. 2003. *An End to Evil: How to Win the War on Terror.* New York: Random House.

Fujita, Hisakazu. 2003. "International Humanitarian Law: 'War on Terror' in Afghanistan." *Indian Society of International Law Year Book on International Humanitarian and Refugee Law* 3: 59–82.

G-8. 2002. "G8 Recommendations on Counter-Terrorism." G-8 Foreign Ministers Meeting, Whistler, B.C., June 12–13, rev. October 4 (www.dfait-maeci.gc.ca/g8fmm-g8rmae/counter-terrorism-en.asp).

———. 2003. "Building International Political Will and Capacity to Combat Terrorism." G-8 Summit, Evian, France, June 1–3 (www.g8.fr/evian/english/navigation/2003_g8_summit/summit_documents/building_international_political_will_and_capacity_to_combat_terrorism_-_a_g8_action_plan.html).

———. 2009. "G-8 Statement on Counter-Terrorism." L'Aquila, Italy, July 8 (www.america.gov/st/texttrans-english/2009/July/20090709123904emffen0.3825342.html)

Gaddis, John Lewis. 2004. *Surprise, Security, and the American Experience.* Harvard University Press.

Heupel, Monika. 2007. "Implementing UN Security Council Resolution 1540: A Division of Labor Approach." Carnegie Papers 87. Washington: Carnegie Endowment for International Peace (June).

———. 2008. "Combining Hierarchical and Soft Modes of Governance: The UN Security Council's Approach to Terrorism and Weapons of Mass Destruction after 9/11." *Cooperation and Conflict* 43, no. 1: 7–29.

Hmoud, Mahmoud. 2006. "Negotiating the Draft Comprehensive Convention on International Terrorism: Major Bones of Contention." *Journal of International Criminal Justice* 4, no. 5: 1031–43.

Keohane, Daniel. 2005. "The EU and Counterterrorism." Working paper. London: Centre for European Reform (May).

Mariner, Joanne. 2007. "The UN Security Council's (Slowly) Improving Message on Counterterrorism and Human Rights." *FindLaw*, October 24 (writ.news.findlaw.com/mariner/20071024.html).

Mayer, Jane. 2008. *The Dark Side: The Inside Story of How the War on Terror Turned Into a War on American Ideals.* New York: Doubleday.

Meisels, Tamar. 2008. *The Trouble with Terror: Liberty, Security, and the Response to Terrorism.* Cambridge University Press.

Mueller, Karl, and others. 2006. *Striking First: Preemptive and Preventive Attack in US National Security Policy.* Santa Monica, Calif.: RAND Corporation.

NATO. 2003. International Military Staff. "NATO's Military Concept for Defence against Terrorism." Brussels, October (www.nato.int/ims/docu/terrorism.htm).

———. 2004. "Heads of State and Government Strengthen NATO's Anti-Terrorism Efforts." Brussels, June 29 (www.nato.int/docu/update/2004/06-june/e0629e).

Rosand, Eric. 2009. "The G8's Counterterrorism Action Group." Policy Brief. Washington: Center on Global Counterterrorism Cooperation (May).

Slaughter, Anne-Marie. 2004. *A New World Order*. Princeton University Press.

Thomas, Ward. 2000. "Norms and Security: The Case of International Assassination." *International Security* 25, no. 1: 105–33.

U.S. House of Representatives. 2008. Committee on Foreign Affairs. *The Decline in America's Reputation: Why?* Serial 110-180. Government Printing Office (June 11).

Young, Oran R. 1999. *Governance in World Affairs*. Cornell University Press.

ALAN S. ALEXANDROFF *and* ANDREW F. COOPER

Conclusion

In an earlier related volume on global governance, *Can the World Be Governed? Possibilities for Effective Multilateralism,*[1] the answer to the central question posed in the title was yes, but. . . . In this volume it would be easy to offer an almost identical and equally contingent answer to a similarly posed question, but the context of global governance has changed significantly.

Some institutions or hubs of global governance have become far more focused in form and membership. This trend is particularly salient in the elevation of the G-20, formerly a transgovernmental network of finance ministers, to a summit at the leaders level. Whether viewed as a steering committee with a problem-solving orientation or, more negatively, "as the supreme global economic institution,"[2] the image of this forum is one of concentrated authority in which a core group of states shapes new rules through a (self-)selective mode of club multilateralism.

Yet the rise of this type of new institutionalism has not necessarily created a sense of order. Contemporary global governance has become more chaotic, unstructured, and fragmented since the earlier volume was being written. Why? It seems that as a result of significant shifts in the landscape, global governance is much farther into transition than was evident just a few years ago. Simply put, the G-x process of informal unstructured international organization creation has accelerated. Although the new G-20 Summit enhances governance capabilities with an accent on equality and enhanced membership legitimacy, there perhaps is less informality than before, given the enlarged membership as well as less "likemindedness." It also remains an open question whether this "committee" framework is effective.

1. Alexandroff (2008).
2. Anders Åslund, "The Group of 20 Must Be Stopped," *Financial Times,* November 26, 2009.

A new U.S. administration meanwhile seems to have committed the United States to renewed multilateralism, while leadership is expanding rapidly beyond the traditional powers to include the rising powers of China, India, and Brazil—and others as well. Can the United States adjust to a larger and far more diverse leadership group? Is it willing to share leadership and forgo privileges that adhered to its past hegemonic status? Can the rising powers step up and accept leadership and collective commitment and decisionmaking?

Misreading the Direction of Global Governance

The currents and eddies related to global governance evolution have given rise to a number of exaggerated or misleading conclusions—many are at best arguable; at worst they are simply wrong. Among the "definitive" assertions of commentators and experts (and rather commonplace in the international relations literature as well) are that expanding membership in the G-8 to a wider collective assembly—G-20 or G-20 plus—will bring needed legitimacy to global governance; that the establishment of global governance legitimacy will bring its own effectiveness; that universal membership—the ideal of the "192 club"—is the preferred ultimate architecture of global governance; that formal institutions are better than informal institutions; and that democratic states act in a "likeminded" way and therefore deserve an organization of their own.

A transition is definitely upon us.[3] In both its nature and impact, however, this process of change remains very much a work in progress. On the institutional side global governance remains dedicated to finding the right shape that combines efficiency and capacity for action with adequate inclusiveness.

The G-x Process and the Evolution of Global Governance Architecture

Much of the new architecture of global governance is a product of the G-x process, the emergence of which was unexpected. A global architecture of informal and unstructured leadership—so at odds with the earlier UN and Bretton Woods institutions—has not been accepted by many officials and commentators with any degree of equanimity. They decry the lack of universality and accountability and the absence of officials, staff, and formal structures. But the G-x process emerged because of forces that are driving global affairs. The deadlock over reform and leadership in many Bretton Woods and UN institutions

---

3. See the chapters by Alexandroff and Kirton, and Kirton, in this volume.

was partly the impetus for the growth of informal and arguably non-hierarchical G-x institutions. Crises and new issues also motivated the G-x process.

These organizations have no founding documents, no big buildings, and no permanent staff in most instances. The first G-x Leaders' Summit—then the G-5—met as six (with the addition of Italy) at Rambouillet, France, in 1975. As the U.K. government described the G-7/8 Summit it was about to host in Birmingham in 1998, the series of summits of leading industrial powers is "an informal organization, with no rules or permanent Secretariat staff."[4] The heart of this G-x system is the agreement over the agenda, the meeting themselves, the determination of commitments, and the opportunity for leaders to sit down in a relaxed, informal atmosphere to tackle weighty issues. The meetings allow leaders to know one another on a more personal basis and to understand the domestic political pressures and constraints under which each works.

The G-x process, however, is not just about leaders and their summits; it has also fostered informal transgovernmental networks.[5] Indeed the original founding G-x organization dating back to 1971 was an informal gathering of finance ministers, which grew to a G-5 finance ministers meeting that continued until the first Leaders' Summit and then continued on as a transgovernmental network of finance ministers. Notably the G-20 finance ministers emerged from the Asian financial crisis of the late 1990s, continued through the recent great financial crisis, and now perhaps is the technical committee for the G-20 Leaders' Summit. These networks have brought together ministers from both traditional and rising powers to work on global governance issues.

The G-7/8 Leaders' Summit drew together the leaders of the advanced countries in an informal and non-hierarchical manner, but it was criticized for its narrow membership as the "Club of the Rich." With the rise of the economic power and diplomatic leverage of China, India, and Brazil, however, their absence from the leaders-level meetings became increasingly incongruous. A G-5 of Brazil, China, India, Mexico, and South Africa participated in some of the 2005 G-7/8 Gleneagles Summit, and some European leaders— among them the United Kingdom's Tony Blair and then his successor Gordon Brown as well as France's Nicholas Sarkozy—urged the permanent expansion of the G-7/8 to include at least the G-5, making a Leaders' Summit at least a G-13. The G-8 plus the G-5 began a regular structured dialogue, known as Heiligendamm Process (HP), at the Summit at Heiligendamm, Germany, in 2007; following the July 2009 G-7/8 Summit in L'Aquila, Italy, the dialogue was renamed the Heiligendamm-L'Aquila Process (HAP). It was not until the Pittsburgh G-20

4. Great Britain, Foreign and Commonwealth Office (1998).
5. See the chapter by Slaughter and Hale in this volume.

Leaders' Summit in September 2009, however, that this "pulling and hauling" came to an end with the statement that "Today, we designated the G-20 as *the premier forum for our international economic cooperation*. We have asked our representatives to report back at the next meeting with recommendations on how to maximize the effectiveness of our cooperation."[6]

The transition from a Republican Bush to a Democratic Obama administration raised the prospect of a renewed multilateral effort by the United States. The new president immediately faced a number of summits in quick succession: the G-20 Leaders' Summit in April 2009, the G-8 and G-8 plus G-5 (and others) in the variable geometry of the Italian summit designed by Prime Minister Silvio Berlusconi, and finally the G-20 Leaders' Summit in Pittsburgh in September 2009. Until Pittsburgh the new administration's approach to the G-x architecture came from snatches of comment from President Obama and his key officials. At least on the surface the president and officials such as Susan Rice, U.S. ambassador to the UN, urged a revitalization of the UN and recognition that the summits must include the rising powers.

It appears, however, that the president and his officials returned from the July 2009 L'Aquila Summit frustrated with the mix of meetings and leadership overlap of the summit's variable geometry. U.S. officials thus joined leaders and officials in other countries in promoting an enlargement that would eliminate the duplication of annual G-7/8 meetings and annual or more frequent G-20 meetings. Rather than going for the unpleasant and possibly costly process of disinviting leaders—including some rather significant allies—already attending the G-20 Summit, the U.S. administration chose to leap over any G-13 or G-13 plus and opt for a G-20.

So it would appear that the tighter grouping of the G-13 (G-7/8 and G-5) has been put aside for the larger and more diverse G-20 Summit. But matters are still rather fluid. In June 2010 Canada will host the G-7/8 and co-host the G-20 Leaders' Summit with South Korea. Then in November South Korea alone will host another G-20 Leaders' Summit. In 2011, the G-20 host looks set to be France, which assumed the presidency of the G-7/8 at the July 2009 L'Aquila Summit. In August 2009, French president Nicholas Sarkozy spoke favorably of G-7/8 enlargement: "I note with pleasure that the transformation of the G-8 into the G-14 has taken a decisive step forward."[7] He further stated that he supported Brazil's call for an end to the G-8— of the various rising powers, Brazil has been most dismissive of the G-8 and its bias toward the developed countries. France, holding the current presidency of both clubs, now seems to have

6. G-20 (2009; emphasis added).
7. Nicholas Sarkozy quoted in, "France Will Transform G-8," *Straits Times*, (August 26, 2009).

an opportunity to remold the leaders' summitry process. Indeed French Prime Minister François Fillon has declared that France will oversee the merger of the G-8 and the G-20 when it chairs both in 2011."[8]

Whatever the precise character of enlargement, the G-x will expand to include at least some of the key rising states, bringing with it a new diversity as well as quarrelsome negotiations over global governance subjects such as climate change and energy.

Shaping Global Governance Leadership: The United States

Questions of future global governance leadership are a key inquiry in this volume, with authors focusing on a number of the rising powers.[9] But a focus on leadership requires attention to the United States as well. In his chapter, John Ikenberry presents a historical and analytic examination of current U.S. leadership options. In what directions can, or will, the new administration take global governance in order presumably to promote collaboration and multilateral action? Whatever form it takes, U.S. leadership will have a significant impact on the architecture and effectiveness of global governance.

Even before the recent global financial crisis raised questions about U.S. power and its hegemonic leadership, liberal institutionalism was being questioned. Not only was there growing resentment abroad about U.S. leadership, but the United States itself, especially during the early years of the George W. Bush administration, had begun to doubt the benefits and utility of multilateralism. The Iraq intervention was only the most pointed exception to multilateral accord. Additionally, domestic politics made U.S. multilateral leadership increasingly difficult, as securing congressional approval of treaties—for example, the Comprehensive Test Ban Treaty—and international policies became an increasingly difficult struggle or simply not possible. Is the United States willing to share leadership responsibilities, as Ikenberry proposes in his liberal institutionalism 3.0? Or will U.S. politics and policy dictate efforts to retain the hegemonic rights the United States has enjoyed in earlier versions of liberal institutionalism? Will the United States become less likely to act multilaterally in an expanded Great Power world where leadership includes China and India, notwithstanding the inclinations of the current U.S. administration? With an expanded world of rights makers, will there be a growing challenge to

8. "French PM: G20 Summits Should Discuss Currency Issues, Absorb G8," *Dow Jones,* January 8, 2010.

9. See the chapters in this volume by Chin on China, Narlikar on India, Hurrell on Brazil, and Moravcsik on the European Union.

leadership consensus? Does the example of the World Trade Organization—an expanded leadership but diminished consensus—represent the likely outcome for other global governance organizations, including leaders' clubs?

Extending Global Governance Leadership: The Rising Powers

Each of the "traditional" rising powers—China, India, Brazil—has exhibited slightly "schizophrenic" behavior in its move toward, and inclusion in, a wider global governance leadership. Each appears to desire the recognition that its inclusion in the great power club would signal, but each bridles in some way at the previous traditional leadership and the status quo label implied by collaborative global governance leadership. The leaders of the rising powers are mindful that their countries' international identities have been shaped in part by their predecessors' rhetorical solidarity with the global South, and they express continued support for structural change and greater equality in global governance institutions. Many officials from the rising powers also express the desire that their countries act as "bridges" between the developing and developed states.[10]

To one degree or another all the rising powers criticized the narrow membership of the G-7/8 process and expressed deep skepticism about joining leadership organizations as they were traditionally constituted. As Celso Amorim, Brazil's foreign minister, declared just before the 2008 G-8 Summit, "you simply can't ignore" the emerging countries such as Brazil, India, and China. He further argued that the G-20 Leaders' Summit was a "better model" than the current G-8 leadership, adding that the "G-8 is over as a political decision group."[11]

Chinese commentators and experts also opposed their country's membership in an expanded G-8, but China has warmed to the G-20 Leaders' Summit, where it has an opportunity to influence the G-20 agenda—particularly in support of developing countries—and leverage its own position.[12] For China and the other large emerging market countries, their inclusion in the G-20 also appropriately acknowledges their status as rising powers and their increasing influence on views of global governance leadership.

At the same time the rising powers themselves are grouping in various ways—for example, as IBSA (India, Brazil, and South Africa), the BRICs (Brazil, Russia, India, and China), BRICSAM (the BRICs countries plus South Africa

10. As Alexandroff and Kirton describe in this volume.

11. Quoted in "Brazil Considers the G-8 Is No Longer a Valid Political Decision Group," *MercoPress*, June 12, 2009. Hurrell, in this volume, chronicles Brazil's ambiguity toward the G-7/8 and the traditional power leadership of global governance.

12. For the Chinese approach to loans in Africa that outflanks the approaches of the international financial institutions, see Chin, in this volume.

and Mexico), or the G-5.[13] The question is whether these rising power clubs have any sustained prospect or are simply short-term opposition responses to the traditional clubs such as the G-7/8? For their members, however, these clubs offer ways to integrate into the Great Power constellations of global relations.

Progress toward integration certainly had been made in the HAP 'structured dialogue' among the G-8 and G-5 members.[14] Officials acknowledge that the HAP has built trust among the parties as they explore policy issues without the need to adopt "hard" negotiating stances. At the L'Aquila Summit, a final report was delivered to the G-8 plus G-5 leaders, along with reports from working groups on development (chaired by South Africa and France), energy (India and Canada), cross-border investment and the encouragement of responsible business conduct (Mexico and the United States), and research and innovation, including intellectual property rights (India and the United Kingdom). While the global governance architecture appears to have turned away at the Pittsburgh Summit from a G-13 configuration, the HAP nevertheless appears to have advanced collaboration among the G-8 and G-5 members.

China, India, and Brazil are seen as the archetypical rising powers, but another possible rising power is the European Union.[15] The structural "super state" dimension of the EU leads it to be passed over by experts when assessing the evolution in global governance leadership. Indeed the EU might be regarded as the only other "superpower" in the contemporary international system. Adding the EU to the mix of rising powers has a substantial impact on expanded global governance leadership. While the EU might differ with the United States on some programmatic matters and policy options— with respect to climate change, development, and conflict resolution, for example—there is considerable congruity between the two around most norms and values. This is not the case for the traditional rising powers and the United States, where differences in values could place enormous constraints on efforts to build collaborative leadership in the new liberal institutionalism.

Rising Institutions

This volume has examined a variety of organizations and institutions, many directly the product of the G-x process, but also those arising from the UN and Bretton Woods systems, such as the counterterrorism committees[16] and the International Energy Agency.[17] It has also looked at efforts to enhance rules for

13. See the chapter by Cooper, in this volume.
14. See Cooper and Antkiewicz (2008).
15. See the chapter by Moravcsik, in this volume.
16. See the chapter by Miller, in this volume.
17. See the chapter by Leverett, in this volume.

and conduct of sovereign wealth funds, many of which are located in the rising powers or in the energy-producing and -exporting countries.[18] Many international relations experts presume that structural change is largely impossible without major power war. John Ikenberry in his classic volume *After Victory* traces the efforts of victorious powers to create and maintain order in international relations.[19] But war and its aftermath is not the only setting (and we anticipate that Ikenberry did not mean to suggest this) and it is evident that there is a continuing institutional evolution in international relations. One need only reference the significant revision in global trade in the 1990s as the system moved from the General Agreement on Tariffs and Trade (GATT) to the World Trade Organization (WTO). And it would appear that the Great Recession provides the conditions for institutional creation and organizational revision.

At the informal G-x level, Leaders' Summits and transgovernmental networks have burgeoned in the face of policy deadlocks, resistance to reform, and financial crises. The classic case of deadlock and resistance is the failure to achieve UN Security Council reform in 2005. But reforms of the UN and Bretton Woods systems, while also difficult, have occurred, pushed forward by the 2008 global financial crisis. New organizations also have been created—the Financial Stability Board, for instance, and the counterterrorism committees in the UN. Some institutions have reformed significantly—for example, with the General Agreement on Tariffs and Trade giving way to the World Trade Organization.

The new transgovernmental networks are notably horizontal in form, bringing together ministerial-level officials—from finance, foreign affairs, trade, and the environment, among other policy areas—to focus on technical issues and promote standards of coordination. In the form of the G-20, these new networks also integrate the traditional and the rising powers.[20] While the coordination and transmittal of practices and standards are significant achievements, these networks have limited capacity to make and implement decisions. Commentators decry the fact that the G-x organizations are not treaty based. In our view, however, such formalism is less relevant than a collective willingness to implement commitments.

The Key Dimensions of Global Governance Leadership

Leadership remains murky. The emergence of the G-x process—G-2, G-7/8, G-8 + G-5, G-20 Leaders, and other networks and clubs—has made the architecture of global governance more informal, but also more complex and overlapping.

18. See the chapter by Drezner, in this volume.
19. Ikenberry (2001).
20. See the chapter by Slaughter and Hale, in this volume.

The G-x process has reached out beyond the traditional powers to the rising powers in the G-5 and now the G-20 Leaders' Summit. Various clubs, global and regional governance organizations, and transgovernmental networks have bubbled up in the past few years.

The authors in this volume, in one fashion or another, focus on the core challenge of contemporary global governance: whether, and by what means, an enlarged leaders club can be integrated successfully and achieve collaborative governance over a range of critical global issues, including terrorism, nuclear proliferation, climate change, and economic stability and growth. Why does this challenge seem so difficult to meet in contemporary international relations? Historically the integration of rising states—the "Power Transition" crisis of rising states—into the international system, with the possible exception of the United States in the late nineteenth and early twentieth centuries, but notably in the case of Germany, was fraught with difficulty. Now experts focus on tensions over the rise of China and whether the new power can be integrated peacefully into the global system, although, as we point out in the Introduction to this volume, the analogy of Germany in the twentieth century does not hold up when broad comparisons are made with the rise of China, especially, but also potentially India and others.

What then are the characteristics of the ideal global governance institution? Frequently identified are the dimensions of legitimacy, effectiveness, likemindedness, informality, and equality.

The frequent condemnation of the G-8 for its lack of legitimacy as a club of the advanced countries suggests that global governance institutions will have to be more broadly inclusive and representative of regions and types of states—developed, rising, and developing. But how broad must the membership be? Are twenty countries sufficient? Even after the "permanent" emergence of the G-20 at Pittsburgh, uninvited parties—the Nordic countries, for example—expressed disappointment in not being included. Can only a UN General Assembly–like institution truly satisfy legitimacy?

"Effectiveness" has various elements, one of which is the capacity to reach consensus and agreement. Another is internal accountability and the ability to meet announced commitments. From this perspective, therefore, effectiveness looks beyond collective commitments and addresses national policy implementation, both formally and informally and through both international organizations and national action. Can the G-20 leaders reach this kind of effective global governance?

Likemindedness refers to general agreement on the approach to collective commitments. It is built on similar views with respect to norms, values, and rules, and might extend to policy solutions—although not necessarily. Many

Table 1. *Characteristics of G-x Process Platforms*

Platform	Effective-ness	Legiti-macy	Like-mindedness	Inform-ality	Equality
United States	yes		n.a.	n.a.	n.a.
G-2	yes			yes	yes
G-7	yes		yes	yes	yes
G-8				yes	yes
BRIC				yes	yes
HP/HAP	n.a.	yes	yes	yes	yes
G-13 (G-8 + G-5) or G-13 plus		yes			yes
G-20 Leaders		yes			yes

n.a. Not applicable.

liberal institutionalists and some neoconservatives once presumed that national regime characteristics such as democracy represented the key to likemindedness. Before the 2008 U.S. presidential election there were calls for a club of democracies to promote common action, including on humanitarian intervention. But disagreement over key norms of international relations divides democratic states as well—for example, unlike other democratic countries, neither India nor Brazil encourages or supports humanitarian intervention. European and U.S. views on concrete policy on trade, currency appreciation, human rights, intellectual property, Tibet, North Korea, and Myanmar are far more congruent than those of, say, the United States and China. But this congruity is built on common views of international relations that extend even to policies where the two do not necessarily agree on specific solutions. We return to likemindedness in the next section.

Informality is a characteristic often ignored by commentators and experts. Indeed the identification of, and support for, informality comes principally from the leaders themselves, who express the value of small group settings at which they come to know each other personally. Membership therefore affects informality: the larger the group the more difficult to create the informality leaders favor.

Finally, equality in global governance avoids hierarchy and differentiation. The G-x process is built on a foundation of equality: each leader is accorded the same strength of voice. This contrasts with the UN Security Council's permanent five veto-wielding members or the Bretton Woods institutions, where members have different national quotas or shares. Nevertheless even in, say, the G-20, there might well be implicit hierarchies not readily identifiable. So it is likely that not all states are equal: the United States and a number of other countries likely carry greater voice and influence, notwithstanding the presumption of equality in the G-x process.

A cursory evaluation of the various G-x process platforms reveals some of the difficulties that officials and leaders face in trying to reach consensus on the form of leadership organization (see table 1). Of all the different groupings, only one, the HP/HAP, has all five of the characteristics we discuss—and yet the HAP is the one organization in which no decisionmaking is envisioned, thus reducing its effectiveness. The expanded G-x forms—G-13, G-20—lack several of the favored dimensions, most critically likemindedness and effectiveness.

Likemindedness and Its Influence on the Future of Global Collaboration

A struggle is under way in international relations today over changing values. Critical norms of the Westphalian nation-state system are weakening discernibly, and none is more critical than the principle of national sovereignty and noninterference in the domestic affairs of other states. Yet the "responsibility to protect," now adopted by the UN, permits intervention in a state whose government is unwilling or unable to protect its own people. States have also advocated sanctions and, in the extreme, even intervention—to eliminate the spread of nuclear and other weapons of mass destruction. There has even been, in Iraq, preventive action by the United States to promote regime change in the face of the presumed possession of such weapons. All these proposed or actual actions challenge state sovereignty, the consequences of which states might act perversely to avoid. Thus Iran and North Korea might be driven to undermine nuclear nonproliferation to ward off intervention and deter international pressure.

This tension over the core value of state sovereignty and the limits it places on global governance fractures collective action, imposes costs and constraints on the liberal international agenda, and challenges the enlargement of global governance leadership. The fracture of collective action separates traditional and rising powers—with China a pivotal advocate for traditional, strict, adherence to state sovereignty and noninterference—as well as democratic and authoritarian powers, and even robust rising democratic powers: both India and Brazil are skeptical about actions that would interfere in the domestic affairs of other states.

This sovereignty divide has appeared in circumstances beyond humanitarian intervention and the responsibility to protect—most recently and dramatically in the climate change negotiations in Copenhagen. The United States insisted on transparency—the international verification of announced national cuts in greenhouse gas emissions. China on the other hand saw such an international verification framework as a serious violation of national sovereignty and interference in the domestic affairs of state.

The divide over norms in approaches to global politics is not restricted to the key concept of national sovereignty and noninterference, but extends to at least three other concepts: developmentalism, hierarchy, and universalism.

An example of developmentalism is the more than occasional appeal of the rising powers to the North-South divide and in their demands for greater equality for developing countries. In various circumstances India and China assert their status as developing countries to declare their separateness and to identify with the global South and against traditional powers in Europe and North America.

The G-x process emphasizes equality, but there is a strong view that hierarchy, rather than equality, might prevail in the G-20: some countries and leaders exercise greater authority than others—not a particularly exceptional view. So equality might not be as important a dimension in the G-x process as is sometimes claimed. Yet it might also be the case that smaller and less powerful countries and their leaders exercise influence well above their size or raw power, which suggests that there might be more equality in the process than was the case in traditional diplomacy and in the formal institutions of the Bretton Woods and UN system.

Finally, universalism still dominates views of appropriate global governance decisionmaking: there can be no commitment or legitimacy without universal agreement. As one strong indictment of global governance decisionmaking on any basis other that universalism states, "But the G20 actually violates fundamental principles of international co-operation by arrogating for itself important financial decisions that should be shared by all countries. In so doing it also emasculates the sovereign rights of small countries that have long been the prime defenders of multilateralism and international law as well as the foremost policy innovators. The rule of the big powers over the rest is in danger of becoming unjust and reactionary."[21]

A Last Word

The challenges facing the global system are great. Some—including possibly climate change and nuclear proliferation—might even be existential. The weakening of the foundation of the state system is making it more difficult to construct a global governance system that encourages states to overcome the collective action dilemma and undertake the collective effort needed to tackle these global challenges. Even without the gulf over global norms, finding the means to integrate the rising powers and to keep "in harness" traditional powers such as the United States poses daunting problems. While it might be true that the

21. Åslund, "The Group of 20 Must Be Stopped."

transformation of rising states from authoritarian to democratic structures is a significant way to promote collaboration—or at least to avoid conflict engendered by the transition of power—it also might take longer to bring about that transformation than the international system can safely permit. And it is evident from contemporary global politics that democratic form does not create necessarily likemindedness.

Meanwhile the system generates new institutions and new forms in seeking to promote the necessary global governance collaboration. Overhanging the current global governance architecture is continuing doubt that institutions created or proposed by the Great Powers will be able to reach collective commitments and find ways to implement policies to meet global challenges. An enlarged leaders' summit, whether a G-13 or a G-20, might be more legitimate but still be unable to effect policy.

Where would such an outcome lead the Great Powers? The history of the G-x process suggests that, in the face of crises, leading states will act together, if only in informal, ad hoc groups. Legitimacy without effectiveness might well result in the transformation of the global governance system into informal, influential, likeminded groups, focused on a specific issue and prepared to press forward on global policy notwithstanding the inability to reach a wider consensus. Thus the Major Economies Forum on Energy and Climate (MEF)—the seventeen major greenhouse gas producers, brought together at the invitation of the United States—could be the model for future global governance institutions, especially after the experience of the Copenhagen climate conference. Global governance could be in for an extended period of ad hoc institutional creation and action in the face of rising states and new challenges.

The circumstances are changing quickly, but this volume's answer to the question posed by the earlier related volume—*Can the World Be Governed?*—is again yes, but. . . .

References

Alexandroff, Alan S., ed. 2008. *Can the World Be Governed? Possibilities for Effective Multilateralism.* Wilfrid Laurier University Press.

Cooper, Andrew F., and Agata Antkiewicz, eds. 2008. *Emerging Powers in Global Governance: Lessons from the Heiligendamm Process.* Wilfred Laurier University Press.

G-20. 2009. "Leaders' Statement." Pittsburgh, September 24–25.

Great Britain, Foreign and Commonwealth Office. 1998. "G8 Structure: An Informal Club" (http://birmingham.g8summit.gov.uk/brief0398/what.is.g8.shtml).

Ikenberry, G. John, 2001. *After Victory: Institutions, Strategic Restraint, and the Rebuilding of Order After Major Wars.* Princeton University Press.

Contributors

ALAN S. ALEXANDROFF is a senior fellow at the Centre for International Governance Innovation (CIGI) in Waterloo, Ontario, and the research director of the Program on Conflict Management and Negotiation at the Munk Centre for International Studies, University of Toronto. Dr. Alexandroff received his B.A., *cum laude* with distinction in all subjects, from Cornell University, an M.A. and Ph.D. in government from Cornell University, an M.A. in International History from the London School of Political Science and Economics, and an L.L.B. from the McGill University Law School.

GREGORY CHIN is a senior fellow at the Centre for International Governance Innovation in Waterloo, Ontario, and an assistant professor in the Department of Political Science and Faculty of Graduate Studies at York University, Toronto, where he teaches global politics, comparative politics, and East Asian political economy.

ANDREW F. COOPER is associate director and distinguished fellow, the Centre for International Governance Innovation, and professor in the Department of Political Science, University of Waterloo. Dr. Cooper received his doctorate from Oxford University. In 2009 he was the Canada-U.S. Fulbright Research Chair, Center on Public Diplomacy, University of Southern California.

DANIEL W. DREZNER is professor of international politics at the Fletcher School of Law and Diplomacy, Tufts University, and a senior editor at *The National Interest*. He has published numerous books, as well as articles in scholarly journals and the *New York Times, Wall Street Journal, Washington Post, Foreign Policy,* and *Foreign Affairs*. He is an occasional commentator for *Newsweek* International and NPR's *Marketplace,* and keeps a daily weblog for *Foreign Policy* magazine.

THOMAS HALE is a Ph.D. candidate in the Department of Politics at Princeton University. His research focuses on the governance of transnational problems such as climate change and financial regulation. He has written on the role of private actors in global governance, the accountability of international organizations, East Asian regionalism, innovative governance mechanisms, and transnational democracy. He holds a masters degree in global politics from the London School of Economics and an AB in public policy from Princeton's University's Woodrow Wilson School of Public and International Affairs.

ANDREW HURRELL is the Montague Burton Professor of International Relations at Oxford University and a fellow of Balliol College. During the 2009/10 academic year he is an inaugural fellow at the newly created Straus Institute for the Advanced Study of Law and Justice at NYU Law School. His book, *On Global Order: Power, Values and the Constitution of International Society* (Oxford, 2007) won the International Studies Association prize for best book in the field of international relations in 2009.

G. JOHN IKENBERRY is the Albert G. Milbank Professor of Politics and International Affairs at Princeton University in the Department of Politics and the Woodrow Wilson School of Public and International Affairs. He is the author of *After Victory: Institutions, Strategic Restraint, and the Rebuilding of Order after Major Wars* (Princeton, 2001), which won the 2002 Schroeder-Jervis Award presented by the American Political Science Association (APSA) for the best book in international history and politics. He has published in all the major academic journals of international relations and has written widely in policy journals.

JOHN KIRTON is director of the G-8 Research Group, co-director the G-20 Research Group, an associate professor of political science, and a research fellow at the Munk Centre for International Studies, University of Toronto. He has advised the Canadian and Russian governments, the World Health Organization, and the International Bankers' Federation on G-7/8 and G-20 participation, international trade, and sustainable development, and has written widely on G-7/8 and G-20 summitry.

FLYNT LEVERETT is a senior research fellow at the New America Foundation in Washington, where he directs initiatives on the geopolitics of energy and Iran. He also teaches at Pennsylvania State University's School of International Affairs and, with Hillary Mann Leverett, publishes www.TheRaceForIran.com. From 1992 to 2003 he served in the U.S. government as a senior analyst at the Central Intelligence Agency, a member of the State Department's Policy Planning Staff, and senior director for Middle East affairs at the National Security Council.

STEVEN E. MILLER has spent 25 years at Harvard University's Kennedy School of Government, where he has been a member of the Belfer Center for Science and International Affairs. He currently serves as director of the International Security Program, editor-in-chief of the scholarly journal, *International Security*, and co-editor of the International Security Program's book series, BCSIA Studies in International Security, published by MIT Press. He is among the leaders of the Pugwash Conferences on Science and World Affairs, an international scholarly association based in Rome. Miller has written extensively on nuclear weapons issues, U.S. security policy, and U.S. foreign policy.

ANDREW MORAVCSIK is professor of politics and international affairs and director of the European Union Program at Princeton University's Woodrow Wilson School of Public and International Affairs. He has authored over one hundred academic publications on European integration, transatlantic relations, international organization, global human rights, international relations theory, and Asian regionalism. His history of the European Union, *The Choice for Europe,* has been called "the most important work in the field" (*American Historical Review*).

AMRITA NARLIKAR is university senior lecturer at the Department of Politics and International Studies, University of Cambridge, and official fellow at Darwin College. Her recent single-authored books include *New Powers: How to Become One and How to Manage Them* (Columbia University Press, 2010). She is also co-editor of *Leadership and Change in the Multilateral Trading System* (Martinus Nijhoff, 2009).

ANNE-MARIE SLAUGHTER is the Bert G. Kerstetter '66 University Professor of Politics and International Affairs at Princeton University. She is presently on leave, serving as director of policy planning for the U.S, Department of State. She was dean of the Woodrow Wilson School of Public and International Affairs at Princeton University from 2002 to 2009. Slaughter has written and taught broadly on global governance, international criminal law, and U.S. foreign policy. Her most recent book is *The Idea that Is America: Keeping Faith with Our Values in a Dangerous World* (Basic Books, 2007).

Index

311

CPSIA information can be obtained at www.ICGtesting.com
Printed in the USA
BVOW031029280113

311747BV00001B/140/P